CITIZEN AND SUBJECT

EDITORS

Sherry B. Ortner, Nicholas B. Dirks, Geoff Eley

A LIST OF TITLES

IN THIS SERIES APPEARS

AT THE BACK OF

THE BOOK

PRINCETON STUDIES IN
CULTURE / POWER / HISTORY

CITIZEN AND SUBJECT

CONTEMPORARY AFRICA
AND THE LEGACY OF
LATE COLONIALISM

Mahmood Mamdani

PRINCETON UNIVERSITY PRESS
PRINCETON, NEW JERSEY

Library of Congress Cataloging-in-Publication Data

Mamdani, Mahmood, 1946–
Citizen and subject : contemporary Africa
and the legacy of late colonialism / Mahmood Mamdani.
p. cm. — (Princeton studies in culture/power/history)
Includes bibliographical references and index.
ISBN-13: 978-0-691-02793-7 (alk. paper)
ISBN-10: 0-691-02793-5 (pbk.: alk. paper)
1. Colonies—Africa—Administration.
2. Africa—Colonial influence.
3. Africa—Politics and government.
4. Despotism—Africa. 5. Democracy—Africa.
6. Apartheid—Africa. 7. Indigenous peoples—Africa.
I. Title II. Series.
JV246.M35 1996
320.96'09'045—dc20 95-25318

This book has been composed in Galliard

http://pup.princeton.edu

Printed in the United States of America

15 14 13

For Mira and Zohran

Contents

Acknowledgments

THE PUBLICATION OF A BOOK is a convenient time to acknowledge publicly the debt incurred in the course of its writing. I welcome this opportunity, knowing fully well that such debts can never be repaid, only reciprocated.

It is difficult for me to retrace the history of this endeavor with precision, especially since its contours do not quite fit a formal program of research and writing. This is particularly true of the questions that came to guide the process of inquiry. More than any other, the contexts giving rise to these questions coincided with three turning points in my personal life. The first was the 1972 Asian expulsion from Uganda, which set me thinking about the relationship between deracialization and democratization. The second was a two-year term, from 1986 to 1988, as chair of the National Commission of Inquiry into the Local Government System, a commission that the National Resistance Movement (NRM) appointed upon coming to power in Uganda in 1986. This experience focused my mental energies on what democratization would mean in the context of rural Uganda. The third was a series of visits to South Africa, beginning with a two-week tour in 1991 as one of a team of African scholars and ending with a six-month family stay in 1993. This encounter with apartheid both made me rethink the claim of its being exceptional and raised the final question, to which this manuscript is a response: how to transcend the urban-rural divide that even this otherwise far-reaching democratic struggle shares with other movements on the continent.

In retrospect, I can trace the beginnings of the research process to a series of studies I carried out in the Ugandan countryside, from 1981 to 1985. During an earlier stay at the University of Dar-es-Salaam (1973–79), I had come to take it for granted that social research did not always require special funding: we used our modest salaries and informal networks to do field research. But all that changed as structural adjustment programs dramatically undercut our real incomes and forced us to become truly market responsive. I have to admit that only research grants—at first a small grant from IDRC on the commercialization of agriculture, later a more generous "reflections on development" grant from Rockefeller/CODESRIA—saved me from having to double as a Kampala taxi driver to ensure enough income for a decent living. Although I dutifully submitted research reports to both funders at the end of a duly specified period, I can remember only two individuals—David

Court, in charge of Rockefeller's Nairobi office, and Thandika Mkandawire, at CODESRIA's Dakar office—cautioning more performance-minded colleagues that the process set in motion by a research grant may take longer to complete. In this case it took a decade. But then both David Court and Thandika Mkandawire—incorrigible social scientists that they are—always suspected that the more significant consequences of social action are often those unintended. For that bit of wisdom, and its unintended consequence, I thank them.

As I think of those who assisted me with the research process in various villages in the first half of the eighties, the feeling that overwhelms me is one of humility more than of gratitude. As many before them, these research assistants—Syahuka Muhindo in the Ruwenzoris, George Ocwa Okello in Lango, and James Serugo in Buganda—introduced me to their home villages and communities and waited patiently as I blundered time and again, good-naturedly acknowledging that this indeed is what a learning process must look like from the outside. Their guidance no doubt prepared me for the work I would have to do as chair of the 1986–88 Local Government Commission. The learning process continued through those years, formally as we held evidence-gathering sessions in village after village and district after district, and informally through discussions stretching over long country drives in the daytime and drinking sessions late at night. My most frequent and formidable companions in those years were Francis Lubanga, the Commission's Secretary, and Margaret Odeke, fellow member. To them, too, many thanks.

The last phase of my formal field research was in 1993 in South Africa. My stay began in Durban and was made possible by a six-month visiting research professorship in the Department of Philosophy at the University of Durban-Westville. Conscious of the bureaucratic and discipline-focused anti-intellectual legacy of administrations in South Africa's historically black universities, the rector of the university, Jairam Reddy, was generous and indulgent toward researchers. Mala Singh, the head of the Department of Philosophy, was helpful while remaining watchful, maintaining a judicious balance between generosity and judgment, lest meager performances be masked by professed commitments. In time, both Jairam and Mala became friends with whom I had regular discussions every time an issue intrigued or irked me.

I began my hostel research with a helping hand from Ari Sitas, a fellow academic from the University of Natal, who invited me to join the Culture and Working Life project of the Congress of South African Trade Unions (COSATU) and introduced me to its union organizer, Alfred Qabula, also a famed worker-poet. As we persisted to organize, at first a workshop, then meetings with individual hostel dwellers—often with paltry results, I am sorry to say—Qabula taught me a lesson in perseverance and stamina that I hope never to forget. In contrast to the semiarid research environment in the Durban hostels of Dalton and Thokoza, I reaped an almost instant and substantial fortune in the larger Johannesburg area: in the hostels of Wolhuter (Johannesburg) and Mzimhlope (Soweto) and the Alexandra civic. That fortune would surely have bypassed me without the generosity of three key individuals: Cas Cavadia of the Civic Associations of Johannesburg, David Letsei of the Alexandra civic, and Sakkie Steyn of the Transvaal Hostel Dwellers' Association.

Outside of the hostel context, I met and discussed—on a regular and informal basis—with several academics, many of whom doubled as militants: Ari Sitas, Blade Nzimande, Mike Morris, Adam Habib, Bill Freund, Ahmed Bawa, Nick Amin, Yvonne Muthein, Sandra Africa, Prem Singh, and Vishnu Padyachee in Durban; Niko Cloete, Rahmat Omar, Hassan Lorgat, Babylon Xeketwane, Eddie Webster, and Phil Bonner in Johannesburg; and Neville Alexander and Abdou Maliqalim Simone in Cape Town, all of whom helped me find my bearings in the rapidly changing South African situation.

I had gone to South Africa with one research objective in mind: to understand the methods of native control the South African state employed. It was a question with which I became preoccupied following my work in the Local Government Commission in Uganda. To explore its historical dimension, I researched collections at several libraries, both within and outside South Africa: at the Legal Resources Centre and the University of Natal in Durban, at the African Studies Centre and the Law Faculty of the University of Witwatersrand, at the Centre for Basic Research and Makerere University's Law Development Centre in Kampala, and finally at Harlem's Schoenberg Center, Columbia University, and the New York City Public Library. Often I stumbled through collections as would a pedestrian through urban concentrations, but at times I benefited from expert guidance: from Sue Clerk at Durban's Legal Resources Centre, John Kateeba and Charles Ndyabawe at the Centre for Basic Research, and John Nsereko at the Law Development Centre.

Most of the writing of this manuscript was done in Kampala, mainly in the congenial atmosphere of our home and of the Centre for Basic Research. Some revision was done at Columbia University's Center for African Studies, into the corridors of which I walked in one day—without warning. George Bond, the director, and Ron Kassimir, his deputy, generously extended to me the hospitality of the center for nearly three months in 1994. It was a collegial gesture that one does not quite expect in today's network-infested world of academia.

As the manuscript took shape, I leaned on several colleagues and friends for critical feedback. Joe Oloka-Onyango and Expedit Ddungu at the Centre for Basic Research, Yash Ghai at the University of Hong Kong, and Niveditta Menon at Lady Shriram College in Delhi read and commented on selected parts. Ben Parker and Adam Habib at the University of Durban-Westville, Bill Freund and Ari Sitas at the University of Natal, Mike Neocosmos in Roma (Lesotho), Peter Gibbons at the African Studies Center in Uppsala (Sweden), and Norman O. Brown in Santa Cruz (California) read and commented on the entire first draft. Henry Bernstein at the University of Manchester and Zene Tadesse in Addis Ababa sent me pages of comments, often with a critique so convincing as to spur me on to yet another draft. Four friends and colleagues—Mamadou Diouf and Thandika Mkandawire at CODESRIA in Dakar, Talal Asad at the New School in New York, and Bob Meister at the University of California in Santa Cruz—combined written comments with discussions that were as drawn-out as I called for. Thandika was relentless with his criticism, I must admit, to some good effect. Both Bob Meister and Talal Asad read several drafts and bountifully gave of their time, energy, and intellect. Through these encounters, critical and understanding, I have come to appreciate that sympathy alone is indeed a poor substitute for friendship and solidarity.

Several persons helped me with the publication process. Ari Zolberg of the New School in New York listened to a breakfast sum-up of the main thesis and undertook to put me in touch with the most suitable publishers. Jane Gelfman intervened as a friend to ensure that I had a fair deal with the publishers. Two named readers, Abdellah Hammoudi at Princeton and Nicholas B. Dirks at Ann Arbor, Michigan, sent in detailed comments with a judicious mix of encouragement and revision suggestions. Mary Murrell, the editor at Princeton University Press, was a helpful guide as I prepared the final manuscript. Finally, I hope that the pen of Dalia Geffen, the copy editor, has eliminated any traces of my incorrigible partiality to exclamation marks!

I dedicate this book to my wife, Mira, and to our son, Zohran. Mira continues to inspire by example, living life to its brim, making light of the most strenuous moments, gently reminding me that I write for an audience, not just for myself. Zohran, in his own small but captivating ways, daily takes us along the trail that is his discovery of life, teaching us to see things through the eyes of a child, as if for the first time. To be sure, I cannot credit either with direct assistance in preparing this book. But I do know that without their companionship it would have been difficult to muster the tenacity and stamina to bring this work to conclusion—and enjoy doing it.

CITIZEN AND SUBJECT

CHAPTER ONE

Introduction:
Thinking through Africa's Impasse

DISCUSSIONS on Africa's present predicament revolve around two clear tendencies: modernist and communitarian. Modernists take inspiration from the East European uprisings of the late eighties; communitarians decry liberal or left Eurocentrism and call for a return to the source. For modernists, the problem is that civil society is an embryonic and marginal construct in Africa; for communitarians, it is that real flesh-and-blood communitites that comprise Africa are marginalized from public life as so many "tribes." The liberal solution is to locate politics in civil society, and the Africanist solution is to put Africa's age-old communities at the center of African politics. One side calls for a regime that will champion rights, and the other stands in defense of culture. The impasse in Africa is not only at the level of practical politics. It is also a paralysis of perspective.

The solution to this theoretical impasse—between modernists and communitarians, Eurocentrists and Africanists—does not lie in choosing a side and defending an entrenched position. Because both sides to the debate highlight different aspects of the same African dilemma, I will suggest that the way forward lies in sublating both, through a double move that simultaneously critiques and affirms. To arrive at a creative synthesis transcending both positions, one needs to problematize each.

To do so, I will analyze in this book two related phenomena: how power is organized and how it tends to fragment resistance in contemporary Africa. By locating both the language of rights and that of culture in their historical and institutional context, I hope to underline that part of our institutional legacy that continues to be reproduced through the dialectic of state reform and popular resistance. The core legacy, I will suggest, was forged through the colonial experience.

In colonial discourse, the problem of stabilizing alien rule was politely referred to as "the native question." It was a dilemma that confronted every colonial power and a riddle that preoccupied the best of its minds. Therefore it should not be surprising that when a person of the stature of General Jan Smuts, with an international renown rare for a South African prime minister, was invited to deliver the prestigious Rhodes

Memorial Lectures at Oxford in 1929, the native question formed the core of his deliberation.

The African, Smuts reminded his British audience, is a special human "type" with "some wonderful characteristics," which he went on to celebrate: "It has largely remained a child type, with a child psychology and outlook. A child-like human can not be a bad human, for are we not in spiritual matters bidden to be like unto little children? Perhaps as a direct result of this temperament the African is the only happy human I have come across." Even if the racism in the language is blinding, we should be wary of dismissing Smuts as some South African oddity.

Smuts spoke from within an honorable Western tradition. Had not Hegel's *Philosophy of History* mythologized "Africa proper" as "the land of childhood"? Did not settlers in British colonies call every African male, regardless of age, a "boy"—houseboy, shamba-boy, office-boy, ton-boy, mine-boy—no different from their counterparts in Francophone Africa, who used the child-familiar *tu* when addressing Africans of any age? "The negro," opined the venerable Albert Schweitzer of Gabon fame, "is a child, and with children nothing can be done without authority." In the colonial mind, however, Africans were no ordinary children. They were destined to be so perpetually—in the words of Christopher Fyfe, "Peter Pan children who can never grow up, a child race."[1]

Yet this book is not about the racial legacy of colonialism. If I tend to deemphasize the legacy of colonial racism, it is not only because it has been the subject of perceptive analyses by militant intellectuals like Frantz Fanon, but because I seek to highlight that part of the colonial legacy—the institutional—which remains more or less intact. Precisely because deracialization has marked the limits of postcolonial reform, the nonracial legacy of colonialism needs to be brought out into the open so that it may be the focus of a public discussion.

The point about General Smuts is not the racism that he shared with many of his class and race, for Smuts was not simply the unconscious bearer of a tradition. More than just a sentry standing guard at the cutting edge of that tradition, he was, if anything, its standard-bearer. A member of the British war cabinet, a confidant of Churchill and Roosevelt, a one-time chancellor of Cambridge University, Smuts rose to be one of the framers of the League of Nations Charter in the post–World War I era.[2] The very image of an enlightened leader, Smuts opposed slavery and celebrated the "principles of the French Revolution which had emancipated Europe," but he opposed their application to Africa, for the African, he argued, was of "a race so unique" that "nothing could be worse for Africa than the application of a policy" that would "de-Africanize the African and turn him either into a beast of the field or into a pseudo-European." "And yet in the past," he lamented, "we have tried both alternatives in our dealings with the Africans."

> First we looked upon the African as essentially inferior or sub-human, as having no soul, and as being only fit to be a slave. . . . Then we changed to the opposite extreme. The African now became a man and a brother. Religion and politics combined to shape this new African policy. The principles of the French Revolution which had emancipated Europe were applied to Africa; liberty, equality and fraternity could turn bad Africans into good Europeans.[3]

Smuts was at pains to underline the negative consequences of a policy formulated in ignorance, even if coated in good faith.

> The political system of the natives was ruthlessly destroyed in order to incorporate them as equals into the white system. The African was good as a potential European; his social and political culture was bad, barbarous, and only deserving to be stamped out root and branch. In some of the British possessions in Africa the native just emerged from barbarism was accepted as an equal citizen with full political rights along with the whites. But his native institutions were ruthlessly proscribed and destroyed. The principle of equal rights was applied in its crudest form, and while it gave the native a semblance of equality with whites, which was little good to him, it destroyed the basis of his African system which was his highest good. These are the two extreme native policies which have prevailed in the past, and the second has been only less harmful than the first.

If "Africa has to be redeemed" so as "to make her own contribution to the world," then "we shall have to proceed on different lines and evolve a policy which will not force her institutions into an alien European mould" but "will preserve her unity with her own past" and "build her future progress and civilization on specifically African foundations." Smuts went on to champion "the new policy" in bold: "The British Empire does not stand for the assimilation of its peoples into a common type, it does not stand for standardization, but for the fullest freest development of its peoples along their own specific lines."

The "fullest freest development of [its] peoples" as opposed to their assimilation "into a common type" required, Smuts argued, "institutional segregation." Smuts contrasted "institutional segregation" with "territorial segregation" then in practice in South Africa. The problem with "territorial segregation," in a nutshell, was that it was based on a policy of institutional homogenization. Natives may be territorially separated from whites, but native institutions were slowly but surely giving way to an alien institutional mold. As the economy became industrialized, it gave rise to "the colour problem," at the root of which were "urbanized or detribalized natives." Smuts's point was *not* that racial segregation ("territorial segregation") should be done away with. Rather it was that it should be made part of a broader "institutional segregation" and thereby set on a secure footing: "Institutional segregation carries with it territorial segregation." The way to preserve native institutions while meeting the labor demands of a growing economy was through the institution of migrant labor, for "so long as the native family home is not with the white man but in his own area, so long the native organization will not be materially affected."

> It is only when segregation breaks down, when the whole family migrates from the tribal home and out of the tribal jurisdiction to the white man's farm or the white man's town, that the tribal bond is snapped, and the traditional system falls into decay. And it is this migration of the native family, of the females and children, to the farms and the towns which should be prevented. As soon as this migration is permitted the process commences which ends in the urbanized detribalized native and the disappearance of the native organization. It is not white employment of native males that works the mischief, but the abandonment of the native tribal home by the women and children.[4]

Put simply, the problem with territorial segregation was that it rendered racial domination unstable: the more the economy developed, the more it came to depend on the "urbanized or detribalized natives." As that happened, the beneficiaries of rule appeared an alien minority and its victims evidently an indigenous majority. The way to stabilize racial domination (territorial segregation) was to ground it in a politically enforced system of ethnic pluralism (institutional segregation), so that everyone, victims no less than beneficiaries, may appear as minorities. However, with migrant labor providing the day-to-day institutional link between native and white society, native institutions—fashioned as so many rural tribal composites—may be conserved as separate but would function as subordinate.

At this point, however, Smuts faltered, for, he believed, it was too late in the day to implement a policy of institutional segregation in South Africa; urbanization had already proceeded too far. But it was not too late for less developed colonies to the north to learn from the South African experience: "The situation in South Africa is therefore a lesson to all the younger British communities farther north to prevent as much as possible the detachment of the native from his tribal connexion, and to enforce from the very start the system of segregation with its conservation of separate native institutions."

The Broederbond, however, disagreed. To this brotherhood of Boer supremacists, to stabilize the system of racial domination was a question of life and death, a matter in which it could never be too late. What Smuts termed institutional segregation the Broederbond called apartheid. The context in which apartheid came to be implemented made for its particularly harsh features, for to rule natives through their own institutions, one first had to push natives back into the confines of native institutions. In the context of a semi-industrialized and highly urbanized South Africa, this meant, on the one hand, the forced removal of those marked unproductive so they may be pushed out of white areas back into native homelands and, on the other, the forced straddling of those deemed productive between workplace and homeland through an ongoing cycle of annual migrations. To effect these changes required a degree of force and brutality that seemed to place the South African colonial experience in a class of its own.

But neither institutional segregation nor apartheid was a South African invention. If anything, both idealized a form of rule that the British Colonial Office dubbed "indirect rule" and the French "association." Three decades before Smuts, Lord Lugard had pioneered indirect rule in Uganda and Nigeria. And three decades after Smuts, Lord Hailey would sum up the contrast between forms of colonial rule as turning on a distinction between "identity" and "differentiation" in organizing the relationship between Europeans and Africans: "The doctrine of identity conceives the future social and political institutions of Africans as destined to be basically similar to those of Europeans; the doctrine of differentiation aims at the evolution of separate institutions appropriate to African conditions and differing both in spirit and in form from those of Europeans."[5] The emphasis on differentiation meant the forging of specifically "native" institutions through which to rule subjects, but the institutions so defined and enforced were not racial as much as ethnic, not "native" as much as "tribal." Racial dualism was thereby anchored in a politically enforced ethnic pluralism.

To emphasize their offensive and pejorative nature, I put the words *native* and *tribal* in quotation marks. But after first use, I have dropped the quotation marks to avoid a cumbersome read, instead relying on the reader's continued vigilance and good sense.

This book, then, is about the regime of differentiation (institutional segregation) as fashioned in colonial Africa—and reformed after independence—and the nature of the resistance it bred. Anchored historically, it is about how Europeans ruled Africa and how Africans responded to it. Drawn to the present, it is about the structure of power and the shape of resistance in contemporary Africa. Three sets of questions have guided my labors. To what extent was the structure of power in contemporary Africa shaped in the colonial period rather than born of the anticolonial revolt? Was the notion that they introduced the rule of law to African colonies no more than a cherished illusion of colonial powers? Second, rather than just uniting diverse ethnic groups in a common predicament, was not racial domination actually mediated through a variety of ethnically organized local powers? If so, is it not too simple even if tempting to think of the anticolonial (nationalist) struggle as just a one-sided repudiation of ethnicity rather than also a series of ethnic revolts against so many ethnically organized and centrally reinforced local powers—in other words, a string of ethnic civil wars? In brief, was not ethnicity a dimension of both power and resistance, of both the problem and the solution? Finally, if power reproduced itself by exaggerating difference and denying the existence of an oppressed majority, is not the burden of protest to transcend these differences without denying them?

I have written this book with four objectives in mind. My first objective is to question the writing of history by analogy, a method pervasive in contemporary Africanist studies. Thereby, I seek to establish the historical legitimacy of Africa as a unit of analysis. My second objective is to establish that apartheid, usually considered unique to South Africa, is actually the generic form of the colonial state in Africa. As a form of rule, apartheid is what Smuts called institutional segregation, the British termed indirect rule, and the French association. It is this common state form that I call decentralized despotism. A corollary is to bring some of the lessons from the study of Africa to South African studies and vice versa and thereby to question the notion of South African exceptionalism. A third objective is to underline the contradictory character of ethnicity. In disentangling its two possibilities, the emancipatory from the authoritarian, my purpose is not to identify emancipatory movements and avail them for an uncritical embrace. Rather it is to problematize them through a critical analysis. My fourth and final objective is to show that although the bifurcated state created with colonialism was deracialized after independence, it was not democratized. Postindependence reform led to diverse outcomes. No nationalist government was content to reproduce the colonial legacy uncritically. Each sought to reform the bifurcated state that institutionally crystallized a state-enforced separation, of the rural from the urban and of one ethnicity from another. But in doing so each reproduced a part of that legacy, thereby creating its own variety of despotism.

These questions and objectives are very much at the root of the discussion in the chapters that follow. Before sketching in full the outlines of my argument, however, I find it necessary to clarify my theoretical point of departure.

BEYOND A HISTORY BY ANALOGY

In the aftermath of the Cuban Revolution, dependency theory emerged as a powerful critique of various forms of unilinear evolutionism. It rejected both the claim that the less developed countries were traditional societies in need of modernization and the conviction that they were backward precapitalist societies on the threshhold of a much-needed bourgeois revolution. Underdevelopment, argued proponents of dependency, was historically produced; as a creation of modern imperialism, it was as modern as industrial capitalism. Both were outcomes of a process of "accumulation on a world scale."[6]

Its emphasis on historical specificity notwithstanding, dependency soon lapsed into yet another form of ahistorical structuralism. Alongside modernization theory and orthodox Marxism, it came to view social reality through a series of binary opposites. If modernization theorists thought of society as modern or premodern, industrial or preindustrial, and orthodox Marxists conceptualized modes of production as capitalist or precapitalist, dependency theorists juxtaposed development with underdevelopment. Of the bipolarity, the lead term—"modern," "industrial," "capitalist," or "development"—was accorded both analytical value and universal status. The other was residual. Making little sense without its lead twin, it had no independent conceptual existence. The tendency was to understand these experiences as a series of approximations, as replays not quite efficient, understudies that fell short of the real perfomance. Experiences summed up by analogy were not just considered historical latecomers on the scene, but were also ascribed a predestiny. Whereas the lead term had analytical content, the residual term lacked both an original history and an authentic future.

In the event that a real-life performance did not correspond to the prescribed trajectory, it was understood as a deviation. The bipolarity thus turned on a double distinction: between experiences considered universal and normal and those seen as residual or pathological. The residual or deviant case was understood not in terms of what it was, but with reference to what it was not. "Premodern" thus became "not yet modern," and "precapitalism" "not yet capitalism." But can a student, for example, be understood as not yet a teacher? Put differently, is being a professional teacher the true and necessary destiny of every student? The residual term in the evolutionary enterprise—"premodern," "preindustrial," "precapitalist," or "underdeveloped"—really summed up the "etc." of unilinear social science, that which it tended to explain away.

A unilinear social science, however, involves a double maneuver. If it tends to caricature the experience summed up as the residual term, it also mythologizes the experience that is the lead term. If the former is rendered ahistorical, the latter is ascribed a suprahistorical trajectory of development, a necessary path whose main line of development is unaffected by struggles that happened along the way. There is a sense in which both are robbed of history.

The endeavor to restore historicity, agency, to the subject has been the cutting edge of a variety of critiques of structuralism. But if structuralism tended to straitjacket agency within iron laws of history, a strong tendency in poststructuralism is to diminish the significance of historical constraint in the name of salvaging agency. "The dependent entry of African societies into the world system is not especially unique," argues the French Africanist Jean-Francois Bayart, "and should be *scientifically* de-dramatised."[7] On one hand, "inequality has existed throughout time, and—it should be stressed *ad nauseum*—does not negate historicity"; on the other hand, "deliberate recourse to the strategies of extraversion" has been a "recurring phenomenon in the history of the continent." Dependency theory is thereby stood on its head as modern imperialism is—shall I say celebrated?—as the outcome of an African initiative! Similarly, in another recent historical rewrite, slavery too is explained away as the result of a local initiative. "The African role in the development of the Atlantic," promises John Thornton, "would not simply be a secondary one, on either side of the Atlantic," for "we must accept" both "that African participation in the slave trade was voluntary and under the control of African decision makers" on this side of the Atlantic and that "the condition of slavery, by itself, did not necessarily prevent the development of an African-oriented culture" on the far side of the Atlantic.[8] It is one thing to argue that nothing short of death can extinguish human initiative and creativity, but quite another to see in every such gesture evidence of a historical initiative. "Even the inmates of a concentration camp are able, in this sense, to live by their own cultural logic," remarks Talal Asad. "But one may be forgiven for doubting that they are therefore 'making their own history.'"[9]

To have critiqued structuralist-inspired binary oppositions for giving rise to walled-off sciences of the normal and the abnormal, the civilized and the savage, is the chief merit of poststructuralism. To appreciate this critique, however, is not quite the same as to accept the claim that in seeking to transcend these epistemological oppositions embedded in notions of the modern and the traditional, poststructuralism has indeed created the basis of a healthy humanism. That claim is put forth by its Africanist adherents; scholarship, they say, must "deexoticize" Africa and banalize it.

The swing from the exotic to the banal ("Yes, banal Africa—exoticism be damned!")[10] is from one extreme to another, from seeing the flow of events in Africa as exceptional to the general flow of world history to seeing it as routine, as simply dissolving in that general flow, confirming its trend, and in the process presumably confirming the humanity of the African people. In the process, African history and reality lose any specificity, and with it, we also lose any but an invented notion of Africa. But it is only when abstracted from structural constraint that agency appears as lacking in historical specificity. At this point, abstract universalism and intimate particularism turn out to be two sides of the same coin: both see in the specificity of experience nothing but its idiosyncrasy.

The Patrimonial State

Whereas poststructuralists focus on the intimate and the day-to-day, shunning metatheory and metaexperience, the mainstream Africanists are shy of neither. The presumption that developments in Africa can best be understood as mirroring an earlier history is widely shared among North American Africanists. Before the current preoccupation with civil society as the guarantor of democracy—a notion I will comment on later—Africanist political science was concerned mainly with two issues: a tendency toward corruption among those within the system and toward exit among those marginal to it.

The literature on corruption makes sense of its spread as a reoccurrence of an early European practice: "patrimonialism" or "prebendalism."[11] Two broad tendencies can be discerned.[12] For the state-centrists, the state has failed to penetrate society sufficiently and is therefore hostage to it; for the society-centrists, society has failed to hold the state accountable and is therefore prey to it. I will argue that the former fail to see the form of power, of how the state does penetrate society, and the latter the form of revolt, of how society does hold the state accountable, because both work through analogies and are unable to come to grips with a historically specific reality.

Although I will return to the society-centrists, the present-day champions of civil society as the guarantor of democracy, it is worth tracing the contours of the state-centrist argument. Overwhelmed by societal pressures, its institutional integrity compromised by individual or sectional interest, the state has turned into a "weak Leviathan,"[13] "suspended above society."[14] Whether plain "soft"[15] or in "decline" and "decay,"[16] this creature may be "omnipresent" but is hardly "omnipotent."[17] Then follows the theoretical conclusion: variously termed as the "early modern authoritarian state," the "early modern absolutist state," or "the patrimonial autocratic state," this form of state power is likened to its ancestors in seventeenth-century Europe or early postcolonial Latin America, often underlined as a political feature of the transition to capitalism.

What happens if you take a historical process unfolding under concrete conditions—in this case, of sixteenth- to eighteenth-century Europe—as a vantage point from which to make sense of subsequent social development? The outcome is a history by analogy rather than history as process. Analogy seeking turns into a substitute for theory formation. The Africanist is akin to those learning a foreign language who must translate every new word back into their mother tongue, in the process missing precisely what is new in a new experience. From such a standpoint, the most intense controversies dwell on what is indeed the most appropriate translation, the most adequate fit, the most appropriate analogy that will capture the meaning of the phenomenon under observation. Africanist debates tend to focus on whether contemporary African reality most closely resembles the transition to capitalism under seventeenth-century European absolutism or that under other Third World experiences,[18] or whether the postcolonial state in Africa should be labeled Bonapartist or absolutist.[19] Whatever their differences, both sides agree that African reality has meaning only insofar as it can be seen to reflect a particular stage in the development of an earlier history. Inasmuch as it privileges the European historical experience as its touchstone, as the historical expression of the universal, contemporary unilinear evolutionism should more concretely and appropriately be characterized as a Eurocentrism. The central tendency of such a methodological orientation is to lift a phenomenon out of context and process. The result is a history by analogy.

The Uncaptured Peasantry

Whereas the literature on corruption is mainly about the state in Africa, that on exit is about the peasantry. Two diametrically opposed perspectives can be discerned here. One looks at the African countryside as nothing but an ensemble of transactions in a marketplace; the other sees it as a collection of households enmeshed in a nonmarket milieu of kin-based relations. For the former, the market is the defining feature of rural life; for the latter, the intrinsic realities of village Africa have little to do with the market. The same tendency can appear clothed in sharply contrasting ideological garb. Thus, for example, the argument that rural Africa is really precapitalist, with the market an external and artificial imposition, was first put forth by the proponents of African socialism, most notably Julius Nyerere. Largely discredited in the mid-seventies, when dependency theory reigned supreme, this thesis was resurrected in the eighties by Goran Hyden,[20] who echoed Nyerere—once again relying on empirical material from Tanzania—that the "intrinsic realities" of "Africa" have little to do with market relationships. Instead, he argued,

they are a unique expression of a premarket "economy of affection."
Market theories were championed by IMF theorists who claimed that
the rationality of ground-level markets was being simultaneously suppressed and distorted by clientele-ridden but all-powerful states. The
argument was given academic respectability by Robert Bates's widely
circulated study *Markets and States in Africa*. Whereas the latter tendency continues to enjoy the status of an official truth in policy-making
circles, the former survives as a marginal but fashionable preoccupation
in academia.

My interest is in the method that guides these contending perspectives. With market theorists, the method is transparent. They presume
the market to exist, as an ahistorical and universal construct: markets are
not created, but freed; African countries are market societies, like those
in Europe, period. Goran Hyden, however, claims to be laying bare the
intrinsic realities of Africa. Yet he proceeds not by a historical examination of these realities but by formal analogies. Searching for the right
analogy to fit Africa, he proceeds by dismissing, one after another, those
that do not fit. In the process, he establishes his main conclusion: Africa
is *not* like Europe, where the peasantry was "captured" through wage
labor; nor is it like Asia or Latin America, where it was "captured"
through tenancy arrangements. But this search stops at showing what
does *not* exist. "It is the argument of this book," writes Hyden, "that
Africa is the only continent where the peasants have not been captured
by other social classes."[21] In hot pursuit of the right historical analogy—
the point will become clear later—Hyden misses precisely the relations
through which the "free" peasantry is "captured" and reproduced.

In this book, I seek neither to set the African experience apart as exceptional and exotic nor to absorb it in a broad corpus of theory as routine and banal. For both, it seems to me, are different ways of dismissing
it. In contrast, I try to underline the specificity of the African experience,
or at least of a slice of it. This is an argument not against comparative
study but against those who would dehistoricize phenomena by lifting
them from context, whether in the name of an abstract universalism or
of an intimate particularism, only to make sense of them by analogy. In
contrast, my endeavor is to establish the historical legitimacy of Africa as
a unit of analysis.

Civil Society

The current Africanist discourse on civil society resembles an earlier discourse on socialism. It is more programmatic than analytical, more ideological than historical. Central to it are two claims: civil society exists as
a fully formed construct in Africa as in Europe, and the driving force of

democratization everywhere is the contention between civil society and the state.[22] To come to grips with these claims requires a historical analysis, for these conclusions are arrived at through analogy seeking.

The notion of civil society came to prominence with the Eastern European uprisings of the late 1980s. These events were taken as signaling a paradigmatic shift, from a state-centered to a society-centered perspective, from a strategy of armed struggle that seeks to capture state power to one of an unarmed civil struggle that seeks to create a self-limiting power. In the late 1980s, the theme of a society-state struggle reverberated through Africanist circles in North America and became the new prismatic lens through which to gauge the significance of events in Africa. Even though the shift from armed struggle to popular civil protest had occurred in South Africa a decade earlier, in the course of the Durban strikes of 1973 and the Soweto uprising of 1976, the same observers who tended to exceptionalize the significance of these events eagerly generalized the import of later events in Eastern Europe!

For the core of post-Renaissance theory,[23] civil society was a historical construct, the result of an all-embracing process of differentiation: of power in the state and division of labor in the economy, giving rise to an autonomous legal sphere to govern civil life. It is no exaggeration to say that the Hegelian notion of civil society is both the summation and the springboard of main currents of Western thought on the subject.[24] Sandwiched between the patriarchal family and the universal state, civil society was for Hegel the historical product of a two-dimensional process. On one hand, the spread of commodity relations diminished the weight of extra-economic coercion, and in doing so, it freed the economy—and broadly society—from the sphere of politics. On the other hand, the centralization of means of violence within the modern state went alongside the settlement of differences within society without direct recourse to violence. With an end to extra-economic coercion, force ceased to be a direct arbiter in day-to-day life. Contractual relations among free and autonomous individuals were henceforth regulated by civil law. Bounded by law, the modern state recognized the rights of citizens. The rule of law meant that law-governed behavior was the rule. It is in this sense that civil society was understood as civilized society.

As a meeting ground of contradictory interests, civil society in Hegel comprises two related moments, the first explosive, the second integrative; the first in the arena of the market, the second of public opinion. These two moments resurface in Marx and Gramsci as two different conceptions of civil society. For Marx civil society is the ensemble of relations embedded in the market; the agency that defines its character is the bourgeoisie. For Gramsci (as for Polanyi, Talcott Parsons, and later Habermas) the differentiation that underlies civil society is triple and not double: between the state, the economy, and society. The realm of civil society is not the market but public opinion and culture. Its agents are intellectuals, who figure predominantly in the establishment of hegemony. Its hallmarks are voluntary association and free publicity, the basis of an autonomous organizational and expressive life. Although autonomous of the state, this life cannot be independent of it, for the guarantor of the autonomy of civil society can be none other than the state; or, to put matters differently, although its guarantor may be a specific constellation of social forces organized in and through civil society, they can do so only by ensuring a form of the state and a corresponding legal regime to undergird the autonomy of civil society.

The Gramscian notion of civil society as public opinion and culture has been formulated simultaneously as analytical construct and programmatic agenda in Jürgen Habermas's work on the public sphere.[25] Habermas accents both structural processes and strategic initiatives in explaining the historical formation of civil society. In the context of a structural change "embedded in the transformation of state and economy," the strategic initiatives of an embryonic bourgeois class shaped "an associational life" along voluntary and democratic principles.[26] At first, this "public sphere" was largely apolitical, revolving "around literary and art criticism." The French Revolution, however, "triggered a movement" leading to its "politicization," thereby underlining its democratic significance.

Critics of Habermas have tried to disentangle the analytical from the programmatic strands in his argument by relocating this movement in its historical context. Thus, argues Geoff Eley, the "public sphere" was from the very outset "an arena of contested meanings," both in that "different and opposing publics maneuvered for space" within it and in the sense that "certain 'publics' (women, subordinate nationalities, popular classes like the urban poor, the working class, and the peasantry) may have been excluded altogether" from it. This process of exclusion was simultaneously one of "harnessing . . . public life to the interests of one particular group."[27]

The exclusion that defined the specificity of civil society under colonial rule was that of race. Yet it is not possible to understand the nature of colonial power simply by focusing on the partial and exclusionary character of civil society. It requires, rather, coming to grips with the specific nature of power through which the population of subjects excluded from civil society was actually ruled. This is why the focus in this book is on how the subject population was incorporated into—and not excluded from—the arena of colonial power. The accent is on incorporation, not marginalization. By emphasizing this not as an exclusion but as another form of power, I intend to argue that no reform of contemporary civil society institutions can by itself unravel this decentralized despotism. To do so will require nothing less than dismantling that form of power.

THE BIFURCATED STATE

The colonial state was in every instance a historical formation. Yet its structure everywhere came to share certain fundamental features. I will argue that this was so because everywhere the organization and reorganization of the colonial state was a response to a central and overriding dilemma: the native question. Briefly put, how can a tiny and foreign minority rule over an indigenous majority? To this question, there were two broad answers: direct and indirect rule.

Direct rule was Europe's initial response to the problem of administering colonies. There would be a single legal order, defined by the "civilized" laws of Europe. No "native" institutions would be recognized. Although "natives" would have to conform to European laws, only those "civilized" would have access to European rights. Civil society, in this sense, was presumed to be civilized society, from whose ranks the uncivilized were excluded. The ideologues of a civilized native policy rationalized segregation as less a racial than a cultural affair. Lord Milner, the colonial secretary, argued that segregation was "desirable no less in the interests of social comfort and convenience than in those of health and sanitation." Citing Milner, Lugard concurred:

> On the one hand the policy does not impose any restriction on one race which is not applicable to the other. A European is as strictly prohibited from living in the native reservation, as a native is from living in the European quarter. On the other hand, since this feeling exists, it should in my opinion be made abundantly clear that what is aimed at is a segregation of social standards, and not a segregation of races. The Indian or the African gentleman who adopts the higher standard of civilization and desires to partake in such immunity from infection as segregation may convey, should be as free and welcome to live in the civilized reservation as the European, provided, of course, that he does not bring with him a concourse of followers. The native peasant often shares his hut with his goat, or sheep, or fowls. He loves to drum and dance at night, which deprives the European of sleep. He is skeptical of mosquito theories. "God made the mosquito larvae," said a Moslem delegation to me, "for God's sake let the larvae live." For these people, sanitary rules are necessary but hateful. They have no desire to abolish segregation.[28]

Citizenship would be a privilege of the civilized; the uncivilized would be subject to an all-round tutelage. They may have a modicum of civil rights, but not political rights, for a propertied franchise separated the civilized from the uncivilized. The resulting vision was summed up in Cecil Rhodes's famous phrase, "Equal rights for all civilized men."

Colonies were territories of European settlement. In contrast, the territories of European domination—but not of settlement—were known as protectorates. In the context of a settler capitalism, the social prerequisite of direct rule was a rather drastic affair. It involved a comprehensive sway of market institutions: the appropriation of land, the destruction of communal autonomy, and the defeat and dispersal of tribal populations. In practice, direct rule meant the reintegration and domination of natives in the institutional context of semiservile and semicapitalist agrarian relations. For the vast majority of natives, that is, for those uncivilized who were excluded from the rights of citizenship, direct rule signified an unmediated—centralized—despotism.

In contrast, indirect rule came to be the mode of domination over a "free" peasantry. Here, land remained a communal—"customary"— possession. The market was restricted to the products of labor, only marginally incorporating land or labor itself. Peasant communities were reproduced within the context of a spatial and institutional autonomy. The tribal leadership was either selectively reconstituted as the hierarchy of the local state or freshly imposed where none had existed, as in "stateless societies." Here political inequality went alongside civil inequality. Both were grounded in a legal dualism. Alongside received law was implemented a customary law that regulated nonmarket relations, in land, in personal (family), and in community affairs. For the subject population of natives, indirect rule signified a mediated—decentralized— despotism.

Even historically, the division between direct and indirect rule never coincided neatly with the one between settler and nonsettler colonies. True, agrarian settler capital did prefer direct rule premised on "freeing" land while bonding labor, but indirect rule could not be linked to any specific fraction of capital. It came to mark the inclination of several fractions of the bourgeoisie: mining, finance, and commerce. The main features of direct and indirect rule, and the contrast between them, are best illustrated by the South African experience. Direct rule was the main mode of control attempted over natives in the eighteenth and early nineteenth centuries. It is a form of control best exemplified by the Cape experience. The basic features of indirect rule, however, emerged through the experience of Natal in the second half of the nineteenth century. The distinction is also captured in the contrast between the experience of the nineteenth-century coastal enclaves (colonies) of Lagos, Freetown, and Dakar and the twentieth-century inland protectorates acquired in the course of *the Scramble.* The Cape-Natal divide over how to handle the native question was resolved in favor of the Natal model. Key to that resolution was the emergence of the Cape as the largest single reserve for migrant labor in South Africa, for the dominance of mining over agrarian capital in late-nineteenth-century South Africa—and elsewhere—posed afresh the question of the reproduction of autonomous peasant communities that would regularly supply male, adult, and single migrant labor to the mines.

Debated as alternative modes of controlling natives in the early colonial period, direct and indirect rule actually evolved into complementary ways of native control. Direct rule was the form of urban civil power. It was about the exclusion of natives from civil freedoms guaranteed to citizens in civil society. Indirect rule, however, signified a rural tribal authority. It was about incorporating natives into a state-enforced customary order. Reformulated, direct and indirect rule are better understood as variants of despotism: the former centralized, the latter decentralized. As they learned from experience—of both the ongoing resistance of the colonized and of earlier and parallel colonial encounters—colonial powers generalized decentralized despotism as their principal answer to the native question.

The African colonial experience came to be crystallized in the nature of the state forged through that encounter. Organized differently in rural areas from urban ones, that state was Janus-faced, bifurcated. It contained a duality: two forms of power under a single hegemonic authority. Urban power spoke the language of civil society and civil rights, rural power of community and culture. Civil power claimed to protect rights, customary power pledged to enforce tradition. The former was organized on the principle of differentiation to check the concentration of power, the latter around the principle of fusion to ensure a unitary authority. To grasp the relationship between the two, civil power and customary power, and between the language each employed—rights and custom, freedom and tradition—we need to consider them separately while keeping in mind that each signified one face of the same bifurcated state.

Actually Existing Civil Society

The rationale of civil power was that it was the source of civil law that framed civil rights in civil society. I have already suggested that this idealization—also shared by contemporary Africanist discourse on civil society—reminds one of an earlier discourse on socialism. More programmatic than analytical, more ideological than historical, its claims call for a historical analysis. Thus the need—as I have already suggested—for an analysis of actually existing civil society so as to understand it in its actual formation, rather than as a promised agenda for change.

To grasp major shifts in the history of the relationship between civil society and the state, one needs to move away from the assumption of a single generalizable moment and identify different and even contradictory moments in that historical flow. Only through a historically anchored query is it possible to problematize the notion of civil society, thereby to approach it analytically rather than programatically.

The history of civil society in colonial Africa is laced with racism. That is, as it were, its original sin, for civil society was first and foremost the society of the colons. Also, it was primarily a creation of the colonial state. The rights of free association and free publicity, and eventually of political representation, were the rights of citizens under direct rule, not of subjects indirectly ruled by a customarily organized tribal authority. Thus, whereas civil society was racialized, Native Authority was tribalized. Between the rights-bearing colons and the subject peasantry was a third group: urban-based natives, mainly middle- and working-class persons, who were exempt from the lash of customary law but not from modern, racially discriminatory civil legislation. Neither subject to custom nor exalted as rights-bearing citizens, they languished in a juridical limbo.

In the main, however, the colonial state was a double-sided affair. Its one side, the state that governed a racially defined citizenry, was bounded by the rule of law and an associated regime of rights. Its other side, the state that ruled over subjects, was a regime of extra-economic coercion and administratively driven justice. No wonder that the struggle of subjects was both against customary authorities in the local state and against racial barriers in civil society. The latter was particularly acute in the settler colonies, where it often took the form of an armed struggle, but it was not confined to settler colonies. Its best-known theoretician was Frantz Fanon. This then was the first historical moment in the development of civil society: the colonial state as the protector of the society of the colons.

The second moment in that development saw a marked shift in the relation between civil society and the state. This was the moment of the anticolonial struggle, for the anticolonial struggle was at the same time a struggle of embryonic middle and working classes, the native strata in limbo, for entry into civil society. That entry, that expansion of civil society, was the result of an antistate struggle. Its consequence was the creation of an indigenous civil society. A process set into motion with the postwar colonial reform, this development was of limited significance. It could not be otherwise, for any significant progress in the creation of an indigenous civil society required a change in the form of the state. It required a deracialized state.

Independence, the birth of a deracialized state, was the context of the third moment in this history. Independence tended to deracialize the state but not civil society. Instead, historically accumulated privilege, usually racial, was embedded and defended in civil society. Wherever the struggle to deracialize civil society reached meaningful proportions, the independent state played a central role. In this context, the state–civil society antagonism diminished as the arena of tensions shifted to within civil society.

The key policy instrument in that struggle was what is today called affirmative action and what was then called Africanization. The politics of Africanization was simultaneously unifying and fragmenting. Its first moment involved the dismantling of racially inherited privilege. The effect was to unify the victims of colonial racism. Not so the second moment, which turned around the question of redistribution and divided that same majority along lines that reflected the actual process of redistribution: regional, religious, ethnic, and at times just familial. The tendency of the literature on corruption in postindependence Africa has been to detach the two moments and thereby to isolate and decontextualize the moment of redistribution (corruption) from that of expropriation (redress) through ahistorical analogies that describe it as the politics of patrimonialism, prebendalism, and so on. The effect has been to caricature the practices under investigation and to make them unintelligible. Put back in the context of an urban civil society encircled by a countryside under the sway of so many customary powers—thus subject to the twin pressures of deracialization and retribalization—patrimonialism, as we will see, was in fact a form of politics that restored an urban-rural link in the context of a bifurcated state, albeit in a top-down fashion that facilitated the quest of bourgeois fractions to strengthen and reproduce their leadership.

There is also a second contextualized lesson one needs to draw from that period. The other side of the politics of affirmative action was the struggle of the beneficiaries of the colonial order—mainly colons in the settler colonies and immigrant minorities (from India and Lebanon) in nonsettler colonies—to defend racial privilege. This defense, too, took a historically specific form, for with the deracialization of the state, the language of that defense could no longer be racial. Racial privilege not only receded into civil society, but defended itself in the language of civil rights, of individual rights and institutional autonomy. To victims of racism the vocabulary of rights rang hollow, a lullaby for perpetuating racial privilege. Their demands were formulated in the language of nationalism and social justice. The result was a breach between the discourse on rights and the one on justice, with the language of rights appearing as a fig leaf over privilege and power appearing as the guarantor of social justice and redress.

This is the context of the fourth moment in the history of actually existing civil society. This is the moment of the collapse of an embryonic indigenous civil society, of trade unions and autonomous civil organizations, and its absorption into political society. It is the moment of the marriage between technicism and nationalism, of the proliferation of state nationalism in a context where the claims of the state—both developmentalist and equalizing—had a powerful resonance, particularly for the fast-expanding educated strata. It is the time when civil society–based social movements became demobilized and political movements statized.[29]

To understand the limits of deracialization of civil society, one needs to grasp the specificity of the local state, which was organized not as a racial power denying rights to urbanized subjects, but as an ethnic power enforcing custom on tribespeople. The point of reform of such a power could not be deracialization; it could be only detribalization. But so long as the reform perspective was limited to deracialization, it looked as though nothing much had changed in the rural sphere, whereas everything seemed to have changed in the urban areas. We will see that wherever there was a failure to democratize the local state, postindependence generations had to pay a heavy price: the unreformed Native Authority came to contaminate civil society, so that the more civil society was deracialized, the more it took on a tribalized form.

True, the deracialization of the central state was a necessary step toward its democratization, but the two could not be equated. To appreciate what democratization would have entailed in the African context, we need to grasp the specificity of tribal power in the countryside.

Customary Authority

Late colonialism brought a wealth of experience to its African pursuit. By the time the Scramble for Africa took place, the turn from a civilizing mission to a law-and-order administration, from progress to power, was complete. In the quest to hold the line, Britain was the first to marshal authoritarian possibilities in native culture. In the process, it defined a world of the customary from which there was no escape. Key to this was the definition of land as a customary possession, for in nonsettler Africa, the Africa administered through Native Authorities, the general rule was that land could not be a private possession, of either landlords or peasants. It was defined as a customary communal holding, to which every peasant household had a customary access, defined by state-appointed customary authorities. As we will see, the creation of an all-embracing world of the customary had three notable consequences.

First, more than any other colonial subject, the African was containerized, not as a native, but as a tribesperson. Every colony had two legal systems: one modern, the other customary. Customary law was defined in the plural, as the law of the tribe, and not in the singular, as a law for all natives. Thus, there was not one customary law for all natives, but roughly as many sets of customary laws as there were said to be tribes. The genius of British rule in Africa—we will hear one of its semiofficial historians claim—was in seeking to civilize Africans as communities, not as individuals. More than anywhere else, there was in the African colonial experience a one-sided opposition between the individual and the group, civil society and community, rights and tradition.

Second, in the late-nineteenth-century African context, there were several traditions, not just one. The tradition that colonial powers privileged as the customary was the one with the least historical depth, that of nineteenth-century conquest states. But this monarchical, authoritarian, and patriarchal notion of the customary, we will see, most accurately mirrored colonial practices. In this sense, it was an ideological construct.

Unlike civil law, customary law was an administratively driven affair, for those who enforced custom were in a position to define it in the first place. Custom, in other words, was state ordained and state enforced. I wish to be understood clearly. I am not arguing for a conspiracy theory whereby custom was always defined "from above," always "invented" or "constructed" by those in power. The customary was more often than not the site of struggle. Custom was often the outcome of a contest between various forces, not just those in power or its on-the-scene agents. My point, though, is about the institutional context in which this contest took place: the terms of the contest, its institutional framework, were heavily skewed in favor of state-appointed customary authorities. It was, as we will see, a game in which the dice were loaded.

It should not be surprising that custom came to be the language of force, masking the uncustomary power of Native Authorities. The third notable consequence of an all-embracing customary power was that the African colonial experience was marked by force to an unusual degree. Where land was defined as a customary possession, the market could be only a partial construct. Beyond the market, there was only one way of driving land and labor out of the world of the customary: force. The day-to-day violence of the colonial system was embedded in customary

Native Authorities in the local state, not in civil power at the center. Yet we must not forget that customary local authority was reinforced and backed up by central civil power. Colonial despotism was highly decentralized.

The seat of customary power in the rural areas was the local state: the district in British colonies, the *cercle* in French colonies. The functionary of the local state apparatus was everywhere called the chief. One should not be misled by the nomenclature into thinking of this as a holdover from the precolonial era. Not only did the chief have the right to pass rules (bylaws) governing persons under his domain, he also executed all laws and was the administrator in "his" area, in which he settled all disputes. The authority of the chief thus fused in a single person all moments of power: judicial, legislative, executive, and administrative. This authority was like a clenched fist, necessary because the chief stood at the intersection of the market economy and the nonmarket one. The administrative justice and the administrative coercion that were the sum and substance of his authority lay behind a regime of extra-economic coercion, a regime that breathed life into a whole range of compulsions: forced labor, forced crops, forced sales, forced contributions, and forced removals.

ETHNICITY AND THE ANTICOLONIAL REVOLT

To understand the nature of struggle and of agency, one needs to understand the nature of power. The latter has something to do with the nature of exploitation but is not reducible to it. I started writing this book with a focus on differentiated agrarian systems on the continent. From the perspective that has come to be known as political economy, I learned that the nature of political power becomes intelligible when put in the context of concrete accumulation processes and the struggles shaped by these.[30] From this point of view, the starting point of analysis had to be the labor question.

I began to question the completeness of this proposition when I came to realize that the form of the state that had evolved over the colonial period was not specific to any particular agrarian system. Its specificity was, rather, political; more than anything else, the form of the state was shaped by the African colonial experience. More than the labor question, it was the native question that illuminated this experience. My point is not to set up a false opposition between the two, but I do maintain that political analysis cannot extrapolate the nature of power from an analysis of political economy. More than the labor question, the organization and reorganization of power turned on the imperitive of maintaining political order. This is why to understand the form of the state forged under colonialism one had to place at the center of analysis the riddle that was the native question.

The form of rule shaped the form of revolt against it. Indirect rule at once reinforced ethnically bound institutions of control and led to their explosion from within. Ethnicity (tribalism) thus came to be simultaneously the form of colonial control over natives and the form of revolt against it. It defined the parameters of both the Native Authority in charge of the local state apparatus and of resistance to it.

Everywhere, the local apparatus of the colonial state was organized either on an ethnic or on a religious basis. At the same time, one finds it difficult to recall a single major peasant uprising over the colonial period that has not been either ethnic or religious in inspiration. Peasant insurrectionists organized around what they claimed was an untainted, uncompromised, and genuine custom, against a state-enforced and corrupted version of the customary. This is so for a simple but basic reason: the anticolonial struggle was first and foremost a struggle against the hierarchy of the local state, the tribally organized Native Authority, which enforced the colonial order as customary. This is why everywhere—although the cadres of the nationalist movement were recruited mainly from urban areas—the movement gained depth the more it was anchored in the peasant struggle against Native Authorities.

Yet tribalism as revolt became the source of a profound dilemma because local populations were usually multiethnic and at times multireligious. Ethnicity, and at times religion, was reproduced as a problem inside every peasant movement. This is why it is not enough simply to separate tribal power organized from above from tribal revolt waged from below so that we may denounce the former and embrace the latter. The revolt from below needs to be problemized, for it carries the seeds of its own fragmentation and possible self-destruction.

I have already suggested that the fragmentation is not just ethnic. Rather, the interethnic divide is an effect of a larger split, also politically enforced, between town and country. Neither was this double divide, urban-rural and interethnic, fortuitous. My claim is that every movement against decentralized despotism bore the institutional imprint of that mode of rule. Every movement of resistance was shaped by the very structure of power against which it rebelled. How it came to understand this historical fact, and the capacity it marshaled to transcend it, set the tone and course of the movement. I will make this point through an analysis of two types of resistance: the rural in Uganda and the urban in South Africa.

We are now in a position to answer the question, What would democratization have entailed in the African context? It would have entailed the deracialization of civil power and the detribalization of customary power, as starting points of an overall democratization that would transcend the legacy of a bifurcated power. A consistent democratization would have required dismantling and reorganizing the local state, the array of Native Authorities organized around the principle of fusion of power, fortified by an administratively driven customary justice and nourished through extra-economic coercion.

In addition to setting the pace in tapping authoritarian possibilities in culture and in giving culture an authoritarian bent, Britain led the way in fashioning a theory that claimed its particular form of colonial domination to be marked by an enlightened and permissive recognition of native culture. Although its capacity to dominate grew through a dispersal of its own power, the colonial state claimed this process to be no more than a deference to local tradition and custom. To grasp the contradiction in this claim, I have suggested, needs the analysis of the institutions within which official custom was forged and reproduced. The most important institutional legacy of colonial rule, I argue, may lie in the inherited impediments to democratization.

VARIETIES OF DESPOTISM
AS POSTINDEPENDENCE REFORM

Clearly, the form of the state that emerged through postindependence reform was not the same in every instance. There was a variation. If we start with the language that power employed to describe itself, we can identify two distinct constellations: the conservative and the radical. In the case of the conservative African states, the hierarchy of the local state apparatus, from chiefs to headmen, continued after independence. In the radical African states, though, there seemed to be a marked change. In some instances, a constellation of tribally defined customary laws was discarded as a single customary law transcending tribal boundaries was codified. The result, however, was to develop a uniform, countrywide customary law, applicable to all peasants regardless of ethnic affiliation, functioning alongside a modern law for urban dwellers. A version of the bifurcated state, forged through the colonial encounter, remained. Whereas the conservative regimes reproduced the decentralized despotism that was the form of the colonial state in Africa, the radical regimes sought to reform it. The outcome, however, was not to dismantle despotism through a democratic reform; rather it was to reorganize decentralized power so as to unify the "nation" through a reform that tended to centralization. The antidote to a decentralized despotism turned out to be a centralized despotism. In the back-and-forth movement between a decentralized and centralized despotism, each regime claimed to be reforming the negative features of its predecessor. This, we will see, is best illustrated by the seesaw movement between civilian and military regimes in Nigeria.

The continuity between the form of the colonial state and the power fashioned through radical reform was underlined by the despotic nature of power. For inasmuch as radical regimes shared with colonial powers the conviction to effect a revolution from above, they ended up intensifying the administratively driven nature of justice, customary or modern. If anything, the radical experience built on the legacy of fused power enforcing administrative imperatives through extra-economic coercion—except that, this time, it was done in the name not of enforcing custom but of making development and waging revolution. Even if there was a change in the title of functionaries, from chiefs to cadres, there was little change in the nature of power. If anything, the fist of colonial power that was the local state was tightened and strengthened. Even if it did not employ the language of custom and enforce it through a tribal authority, the more it centralized coercive authority in the name of development or revolution, the more it enforced and deepened the gulf between town and country. If the decentralized conservative variant of despotism tended to bridge the urban-rural divide through a clientelism whose effect was to exacerbate ethnic divisions, its centralized radical variant tended to do the opposite: de-emphasizing the customary and ethnic difference between rural areas while deepening the chasm between town and country in the pursuit of an administratively driven development. The bifurcated state that was created with colonialism was deracialized, but it was not democratized. If the two-pronged division that the colonial state enforced on the colonized—between town and country, and between ethnicities—was its dual legacy at independence, each of the two versions of the postcolonial state tended to soften one part of the legacy while exacerbating the other. The limits of the conservative states were obvious: they removed the sting of racism from a colonially fashioned stronghold but kept in place the Native Authorities, which enforced the division between ethnicities. The radical states went a step further, joining deracialization to detribalization. But the deracialized and detribalized power they organized put a premium on administrative decision-making. In the name of detribalization, they tightened central control over local authorities. Claiming to herald development and wage revolution, they intensified extra-economic pressure on the peasantry. In the process, they inflamed the division between town and country. If the prototype subject in the conservative states bore an ethnic mark, the prototype subject in the radical states was simply the rural peasant. In the process, both experiences reproduced one part of the dual legacy of the bifurcated state and created their own distinctive version of despotism.

SOUTH AFRICAN EXCEPTIONALISM

The bittersweet fruit of African independence also defines one possible future for postapartheid South Africa. Part of my argument is that apartheid, usually considered the exceptional feature in the South African experience, is actually its one aspect that is uniquely African. As a form of the state, apartheid is neither self-evidently objectionable nor self-evidently identifiable. Usually understood as institutionalized racial domination, apartheid was actually an attempt to soften racial antagonism by mediating and thereby refracting the impact of racial domination through a range of Native Authorities. Not surprisingly, the discourse of apartheid—in both General Smuts, who anticipated it, and the Broederbond, which engineered it—idealized the practice of indirect rule in British colonies to the north. As a form of rule, apartheid—like the indirect rule colonial state—fractured the ranks of the ruled along a double divide: ethnic on the one hand, rural-urban on the other.

The notion of South African exceptionalism is a current so strong in South African studies that it can be said to have taken on the character of a prejudice. I am painfully aware of the arduous labor of generations of researchers that has gone into the making of South African studies: someone new to that field must tread gingerly and modestly. Yet we all know of the proverbial child who combines audacity with the privilege of seeing things anew; perhaps this child's only strength is to take notice when the emperor has no clothes on. My claim, simply put, is that South Africa has been an African country with specific differences.

The South African literature that has a bearing on the question of the state comprises three related currents. The first is a body of writings largely economistic. It focuses on the rural-urban interface and the diminishing significance of the countryside as a source of livelihood for its inhabitants. Its accent is on the mode of exploitation, not of rule. With its eye on an irreversible process of proletarianization, it sees rural areas as rapidly shrinking in the face of a unilinear trend. Because it treats rural areas as largely residual, it is unable fully to explain apartheid as a form of the state. It is only from an economistic perspective—one that highlights levels of industrialization and proletarianization one-sidedly—that South African exceptionalism makes sense. Conversely, the same exceptionalism masks the colonial nature of the South African experience.

The point is worth elaborating. It is only from a perspective that focuses single-mindedly on the labor question that the South African experience appears exceptional. For the labor question does illuminate that which sets South Africa apart more or less in a category of its own: semi-industrialization, semi-proleterianization, semi-urbanization, capped by a strong civil society. This is why it takes a shift of focus from the labor question to the native question to underline that which is African and unexceptional in the South African experience. That commonality, I argue, lies not in the political economy but in the form of the state: the bifurcated state. Forged in response to the ever present dilemma of how to secure political order, the bifurcated state was like a spidery beast that sought to pin its prey to the ground, using a minimum of force—judicious, some would say—to keep in check its most dynamic tendencies. The more dynamic and assertive these tendencies, as they inevitably were in a semi-industrial setting like South Africa, the greater the force it unleashed to keep them in check. Thus the bifurcated state tried to keep apart forcibly that which socioeconomic processes tended to bring together freely: the urban and the rural, one ethnicity and another.

There is a second body of scholarship, which is on the question of chiefship and rural administration. It is a specialized and ghettoized literature on a particular institutional form or on local government, whose findings and insight are seldom integrated into a comprehensive analysis of the state. And then, finally, there is a corpus of general political writings that is wholistic but lacks in depth and explanatory power. This is the literature on "internal colonialism," "colonialism of a special type" and "settler colonialism." No longer in vogue in academia, this kind of writing has tended to become increasingly moralistic: it is preoccupied with the search for a colonizer, not the mode of colonial control. With a growing emphasis on non-racialism in the mainstream of popular struggle in South Africa, it appears embarrassing at best and divisive at worst. As a failure to analyze apartheid as a form of the state, this triple legacy is simultaneously a failure to realize that the bifurcated state does not have to be tinged with a racial ideology. Should that analytical failure be translated into a political one, it will leave open the possibility for such a form of control and containment to survive the current transition.

The specificity of the South African experience lies in the strength of its civil society, both white and black. This is in spite of the artificial deurbanization attempted by the apartheid regime. The sheer numerical weight of white settler presence in South Africa sets it apart from settler minorities elsewhere in colonial Africa. Black urbanization, however, has been a direct by-product of industrialization, first following the discovery of gold and diamonds at the end of the nineteenth century, then during the decades of rapid secondary industrialization under Boer "nationalist" rule. One testimony to the strength of black civil society was the urban uprising that built wave upon wave following Soweto 1976 and that was at the basis of the shift in the paradigm of resistance from armed to popular struggle. The strength of urban forces and civil society–based movements in South Africa meant that unlike in most African countries, the center of gravity of popular struggle was in the townships and not against Native Authorities in the countryside. The depth of resistance in South Africa was rooted in urban-based worker and student resistance, not in the peasant revolt in the countryside. Whereas in most African countries the formation of an indigenous civil society was mainly a postindependence affair, following the deracialization of the state, in South Africa it is both cause and consequence of that deracialization. Yet civil society–based movements in apartheid South Africa mirror the key weakness of similar prodemocracy movements to the north: shaped by the bifurcated nature of the state, they lack an agenda for democratizing customary power gelled in indirect rule authorities and thereby a perspective for consistent democratization.

The contemporary outcome in South Africa reflects both features, those generically African and those specifically South African. The situation leading to the nonracial elections of 1994 is a confluence of five historical developments. The first is the shift to apartheid rule in the late 1940s. Most analysts have seen this as an exception to the "wind of change" then blowing across the continent, a wind that in its wake brought state independence to nonsettler colonies. In retrospect, though, apartheid—the upgrading of indirect rule authority in rural areas to an autonomous status combined with police control over "native" movement between the rural and the urban, an attempt to convert a racial into an ethnic contradiction—was the National Party's attempt to borrow a leaf from the history of colonial rule to the north of the Limpopo. What gave apartheid its particularly cruel twist was its attempt artificially to deurbanize a growing urban African population. This required the introduction of administratively driven justice and fused power in African townships; the experience can be summarized in two words, *forced removals*, which must chill a black South African spine even today.

Second, forced removals notwithstanding, the processes of urbanization and proletarianization continued. The repression that administratively driven justice and fused power made possible—particularly in the "decade of peace" that followed the Sharpeville massacre of 1960—

created a climate of great investor confidence. As rates of capital accumulation leaped ahead of previous levels, so did rates of African proletarianization and urbanization.

Third, the decade of peace ended with the Durban strikes of 1973 and the Soweto uprising of 1976. For the next decade, South Africa was in the throes of a protracted and popular urban uprising. The paradigm of resistance shifted from an exile-based armed struggle to an internal popular struggle.

Fourth, the original and main social base of independent unionism that followed the Durban strikes of 1973 was migrant labor. The trajectory of migrant-labor politics illuminates the broad contours of the politics of resistance in apartheid South Africa. From being the spearhead of rural struggles against newly upgraded Native Authorities in the 1950s, migrant labor provided the main energy that propelled forward the independent trade union movement in the decade following the Durban strikes. But by the close of the next decade, hostel-based migrants had become marginal to the township-based revolt. As tensions between these two sectors of the urban African population exploded into antagonism in the Reef violence of 1990–91, hostels were exposed as the soft underbelly of both unions and township civics. Seen in the 1950s as urban-based militants spearheading a rural struggle—an explosion of the urban in the rural—by 1990 migrants appeared to many an urban militant as tradition-bound country bumpkins bent on damming the waters of urban township resistance: the rural in the urban.

If my objective in looking at the South African experience were simply to bring to it some of the lessons from African studies, the result would be a one-sided endeavor. If it is not to turn into a self-serving exercise, the objective must be—and indeed is—also to bring some of the strengths of South African studies to the study of Africa. For if the problem of South African studies is that it has been exceptionalized, that of African studies is that it was originally exoticized and is now banalized. But unlike African studies, which continues to be mainly a turnkey import, South African studies has been more of a homegrown import substitute. In sharp contrast to the rustic and close-to-the-ground character of South African studies, African studies have tended to take on the character of a speculative vocation indulged in by many a stargazing academic perched in distant ivory towers.

This lesson was driven home to me with the forceful impact of a dramatic and personal realization in the early 1990s, when it became possible for an African academic to visit South Africa. At close quarters, apartheid no longer seemed a self-evident exception to the African colonial experience. As the scales came off, I realized that the notion of South African exceptionalism could not be an exclusively South African creation. The argument was also reinforced—regularly—from the northern side of the border, both by those who hold the gun and by those who wield the pen. This is why the creation of a truly African studies, a study of Africa whose starting point is the commonality of the African experience, seems imperative at this historical moment. To do so, however, requires that we proceed from a recognition of our shared legacy which is honest enough not to deny our differences.

If the reader should wonder why I have devoted so much space to South African material, I need to point out that the South African experience plays a key analytical and explanatory role in the argument I will put forth. It is precisely because the South African historical experience is so different that it dramatically underlines what is common in the African colonial experience. Its brutality in a semi-industrialized setting notwithstanding, apartheid needs to be understood as a form of the state, the result of a reform in the mode of rule which attempted to contain a growing urban-based revolt, first by repackaging the native population under the immediate grip of a constellation of autonomous Native Authorities so as to fragment it, and then by policing its movement between country and town so as to freeze the division between the two. Conversely, it is precisely because black civil society in South Africa is that much stronger and more tenacious than any to the north that it illustrates dramatically the limitations of an exclusively civil society-based perspective as an anchor for a democratic movement: the urban uprising that unfolded in the wake of Durban 1973 and Soweto 1976 lacked a perspective from which to understand and transcend the interethnic and the urban-rural tensions that would mark its way ahead.

Finally, the seesaw struggle between state repression and the urban uprising had reached a stalemate by the mid-1980s. It was as if the waters of the protracted uprising had been checked and frustrated by the walls of indirect rule Native Authorities. The uprising remained a predominantly urban affair. At the same time, the international situation was changing fast with glasnost coming to the Soviet Union and the cold war thawing. In this context the South African government tried to recoup a lost initiative through several dramatic reforms. The first was the 1986 removal of influx control and the abolition of pass laws, thereby reversing the legacy of forced removals. It was as if the government, by throwing open the floodgates of urban entry to rural migrants, hoped they would flock to townships and put out the fires of urban revolt. And so they flocked: by 1993, according to most estimates, the shanty population encircling many townships was at around seven million, nearly a fifth of the total population. Many were migrants from rural areas.

The second initiative came in 1990 with the release of political prisoners and the unbanning of exile-based organizations. The government had identified a force highly credible in the urban uprising but not born of it and sought to work out the terms of an alliance with it. That force was the African National Congress (ANC) in exile. Those terms were worked out in the course of a four-year negotiation process, called the Convention for a Democratic South Africa (CODESA). The resulting constitutional consensus ensured the National Party substantial powers in the state for at least five years after the non-racial elections of 1994. Many critiques of the transition have focused on this blemish, but the real import of this transition to nonracial rule may turn out to be the fact that it will leave intact the structures of indirect rule. Sooner rather than later, it will liquidate racism in the state. With free movement between town and country, but with Native Authorities in charge of an ethnically governed rural population, it will reproduce one legacy of apartheid—in a nonracial form. If that happens, this deracialization without democratization will have been a uniquely African outcome!

SCOPE AND ORGANIZATION

This book is divided into two parts. The first focuses on the structure of the state. Following this introduction is a chapter that reconstructs the moment of the late-nineteenth-century scramble as a confluence of two interrelated developments. The first was the end of slavery, both in the Western hemisphere and on the African continent. This shift of historical proportions both underlined the practical need for a new regime of compulsions and cleared the ground for it. The second contributory factor was the set of lessons that late colonialism drew from its Asian experience. The historical context illuminates what was distinctive about the nature of colonial power in Africa.

The political history of indirect rule, from its genesis in equatorial Africa to its completion in South Africa, is traced in chapter 3. I should perhaps clarify at this point that I do not claim to have written a book that is encyclopedic and panoramic in its empirical reach. The point of the examples I narrate is illustrative. As a mode of rule, decentralized despotism was perfected in equatorial Africa, the real focus of the late-nineteenth-century scramble. Only later did its scope extend north and south, parts of the continent colonized earlier. The examples I use from the colonial period are clustered around the period of incubation of indirect rule in equatorial Africa, with an extended discussion of South Africa, which is usually presumed to be an exception to the African experience and which I contend was the last to implement a version of decentralized despotism.

As its pioneers, the British theorized the colonial state as less a territorial construct than a cultural one. The duality between civil and customary power was best described in legal ideology, the subject of chapter 4. Legal dualism juxtaposed received (modern) law with customary law. But customary law was formulated not as a single set of native laws but as so many sets of tribal laws. Conversely, colonial authorities defined a tribe or an ethnic group as a group with its own distinctive law. Referred to as custom, this law was usually unwritten. Its source, however, was the Native Authority, those in charge of managing the local state apparatus. Often installed by the colonizing power and always sanctioned by it, this Native Authority was presented as the traditional tribal authority. Where the source of the law was the very authority that administered the law, there could be no rule-bound authority. In such an arrangement, there could be no rule of law.

This first part of the book closes with a chapter (5) on the relation basic to decentralized despotism, that between the free peasant and the Native Authority. Through an illustrative exploration of extra-economic coercion, chapter 5 sums up the distinctive feature of the economy of indirect rule. Together, chapters 3, 4, and 5 sum up the institutional triad through which this decentralized mode of rule operated: a fusion of power, an administratively driven notion of customary law, and a range of extra-economic compulsions. Each chapter also closes with a discussion of the variety and the overall limit of postindependence reform.

The second part of the book explores the changing shape of oppositional movements as they grow out of the womb of the bifurcated state. I focus on two paradigm cases to illuminate the rural and urban contexts of resistance: Uganda and South Africa. Within the context of exploring different ways of bridging the urban-rural divide, my objective is twofold: first, to counterpose the earlier discussion of authoritarian possibilities in culture (customary law) to a discussion of emancipatory possibilities in ethnicity; second, to problematize ethnicity as resistance, precisely because it occurs in multiethnic contexts.

The Ugandan material forms the bulk of case studies in chapter 6 on rural-based movements in equatorial Africa. My primary accent is on movements that seek to reform customary power in rural areas, so as to bring out both their creative moments and their limitations. The South African material in chapter 7 focuses on urban-based movements, organized the first time as trade unions and the second time as political parties. Through a combination of secondary source material and primary interviews, mainly in some of the "violent" hostels in Johannesburg, Soweto, and Durban, I explore the dialectics of migrant politics (the rural in the urban) through the turning points of the 1970s and the early 1990s in the overall context of the politics of South Africa.

The conclusion (chapter 8) is a reflection on how oppositional movements and postindependence states have tried to come to terms with the tensions that the structure of power tends to reproduce in the social anatomy. My point is that key to a reform of the bifurcated state and to any theoretical analysis that would lead to such a reform must be an endeavor to link the urban and the rural—and thereby a series of related binary opposites such as rights and custom, representation and participation, centralization and decentralization, civil society and community—in ways that have yet to be done.

Part One

THE STRUCTURE OF POWER

CHAPTER TWO

Decentralized Despotism

THE TARGET of the late-nineteenth-century European Scramble was equatorial Africa. Prior to that, the European colonial presence in Africa was mainly to the north (Algeria) and the south (South Africa). Otherwise, it was restricted to a few coastal enclaves. It is not in the early colonies, but in equatorial Africa that the African form of the colonial state was forged, first and foremost by Britain, with other powers following suit. The lessons of equatorial Africa would then be applied to colonies with an earlier history.

The purpose of this chapter is, first, to reconstruct the moment of the Scramble as a confluence of several developments. Together, these set the parameters within which colonial policy in the newly acquired possessions evolved. Second, it is to sketch the contours of the form of power that emerged by the end of the colonial period. I describe this state form as a *decentralized despotism.*

The moment of the Scramble was a meeting point of several interrelated developments, both internal and external. The end of slavery in the Western hemisphere underlined the practical need for organizing a new regime of compulsions, except this time within newly acquired African possessions. From being a humanitarian impulse, the movement to abolish the slave trade gained practical immediacy in the aftermath of the American Civil War. A direct effect of that war—which rerouted the supply of southern cotton to the north—was an acute shortage of cotton for textile production elsewhere, the "cotton famine," as it came to be known. To address the dilemma this vital shortage posed for its leading industry, the British Cotton Growing Association was formed in 1902. By 1904, the cotton question had become sufficiently important to be included in the king's speech. "The insufficiency of the supply of raw material upon which the great cotton industry depends has inspired me with deep concern," noted His Majesty and then drove the point home. "I trust that the efforts which are being made in various parts of the Empire to increase the area under cultivation may be attended with a large measure of success!"[1] This changing context helped swing important sections of manufacturing opinion against slavery and in favor of colonization, so that Africans who yesterday were transported to the New World could now stay at home—in both instances to produce cotton for "the Satanic mills."

Colonial crops ranged beyond cotton, from sugar and sisal to rubber and coffee. All of them tropical agricultural products, their significance was either strategic or simply economic. Yet in this constellation of raw materials that would feed European manufacturing, the pride of place belonged to cotton. The three *c*'s that Livingstone claimed would together rejuvenate Africa were cotton, Christianity, and civilization. The prototype organization lobbying for an official policy that would encourage the cultivation of industrial crops in the equatorial colonies was the British Cotton Growing Association in London.

If the end of slavery in the American South underlined the practical need for a regime of compulsions in equatorial Africa, the human and organizational fabric from which to fashion such a regime could be made available only by actual developments on the African continent. Key to these developments was the defeat of nineteenth-century slave-based conquest states. As this development brought to a close the regime of formal slavery on the continent, it opened the possibility of a new era of compulsions short of formal slavery.

Every colonial power with experience understood that a colony was not akin to a blank slate; there was no choice but to work with the material available on the ground. This practical limitation, however, did not mean the absence of choice. For developments in precolonial Africa were not uniform and consistent, but heterogeneous and even contradictory. The choice that colonial powers did make from a limited menu was a result of both practical necessity and vision shaped by experience. If the nature of practical necessity was underlined most acutely by the "cotton famine" following the American Civil War, the vision of late colonialism was marked by its experience in older nineteenth-century colonies, particularly in Asia.

More than any other influence, it is the nature of developments in late-nineteenth-century Africa and the experience of late colonialism in Asia that made for how colonial powers pursued practical necessity in their equatorial possessions. In what follows, I will try to disentangle these two influences. When it comes to nineteenth-century African developments, I will sketch these as a mixed menu that offered different possibilities to conquering powers, before going on to sketch the alternative that colonial powers actually built on and privileged as customary and traditional Africa. I say built on because at no point did colonial powers simply reproduce a nineteenth-century mix. If the starting point of a colonial initiative was a possibility actually on the ground, what colonial powers made of it—the scope and force they gave to the customary and to tradition—was shaped by the lessons late colonialism drew from its primarily Asian experience. The customary, in this sense, was neither just arbitrarily invented—like the Christian God creating the world in six days and resting on the seventh—nor faithfully reproduced. It was crafted out of raw material on the ground and in contention with it. Out of this process, this statecraft, was forged the decentralized despotism that came to be the hallmark of the colonial state in Africa.

PRECOLONIAL ANTECEDENTS

Like all colonial powers, the British worked with a single model of customary authority in precolonial Africa. That model was monarchical, patriarchal, and authoritarian. It presumed a king at the center of every polity, a chief on every piece of administrative ground, and a patriarch in every homestead or kraal. Whether in the homestead, the village, or the kingdom, authority was considered an attribute of a personal despotism. To what extent does this conception reflect actual developments in precolonial Africa? To begin with, one needs to realize that notions of a precolonial tradition are far more constraining than illuminating. "How far back do we have to go," asks Catherine Coquery-Vidrovitch, "to find the stability alleged to be 'characteristic' of the pre-colonial period: before the Portuguese conquest, before the Islamic invasion, before the Bantu expansion?"[2] She then answers: "Each of these great turning points marked the reversal of long-term trends, within which a whole series of shorter cycles might in turn be identified." "In short," she concludes, "the static concept of 'traditional' society cannot withstand the historian's analysis."

I will confine myself to the backdrop to the scramble and argue that the tendencies that went into the making of nineteenth-century Africa were multiple rather than singular, diverse rather than uniform, contradictory rather than consistent. Of these the one that came closest to echoing these notions was also the least traditional, itself being a product of nineteenth-century conquest history. More than reflecting a slice of reality in the collage that was nineteenth-century Africa, the colonial notion of the precolonial was really a faithful mirror reflection of the decentralized despotism created under colonial rule.

To bring out the diversity of the precolonial experience is important, if only because of a widespread tendency to present that experience as uniform, whether the point is to demonize or to idealize it. Counter to notions of a tyranny-ridden Dark Continent, one can find characterizations of a continent where noble savages lived freely and without restraint. "Africa," argues a study, *Blank Darkness: Africanist Discourse in French*, "has been made to bear a double burden, of monstrousness and nobility," for "throughout the history of Africanist writing there is a striking tendency towards dual, polarized evaluations which are too often hastily ascribed to this or that historical trend."[3] One example from Anglophone literature will suffice to make the point. In his recent summation of decades of research on the subject, Basil Davidson has argued that although the historical paths to state formation and the resulting state forms were various, a common feature underpinned the political life of African states: the quest for "a unifying force," depending on "a system of participation that must not only work, but must publicly be seen to work," combined with "a systematic distrust of power."[4] Together, these amounted to "an insistence on the distribution of executive power," a theme that Davidson argues regulated the life "of pre-colonial political institutions in every African region where stable societies produced one or other form of central government." The statements are categorical, and Davidson goes on to build a general theory on one set of experiences while ignoring discordant notes. His account accurately sums up the historical experience of the Akan states, as it does the main tendency in instances where state formation was the result of internal differentiation, but it is difficult to find in the text a single reference to the conquest states of nineteenth-century Africa or to the experience of degrees of unfreedom that was the lot of a growing number of Africans in the time of turmoil that was the nineteenth century. The fact that these states hardly exemplified a deeply rooted African tradition or that the colonial powers built on that nineteenth-century tradition of administratively appointed chiefs keeping in place a regime of force is hardly reason enough to remain silent about it.

To understand the historical roots of unfreedom in the African experience, one needs to recognize that experience as not just diverse but also contradictory: state power was built not only as a consequence of processes of internal differentiation, but also as the direct result of conquest. Similarly, precolonial chiefship was not only the traditional variant constrained by kin-based obligations; there were also administrative chiefs who acted relatively independently of these restraints. Just as conquest did not begin with colonialism, administrative chiefship was not confined to the conquest states. Yet the point about colonialism was that it generalized both the conquest state and the administrative chiefship, and in doing so it wrenched both free of traditional restraint.

Stateless Communities

Ifi Amadiume recently has underlined the need to appreciate the contradictory character of the African experience.[5] In an effort to grasp the flux of gender relations in precolonial Africa and the colonial impact on it, she has argued for the need to move away from an understanding of matriarchy and patriarchy as two mutually exclusive systems of descent and inheritance, with associated implications of king or queen rule, toward a conceptualization of them as systems of power and ideology that could and did coexist in tension. Matriarchy, in this sense, was a system of autonomous female organization and an associated ideology that crystallized and defended this autonomy—and so coexisted with similarly autonomous forms of male organization, as in Igboland. This autonomous space was uniformly destroyed by colonial rule. And in this sense the "world historical defeat" of the female gender was experienced in Africa not as much with the onset of state organization as with the consolidation of the colonial state.

In the political literature on Africa, Igboland is the prototype of not only a nonmonarchical order but also of a nonstate one. The "decentralized village self-government"[6] characteristic of Igboland is, in this sense, representative of similar decentralized and democratic forms of organization operative in other contexts: for example, among the slash-and-burn agriculturalists of northern Uganda[7] or the extensively grazing pastoral communities of Karamoja and the East African Rift Valley.[8] In these stateless communities, colonial imposition could not resonate with any aspect of tradition. Often tribes were created on the basis of territorial contiguity as villages were brought together under a single administrative authority. Chiefship was similarly manufactured and chiefs were imposed. If marginal men who shifted alliances at the sight of a more powerful invader could not be found, others were brought in from the outside. The two great revolts against the imposition of a state hierarchy in the colonial period was the Maji Maji rebellion in Tanganyika and the great revolt against the warrant chiefs in Igboland, so-called because these were chiefs created by warrant of the colonial governor. Similar revolts echoed across the range of stateless communities, even if the protest did not always break into the open with an equivalent force.

Traditional Chiefs

The transition from tribal to state organization has often been conceptualized as one from a kinship to a territorially based authority. Although tribes organized under the domination of elders, they contained redistributive mechanisms that thwarted tendencies to reproduce inequalities in a cumulative fashion. The nature of the relationship between elders on the one hand and juniors and women on the other is still the subject of debate. Was it an exploitative relationship? If so, did elders constitute a class?[9]

The conflict between the clan (kinship) and the administrative (territorial) mode of organization is brought out by studies on the intralacustrine region of eastern Africa.[10] They conclude not only that the conflict between the two modes of political organization existed at varying degrees of intensity, but also that the outcome varied. In the midst of variation, one needs to keep in mind a distinguishing feature of the African landscape. To the extent that kin groups were able to defend their custodianship over land and keep it from being turned into private property—and this was the overwhelming tendency continentally—state authority remained significantly circumscribed by that of clans and lineages.

Similarities notwithstanding, each outcome had a unique dimension. Contrast, for example, the cases of Buganda and Bunyoro, where the centralizing tendency had gone the furthest. In Buganda, the king emerged supreme with control over land but with an administrative hierarchy whose personnel came from both humble and noble origins: the line of chiefs recruited from ordinary citizens predominated over hereditary chiefs.[11] Traditional chiefs, those in office by right of descent, had been eclipsed by administratively appointed commoner chiefs. In Bunyoro, however, the tendency was toward the consolidation of a landed aristocracy with heritable wealth. The landed nobility continued to check the centralizing ambitions of the king, in the most extreme case leading to secession, as in Toro. But even when centralization had gone far, as far as in Buganda, the organized power of clans continued to function as a popular check on both the king and the appointed administration.

The tension between administrative authority and kin groups gave rise to a differentiation within the institutions of chiefship: between kin-based, hereditary traditional chiefs and state-appointed administrative chiefs. Both were in turn checked by clan- and lineage-based councils that in most places retained the right of access to land and all other natural resources: village councils made and enforced rules of access that regulated the balance between livestock, water, and forage, ensuring a sustainable use of sustainable resources; local councils regulated the movement of herds and the protection of crops; others organized vast markets and sustained long-distance trade; still others regulated bride-wealth and obligations between families and spouses, ensuring personal rights for the children and the aged.[12]

These were the traditional institutions of traditional Africa through which village-based communities regulated social and economic affairs, but they were not its only institutions. This is particularly clear with the nineteenth century, which was hardly a period of stable reproduction of customary relations. Ngoni conquest in central Africa, for example, was experienced as the dominance of patriarchal over matriarchal societies, leading to a proliferation of internal "slavery," including "slave marriages," terms put in quotation marks because they refer to a diversity of relations embodying degrees of personal unfreedom contained within familial and clan relations, but none a subjugation as total as the market-driven slavery unleashed by the acute demand for labor in New World mines and plantations organized along capitalist lines. The West African counterpart to the Ngoni *mfacane* was the Fulani *jihad*, which subjugated peasant societies to a range of similarly enforced tributary relations.

Administrative Chiefs

The rise of nineteenth-century conquest states gave a fillip to the administrative variant of chiefship, but it was not until the colonial period that the administrative chief emerged as the full-blown village-based despot, shorn of rule-based restraint. Restraint on precolonial authority flowed from two separate though related tendencies: one from peers, the other from people. The first was a tendency internal to state organization, exemplified by the tension between kings and chiefs, particularly traditional chiefs, who were not likely to be royal appointees. This tension was the driving force behind the king's trying to offset hereditary traditional chiefs with a hierarchy of appointed administrative chiefs. To the extent that they could claim a nineteenth-century precedent, the chiefship that the colonial powers created was built on the administrative variant, not the traditional. Even then, what is impressive is not the continuity in tradition, even if a nineteenth-century one, but the break in continuity. To begin with, even if nineteenth-century administrative chiefs were the king's appointees who could not stay in office without the king's pleasure, their power was not just circumscribed by the will and capacity of the king. It was also constrained by tradition as embodied in the traditional chiefs alongside whom they functioned in tension. Besides this peer restraint, there was also a popular constraint, that of the people, the result of the second tendency that shaped developments in the nineteenth century. This was the tension between state authority in all its forms (traditional and administrative) and clan organization. By undermining both popular (clan) checks on state authority and traditional constraints as embodied in traditional chiefs, the colonial state really liberated administrative chiefs from all institutionalized constraint, of peers or people, and laid the basis of a decentralized despotism. In what follows, I will try to illustrate the two forms of constraint on nineteenth-century administrative chiefs. My examples will be taken from south-central (Zulu, Xhosa, Swazi, and Tswana) and western (Fanti and Ashanti) African state formations.

The Zulu kingdom is often held up as an instance of the most centralized and despotic form of political authority in nineteenth-century Africa. In 1881, the Cape Native Laws and Customs Commission interviewed Cetshwayo, the former king of the Zulus, on the position of the Zulu monarch.[13] The line of questioning suggests that the interviewers expected their prejudices regarding an absolutist kingship in Africa to be confirmed. The answers are even more revealing. We can divide the questions into two sets: those which probe the relation between the king ("supreme chief") and his chiefs, and those which concern relations with peasants.

The King and the Chiefs

144. As the king of the Zulus, was all power invested in you, as king, over your subjects?
– In conjunction with the chiefs of the land.

145. How did the chiefs derive their power from you as king?
– The king calls together the chiefs of the land when he wants to elect a new chief, and asks their advice as to whether it is fit to make such a man a large chief, and if they say "yes" the chief is made.

146. If you had consulted the chiefs, and found they did not agree with you, could you appoint a chief by virtue of your kingship?
– In some cases, if the chiefs don't approve of it, the king requires their reasons, and when they have stated them he often gives it up. In other cases he tries the man to see whether he can perform the duties required of him or not.

147. In fact, you have the power to act independently of the chiefs in making an appointment, although you always consult them?
– No; the king has not the power of electing an officer as chief without the approval of the other chiefs. They are the most important men. But the smaller chiefs he can elect at his discretion.

The King and the Subjects

90. Is compassing the death of a chief a crime punishable with death?
-- No, only a fine of cattle.

91. Is a man killed for trying to kill a king?
– He is simply fined cattle, and is talked to very severely.

92. Is a man punished with death for disobeying a direct order of the king?
– He is simply fined when he has committed the offence twice before.

93. What is the punishment for a man deserting from his tribe?
– If the chief of his district had given him any property he would be asked by the chief to return that property, and then he would be at liberty to go.

The parameters of the questions are clearly narrow, reflecting the interest of the commission in such issues as what happens when authority is challenged (disobedience, desertion, up to regicide) by ordinary persons not in their rights. But even this limited query shows that, when defied, power could not respond with impunity.

A recent document prepared by a Transkei-based community organization contrasts the nature of traditional chiefship in the preconquest period with the one under colonial rule.[14] Notwithstanding its tendency to equate the precolonial with the traditional and the colonial with the administrative, the document illuminates the contrast between the two forms of chiefship. The traditional chief functioned in "an advisory and consultative context, unlike the bureaucratic model imposed under colonialism." The administrative power of such a chief consisted mainly in "the right to allocate land," but it was a right exercised through a double consultation: "with his (sometimes her) counselors, but primarily in consultation with the wider community," for the chief was "the custodian" of the land, not its proprietor. And custody "could only be exercised through a consensus of the community as a whole." The ultimate popular sanction against a despotic chief was desertion: "You tried to increase your following, rather than encouraging desertion to a neighboring chief, or to a rival relative." Colonial conquest built on the administrative powers of the chief, introducing "a highly bureaucratic command-and-control system." Under apartheid, "the administrative powers of the chief were systematically strengthened" but were made accountable to "a new consensus," one that "emphasized the state as the determiner of the consensus."

The check on administrative authority by one's peers was perhaps more highly developed in Swazi than in any other Ngoni society.[15] The distribution of authority, leading to a form of checks and balances, was practiced at every level, from the royal house to the village. The queen mother (*indlovukazi*) came to occupy a position both independent of the king (*ingwenyama*) and strategic enough to act as a check on any absolutist royal pretensions. The king controlled the army, and the commander-in-chief resided at the queen mother's village. The king's centralizing ambitions led to the creation of an administratively appointed hierarchy of princes. Based in the provinces, their function was to oversee the activities of traditional local chiefs and their headmen. The king ruled with the advice of an "inner council" (the *liqoqo*).

Though appointed by the king himself, it was drawn primarily from "members of the royal clan, as well as principal headmen and trusted commoners."

This whole state structure, the community of peers—the king and his council, the queen mother, the princes, chiefs, and headmen—was constrained by a popular institution called the *libandla*. A "national council" chaired by "a senior prince from the *liqoqo*," the libandla's membership comprised both commoners and nobles. The difference lay in this: whereas attendance for commoners was voluntary, it was compulsory for the entire state hierarchy—the king and queen mother, all chiefs, princes, and headmen. Its sanction was required "on all important matters." These structures did not function just at the center; both the liqoqo and the libandla were mirrored at local levels, requiring the traditional chief to consult the corresponding council "on various aspects of local importance." But the assembly's limitations are also clear: it was limited to adult males among commoners, and it met only once a year.[16]

The changing relationship between popular (clan) and administrative (state) organs through the colonial period is well illustrated by the example of Botswana. Alongside administration by state officials, there developed in the precolonial period the institution of the *Kgotla*, "a place where the community meets to discuss openly issues of common interest with the chief." As a clan-based institution, the Kgotla, like the libandla in Swaziland, had one clear shortcoming. Neither women nor subject nationalities were allowed to participate in its deliberations. Yet this popular institution of Tswana adult males represented a check on the authority of the chief. It was a public assembly that could discuss any public issue, one where administration by public officials was subject to public scrutiny, including strong criticism in the "highly stylized form of songs or poems."[17] At the same time, the Kgotla also functioned "as a judicial court where the community as a whole could participate in the process of adjudication."[18]

In the colonial period, this public assembly was turned into a forum where decisions were announced but not debated. A reform was initiated in 1920. Its point was not to restore the powers of the Kgotla but to reduce the autonomy of chiefs vis-à-vis the colonial power. Once this was achieved, the chiefs' powers over the local population were reinforced in phases, starting in 1938. The 1938 law allowed chiefs to appoint a finance committee to supervise the local treasury; it also gave them powers to make bylaws "with the agreement of the *Kgotla*." The 1954 African Administration Proclamation gave the chiefs "legislative and executive authority, as long as they exercised it with the consent of the *Kgotla*." But the "consent of the *Kgotla*" was by now a euphemism for the veto power the colonial state exercised over all chiefly decisions,[19] for it was colonial authority that had the ultimate power to decide what the real interests of the Kgotla (the people) were. In relation to the peasant, however, the chiefs were all-powerful. They had the powers to allocate land and administer schools; to approve the appointment of clerks, police, and messengers; to make bylaws; and to adjudicate cases.[20]

At the other extreme of the conquest states of nineteenth-century Africa were the loose confederations arrived at among the Akan peoples of West Africa, particularly the Ashanti and the Fanti. Rattray argued that at the heart of "the whole success and wonder of this loosely bound confederacy" was the practice of "decentralization."[21] Over time, the authority of the chief had come to be so "limited and severely defined" that "a whole series of injunctions . . . were publicly recited before him on his enstoolment." The "most important" of these was "never to act without the advice and full concurrence of his counselors, who were in turn subject to similar restraints." Policy was discussed at various levels: in "the old Oman or national councils" as in the "Omansin (sub-tribal division) before a final decision could be taken constitutionally." At such gatherings, "a Paramount Chief and such of his counselors as attended with him were never anything more . . . than vehicles of communication." Should a chief make "the least attempt to act on his own initiative," it was considered "a legitimate cause for destoolment." The community of freemen (for there were others who lived in degrees of unfreedom) among the Akan constituted a genuine "public opinion."

Both the Ashanti and the Fanti confederations were subordinated to British power by the last quarter of the nineteenth century. But before that happened, the Fanti made an extraordinary attempt to safeguard their independence as a people by reforming the constitution of government so as to cement a national alliance between the traditional chiefs and the elite educated in Western institutions. The Fanti confederation "assumed a political nature" in 1871 "with the promulgation of the *Mankessim* constitution." "Based on the blueprint set out by Dr. James Africanus Beale Horton in his *Letters on the Political Condition of the Gold Coast* published in London in 1871," this document provided for "a legislative assembly in which both the traditional and educated elements would be represented."[22] When the British proclaimed a formal protectorate over Fantiland in 1874 and assumed the right to dismiss chiefs—"a right which traditionally belonged to the Oman Council of chiefs or the people"—resentment grew among the traditional leadership and the Western-educated stratum. Indeed, once this violation of tradition was formalized in the 1883 Native Jurisdiction Ordinance, the Western-educated elite saw it as imperative "to study and interpret the traditional institutions and customs for the purpose of defending them effectively against British encroachment." Perhaps the most notable expression of that effort was the 1897 treatise on Fanti customary law by John Mensah Sarbah, the first indigenous barrister of the Gold Coast. Sarbah called for the dispensing of "customary law," which he defined in the Augustinian sense as having "sprung from usage, as well as laws or commands made by chiefs or rulers, headmen, the village council, headmen of clans, and company captains."[23] He called for its enforcement "either by means of the village council sitting and acting judicially as a local tribunal" or by invoking "the silent force of the popular sanction according to an usage long established or well known."[24]

Just as the colonial state usurped the erstwhile right of the people or the peers to destool an errant chief, so it now replaced the village council with the administratively appointed village chief as the local tribunal. The impact of this shift was enormous. For nowhere in Africa did there exist centralized judicial institutions with exclusive jurisdiction over an area, something that colonialism created as customary. Like with rights over land and natural resources, jurisdiction over persons was likely to be multiple and not exclusive. Certainly, the jurisdiction over family disputes was a matter for lineage members and elders, not really for chiefs. There was nothing customary about a Native Authority whose rights extended to settling domestic disputes.

To sum up this discussion, we need to bear in mind that precolonial Africa comprised neither just pristine stateless communities nor only tyranny-ridden conquest states. Even in the nineteenth century, the conquest states did not exhaust the experience in state formation. External conquest was one route to state formation, and the other was through internal differentiation. The latter and not the former experience is the more fruitful ground for recapitulating custom and tradition. We will see that although it abolished formal slavery, colonialism crystallized, formalized, and built on the range of unfreedoms unleashed in nineteenth-century conquest states, only to generalize them. From African tradition, colonial powers salvaged a widespread and time-honored practice, one of a decentralized exercise of power, but freed that power of restraint, of peers or people. Thus they laid the basis for a decentralized despotism.

THE LESSONS OF LATE COLONIALISM:
CREATING A FREE PEASANTRY

The division between the citizen and the subject, the nonnative and the native, was characteristic of all colonial situations. It was not unique to Africa. Specific to Africa, though, was the closeting of the subject population in a series of separate containers, each under the custody of a Native Authority said to be the rightful bearer and enforcer of an age-old custom and tradition. Britain, more than any other power, keenly glimpsed authoritarian possibilities in culture. Not simply content with salvaging every authoritarian tendency from the heterogeneous historical flow that was precolonial Africa, Britain creatively sculpted tradition and custom as and when the need arose. In this endeavor, other European powers followed it. By this dual process, part salvage and part sculpting, they crystallized a range of usually district-level Native Authorities, each armed with a whip and protected by the halo of custom.

Defining the Customary

In his influential *African Survey*, published in 1938, Lord Hailey attempted to put Britain's Africa policy in a broad historical perspective. Inspired by a suggestion of General Smuts in his 1929 Rhodes lecture, funded by the Carnegie Corporation of New York and the Rhodes trustees—and officially endorsed by a Government of United Kingdom White Paper of 1940—*An African Survey* took on the status of a quasi-official document.[25] As prelude to a discussion of the "system of law" in colonial Africa, Hailey provided a sum-up of "the evolution of law in the Roman and British empires."

> Expressed in the briefest of terms, the chief problem of Rome was one of assimilation, and in this respect the Latin mind tended to regard identity of legal rights as a more important element than equality of political powers. The problem of the British in India was primarily to find a system of law which would avoid emphasizing the fact that the country was passing under the dominion of a Power professing an alien faith.[26]

This, argued Hailey, was why the British were "strongly moved by the need for maintaining a customary law based on the religious and social life of India." But emphasis on the customary did not run like an even thread through the course of British rule in India. Rather, British rule at its inception was more a repudiation of the customary, more a commitment to a "civilizing mission" through which to "rejuvenate" society. The shift from "rejuvenating" to "conserving" society, from repudiating to confirming tradition, was really a latter-day development. In the history of British rule in India, there were several dividing lines between the emphasis on rejuvenating and conserving society, but none as decisive as the Indian Mutiny of 1857. In a series of writings, the best known of which is *Ancient Law*, Sir Henry Maine, law member of the government of India between 1862 and 1869, put forth the view that subject peoples should be ruled through their own customs. The notion of the customary was part of the continuity in British colonial thinking in its transcontinental sweep, from Asia to Africa. Wherein, then, lay the specificity of the African colonial experience?

Africa, after all, was Europe's last colonial possession. To that venture, European powers brought a wealth of experience. This was truer of Britain than of any other power. "British thinking about Africa was much more closely related to British thinking about India than is generally realized," sums up a careful historian of British rule in Asia and Africa, and then goes on to qualify: "If there was a difference, perhaps it was this: in India the actions which the British took to prevent 'the dissolution of society' were essentially curative, in Africa preventive."[27] The shift in perspective from the curative to the preventive was really one from rejuvenating to conserving society. It was rather a turnaround: from a conviction that Europe had a "civilizing mission" in the colonies to a law-and-order obsession with holding the line. This change in preoccupation from progress to power took place early in Africa's colonial history. The shift from the curative to the preventive involved both continuity and discontinuity. It is the latter that defines the specificity of the African colonial experience.

European rule in Africa came to be defined by a single-minded and overriding emphasis on the customary. For in the development of a colonial customary law, India was really a halfway house. Whereas in India the core of the customary was limited to matters of personal law, in Africa it was stretched to include land. Unlike the variety of land settlements in India, whether in favor of landlords or of peasant proprietors, the thrust of colonial policy in Africa was to define land as a communal and customary possession. Just as matters like marriage and inheritance were said to be customarily governed, so procuring basic sustenance required getting customary access to communal land. With this development, there could be no exit for an African from the world of the customary. In other words, although the notion of the customary was not unique to the African encounter with Western colonialism, distinctive about that encounter was the *scope* of the customary. Including both personal relations (marriage, succession, movement) and access to productive resources (land), the realm of the customary was rounded off into a full circle.

Lest one think that the tag "customary" was a shorthand for letting things be as they always had been, that this was a permissive gesture of powers tired and reluctant to execute a mission, we need to bear in mind that there was nothing voluntary about custom in the colonial period. More than being reproduced through social sanction, colonial custom was enforced with a whip, by a constellation of customary authorities— and, if necessary, with the barrel of a gun, by the forces of the central state. Said to have the breadth of community sanction and the depth of historical usage, the customary was given precedence over any received law, provided it was not "repugnant." This benign term, we will see, was a concession more to power than to polite society.

The bearer of custom was said to be the tribe. Defined and marked as a member of a tribe, the colonized African was more fully encapsulated in customarily governed relations than any predecessor or, for that matter, any contemporary in the colonized world. The more custom was enforced, the more the tribe was restructured and conserved as a more or less self-contained community—autonomous but not independent— as it never had been before. Encased by custom, frozen into so many tribes, each under the fist of its own Native Authority, the subject population was, as it were, containerized. That imperative, the containerization of a subject people, was the core lesson that Britain learned from its Indian encounter and France from its Indochinese experience. It was the preventive aspect of colonial rule in Africa.

This dimension, which differentiated colonial rule in Africa from other experiences, was often explained away by sympathetic observers as a necessary paternalism. "The objective of African customary law," claimed Lord Hailey citing the authority of anthropologists and legal scholars—from Driberg, Radcliffe-Brown, and Malinowsky to Hogbin, Seagle, and Paton—is "primarily designed to maintain the social equilibrium." Dame Margery Perham, another quasi-official historian of indirect rule, congratulated British rulers on having "corrected the nineteenth century complacency about the universal superiority of our own ideas and institutions."[28] While frankly acknowledging "the comprehensive despotism" allowed "the political officer" in a colony as "the father of his people," she hailed "the district officer" who supervised the Native Authority as "one of those supreme types which history throws up when the opportunity and the genius of a race combine." "The preservation of native law and custom is not an end in itself," she counseled, "but a transitional stage by which Africans may in their own right become members of the civilized world, not as individuals, but as communities."

To be civilized "not as individuals but as communities," to be subject to a process that one-sidedly opposed the community to the individual, and thereby encapsulated the individual in a set of relations defined and enforced by the state as communal and customary, indeed summed up "the opportunity and the genius" of British colonialism in Africa. Key to this enterprise was the question of land. Everywhere—we will look at the few exceptions later—land was defined as a customary and communal possession. Instead of becoming a peasant freehold or a possession of landed classes, access to land came to be controlled by customary authorities. To the extent that this remained the case, land remained outside the scope of the market; to the extent that peasant households remained in customary possession of land, without the right to alienate it, the sway of market forces was limited. Beyond that limit, nothing short of force could push labor and its products into the realm of the market. Rather than being its antithesis, force came to be complementary to the market. Customary access to land defined the free peasantry in colonial Africa, and a regime of compulsions simultaneously breached and marked the limits of that freedom in the name of indirect rule. We will see that the colonial experience in Africa was marked by force to an unusual degree. More than the force of tradition, the colonial legacy came to signify a tradition of force.

A DECENTRALIZED DESPOTISM

The decentralized arm of the colonial state was the Native Authority, comprising a hierarchy of chiefs. It is the regime of extra-economic coercion—the compulsion by which free peasants with customary access to land may otherwise be conscripted, forced to labor, or to cultivate—that makes intelligible the powers chiefs wielded over peasants. We will see that without Native Courts that enabled Native Administrations to turn their writ into law, the Native Authority would have been emasculated as an active agent. The scope of this agency was sometimes defined in formal agreements or codes issued at the onset of colonial rule but mostly evolved through practice. As early as 1891, the Natal Native Code in South Africa had specified the ends to which the powers of the chief may be used. Prominent among these was forced labor: "The prompt supply of men for purposes of defense, or to suppress disorder or rebellion, or as laborers for public works, or for the general needs of the colony, as and when ordered by the Supreme Chief to supply the same" [S.46(b)]. Clause 9 of the Buganda Agreement of 1900 specified "the upkeep of the main roads" as a task to be supervised by the chief, alongside "the assessment and collection of taxes," "administering justice amongst the natives," and "the general supervision of native affairs." Clause 13 explained how this may be done, for it gave every chief powers to call upon one laborer for every three households for up to a month in a year "to assist in keeping the established roads in repair." In his study of indirect rule in Nigeria, Padmore observed that "so long as the chiefs collect the amount of taxes assigned to them and supply labor when ordered to do so, the European officials seldom interfere."[29] Jean Suret-Canale has put together the duties of a chief in French colonies: "Collection of taxes, requisitioning labor, compulsory crop cultivation and provision of military recruits."[30] From the time of company rule, it was part of the duty of chiefs in Belgian-controlled Congo to enforce such measures as "forced labor, compulsory cultivation, conscription, labor recruitment and other state requirements."[31]

"The first step" in building a regime of "indirect rule," counseled its architect, Lord Lugard, "is to *endeavour* to find a man of influence as chief, and to group under him as many villages or districts as possible, to teach him to delegate powers, and to take an interest in his 'Native Treasury,' to support his authority, and to inculcate a sense of responsibility."[32] In the edifice of Native Authority, the chief was the pillar. The tendency was to define the customary powers of the chief in a way so embracing as to fortify him from any external threat. If the Native Authority was akin to a colonial fortress in a hostile wilderness, the chief was its knight whose armor must not be allowed to be breached at any point. Consider the 1891 Natal Native Code, which empowered the chief to demand "respect and obedience" (S.57) and "to try all civil cases (divorces excepted) between natives" (S.49), to impose a fine within limits (S.51), and to arrest (S.55) those who transgress orders; or chiefs in colonial Mozambique whose jurisdiction over residents covered the usual range of practices, from petty theft to drunkenness, from tax evasion to adultery. Padmore wrote of the chief in Nigeria:

> The chief is the law, subject to only one higher authority, the white official stationed in his state as advisor. The chief hires his own police . . . he is often the prosecutor and the judge combined and he employs the jailer to hold his victims in custody at his pleasure. No oriental despot ever had greater power than these black tyrants, thanks to the support which they receive from the white officials who quietly keep in the background.[33]

As an institution, the Native Authority bore little resemblance to a local administration authority, say in Britain. Its personnel functioned without judicial restraint and were never elected. Appointed from above, they held office so long as they enjoyed the confidence of their superiors. Their powers were diffuse, with little functional specificity. The three pillars that Lugard claimed as upholding the system of indirect rule—Native Courts, Native Administration, and a Native Treasury—together crystallized the ensemble of powers merged in the office of the chief. As we will see, these powers also included a fourth: making rules.

The central fact about political power as it confronted—and still confronts—the peasant producer is the single and fused nature of authority: the chief. Place yourself in the position of a poor peasant in the rural Uganda of the early 1980s, confronted by the chief at the time of tax collection, or for that matter at any of several occasions when a compulsion is decreed. It is the chief who has the right to make a bylaw governing his locality, who assesses the value of your petty property and therefore how much tax you must pay, who comes to collect that tax, who fines you if you fail to pay that tax, who jails you if you fail to pay the tax and the fine, who decides where you labor when in jail, and who releases you upon termination of the sentence. The chief is the petty legislator, administrator, judge, and policeman all in one. Every moment of power—legislative, executive, judicial, and administrative—is combined in this one official. Here there is no question of any internal check and balance on the exercise of authority, let alone a check that is popular and democratic. The chief is answerable only to a higher administrative authority. An unwritten norm of indirect rule was that the lower authority must never be short-circuited. To entertain any complaints behind the chief's back would be to humiliate him. To so weaken a subordinate officer and compromise his prestige would be to endanger patiently accumulated gains in years of administrative labor. Therefore nothing must be done that would bring disrespect to authority. It is the agent of this fused authority, this clenched fist, who is usually called the chief. To the peasant, the person of the chief signifies power that is total and absolute, unchecked and unrestrained.

No doubt such a fusion of power in the person of a state functionary was bound to lend itself to abuse, often considerable and repeated. Early colonial legislation had invited chiefs—most likely out of practical consideration—to share with government authorities whatever dues, fines, and fees they had collected. Like every instance of tax farming, this too turned out to be an invitation to chiefs to add personal demands to systemic ones on the peasantry. As instances of abuse came to light and accumulated, concern focused on how to discipline the functionaries of Native Authorities from above. The twofold answer to this question sums up the internal history of indirect rule between the two world wars: one, if a Native Treasury was created and chiefs paid a regular salary from its proceeds, they would not have to resort to exacting tribute; and two, if chiefs were subject to appointment and dismissal, the few bad ones could be replaced and the rest kept in check.

Lugard argued that the creation of a Native Treasury, from which the salaries of Native Administration personnel would be paid, would put an end to such abuse. "The tax—which supersedes all former 'tribute,' irregular imposts and forced labor—is, in a sense, the basis of the whole system, since it supplies the means to pay the Emir and all officials," explained Lugard with reference to northern Nigeria, held up as a pathbreaking success in indirect rule. "It is obvious," he argued in his influential 1919 "Report on the Amalgamation of Northern and Southern Nigeria," "that it [the system] depends essentially on the principle of direct taxation, which provides the means whereby Native Administration can pay salaries to the paramount chief and all other officials, and so put an end to the unlimited exactions on which they had previously lived, and reduce their number to those actually required for the service of the Native Administration."[34]

But abuse continued and fueled popular discontent. In response, the central state implemented yet another so-called reform: in addition to being salaried, the position of a chief was made subject to appointment, transfer, and dismissal, thereby reducing to a minimum his individual autonomy vis-à-vis the colonial power. Even the British, the high priests of indirect rule through traditional authority, asserted that the agent of tradition be not a hereditary but a colonial appointment; once the colonial order stabilized, even the position of precolonial kings and native aristocracies was made subject to appointment and dismissal. In Buganda, for example, the struggle over the right of the Kabaka's government to appoint chiefs reached a climax in 1926, when the Katikiro (prime minister) was compelled to resign over the issue. The case of Sir Apollo Kaggwa is instructive, for he was no ordinary native official. The Colonial Office file on the subject recognizes that he "rendered invaluable help to the British during the perilous days of the mutiny, as well as, finally, against the remnants of the Sudanese," and goes on to confirm: "It is no overstatement to say that had his prestige and authority been cast at that time into the balance against the British raj, European influence would have been entirely, if not temporarily, eclipsed."[35] As the court ruled in a key case in Rhodesia a decade later, "the Native Affairs Act 1927 gave the Governor-in-Council an unqualified right to appoint who[m]soever he considered suitable to a chiefship," and "accordingly, hereditary rights of succession to the chiefship under African law and custom have been expressly abolished."[36] Compare this with French practice, for example, in Futa-Jalon in Guinea, where the French set up an assembly of chiefs under the protectorate treaty signed in 1897. Article 2 of that treaty specified that "France pledged to respect the existing constitutions of Futa-Jalon." But the assembly functioned under the direct supervision of the resident, who removed all ambiguity from the nature of this pledge: "The chief will attend to the tax and furnish manpower, or he will be smashed like a glass."[37] The point was that, no matter what the official claims about the traditional nature of Native Authority were, its officials were considered the lowest rung of the colonial administrative ladder. Although they practiced decentralized administration in all other matters, both the British and the French reserved the right to appoint "the right man"—whether white or native—to every spot. In this matter, there was no concession to tradition.

Once the appointment was made, central supervision over local administration and local officials was effected mainly through the organization of financial relations between the two. Both the British and the French practiced a policy of fiscal autonomy. So long as a colony could balance its books, its administration remained a highly decentralized affair. If it failed to do so, a British colony, for example, would pass under the supervision of the Treasury.[38] Every line item would be carefully screened, and every excess mercilessly cut so as to balance the budget. This practice held in relations between the Colonial Office and the governor-in-council, as it did between the central state in the colony and local officialdom. District-level autonomy at times reached the level of a fetish, as we will see with the food policy in the British colonies. The result was a pervasive revenue hunger all along the chain of command, from the central to the local state, leading to efforts to tax or impose fees on anything that moved. Even the performance of chiefs was judged—and their salary levels established—on the basis of the tax revenue they were able to collect, not the number of persons under their administration. This was true even in the poorest districts, such as Karamoja in Uganda.

Not surprisingly, chiefs used their customary powers to keep order and exact labor to help themselves along the way. In German times, the chiefs in Tanganyika collected tribute in various forms: labor, cattle, meat, and beer, all in addition to what a peasant was required to give to the government. A German missionary "estimated that the chief was paid seven times as much as the colonial government in the process." What disturbed this observer greatly was "the extremes to which the chiefs took the custom of using the children of commoners as servants in their households"; if the chief requested, he always had the right to the third child of a man.[39] In the French-controlled parts of Cameroon, a researcher recently collected stories of "not only the ruthlessness of the chiefs in levying labor on government's orders but also the practice of putting them to work on their plantations." But "the main theme in the stories about the chiefs," he found, "is the ruthless way they appropriated women throughout their area."[40] In colonial Mozambique, peasants who failed to meet their tax obligations often ended up working the personal plantation of the chief. "My father had eight hectares of cotton," reminisced the son of a chief, "worked entirely by convicted criminals and widows who were unable to pay their taxes."[41]

More than forced labor, forced contributions were the real stuff of extralegal extortion that chiefs resorted to for personal enrichment. Take, for example, the range of compulsions the chiefs of Fouta (Guinea) levied on the population in 1953: 50 francs per family for each feast day, 25 per head for 14 July and 11 November, and 15 per head on the occasion of the census; in addition, a death levy on all persons above the age of seven, but for an adult over twenty-five, a levy of 10,000 francs or two oxen to confirm "the right of succession," "failing which the lands of the deceased were confiscated, and sometimes the empty granaries, without anything being left for the surviving spouse." The point was to ensure that the chief in question be able to purchase a house and an American car and finance a pilgrimage to Mecca.[42]

In her review of case reports from Native Authority courts in Kilimanjaro—from a period when chiefs were already paid regular salaries—Sally Falk Moore concluded that "to an important extent the court must be seen as having once been an arm of personal chiefly power"; for instance, a man who failed to come to the *baraza* (public assembly) to pay tax was sentenced to five strokes.[43] That same year, 1936, when a casebook recorded that a village headman was fined five shillings "for not having seized the property of a tax defaulter when ordered to do so," the district officer wrote in red in the margin, "Do not enter such cases in this register. . . . This case is neither civil nor criminal."

The combination of financial autonomy for local units and administrative absolutism for its agents created a decentralized despotism. Their salaried status made for little change in the relation between the chief and the peasant under his jurisdiction. The most effective way for local officials to exact additional revenues from subjects was to tighten the regime of extra-economic coercion. This is the reason, Lugard's stated intentions notwithstanding, that chiefs continued to be able to exact and extort benefits from peasants. This is why, wherever the power of a local authority remained fused, chiefs or cadres were in a position to coerce favors from peasants. So long as the fused powers of chiefs remained intact, this continued to be the case, as much after colonial reforms that paid chiefs regular salaries as before it, as much after chiefs were abolished and replaced with another category of personnel as before it. The point can be illustrated with a few contemporary instances: from Uganda, South Africa, and Zaire.

In the Uganda of Amin and Obote II, it was customary for chiefs to hire out tax defaulters as labor gangs to commercial farmers and pocket their payment as personal gain.[44] The 1987 Commission of Inquiry into the Local Government System in Uganda found that peasants traveling but ten miles to markets in the capital had to pay market dues at least three times, twice when crossing a district boundary and a third time upon entering the market![45] The same commission noted a direct link between the incredible range of *empooza* (Luganda, from "to impose") levied by cash-starved local authorities and extralegal extortion by its on-the-ground officials. Take, for example, the compulsion to contribute to a "hospitality fund" because a state official (from the higher chief to the minister to the president himself) was coming to visit one's area or because a presidential lodge needed to be constructed in the region. One such instance occurred in October 1993, when, overwhelmed by the prospect of a presidential visit, local officialdom in a poor district in northeastern Uganda ended up spending more than seven million shillings ($6,000). When the president left after a few days, the district coffers were in the red. Seven months later, the same district was in the throes of a famine. After a survey of "these systems of contribution and imposition" observed during field research in a village west of Ibadan in Nigeria, a researcher concluded: "All in all, the value of the resources devoted by ordinary citizens to issues that in other systems would fall within the purview of the local state are far in excess of the official tax rate."[46] Legal and extralegal, systemic and individual, these exactions serve not only to beef up the lean purses of the local authority but also to line the pockets of its individual functionaries.

The debates in the KwaZulu Legislative Assembly give revealing information on how matters stood in Zululand in the 1970s. As the eviction of labor tenants from white-owned farms increased, chiefs cashed in on the displaced people's hunger for land. Legislative records from 1975 contain warnings to chiefs "not to continue with the unlawful practice of receiving money or kind in return for the allocation of a site." In 1978 newspapers reported Buthelezi attacking chiefs for "fleecing" the people, that is, charging for sites, arable land, and services such as collecting pension checks. In a research carried out in the early 1980s, Paulus Zulu concluded that nine out of every ten respondents who acquired a site on which to build a house had to make some monetary payment either to the chief or to the local *induna* (headman). In some cases, they even had to pay an annual rent. Forty percent of those he interviewed had to pay for an induna to approve pension or disability grant applications. Chiefs demanded contributions "as a common practice" for anything, even "purchasing a new car, or a new building, or a son's marriage."[47] As late as 1987, Buthelezi could complain to chiefs in the KwaZulu Legislative Assembly: "Someone was informing me that he had to pay 1000 Rand for a site and . . . bottles of whisky."[48]

In the absence of democratic forms of accountability, autonomy and decentralization turned into a license for on-the-ground functionaries freely to augment the local treasury and supplement their own meager salaries through extortion from local residents. In independent Zaire, for example, it became customary for local officials to extort levies from residents in the eight hundred collectivities of the "reformed" local administration. This "financial autonomy" was legally abolished with the territorial reform enacted on 5 January 1973. But the law was never implemented, for the center never had funds to take over the financial administration of Zaire's more than eight hundred collectivities.[49] The collectivities continued to enjoy financial autonomy, meaning they continued to levy a diverse panoply of taxes on residents with the consent of the subregional commissioner. In the city of Lisala in 1974–75, for example, a series of incidents of taxation put together by a researcher "from a long list . . . illustrative of the general pattern" included taxes pertaining to birth, marriage, and divorce certificates, transit permits, land tax, water consumption tax, social tax, and even a boutique tax. The range of taxes would expand (but seldom contract) in a fashion totally arbitrary. Thus, for example, in 1975 the city set up barricades on main roads leading into it and required a "supplementary road tax" from all those coming into town either to sell produce or to visit the hospital. A neighboring collectivity imposed a tax on all cassava (manioc) sellers; another imposed a tax on concubinage.[50]

Financial autonomy also provides the framework in which lower-level functionaries such as chiefs, police officers, and party youth, often not even paid their meager salaries because of high-level corruption, "resort to violence to extract money from the population." One chief defined "education work" to mean forced labor on his own plantation. The most opportune time for extralegal extortion is when the tax is due. "Tax collection in Zaire," concludes the author of the study from which I have been quoting extensively, "is a brutal affair in which the police and party youth wing often collaborate with great gusto. In no society is the tax collector a well-liked figure. In Zaire, however, people literally run when they see him approach. Once again, the *avantages* of the chief results in brutality by the bureaucrats and suffering for the people."[51] Yet this collectivity chief is beyond the reach of any legally initiated action. For the Ordonnance-Loi no. 74-255 of 6 November 1974 stipulates that collectivity chiefs cannot be brought to justice without the express written consent of the state commissioner for political affairs![52]

Such is the banal violence of indirect rule in its day-to-day operation. We will see that the weaker, the less resourceful, and the less experienced a colonial power was, the harsher was the reality of its rule, as in the Belgian possessions of the Congo and Ruanda-Urundi or the Portuguese possessions of Mozambique, Angola and Guinea-Bissau. But everywhere, the minute order faced opposition, power shifted gear, from a normal to a crisis-driven response. The tendency for cadres of the decentralized structure of administrative coercion was to turn into foot soldiers run amock. One has only to turn to an account of colonial pacification—say, of the Mau Mau—to fill in the grisly details. In the event of a crisis, the routine violence of indirect rule exploded like the fragments of a cluster bomb, leaving in its wake blood-soaked homes and fields. No matter how gruesome they were, one needs to understand such events as an extreme manifestation of the crisis of indirect rule and not as exceptional episodes.

We will see that indirect rule was never just a commonsense, pragmatic, and cost-efficient administrative strategy that utilized local personnel to fill its lowest tiers. Its point was to create a dependent but autonomous system of rule, one that combined accountability to superiors with a flexible response to the subject population, a capacity to implement central directives with one to absorb local shocks. The distinction between civic and customary power appeared at all levels. Institutionally, civic power was organized along the principle of differentiation, the customary on the basis of the fusion of power. Ideologically, civic power claimed to defend rights, and customary power to enforce custom. Economically, civic power regulated market transactions and ensured the reproduction of market relations, and customary power was located at the interstices of the market and nonmarket relations, mediating the link through extra-economic coercion.

Yet civic and customary power were always joined under the same overall colonial authority. Without taking into account the backing of civic power, one cannot understand the stamina of customary power. This is why the contradiction between the two was not quite synonymous with the one between the local and the central state. The contradiction appeared within each. The local state, for example, was not just the Native Authority. It also included the representative of the central power, the British district commissioner or the French cercle commander. The local state, in turn, both functioned as a conveyor belt for central state policies and possessed a degree of autonomy. As representatives of the center in the local, the district commissioner and the cercle commander stood in charge of the local state apparatus. Yet neither could be confused with the chiefly hierarchy that was the Native Authority and its autonomy.

The contradiction similarly appeared within the central state. Take, for example, the contemporary organization of the central state in Uganda, which is said to be along modern functional lines, with each ministry of the state designed to execute a specialized function, but in most instances with a scope strictly urban. Thus, the Ministry of Education is responsible for all postprimary education, whereas primary education remains the responsibility of the Ministry of Local Government; the Ministry of Health takes responsibility for all hospitals, leaving pre-hospital services the responsibility of the Ministry of Local Government; similarly, the Ministry of Transport looks after the main arteries of communication, whereas feeder roads are left with the Ministry of Local Government; and so on. Although an administrative division in the central government has created a number of functionally based line ministries as would be the case in the government of any modern state, the domain of most ministries is by and large urban; correspondingly, a single central ministry presides over all affairs concerned with peasants. This octopuslike structure is a state apparatus complete in itself, only it is subordinate; it is autonomous but not independent. In apartheid South Africa, this ministry used to be called the Ministry of Bantu Affairs; in the Africa of free peasants, it bears a name far more anesthetized: the Ministry of Local Government or an equivalent. In both, it watches over a constellation of Native Authorities.

To stretch reality, but without stepping outside the bounds of the real, the Africa of free peasants is trapped in a nonracial version of apartheid. What we have before us is a bifurcated world, no longer simply racially organized, but a world in which the dividing line between those human and the rest less human is a line between those who labor on the land and those who do not. This divided world is inhabited by subjects on one side and citizens on the other; their life is regulated by customary law on one side and modern law on the other; their beliefs are dismissed as pagan on this side but bear the status of religion on the other; the stylized moments in their day-to-day lives are considered ritual on this side and culture on the other; their creative activity is considered crafts on this side and glorified as the arts on the other; their verbal communication is demeaned as vernacular chatter on this side but elevated as linguistic discourse on the other; in sum, the world of the "savages" barricaded, in deed as in word, from the world of the "civilized."

Does not this divided world—on one side free peasants closeted in separate ethnic containers, each with a customary shell guarded over by a Native Authority, on the other a civil society bounded by the modern laws of the modern state—reflect the general contours of apartheid? Was not the colonial state the basic form of the apartheid state? Has not the deracialization of that state structure through independence failed to come to terms fully with the institutional legacy of colonialism? It is in this sense that independent Africa shows apartheid South Africa one possible outcome of a reformed state structure, deracialized but not democratized—whether achieved through armed struggle or through negotiations, through independence from a foreign colonial power or through strategic engagement with an erstwhile colonizing resident minority: a deracialized but decentralized despotism.

CHAPTER THREE

Indirect Rule:
The Politics of Decentralized Despotism

KEY TO UNDERSTANDING the state in contemporary Africa is the historical fact that it was forged in the course of a colonial occupation. The form of the state that contained the free peasant was comprehensively thought through by Lord Lugard, the architect of indirect rule. But this system did not spring full-blown from the mind of a colonial architect, for although Lugard theorized it as the British colonial system, its origins predated Lugard's reflection on it; also, the practice it summed up was not confined to British colonies.

The creation of a separate but subordinate state structure for natives first developed in the southern African colonies and not in West Africa. Here, first and foremost in the colony of Natal, was created a dual system: one for colonizers, the other for natives; one modern, the other customary. The system emerged through trial and error. It was a good half-century before it could be codified as law in Natal (1891) and another three and a half decades before it was generalized to the rest of South Africa (1927). As we will see, this system of control did not yet conform to a full-fledged regime of indirect rule. It lacked certain key features: an autonomous Native Administration with powers to make bylaws or rules, and a Native Treasury to pay its personnel and finance its activities; in sum, a native state apparatus that was not only dependent but also autonomous. It lacked these, at least until the creation of homelands under apartheid.

In this chapter, I will trace the development of institutions of indirect rule, from their South African genesis to their equatorial African completion, returning to the belated South African reform—apartheid—that was the final step in a long and drawn-out deepening of indirect rule institutions in that country. The chapter closes with a discussion of postwar and postindependence attempts to reform the institutions of indirect rule.

THE SOUTH AFRICAN GENESIS

Great Britain annexed the colony of Natal in 1843. An 1846 commission summed up with alarm the existing state of affairs: "The natives' own laws are superseded; the restraints which they furnish are removed. The government of their own chiefs is at an end; and, although it is a fact that British rule and law have been substituted in their stead, it is not less true that they are almost as inoperate as if they had not been proclaimed, from a want of the necessary representatives and agents to carry them out." "The danger of such a state of things," the commission concluded, "scarcely needs our pointing out."[1] Practical as they were, the commission's recommendations formed the starting point of a decades-long search for an inexpensive but efficient mode of control over natives.

The commission's core recommendations were twofold: aggregating the natives in separate locations and administering their day-to-day activities under a "system of justice" that "should conform as much to their own law as is compatible within the principle of ours." The roughly one hundred thousand natives were brought together in ten separate locations. The residential and farming land of these locations, amounting to more than two and a quarter million acres, was brought under the control of the Natal Native Trust, set up in 1864 under the control of the governor and his executive council. Here, in embryonic form, was the first of two legs on which would stand the policy of native control: segregation. The colonial secretary directed that within the "locations" customary law would hold provided it was not "repugnant to the general principles of humanity, recognized throughout the whole civilized world." Because the colonial power held itself to be the representative of the "civilized" world and the custodian of "general principles of humanity," this proclamation—reproduced in some form in every colonial context—underlined the legitimacy of its claim to modify and even remake the customary.

Together, segregation and customary law would create something more than just territorial segregation between the colonizer and the colonized, the settler and the native; it would create an embryonic "institutional segregation." The agents administering customary law would be the chiefs, but with newly defined powers and accountability. So, ordinance 3 of 1849 defined the lieutenant governor as the "supreme or paramount native chief, with full powers to appoint all subordinate chiefs, or other authorities among them" (clause 3). To codify customary law, the second leg of the policy of native control that came to be called native administration, a commission was appointed. The Code of Native Law it recommended was adopted as a set of guidelines in 1878 and then made legally binding in 1891.[2]

Known as the Natal Code of Native Law, the 1891 statute was a draconian piece of legislation by any standard. The powers it defined for the "Supreme Chief" (according to S.5, "the officer for the time being administering the Government of the Colony of Natal") far exceeded those of any precolonial despot. He could fix "the least number of houses which shall compose a kraal" (S.42) or forcibly move any "tribe, portion thereof," or individual to any part of the colony (S.37). He could "amalgamate" or "divide" any tribe(s) (S.33), appoint all chiefs (S.33), or remove any for "political offence, or for incompetency, or other just cause" (S.34). He had "absolute power" to call upon all "natives" to supply "armed men or levies" to defend the colony from external aggression or internal rebellion (S.35) and "to supply labor for public works or the general needs of the colony" (S.36).

The regime of total control the 1891 code laid out applied from top to bottom. It laid out the legal basis for not only absolute authority over natives in the colony, but also patriarchal control over minors and women in each kraal. The code specified that the kraal head was to be the "absolute owner of all property belonging to his kraal," and it was his duty to "settle all disputes" within (S.68). It laid out as a "general rule" that "all the inmates of a kraal are minors in law," the exception being married males or widowers or "adult males not related to the kraal head" (S.72). The section on "personal status" ordained that unless exempted by the High Court, "females are always considered minors and without independent power" (S.94). They can "neither inherit nor bequeath" (S.143). All income was to be controlled by the head of the kraal (S.138), who was given powers to disinherit any son who may disobey him (S.140). Short of that, kraal heads were to "rank as constables within the precincts of their own kraals and are authorized to arrest summarily any person therein" (S.74). To complete this declaration by which "general principles of humanity, recognized throughout the civilized world," were to be brought to natives, kraal heads were also given powers to "inflict corporal punishment upon inmates of their kraals" for "any just cause"!

So routinely and completely was the native to be subjugated that the code even specified the type of salute natives must give to and the manner in which they must hail each category of officialdom, from the white supreme chief to the native headman (S.219). The totality of subjection was spelled out in the powers of the supreme chief. The supreme chief possessed not only rule-making but also judicial powers—the "authority to punish by fine or imprisonment or both" (S.39)—and yet stood above any law: "The Supreme Chief is not subject to the Supreme Court, or to any other court of law" for any action "done either personally or in Council" (S.40). This then was the essence of colonial absolutism, rule by decree, rule without judicial or parliamentary restraint.

When South Africa was unified in 1910, section 147 of the (South Africa) Act vested control and administration of native affairs throughout the union in the governor-general, who was to act with the advice of the Executive Council, not Parliament. The union was forged around one key principle, rule by decree over natives; in the person of the governor, the union was like an armed fist over native heads. In the evolution of native policy in South Africa, 1910, 1927, and 1951 stand out as three pivotal points, each the bearer of a key principle in a growing consensus that would eventually be summed up under apartheid as a unified and generalized policy of native control. If 1910 was an agreement to subject natives to a rule by decree, 1927 generalized customary law as the form that rule must take throughout the Union of South Africa, and 1951 crystallized the final point of that consensus, that native control must be mediated at the level of the tribe, not the village, not through headmen but through a full-fledged, even if subordinate, state apparatus organized around the institution of chiefship. At the same time, the movement from 1910 to 1951 reflected a shift in perspective, from one of direct to indirect rule.

The Cape versus Natal

In the intervening period, from 1910 to 1951, a spirited tug-of-war was waged between two different legal and administrative philosophies: that of the Cape and that of Natal, that of direct and indirect rule. Because much has been made of the liberalism of the Cape system, it is important to underline the parameters that both shared and point out where difference was the result of principle and where of circumstance. It would be a mistake to think of the Cape experience as marking an exception in the general flow of native policy in South Africa. Although the pace at which the shift took place was slower in the Cape, the trend was ultimately not different. To underline that shift is to illustrate the main contours of the flow and to define the conditions that shaped its trend and pace. The thrust of native policy in the Cape is marked by three phases. As the mode of control shifts from one to another, the overall framework of policy shifts from the race model of the early Cape to the tribal option exemplified by the Natal model all along, from a direct to an indirect mode of rule.

When the English took charge of the Cape, it was a multiracial society marked by a single legal order. In this first phase, the colonized were the indigenous Khoikhoi and the imported Malay slaves, forming a small minority of the Cape population. But the colonized swelled into an overwhelming majority in the second phase, which began with the conquest of the Xhosa people. It was a conquest that took a century to make, from what the victors termed the First Kaffir War to the west of the Fish River in 1779 to the Ninth Kaffir War against the Gcaleka in the

Transkei in 1877–78. Up to the Seventh Kaffir War, the British had tried to force natives off the land into remote areas. In 1847, they abandoned the attempt, annexed the territory west of the Great Kei, and gave it the highly illuminating name British Kaffraria.[3] The trauma of eight decades of colonial aggression was vividly registered in the prophecy that led to a generalized cattle killing, breaking the back of the Xhosa and Thembu peoples who lived in British Kaffraria. In this context Sir George Grey, that torchbearer of Cape liberalism who was then the governor of the Cape, marked in flesh and blood the essentials of legal integration in a multiracial colonial society. Taking advantage of the changed situation, Grey confiscated much of the Xhosa and Thembu peoples' land and settled thousands of whites on farms between scattered reserves. The authority of chiefs was undermined, as all judicial and administrative functions were transferred to white magistrates. Thus was established the social prerequisite of a single legal order in a colonial settler society: appropriation of land, destruction of communal autonomy, and establishment of the "freedom" of the individual to become a wage worker.[4] Also, the single legal order was confined to matters of personal law; in the public realm, natives were ruled by proclamation and magistrates held absolute power. This was direct rule.

The policy of legal integration was shaped by both the long history of colonial wars and the eventual defeat and dispersal of the natives. The background of armed resistance had stiffened the resolve of masters of the Cape—proverbially once bitten, twice shy—in favor of a policy of nonrecognition of native institutions. At the same time, defeat and dispersal made it possible to integrate and dominate natives within a single legal order. In this, there was little difference between the Boers and the early British settlers. The zeal of a "civilizing mission" combined with the very real threat that tribes were seen to represent, not only to the civilizing mission, but to the civilizers themselves. For the tribe not only signified the territorial parameter of defense, but was also the ideological reference point for an independent way of life. After all, it had taken the Cape settlers more than a century to tame the tribes. Tribalism was rightly perceived as the anchor of native resistance. If the military capacity of the tribes had to be eroded, the chiefs would have to go—so went settler logic of the time.[5] The institutional backbone of the tribe had to be smashed, and so it was.

Yet we must remember that this smashing could never be complete. Even when the Cape Parliament is said to have "reluctantly annexed Kaffraria" in 1865 and resolved to maintain a single legal system for all its inhabitants, its prerequisite—capitalist relations and the sway of market relations—did not quite obtain. In the scattered reserves that punctuated the space between one settler farm and another, "tribal courts and tribal law continued to operate under makeshift arrangements."[6] In spite of prevailing notions that contrast direct rule in the Cape with in direct rule in Natal, it never was possible for the colonists to rule directly over natives. The smashing was more a lobbing off of the political superstructure of the tribes: the settlers ruled through village-based headmen instead of tribal chiefs. Although the control over natives remained indirect, the consequence was to fragment the nature of the mediating Native Authority on the ground, confining each to a village. In this second phase, then, the claim to legal integration was partly a fiction.

The point was to be driven home seven years later, in 1871, when the Cape annexed Basutoland; official policy changed dramatically and ushered in the third phase in the evolution of native policy in the Cape. Arguing that its inhabitants were "not yet sufficiently advanced in civilization and social progress" to assume full responsibility as citizens, the Cape authorities rejected legal assimilation for the natives of Basutoland. For the first time, then, dualism in personal law and political inequality went hand in hand. But the Sotho petitioned for a parliamentary franchise in 1872. The governor's response was revealing. Rejecting the appeal, he warned them of the entire range of consequences if legal assimilation were to hold: "Colonial law would have to supersede Sotho law, the unoccupied land would be appropriated and sold, and whites be allowed to acquire land and settle in Basutoland."[7]

The wisdom of the new policy was to be confirmed in the following decade. Resistance to colonial occupation did not cease: the Ninth Kaffir War took place in 1877–78 against the Gcaleka and the Ngqika in the Transkei, not to mention the defeat suffered at the hands of the Sotho in the Disarmament War of 1880–81. The lesson was clear: it was not possible to scatter and break peasant communities, and without that, it would not be possible to break their will and their capacity to resist outright imperial occupation. The Cape Native Laws and Customs Commission of 1880–83 warned the government against "excessive interference in the affairs of recently conquered communities." From across the Natal border, Shepstone also offered advice. "The main object of keeping natives under their own law," he told the Cape Commission of 1883, "is to ensure control of them." To drive the point home, he reminded the commission that Natal's African population "has never taken up arms against us, while your people have; and that, in my opinion, alters the position of things very much."[8]

These lessons were formalized in law when the Cape annexed the Transkei and Griqualand East (1879), the Gcalekaland and Thembuland (1884), and Pondoland (1894). The pace was set by the Transkeian Annexation Act of 1877, which gave the governor the power to legislate by proclamation; no Cape statute was to hold within its borders unless specifically extended. The courts, even if operated by white commissioners, were to apply tribal law to all cases between natives, subject to the proviso that it not be "repugnant to justice and equity" or "contrary to good policy and public morals." Unlike in the other provinces of South Africa, where magistrates were predominantly officials of the Department of Justice, in the Transkei they were set apart—under the control of the Native Affairs Department, an administrative agency of the central state. The lessons of war were clear: among the colonized, there was not to be even the formal pretense to a rule of law. Though chiefship was abolished, local administration was to be mediated through a corps of native headmen. In other words, whereas the writ of headmen held over one or several villages, chiefs with a writ over the entire tribe would not be tolerated. Broken at the tribal level, Native Authority would be harnessed at the village level. Through having to establish control in the face of anticolonial resistance, the governors of the Cape had arrived at a form of rule that would closely approximate French-style indirect rule.

But political wisdom alone could not fully explain the shift from direct to indirect rule. The changing realities of the political economy of the Cape—and with it a rapidly expanding demand for mine labor—had also much to do with it. For whereas white farmers called for the breaking up of tribes to release labor that could be absorbed and controlled on settler farms, the mines required the retention of tribal reserves from which labor would be released when required and to which it could be returned when not needed. The requirements of settler farms called for the appropriation of native lands to release land and labor for settler agriculture, whereas that of the mines called for its retention so that peasant farms would continue to function as productive family units releasing and reabsorbing single male labor in an ongoing series of migration cycles.

The difference is clear if we see how the pass system functioned with reference to settler farms and mines.[9] The pass system was introduced on the Cape following the abolition of the slave trade. The Calendon Code of 1908 made it "compulsory for a Khoisan to have a fixed and registered place of residence and to carry a pass when moving within or between districts of a colony." As in all other British colonies where some version of the Masters and Servants Act was in effect, it required the "compulsory registration of (labour) contracts" and treated their breach as a penal offense. It further "legitimised a system of child labour through compulsory apprenticeship of children born to farm labourers under service contracts." Compulsory attachment—of servants to masters and of their children to an obligatory apprenticeship—suited the needs of labor-starved settler farms. But the pass system the mines fashioned through the Native Labour Regulation Act of 1911 sought to tie family labor not to a single employer, but to the reserve. The difference between settler farms and mines in how each perceived the significance of the pass system lay in this: whereas the pass system was for settler farms a way of tying family labor to employer, for the mines it was a way of preventing the permanent settlement of African families on their property by maintaining worker ties with the reserves. Unlike settler farms, who saw the survival of peasant agriculture as mainly a threat, its reproduction in the reserves was for the mines the sine qua non of a continuing migrant labor system. The two ends of this system of temporary migration were the reserve and the compound; both, as we will later see, organized expressions of indirect rule.

It seems to me that for Cape liberalism to flourish in a colonial context required an all-embracing capitalist market: combining civil inequality based on market differentiation with legal equality based on the rule of law. "Equal rights for all civilized men south of the Zambezi," that clarion call of Cecil Rhodes, was inscribed in a propertied franchise, one that would "naturally" exclude that vast majority of natives on grounds of their propertyless civil status, not on the basis of any legally inscribed racial discrimination. The precondition for legal equality was civil inequality: an end to customary tenure and holdings and the appropriation of land. But where the reach of capitalist relations was limited, and the law facilitated the retention rather than the appropriation of peasant holdings, a propertied franchise could not go hand in hand with colonial control. There, political inequality would have to be grounded in a legal dualism, rather than in market differentiation. It is this reality that the Natal system symbolized in the operation of a dual judicial system, one modern, the other customary, neither quite separate nor quite equal.

As the Cape reserves turned into "the single largest source of migrant labour" in South Africa, the Cape system lost both its liberalizing zeal and its consistency.[10] In the Cape colony proper, the basic terms of a nonracial propertied franchise had been spelled out under the Cape of Good Hope Constitution Ordinance of 1852, and it still held. But this policy of assimilation was modified in the Transkeian territories, where white officials administered customary law. This was reflected in the fact that the governor of the Cape did not rule over the Transkeian territories as he did over the Cape, as presiding officer of a legislature to which he remained answerable. Rather, he ruled these protectorates as a high commissioner, with powers to legislate for them by decree. Whereas the powers of a governor of a colony were circumscribed by the rights of those he governed, however modestly the latter were defined, those of a high commissioner of a protectorate were not; for the essence of protection was not to guarantee rights but to enforce custom. In a colony under direct rule, the guarantee of rights required the rule of civil law, however circumscribed racially. But in a protectorate under indirect rule, custom was enforced through customary law.

In more than a century, native policy in the Cape went through three phases. Of these, only the first can be characterized as direct rule over a colonized minority comprising the indigenous Khoikhoi and Malay ex-slaves. The second period, one in which peasant communities were partly disintegrated as settler farms were set up in British Kaffraria, was clearly one of transition: official claims to a single legal order were belied by an informal tolerance of tribal law in peasant enclaves in the Cape proper. The third and final period is indirect rule. Legal dualism obtained; relations among peasants were regulated through customary law. The key difference with the apartheid period was in the agents who enforced it, white commissioners at the outset and native chiefs under apartheid.

What then were the differences between the Cape and the Natal systems by the onset of this century? At first glance, they seem purely quantitative, with the difference one of terminology. In the Cape, the parameters of civil society were stretched to include a tiny minority of the colonized. Thus emerged the Cape Native Franchise. Not that there were no natives permitted into the ranks of civil society in Natal. There were. But they were exemptions, individually based and even more narrowly defined. The successful petitioner was "exempt from the operation of native law" only, not from discriminatory civil (modern) legislation imposed on all Africans.[11] Whereas those exempted in Natal numbered 851 in 1890 and 5,000 in 1904, by 1905 only 3 had managed to become enfranchised.[12] The other side of individual exemption (Natal) or a group-based civilized franchise (Cape) was the vast majority of those colonized, branded, and confirmed in a captive status as natives (Natal) or uncivilized (Cape).

The common presumption of the two systems was underlined by their acceptance of two key institutions: segregation and customary law. Segregation separated whites from natives. Customary law separated civil from uncivil society: in Natal, nonnatives from natives, except those few exempt individuals; in the Cape, the civilized from the uncivilized. In both instances, the content of customary law, the legal parameters within which native lives had to be lived, was sanctioned by the colonial state in the person of the governor-general. In both instances, the governor-general was the supreme dictator over natives, whether all or almost all. In the traditional nomenclature of Natal, where he administered customary law through native chiefs, the governor-general was called the paramount chief; in the modernizing jargon of the Cape, where the dispensers of customary law were white commissioners and not native chiefs, he was the high commissioner. But in the Cape as in Natal, he ruled with immunity, from parliament or the courts. It was, in modern parlance, an unfettered rule by decree.

The 1927 Consensus

This shared premise of the Natal and Cape systems was written into law in 1927. S.1 of the Native Administration Act designated the governor-general as the supreme chief of all natives. S.25 allowed this supreme chief to rule all natives by decree ("by proclamation in the Gazette"), subject to neither parliamentary nor judicial restraint. He was given the powers to amend the Natal Native Code by proclamation, which he did in 1932. Not only could he "divide" or "amalgamate" tribes, as in the original Native Code of 1891, he was also given powers to "constitute a new tribe" [S.5(1)(a)], literally at will. His edict extended to every individual native, for he could "create and define pass areas within which natives may be required to carry passes" or even "prescribe regulations for the control and prohibition of the movement of natives into, within or from any such areas" (S.28). Not content with establishing colonial control over collective identity and individual movement, the lawmakers made it a crime to "utter any word . . . with intent to promote any feeling of hostility between natives and Europeans" [S.29(1)]. To give teeth to these powers, the supreme chief could appoint a native commissioner (a white man), his assistant, or a chief (S.2)—in other words, the entire Native Administration. He could confer power over civil and criminal jurisdiction to lesser chiefs (S.12). And so, for the first time, courts of chiefs and headmen were established throughout the country on the basis of authority given by government warrant.[13] The powers conferred on the governor-general as supreme chief were despotic to the extreme. Their context was fast-expanding resistance under the leadership of the Industrial and Commercial Workers' Union of Africa (ICU), a trade union with growing support in rural areas. The ICU did not survive that decade, but the Native Administration Act held sway over all of South Africa, substantially unchanged, for the next fifty-eight years.

The 1927 act was qualified in one respect when it came to its application in the Cape. The governor-general did not rule as the supreme chief over Cape natives; he did so as their high commissioner. The difference, we have seen, lay in the fact that the supreme chief ruled through native chiefs, and the high commissioner through white commissioners. Thus, unlike in the other provinces, white commissioners—and not native chiefs—administered customary law in the Cape Province. But then, commissioners in the Cape, unlike in other provinces, were subject to administrative control under the Department of Native Affairs (an executive agency), and not judicial supervision under the Department of Justice. It was the "desperate opposition" of the Cape authorities "to any increase in the judicial powers of the chiefs," whether in Transkei or Ciskei, that was "largely responsible for excluding the Cape Province from the aegis of the 'Supreme Chief.'"[14] We have seen that this desperation was born of concrete historical experience. The tenor of Cape liberalism was largely shaped by the experience of protracted African resistance: the century-long Kaffir wars. Cape liberalism was bent on fragmenting the colonized to the extreme. It combined racial exclusion with a village-level autocracy run through headmen. For the settlers in the Cape, tribalism was synonymous with resistance. Hence their "desperate" opposition to the restoration of chiefs, even if under the supreme chief.

That desperate opposition held until the apartheid era, when the institution of chiefship was restored throughout South Africa as the dispenser of customary law. We will later analyze the conditions that made this possible; but the point at this juncture is that apartheid neither repudiated nor changed the basic thrust of the system of native control in place by 1927. For with the passage of the 1927 Native Administration Act, two elements of the triple consensus that would define native policy under apartheid were already in place: rule by decree and customary law. The first had held together the 1910 Union, and the second was effected through the 1927 act. That act generalized throughout the Union a system of controls that wore an indigenous mask and went by the benign phrase "indirect" rule over "natives" through "customary" law. It set up separate white and African structures, making customary law for native control a preserve of specialized lower courts, of chiefs and commissioners, subject to administrative control. In South Africa that control was through the Department of Native Affairs, but it was a system neither uniquely nor particularly South African.

INDIRECT RULE AS COLONIAL REFORM

How is one to understand the significance of indirect rule? As an inevitable response to prevailing circumstances, no more than a practical necessity that Lugard turned into a theoretical virtue? Or as a creative colonial response to the riddle that simply would not go away: the native question?

Those who have argued that indirect rule was no more than bare necessity have stressed two aspects of the colonial situation in the early part of this century: the lack of personnel that every colonial power faced and the extreme difficulty in communicating over long distances.[15] Both problems were real. In 1903, when Kano and Sokoto came under the control of the British, the population of northern Nigeria was estimated at a little more than seven million.[16] To govern this population, Lugard had at his command 231 civil European officers in 1903–1904. For the next two years, the corresponding numbers were 241 and 266 respectively. In 1906, the ratio of European civil officers was something like 1 to 2,900 square miles and 1 to 45,000 Africans. Subordinate clerical and technical staff from Europe were hard to come by and were often absent. The death rate was high. In the four years from 1903 to 1907, 65 Europeans died and 264 returned home as invalids, victims of black-water fever, dysentery, malaria, anemia, sunstroke, and bronchitis. "In 1900," claims the Nigerian scholar I. M. Okonjo, "the hopelessness of the communications system made the adoption of 'indirect' rule all but inevitable." Given the tortuously slow and difficult pace at which available transport functioned, "it was practically impossible for the high commissioner or the various heads of department to visit more than a third of provincial headquarters" in a tour of twelve months; even then, "nine-tenths of the time of a journey was occupied in actual traveling." The result was "a heavy delegation to residents and a large volume of correspondence."[17]

The situation in other colonies and in other periods was not that different. We can take illustrative examples from two different periods: just after the First World War and roughly two decades later, before the onset of the Second World War. In Kenya, the tightest-governed British colony north of the Limpopo, there were a total of 145 British administrative cadres in 1921 (and even fewer, 114, in 1939). This gave a ratio of 1 per 22,000 natives. The corresponding ratio for Uganda was 1 for every 49,000 and for Nigeria 1 for every 100,000.[18] Writing at the onset of the Second World War,[19] the French colonial officer Robert Delavignette gave figures for European officials and the corresponding native population in the African colonies:

	European Officials	Native Population
British Nigeria	1,315	20,000,000
Belgian Congo	2,384	9,400,000
French Equatorial Africa	887	3,200,000
French West Africa	3,660	15,000,000

A form of decentralized administration came to be characteristic of every colony. The unit of that administration was the district in British colonies and the cercle in French-controlled territories. The real "man on the spot," the white officer who personified colonial authority, was the

British district commissioner and the French cercle commander. The former was the legendary colonial "King in the castle"; the latter an equally famed "*Le roi de la brousse*."[20] Both enjoyed an enormous latitude in the interpretation of policy. The administration of every district or cercle was stamped with the personality, the style, and the point of view of its commissioner or commander. Anyone who has perused archival correspondence between the secretary in London and the governor in the colonial capital, and in turn the governor and the district commissioner in the field, cannot fail to be impressed by the division of labor in the chain of command over native policy: the colonial secretary usually confined himself to outlining the basic thrust of policy in the form of guidelines, the governor and his council established the main lines of policy, and the district commissioner was in charge of interpreting, modifying, and implementing policy in light of local conditions. Van Vollenhoven, the celebrated governor-general of Afrique Occidentale Française (AOF), solemnly declared that "only one's presence, personal contact counts. The circular is zero." "Few general practitioners in human history," concluded Robert Huessler in his study of northern Nigeria, "were as powerful and active in the whole sweep of community life."[21]

Clearly, given this combination of circumstances—the paucity of European administrative personnel available to the colonial administration, the difficulty in effecting rapid and regular communication between administrative centers, and the diversity of ecological and social conditions on the ground—some form of decentralization was inevitable. Thus runs the above argument that indirect rule was a practical necessity for all European powers in Africa at the turn of the century. The facts are compelling, but only insofar as they underline the scarcity of European personnel. They ignore the African personnel—recruited from educated middle strata—and already available to European powers. They ignore the decisive shift in the policy orientation of European powers on the continent at the turn of this century, as they dropped the alliance with literate Africans and began a search for culturally more legitimate allies. For the scarcity of administrative personnel, the key argument in this logical construct, was artificially created; it was not inevitable.

By 1860 the major European powers already controlled enclaves on the West African coast in the form of colonies: the French in the Four Communes of Senegal and the British in the Crown colonies of Sierra Leone, Gold Coast (Ghana), and Lagos (Nigeria). In the British colonies were resettled the "recaptives,"[22] African slaves seized by the British naval blockade that lasted from 1807 until the 1860s and who were returned to these coastal enclaves as freedmen and freedwomen. They numbered in the hundreds of thousands; one estimate of those captured

and resettled in a twenty-six-year period is of 103,000 persons. The recaptives were ardent proponents of Christianity and civilization. They
saw the European powers then on the continent as partners in a joint
mission to civilize traditional Africa. Not only did they create forms of
self-administration in the colonies, but the literate groups along the sea-
board from Lagos Island to Gambia sent their sons and sometimes
daughters to Fourah Bay College, set up by the Church Missionary Society in Sierra Leone as early as 1827, and to London law schools and
courts to acquire the education they believed was the beacon of a civilized life. Many returned to occupy leading positions in colonial administration. Among these educated Creoles could be found educators and
militant intellectuals such as Edward Blyden and James Johnston, doctors such as John Africanus Horton and Broughton Davies, evangelist
bishops such as Samuel Ajayi Crowther, and barristers such as Samuel
Lewis, the first African to be knighted by the queen of England.[23]

In the Gold Coast as in Lagos, Africans sat in the legislature and held
senior offices from the 1850s on. In Egypt and Sudan, an even larger
Turco-Egyptian administration was established. In the Portuguese colonies in the nineteenth century, the mestizos "dominated commerce"
and "provided military commanders and civil governors." Many were
"men of education." Their fortunes were eclipsed in the twentieth century when "their position was continually depressed."[24] In Sierra Leone
in the early 1890s, nearly half the senior posts were held by Africans.
From among the Africans domiciled in the four coastal French communes, it was possible for a general to emerge—like Alfred Dodds, who
helped conquer Dahomey for France.[25] The widespread belief among
the educated strata that a partnership with colonial powers would lead
them to independence and regeneration was understandable in the
1860s, since European powers appeared to be getting ready to abandon
their colonial enterprise.

But that was not to be. The close of the century saw a sharp reversal
in trends as a furious rivalry was unleashed between the same European
powers for colonial possessions on African soil. Instead of withdrawing
from coastal settlements, the trend was to turn these into beachheads for
inland penetration and control. Every little colony was turned into a
gateway to huge inland protectorates. The partnership between literate
coastal Africans and European colonial administrations turned sour in
no time. The end of the nineteenth century saw, as the historian A. E.
Afigbo has shown, not only a "systematic removal of educated Africans
who held positions of responsibility in the earlier decades," but also a
"systematic tightening of conditions under which Africans could become French citizens in Senegal and elsewhere."[26] As colonial powers
"began to exercise restriction on the recruitment of highly skilled Afri-

cans into the administrations," they "created the artificial scarcity of administrative personnel." Although Africans had held nearly half of all senior official posts in Sierra Leone in 1892, their share declined to one in six by 1912.[27] The door that was shut in the face of the educated strata from the start of the scramble remained closed until the final chapter of colonial rule. In the Gold Coast, for example, it was not until 1942 that the first Africans, A. L. Adu and Kofi Busia, came to be appointed to the colonial administrative service.[28] We will later see the same trend surface in other colonies such as Tanganyika on the eastern coast, as German colonialism gave way to British rule.

The scarcity of administrative personnel was not inevitable. It was really the by-product of a larger political problem: the native question. To solve that problem, the educated strata of Africans, those who aspired to self-administration and independence, could be of little help. Ironically, this stratum had been the most pro-Western of any group. It had assimilated culturally while aspiring for administrative autonomy immediately and political freedom eventually. Estranged from the vast mass of natives, who often saw them as no more than cultural fifth columnists, only yesterday the spearhead of European penetration—which they had championed as a prerequisite for cultural rejuvenation—the educated stratum was to be hurled into political oblivion while colonial rule stabilized over the next several decades.

This marginalized educated stratum, excluded from the civil society of the colons but beyond the lash of customary law, articulated the first wave of Africanist thought in response to racism and colonial occupation. Blyden spoke of the need to herald the "African personality" in response to racism. Johnson advocated an "Africa for the Africans," popularizing the demand for Ethiopianism whereby Africa would be "evangelized only by Africans but not by Europeans."[29] This constellation of ideas about Ethiopianism, Pan-Africanism, and the African personality amounted to no less than an intellectual renaissance; yet its political import was by and large limited to the narrow educated stratum.

Faced with the imperative of the native question and the cultural resistance of the African population to the policy of assimilation, the British understood better than any other colonial power the need for a policy that would harness culturally legitimate political allies—and not literate Africans ambivalent or even hostile to tradition. By 1898 Sir George Goldie, the president of the Royal Niger Company, had formulated a dictum that all company officials were required to follow: "The general policy of ruling on African principles through native rulers must be followed for the present."[30] Indirect rule came to be predicated on a form of decentralization that was more cultural than territorial. More than just a search for personnel to augment the few European officials available on the ground, it was a search for institutional forms of control anchored in a historical and cultural legitimacy; summed up in the words of General Jan Smuts, it was a shift from territorial to institutional segregation.

Institutional segregation referred to a policy of native control that would be mediated through native chiefs working through native institutions. But neither the personnel nor the institutions they worked were simply available for the picking. Even where chiefs already existed, they had to be tamed. As usual, Lugard advised on the best practical solution: to "thrash them first, conciliate them afterwards; and by this method our prestige with the native tribes would be certainly greatly increased, and subsequent troubles with them would be less likely."[31] In reality, native institutions were given life and substance through a policy that combined a recognition of existing facts with creative modification and even outright fabrication. Whatever the mix, in every instance institutional segregation involved a shift in native policy from a civilized to a tribal orientation and a corresponding change in its social base from the educated strata to traditional chiefs. Simply put, as the link with traditional authorities was forged, so the alliance with the educated strata was severed.

By 1920 indirect rule could be said to express the general thrust of British colonial policy on the native question. Because indirect rule meant that the real locus of colonial administration was the local state, the district run by the district commissioner, it was imperative that this man on the spot be carefully identified, groomed, and placed. Both Britain and France ended the local recruitment of colonial administrators between 1890 and 1914 and reorganized the colonial administration into a formal service along lines of the upper echelon of the metropolitan bureaucracy.[32] The corollary of district-level decentralization was that the agents of district administration were recruited, trained, and placed from the center. This was not simply a territorial shift, from local to metropolitan recruitment, but also a change in social emphasis. During the 1920s, the Colonial Office began to recruit administrators chiefly from Oxbridge. Applicants were screened through interviews and references designed to identify "those qualities of character and personality so essential in dealing with native peoples."[33] The rationale for recruiting the new class of colonial officials from the upper classes at home was that they could be "chiefs in their own country"—men who considered it their birthright to rule, and who did so by habit.

Although Smuts may have expressed the political rationale and the theoretical gist of indirect rule most succinctly, it was Lugard who had earlier characteristically summed up the new policy in terms that would make it accessible to the practically inclined administrator. By the time he came to West Africa, Lugard had already accumulated a significant African experience. His baptism had been in East Africa, in the service of Sir William Makinnon's East Africa Company in 1888 and 1892. On its behalf, Lugard concluded a treaty in 1892 with the Kabaka of Buganda, one that would become the basis of British indirect rule in the next century. This experience was reinforced by his next assignment, when as a servant of Sir George Goldie's Royal Niger Company in 1894–95 he secured the Borgu regions of northern Nigeria for the British against the French. As in Buganda, Lugard held the view that the highly organized native rulers in Borgu "should be used as the main agency for administering the territory."[34]

In the Lugardian scheme, indirect rule was a single and coherent edifice resting on three pillars: a Native Court, a Native Administration, and a Native Treasury. I will argue that an important complement to the judicial, administrative, and financial dimensions of this authority was a fourth, rule making. Lugard saw this ensemble as dependent but autonomous. In his well-known 1919 "Report on the Amalgamation of Northern and Southern Nigeria," Lugard explained the autonomy of this Native Authority in some detail.

> The policy of the Government was that these chiefs should govern their people, not as independent but as dependent Rulers. The orders of Government are not conveyed to the people through them, but emanate from them in accordance where necessary with instructions received through the Resident. While they themselves are controlled by Government in matters of policy and importance, their people are controlled in accordance with that policy by themselves. A Political Officer would consider it as irregular to issue direct orders to an individual native, or even to a village head, as a General commanding a division would to a private soldier, except through his commanding officers. The courts administer native law, and are presided over by native judges (417 in all). Their punishments do not conform to the criminal code, but on the other hand, native law must not be in opposition to the Ordinances of Government, which are operative everywhere, and the courts . . . are under the close supervision of the District Staff. Their rules of evidence and their procedure are not based on British standards, but their sentences, if manifestly faulty, are subject to revision. Their prisoners are confined in their own native goals, which are under the supervision of the British staff. The taxes are raised in the name of the native ruler and by his agents, but he surrenders the fixed proportion to government, and the expenditure of the portion assigned to the Native Administration, from which fixed salaries to all native officials are paid, is subject

to the advice of the Resident, and the ultimate control of the Governor. The attitude of the Resident is that of a watchful advisor not of an interfering ruler, but he is ever jealous of the rights of the peasantry, and of any injustice towards them.[35]

Although this system was to be applied "in its fullest" only "to communities under the centralized rule of a paramount chief, with some administrative machinery at his disposal," Lugard had no doubt that "its underlying principles" needed to be applied "to the varying extent to which it is possible to apply them, even to the most primitive communities." Lugard's point was that the implementation of indirect rule would be greatly facilitated by the prior existence of a native state apparatus, but indirect rule did not have to be restricted to these areas. For it was possible to build a native state apparatus where none had existed before. The important point was to ensure that the parameters of this state authority corresponded with that of the native community, the tribe, and then to rule through it. Between culture and territory, the former must define the parameters of decentralized rule: the boundaries of culture would mark the parameters of territorial administration. This is why to install a state apparatus among communities whose lives had never before been shaped by one was literally to invent tribes!

Not surprisingly, the tendency was for the tribe to be defined as the unit of indirect rule administration. As George Padmore noted in Nigeria, the Mecca of indirect rule, administrative units corresponded "roughly to ethnic or tribal groupings."[36] "The notion of tribe," argues the historian John Iliffe, "lay at the heart of 'indirect' rule in Tanganyika."[37] A 1930 *Native Administration Memorandum on Native Courts*, issued in Tanganyika, explained that tribes were cultural units "possessing a common language, a single social system, and an established customary law." Based on the belief that "every African belonged to a tribe, just as every European belonged to a nation," a provincial commissioner summarized official policy: "Each tribe must be considered a distinct unit. . . . Each tribe must be under a chief." Yet "most administrators knew that many peoples had no chiefs." The solution of this riddle was Governor Cameron's major contribution to indirect rule administration in Tanganyika. He gave to the chiefless peoples chiefs. Admonishing an official who could not see the trees for the wood, Cameron summed up the policy in a nutshell: "Mr. Thompson must take the tribal unit." In other words, if there did not exist a clearly demarcated tribe with a distinct central authority, then one had to be created in the interest of order.

As the mission to give the stateless communities a centralized administration under their "own" chiefs got under way, a clear demarcation took place between German methods of colonial administration implemented in the pre–World War I period and British indirect rule.[38] Until 1925, the British had preserved the German administrative structure, which was based on a form of territorial decentralization served by a centrally organized civil service whose complexion was both European and African. The twenty-two district officers who reported to the secretariat in Dar es Salaam used a gradation of officials trained in government-run schools. Initially, these school graduates were used mainly as senior (*liwali*) and intermediate (*akida*) administrative officers, particularly in areas where no administrative structure had existed prior to colonialism. Later, however, they also came to replace those Arab and African chiefs who initially had served alongside them.

In 1924 a conference of district officers unanimously recommended that administrative decentralization take a provincial form, with each area being run by "an autonomous local native Government having its own legislation, treasury and authorities." To implement that agenda was the mandate of Sir Donald Cameron, appointed governor in 1925. "It is our duty," wrote Cameron soon after arriving in Tanganyika, "to do everything in our power to develop the native on lines which will not Westernize him and turn him into a bad imitation of a European." The point, rather, must be "to make him a good African." To accomplish that, however, required not to "destroy the African atmosphere, the African mind, the whole foundations of his race, and we shall certainly do this if we sweep away all his tribal organizations." Like General Smuts around the same time, Cameron too was averse to the "Europeanized Africans," those he had seen in Lagos; he viewed the political utility of indirect rule in clear terms:

> If we set up merely a European form of administration, the day will come when the people of the Territory will demand that the British form of administration shall pass into their hands—we have India at our door as an object lesson. If we aim at indirect administration through the appropriate Native Authority—Chief or Council—founded on the people's own traditions and preserving their own tribal organization, their own laws and customs purged of anything that is "repugnant to justice and morality" we shall be building an edifice with some foundation to it, capable of standing the shock which will inevitably come when the educated native seeks to gain the possession of the machinery of Government and to run it on Western lines. . . . If we treat them properly, moreover, we shall have the members of the Native Administration on our side.

As Cameron set about realizing his plans for installing indirect rule through Native Authorities, it became clear that the chief obstacle in his path were the stateless peoples. In time, three alternatives emerged as ways of removing this obstacle.[39] One option, as pursued with the Sagara, was to subordinate them to a neighboring chiefdom. A second option was to convert religious leaders into administrative chiefs, as was indeed done with the Masai. A third option, almost always disastrous, as with the Makonde, was to elevate one of several village headmen into a chief. In the process, however, several successes were registered in creating tribes where none had existed before, the most outstanding being the case of the Nyakyusa around Lake Victoria.

"Tak[ing] the tribal unit" as the point of departure for setting up a unit of administration was no simple matter. More than just creating a tribal hierarchy where none had existed previously, this often involved working through a mishmash of ethnic affiliations to create "purer" and clearer tribal identities as the basis for tribal authorities. Early in the history of the two Rhodesias, the governor of Northern Rhodesia wondered in a communiqué to London as to "why the number of native authorities could not be reduced." The secretary of native affairs fell back on "native tradition" and yet argued without hint of contradiction that the same tribal boundaries and organization needed careful nurturing, for when colonial rule came to Northern Rhodesia "the tribes were in a very disorganized state," but since then a tribal organization had been "created."[40]

The implication is that tribes are supposed to be in an organized state, each with its own territory, customs, and leadership. But should the opposite be true, it was clearly the duty of officialdom to create order out of chaos and tribal "purity" out of a tribal patchwork. This was not as formidable a task as may seem at first thought, for colonial officials were generally convinced that the tendency of commoners to run things into one another had a healthy counter in the tendency of rulers to ethnic purity. One only had to identify the leaders, the chiefs, and put them in place for the rest to follow. How things did fall into place, and order was created out of chaos, is illustrated by a study of the "invention" of the Ndebele ethnic identity in colonial Zimbabwe.[41]

Prior to the British conquest, the Ndebele were not an ethnic group but "a conglomeration of peoples who were members of the Ndebele state." Imagine the horror of the native commissioner of Malema District when he realized that the Ndebele did not behave as the Ndebele are supposed to: "Deference is shown by no-one to anyone"; there reigned "a state of anarchy in which the old vital and essential laws and customs were either forgotten or swept away"; and, horror of all horrors, far from a woman being kept in her place, "a girl may chose whom she likes, when she likes, and as often as she likes"! The commissioner's remedy was to teach "the Ndebele" how to be Ndebele by bringing to them a version of the Natal Native Code of 1891. For, reasoned the commissioner, "broadly speaking, it is an established fact that the laws and customs of Natal and Zululand are absolutely the same as in this country." It was an assertion that the assembled chiefs, "attracted by the powers which the Natal Code allocated to them," were in no mood to dispute.

The immediate similarity between the French and British colonial administrations was that neither could dispense with African middlemen. Even though the French had more of a "metropolitan poor white problem" to dispose of through emigration to the colonies, the number of French administrators were still few and far between. In 1912, 341 administrators were in service in all of French-controlled West Africa; in 1937, the number had increased to 385, but "half of them worked in the main towns." The corresponding number in the general administration (administrators and civil servants) of French-controlled Equatorial Africa was 398 in 1913, going down to 366 in 1928.[42] In French-controlled West Africa, eight times the size of France and with a population of around fifteen million by the late 1930s, the territorial administration revolved around 118 cercle commanders who supervised 48,000 village chiefs with the assistance of 2,200 intermediate canton chiefs.[43] "Without the chiefs," admitted the former governor-general of "Overseas France," Robert Delavignette,[44] the French administration "would have been helpless," not only because the chief "represented his community in its dealings with the administration," but "even more importantly," because he represented "the administration vis-à-vis the community."

As with the British, the mere scarcity of personnel could not explain a shift to indirect rule. When the French Republic abolished slavery in 1848, it also conferred citizenship on all the inhabitants of its colonies regardless of color. *Colonies* then referred to the French West Indies and the island of Reunion. In French-controlled Dakar, then but a collection of a few trading posts, the decree was of relevance to some ten thousand slaves.[45] Between 1890 and 1914, the French installed in the African colonies a system officially dubbed "direct administration." To make up for the shortage in personnel, they looked to the native citizens of the Four Communes as allies who would mediate between them and newly conquered subjects in the interior. In another decade, however, both the policy of direct administration and the role of black citizens were under question. Key to understanding the shift of French policy from direct to indirect administration is a reevaluation of the policy of assimilation undertaken after World War I. As the French responded to the balance of forces on the ground—and learned from their own experience in Indochina and Algeria and the British example next door—they came to appreciate the need for a native cultural policy other than assimilation. The experience of the Four Communes showed that native cultural assimilation led to a resurgence rather than to an effective subordination of native political demands. At the same time, the experience of peasant resistance—for example, the one under the leadership of the Islamic marabouts in turn-of-the-century Senegal—showed that those culturally assimilated were hardly the most efficient mediators between colonizers and subjects. The search for traditional as opposed to civilized institutions through which to mediate colonial control was reflected in the shift from assimilation to association as the central thrust of French policy. Let us trace this shift historically.

The difference between early British and French colonial experience is summed up by the following: unlike the British, who in Nigeria and Uganda worked out alliances and "treaties" with rulers of precolonial kingdoms, the French were more often than not in direct conflict with these great aristocracies. When the majority of the great African states—like the kingdoms of Segou and Sikasso and the state of Samory—refused to submit to French claims, they were suppressed. In the words of governor-general W. Ponty in 1910, the point of direct administration was to "suppress the great native polities which are nearly always a barrier between us and our subject."[46] To flatten all mediation between the village and themselves to one, the village chief, came to be the key object of French policy. But in reality, this objective remained elusive. Caught between an acute shortage of European administrators who were concentrated in the main towns and a turn of policy away from the previous assimilationist bent, a de facto recognition of chieftainship beyond the village level became inevitable. By the early 1920s, this shift had gained a theoretical recognition. The older ideal of assimilation was shed as quickly as the newer notion of association was embraced. In his influential work *Domination et Colonisation*, the conservative colonial theorist Jules Harmand distinguished "colonies of settlement from those of *domination* in which European rule was exercised over a large indigenous population." In the latter, he argued, "the social standards of the Native inhabitants were too remote from those of France for assimilation to be practicable."[47] As an alternative, he proposed a "policy of association," which he defined as "indirect administration, with the preservation but improved governance of the institutions of the conquered peoples, and with respect for their past." The publication in 1923 of Sarraut's *La Mise en Valeur des Colonies Françaises* signaled that the policy had indeed received official sanction.[48]

Association, as opposed to assimilation, had originally been suggested for Indochina. Only later was the policy extended to Africa, where the test case was the North African colony of Morocco. The forms of the

Sherifian state were preserved throughout Morocco, as indeed they were by the Spanish colonists in the portion of Morocco they came to control. The practice in France's sub-Saharan colonies fell short of the Lugardian stress on creating an autonomous Native Administration. The degree of autonomy varied from one situation to another, as did the level of mediation through native institutions and personnel. But the general situation was that chiefship could not be confined to the village level; a second tier of canton chiefs was also created, at first in French-controlled West Africa, later extended to French-controlled Equatorial Africa, where the *chef de terre* came to be in charge of "a group of several villages."[49] At the same time, relations among natives came to be regulated under customary law, dispensed by various levels of chiefs under the direct supervision of the French cercle commander, as indeed it was under the supervision of white commissioners in southern Nigeria or the Cape. All in all, indirect administration in France's sub-Saharan African colonies was more a Cape-like affair than a Natal-type administration, closer to British rule in southern Nigeria than in northern Nigeria.

Even in the coastal enclaves of Gorée, St. Louis, Rufisque, and Dakar, which had received a "full mandate" as communes between 1872 and 1889, thereby granting its "originators" the right to elect a general council and to send a deputy to the French parliament, the policy of assimilation was stiffened as black Senegalese organized to wrest the seat of the deputy from the coalition of whites and mulattos who had held it until the election of 1913.[50] Out of a total population estimated at around one million and three quarters, only 78,373 Africans were considered citizens. The rest were classified as subjects. But even the members of the Four Communes straddled assimilation and association, direct and indirect rule: although they had the right to vote, their personal relations were regulated from 1936 on under customary law, Islamic or otherwise.[51] They were beyond the pale of the French civil code.

The shift from direct to indirect rule was perhaps most dramatically illustrated in the volte-face in French relations with Islam, particularly in Senegal. Prior to the 1920s, the French perceived Islam as a militant but reactionary order with leaders—the marabouts of the Sufi brotherhoods—allied to an erstwhile feudal and slave-owning aristocracy. They feared the possibility of a militant Mahdist opposition and responded to Islam in a manner both hostile and sharp. By the late 1920s, however, the French had cultivated a "considerable stake" in Islam, one "so important that it had to be carefully protected." The remarkable history of Sufi Islam in colonial Senegal has been well synthesized in a study of its leading brotherhood, the Mourides.[52] In the early period of French expansion, the warrior marabouts led much of the "most tenacious and effective resistance" to French rule. But the leading warrior marabouts were killed in battle. Even if they inherited prestige and followers, their less militant successors turned the energy of these devotees from warlike purposes to peaceful and economic ones. Although preserving the institutional autonomy of the brotherhood, they changed its orientation: to migration and settlement of virgin lands so as to take full advantage of the newly built railway and to cultivating groundnuts for export so that both followers and marabouts may gain from it. Toward realizing this goal, the brotherhood's major innovation was the *dara*, "a farming community of young men acting in the service of the *Shaikh*." Historically a means whereby followers could collectively seize and settle unoccupied land, the dara evolved into both a Koranic school and a farming group that became the marabouts' "principal source of wealth." The monastic-type discipline of the dara, however, applied to only a small minority of the followers. The great majority remained "independent peasants" who expressed their devotion through offering the marabout occasional labor—"a few days in a month or a year" on the latter's fields—or a regular share of the harvest.

The authority of the marabouts offered something to all social layers of the colonized. To the poor and the downcast, the marabouts provided "patronage of leadership in forms adjusted to the circumstances of colonial rule." To those from a richer station, they offered a possibility of recovering "some of their lost prestige, through marital and other alliances with maraboutic families"; and to all, the possibility of coming "to terms with changes that they had been unable to prevent." From militant anticolonialism at the onset of French rule, the brotherhoods grew into "religious mutual aid association(s) with economic aims."

No doubt this turnaround in the orientation of the brotherhoods provided the context for a similar shift in French policy.[53] The shift became clear at the death of important Islamic leaders like el-Hajj Malick Sy, Sheikh Sidia, and Ahmadu Bamba. Instead of seizing their deaths as an opportunity to "fragment their respective followings and divide the various Sufi orders into their component parts," the French did the opposite. There was "an unprecedented degree of [French] intervention in the internal affairs of the Sufi orders in order to maintain a strong and unified command" (p. 165). Instead of removing native mediation between the village and the French authority at the circle, as had been the policy only a decade before, they sought and cultivated intermediaries.

Association found its way into the field of education with the decree of 1 May 1924, which gave lieutenant governors of Islamized colonies the authority to establish Islamic religious schools (*medersas*) with "the essential aim" of establishing "a point of contact between literate Muslims and our administrators by the training of interpreters, judges and secretaries of native tribunals" (p. 183). The first medersa, established in 1930 in Mauritania, limited entry to the sons of the nobility and had no provision for teaching French. It set the tone for future initiatives. When a French education inspector objected that "a thriving and dynamic system of Qur'anic education would be a very serious challenge to French secular schooling," the lieutenant governor underlined the broader justification of the policy: "A Muslim intellectual foyer will help maintain West African Islam in its present mood which renders it much more malleable and open to our administrative action than in any other region with a Coranic influence" (p. 190).

The lieutenant governor was right on all counts. In the kaleidoscopic reality of Islam in Africa, it would be difficult to find many instances of a lips-and-teeth relationship between an occupying colonial power and an indigenous Islamic hierarchy. Indeed, the near-symbiotic alliance between French political and marabout religious authority was testimony that the objective was realized in practice.[54] Not only did the followers in the brotherhood take to groundnut cultivation as French-organized cooperatives provided marabouts with easy access to seeds and tools, the marabouts also obliged by organizing recruits in the hundreds during wartime. In the referendum of 1958, the marabouts campaigned against independence "with the help and the encouragement of the French administration." The final vote, overwhelmingly in favor of the French community, was popularly termed "the marabouts' Yes." The lesson was not lost on the postindependence leadership of Senegal. With a flimsy party structure "inadequate to reach the mass level directly," they proceeded "through the marabouts." Crucial to President Leopold Senghor's move from a minority position in the Territorial Assembly to a commanding one in the postcolonial order was his ability to "secure the allegiance of a few crucial marabouts."

The British example inspired many lesser colonial powers: from the Belgians in the Congo to the Portuguese in the colonies of Mozambique, Angola, and Guinea to the Italians in Libya and even to the Americo-Liberians. The Belgians introduced indirect rule institutions in the Congo in the 1920s.[55] The reorganization of the administration in 1918 was followed by the creation of a special legal category called native, subject to customary law and to whom the Code Napoléon did not apply. From 1921 on, all Africans were eventually required to return to the rural areas from which they were deemed to have come in the first place. The native must belong to his tribe: the notion of the native as permanently a peasant and only temporarily a worker was given legal reality through a series of decrees between 1931 and 1933.

The Portuguese have a history of colonial assimilation of the civilized natives that predates the French Revolution. Royal ordinances and orders from 1755 on made it a criminal offense to refer to offsprings of mixed marriages as "half-breeds or (by) any other insulting term." If accompanied by "a certain measure of education," the profession of Christianity qualified a native to be treated as civilized, and was considered "sufficient qualification for equal political and judicial rights."[56] Like the French, however, the Portuguese entered this century with a policy designed to reduce all mediation between their field officers and natives to the village headman. The exception to this tendency were the Bakongo in Angola and the Fula in Guinea. Native policy was system atized in the late 1920s and put under charge of the local state, its functionaries being the *chefes de posto* (district officers) and the *regedores* (administrative chiefs). In time, there evolved a hierarchy of African chiefs, from the senior *regulos* to the junior *cabos*. The African population was divided between the *civilisados*—by 1950, five thousand in Mozambique and thirty thousand in Angola—and the *indigena* (natives). The latter group was the proper concern of native policy, systematized as the Estatuto Politico Civil e Criminal des Indigenas in 1929. The statute viewed the native not as an individual but as "part of a community ruled directly by a chief, and subject in the first instance to African customary law." The native was granted access to communal land and, in return, paid the native tax and was "liable to perform a variety of (labour) services."[57]

Similarly, a royal decree in 1929 in Libya divided the nomadic peoples of the colony into tribes and subtribes at the discretion of the governor and on the advice of the regional commissioner.[58] In Liberia, where there was no racially distinct colonizer, "civilized men" were defined as "those who can read and write English."[59] Indirect rule institutions were introduced with the implementation of the Barclay Plan in 1904.[60] The plan contained two main features: administrative chiefs and a paramilitary force to back them up. The indigenous population was reorganized into clans, chiefdoms, and districts: several clans constituted a chiefdom, and several chiefdoms made up a district with its own commissioner. At each level, executive and judicial functions were performed by the same officials. It was the duty of chiefs to "maintain order, recruit labor and collect taxes," a job they accomplished with the help of the newly formed Liberian Frontier Force.

Where there was a significant settler presence, the transition from direct to indirect rule was usually an informal and protracted affair, with legal recognition following rather than clearing the ground for it. In such instances, the point of legal reform was to prune the worst excesses of indirect rule authority brought to light by popular protest.

Take the example of Southern Rhodesia. The "cornerstone of all Southern Rhodesian law" was the provision that "the law to be administered shall, as nearly as the circumstances of the country will permit, be the same as the law for the time being in force in the Colony of the Cape of Good Hope."[61] Here, as in South Africa, the president's power to appoint chiefs included "the right to divide existing tribes into two or more" or "to amalgamate tribes or parts of tribes into one."[62] Likewise, the line of native authority ran from chiefs to headmen to messengers and heads of kraals. As in the French colonies, where the chiefs had no status, Southern Rhodesian law books contained hardly a reference to the powers of native chiefs and headmen, but there was no shortage of clauses on their duties or obligations. Yet even if the law was entirely silent on this question, it had long tolerated chiefs and headmen dispensing customary justice as part of an on-the-ground reality.

Thus, when the 1937 Native Law and Courts Act defined these powers formally and required that customary law be dispensed only by those chiefs or headmen possessing "a warrant from the governor," it was less to inaugurate a new era of indirect rule than to address its problems, by defining and limiting the powers of indirect rule authorities in the face of popular protests against their abuse.[63] Exactly that same "reform" came to Botswana through the Native Courts Proclamation of 1938, and for the same reason. As popular resentment built up against indirect rule authorities in the 1920s and 1930s, a government commission was appointed which confirmed the widespread abuse of powers by chiefs and headmen; to check it, the reform specified that only those chiefs and headmen issued "with warrants by the Resident Commissioner could exercise judicial powers and enforce their decisions."[64] Similarly, the statute recognizing "traditional native organizations" dispensing "traditional law" in the Portuguese colonies was not passed until 1954.[65]

A complete reform of indirect rule leading to its full autonomy was possible only where the weight of settler interests was weak. That was, as one would expect, in the nonsettler colonies. But it was also effected in those settler colonies where the relative strength of settler influence was weakened by other fractions of capital or a powerful peasant movement or some combination of the two. One example of where such a reform was effected in spite of a substantial settler presence was the British colony of Swaziland. Settlers had long opposed autonomous powers for Swazi chiefs, and the British-controlled central state had obliged in a context where Swaziland was assumed to be on a political course that would lead to its eventual absorption into the Republic of South Africa. But the unexpected victory of the National Party in the 1948 elections put into question this assumed trajectory. As the National Party consolidated its hold over the South African state, the Swazi colonial state effected a successful transition in the form of indirect rule from semiautonomy to autonomy and then to independence. The shift is clear if we compare two key legislations from 1944 and 1950.[66] The sharply limited autonomy of native rulers was reflected in the Native Administration Proclamation of 1944 in Swaziland: it gave the British high commissioner the power to appoint and depose all chiefs, including the paramount chief. The tide turned with Proclamation 79 of 1950. It recognized the Swazi king as the sole authority for issuing any of a wide variety of twenty-nine orders enforceable in the customary courts. The king and chiefs were empowered to make rules providing these did not conflict with existing laws in the country. These rules could be enforced in native courts. Another proclamation (the 1950 Native Courts Proclamation) gave the king the right to establish Swazi courts, to prescribe their rules of procedure, and to establish courts of appeal—all subject to ratification by the British resident commissioner.

A similar transition to autonomy—full-fledged indirect rule—and then to independence was attempted in South Africa when the National Party came to power in May 1948. The Bantu Authorities Act (68 of 1951) claimed to restore "the natural native democracy" to the reserves by creating a system of councils controlled by chiefs and headmen. For the first time, an autonomous Native Treasury and a Native Administration paid from it—with powers to make rules in a native legislature—were added to the administration of customary law, in Zululand (Natal) and in other homelands. The pace was set in the Transkei in 1956, when the Transkeian Territorial Authority was created, growing over the next twenty years from "self-government" (1963) to "independence" (1976).[67] The Transkeian example was emulated in three other instances—Ciskei, Venda, and Bophuthatswana—whereas developments in Zululand stopped at the establishment of an autonomous indirect rule regime.

Ironically, it is apartheid that brought to South African natives full-blown indirect rule, that system of control upheld in equatorial Africa as testimony to the true colonial genius of British imperialism; and it was apartheid that tried to keep pace with imperial-style decolonization, particularly in migrant reserve territories like Swaziland, as the "wind of change" blew across the continent. But that is where the parallel ends, for although indirect rule was successfully reformed in colonies to the north of the Limpopo through a deracialization of the state apparatus, such a reform was not within easy grasp of South Africa. Precisely that special feature in the colonial experience of South African natives, that it had come to be a colony of white settlement—a fact most often summed up in the phrase "settler colonialism" or "internal colonialism"—made such a reform difficult. For the deracialization of the system of indirect rule would require a reform of both native communities and hitherto white civil society. Entrenched in civil society and state institutions, white privilege set apart South Africa—and, to a lesser extent, Algeria and Rhodesia—from the rest of Africa. To undermine that privilege and deracialize the state would require a struggle of great depth. I will examine the main features of that struggle in a subsequent chapter. The following section explores the state reform that was possible in the context of racial privilege.

SOUTH AFRICA: TRANSITION TO APARTHEID

On the face of it, the debate on the most efficient mode of native control came to crystallize around two alternatives: race or tribe. The shift from race to tribe was pioneered by the British and articulated as the policy of indirect rule. It was a transition ultimately made by every colonial power. For this there were compelling reasons that flowed from the very nature of the colonial encounter. Occupying powers learned that if popular resistance could not be smashed frontally, it would have to be fragmented through reform. To be effective as a mode of control, reform would have to lead to a redefinition in the very mode of resistance. Race as the main way of defining the social status of the colonized had two important disadvantages: first, it defined the colonized as a racially oppressed majority; and second, it was difficult to legitimate this mode of control by anchoring it in any traditional practice. On both counts, racism tended to accentuate the colonial context of rule rather than to assuage it. As the cutting edge of social life, racism compounded rather than eased the problem of rule in a colonial context, for its thrust was not to divide and rule, but to unite and rule!

The alternative to racism—as the main way of defining the social, legal, and political status of the colonized—was tribalism. On the face of it, tribe as a social litmus had none of the disadvantages that race did. In fact, its advantages were obvious: unlike race, tribe would dissolve the majority of the colonized into several tribal minorities; furthermore, tribal identity could be argued to be both natural and traditional. Over time, those in positions of power came to realize that a debate on the mode of control was simultaneously one on the mode of representation. Control and representation were two sides of the same coin, which would eventually make for a single fit: the mode of representation, whether racial or tribal, would shape the lines along which natives would organize and in turn avail the state corresponding avenues of native control.

Those who argued for tribe over race as the major determinant of native social status, however, did not have an easy ride. For the recognition of natives as belonging to tribes was not without its problems. This, more than anything else, had been at the root of the difference between the French and British systems of native control. It was also the crux of the century-long debate in South Africa between the Cape and the Natal on how best to control natives.

The Changing Face of Tribalism

To the early settlers on the South African landscape, tribes were the defining feature of social reality. Tribalism, settlers generally agreed, was a source of danger, and a great one at that. For tribes may have been subdued, even conquered, but they defined the parameters of an autonomous way of life. This autonomy was multifaceted: the tribal economy was a source of livelihood, tribal ideology a source of identity and common purpose, and tribal institutions a potential locus of peasant resistance. In the face of the tribal way of life, settlers became militant advocates of a "civilized" policy that would emancipate ordinary tribesmen from the tyranny of chiefs, and tribeswomen from female slavery.

"The wives of a man are practically his slaves," argued Natal's governor Pine, "and the more a man has the richer he is." To draw out the practical significance of this moral crusade, the governor added: "How can an Englishman with one pair of hands compete with a native man with five to twenty slave wives?" To drive the point home, the Kaffir Commission of 1852–53 argued that although "the Kaffirs were rapidly becoming rich and independent," this was "evidence of the increasing means of sensual indulgence available to the males." "Their prosperity would be welcome if it were the fruit of men's regular and honest industry, but it flowed in fact from polygamy and female slavery." And so the commission made its most "enlightened" recommendations: that polygamy and *lobolo* (bridewealth) be prohibited by law.[68]

The early Boer republics were the most resistant to recognizing any sort of customary law. For to sanction native law was to underwrite native autonomy, and that would offend not only their Calvinist consciences but also their more urgent and practical demands for land, labor, and security. The Orange Free State did sanction the customary law of inheritance, but "only in administering estates of *de facto* monogamists." Settlers petitioned the Orange Free Volksraad "to prevent evils arising from tribal marriages," evils such as "the exchange, akin to slavery, of women and children, ill-treatment and the theft of cattle for lobolo"—never mind that these memorialists came from a community that habitually raided tribal villages for child labor![69]

The Transvaal Volksraad actually legislated against tribal marriage. Law 13 of 1876 declared in lofty terms: "In furtherance of morality the purchase of women or polygyny among the coloured races is not recognized in this Republic by the law of the land." The supreme court ruled that "polygyny was inconsistent with the general principles of civilization."[70] Similarly, a directive of 1895 barred lobolo claims. In the Boer republics, as in the early Cape, the accent of native control policy was on race, not tribe, and the reason was patently obvious: tribal autonomy had to be destroyed, both to flush land and labor into settler hands and settler-controlled markets and to destroy the capacity of tribal organs to act as vehicles of resistance.

Once land and labor were firmly pushed into settler-controlled markets, the pendulum swung in the opposite direction. Now that tribal autonomy had indeed been compromised, settler opinion became increasingly concerned with the need for tribal stability. Let loose from age-old tribal bonds, the laborer, the professional, the trader, and the intellectual came to symbolize a threat instead of a promise. These products of a civilized native policy made equally modern and civil demands: parity of treatment and equality of civil status. The tribal customs that yesterday were seen as still cementing the bonds of resistance now appeared in a new light: in the words of the South African Native Affairs Commission of 1903–1905, as "keeping young people in check."

Just as the British had done at the close of the nineteenth century, the French and the Belgians in the 1920s, and the Portuguese in subsequent decades, the rulers of South Africa too came to see the culturally civilized native as a growing political threat. To check that threat, the state would try to shore up customary law and tribal chiefs—precisely when changing conditions were fast eroding their role and status. Now that tribalism seemed a spent force, no longer a threat to settler security or a viable alternative to the labor market, new virtues would be discovered in a renewed tribalism. From the early-twentieth-century encounter of shriveled tribal authorities and anxious colonial rulers would be born yet another tribalism, one that should be understood more as the outcome of a specific historical encounter than of a historical residue. To grasp the significance of this shift, we need to recognize that even when colonial governments had earlier recognized customary law, as had the government in Natal, it had defended this as a necessary evil, not a virtue. Even Shepstone's rudimentary form of indirect rule, evolved in late-nineteenth-century Natal, came under question with the turn-of-the-century Bambatha Rebellion in Natal. The 1906–1907 Native Affairs Commission, appointed to underline its causes and draw lessons, wondered aloud why "at this date, after more than sixty years of occupation, we should be in search of the best methods of governing the Natives" (Simons, *African Women*, pp. 42–43). Understandably, that commission recommended that "means should be found for its [tribalism's] silent and unobserved disintegration."

The shift from race to tribe as the main determinant of native social status took decades to be effected. That evolution makes sense as part of a wider search for effective forms of native control. To understand how tribalism, once seen as the focal point of native resistance, could now be looked upon as an efficient mode of native control, we need to place the changing terms of the debate in the context of a shifting social and political landscape.

The Race Option

The cutting edge of liberal segregationist policy was more obvious in urban areas, where a racial mix obtained on the ground. The liberal Cape pioneered the segregation of African urban residents in separate areas called locations. Two locations were set up in 1903, one in Ndabeni (Cape Town) and the other in New Brighton (Port Elizabeth) following the passage of the 1902 Native Reserve Location Act. The Transvaal followed suit in the same year, as did Natal in 1904.[71]

This initiative was generalized on the recommendation of the Stallard Commission of 1922. Deploring the "miscegenation" and the tendency for mainly unemployed poor whites and blacks to live "cheek by jowl" in squalid locations and shantytowns, the commission spelled out the thrust of urban native policy in words that have since been chiseled in stone in the annals of South African history: "The Native should only be allowed to enter urban areas, which are essentially the white man's creation, when he is willing to enter and to minister to the needs of the white man, and should depart therefore when he ceases so to minister."[72] And for those who do get the privileged urban entry, the commission recommended a thoroughgoing municipal segregation on top of the already effected segregation in workplaces and in industrial conciliation.

But the Stallard Commission went a step beyond calling for racial segregation. It made segregation the basis of representation. It recommended that each local authority set up a Native Affairs Department to administer its own segregated residential location; at the same time, this administrative unit would be a unit of representation, being a Native Advisory Board staffed by African legal residents but chaired by a white superintendent of locations. These recommendations were formalized in the 1923 Natives (Urban Areas) Act, a piece of legislation that for the first time crystallized not only residential segregation but a comprehensive administration of urban Africans along separate racial lines, thus constructing a Chinese wall between native and white civil society.[73]

We must remember that race and tribe were seldom seen as mutually exclusive alternatives in the debate on representation and control. The two were always joined together in a single policy, with the debate focusing on where the primary emphasis should lie. This was most evident in the countryside. A race policy would call for racially specific African forums (councils) in which individual representatives would have tribal constituencies. Alternatively, a primary emphasis on tribe would lead to the creation of separate tribal forums (Native Authorities) in the overall context of racial segregation. An African council may be elected in some measure, but its role would be advisory. Native Authorities, however, always functioned with appointed officials, who either had a hereditary claim to status or were conferred such a status. The home of the race option was the Cape, and its high point in South African affairs—also considered a major liberal victory—was the passage of Smuts's Native Affairs Act in 1920.[74] The act implemented a cardinal principle of liberal segregationist policy: consultative forums for Africans under the trusteeship of whites.

A shift of opinion from race to tribe can be discerned in the 1920s. As racially separate councils were set up in the years that followed the passage of the 1920 Native Affairs Act, there was a buildup of concern within the Native Affairs Department (NAD) about the wisdom of constituting transtribal representative institutions that would lead to the disintegration of tribal bonds. So that while the entire native population of the Transkei (with the exception of Mount Ayliff) was included in the Transkei Bunga by 1923, the view that the Bunga would "break down tribal barriers" and "tend to produce a bond of interest among the black vis a vis the white" began to gain the upper hand within the NAD.[75] Enthusiasm for councils waned. No new councils were established between 1920 and 1926. Even though an amending legislation was introduced that year substantially reducing the powers of councils, no general transtribal council was established outside the Transkei.[76]

Liberal white opinion too came to share doubts about the wisdom of a civilized native policy whose inevitable effect was to loosen tribal bonds. We have seen that General Smuts was unequivocal on the issue by the time he came to give the 1929 Rhodes lecture: at the root of "the colour problem" in South Africa, he argued, were "urbanized or detribalized natives."

These lessons were summed up in the 1927 act, whose key provisions also reflected the general drift of opinion in favor of the tribal option. For the 1927 act generalized, for the first time, a dual legal order throughout South Africa. It created separate native courts to administer customary law to natives. It put in place a semiautonomous form of indirect rule, one where customary law was administered by white commissioners, and where native authorities administered single or multiple villages as would headmen or canton chiefs in a French colony, but not the tribe as would a paramount chief in a British colony. We are told that the act was received in Parliament with a degree of enthusiasm that General Hertzog, the minister of native affairs, found "gratifying to the point of being almost an embarrassment." The focus of that enthusiasm was the incitement clause, which made it a crime to act "with intent to promote any feeling of hostility between Natives and Europeans." Members called for repressive measures against the Communists and leaders of the Industrial and Commercial Workers' Union of Africa (ICU). There was a growing feeling that the cutting edge of African resistance was no longer tribal; rather, the very processes that were undercutting tribal isolation and autonomy were giving rise to modern forces with strongly egalitarian demands. "The 'incitement' clause," argued Simons, "sharpened the realization that tribalism might be a bulwark against radical movements."[77]

Not until 1951 did South African ruling circles move decisively to subordinate race to tribe in the formulation of native policy. That move was a recognition that the real threat to racial supremacy came from new class forces engendered by the modern economy, forces that cut across tribal lines and would therefore flourish in the context of a racial mode of representation and control. The answer, argued the architects of apartheid, was to try and rebottle these forces within tribal confines, where they would surely be better contained by traditional authorities backed up by the armed might of the settler state. So the new post-1948 apartheid regime set about implementing a comprehensive program for the restoration of fully autonomous tribal authorities. It was a blueprint whose agenda could have been taken from any British manual on indirect rule in colonial Africa.

How could one explain that although the early-twentieth-century Boer republics had been uncompromising opponents of tribalism, the Boer intelligentsia organized in the Broederbond would only three decades later champion tribalism as a form of "native democracy" that must not only be tolerated as a necessary evil but positively be encouraged to flourish? This change of heart is easier to understand in the context of a changing situation. If the impetus behind the 1927 Parliament's appreciating the virtue of customary law in containing natives within bounds of tradition was the sight of the ICU and its Communist allies in the 1920s, the learning impetus two decades later would come from an urban resistance that seemed to grow rapidly in the teeth of bloody repression.

Key to that lesson was the realization that in the final analysis race and tribe ought to be seen as complementary—and not exclusive—methods of native control. Exclusive reliance on race had led to a superficial mode of control: while strictly demarcating natives from white civil society, it left the former as a majority. To deepen and stabilize the rule of a racially defined minority, it was necessary to split the majority into compartmentalized minorities. But that division could not be an arbitrary invention. To be believable and to stick, it had to be anchored in a historical and cultural experience. To consolidate racial rule required that it be anchored in a tribal mode of control: by defining every native as a Bantu belonging to a particular tribe, subject to regulation under its own customary law, it would be possible to divide natives into a number of tribes, each a minority on its own, and thereby contain all within the parameters of separate tribal institutions. If racial superiority required a form of the state to be enforced and reproduced, so did the tribal separation of the natives; only, that state—the local state, the Native Authority—would be autonomous but dependent. A solution that British imperialism had arrived at as more of a preventive measure in its African colonies, all other colonial powers in the continent arrived at as a curative measure. In learning that lesson, the framers of apartheid were the last, not the first, and certainly not the only ones.

Apartheid: The Tribal Option

The crisis of native control exploded with great intensity in urban areas. This urban revolt was both work- and community-based. Its dimensions were marked by events ranging from the 1946 mineworkers' strike to squatter and commuter struggles. The miners' strike was the most dramatic of this chain of events. Between sixty thousand and one hundred thousand miners stopped work, bringing between seventeen and twenty-one mines to "a virtual standstill."[78] This "largest strike in South African history" was the doing of migrant workers. It was countered by a massive show of force. Compounds were sealed off under armed guard as sixteen hundred police were called to special duty. Twelve Africans were killed and more than a thousand injured. The strike, which began on 12 August, was over by the seventeenth, in spite of a call on the thirteenth by the Transvaal Council of Non-European Trade Unions for a general strike of black workers. Yet this "apparent failure" turned out to be "a milestone in South Africa's social and political development." In dramatically bringing to the surface the changing weight and alignment of forces old and new it triggered a process that "force[d] all groups into a re-examination of their position and responses, producing important political shifts."[79]

The shift in postwar politics was not just from rural to urban resistance. It was also a shift from work-based to community-based action. There was a marked slowdown in strike activity once the miners' strike ended, but at the same time there was an escalation in community-based organizations and protests. These centered either on the provision of poor services, mainly housing and transport, or on the administration of pass laws. Some of the most dramatic ones were transport struggles in the township of Alexandra, outside Johannesburg. Year after year, from 1941 to 1944, building through four boycotts in as many years, the Alexandra bus boycotts displayed a tenacity that was to make of them a legendary phenomenon.

Whereas commuter boycotts were sustained by township-based workers, migrants were more likely to be the moving force behind squatter struggles, whose context was twofold. On the one hand, municipal segregation required that African people be moved from inner-city slums to locations; on the other hand, there was a rapid inflow of migrants into urban areas. Within a decade and a half, between 1939 and 1952, the urban African population doubled.[80] To contain this growing inflow of rural and inner-city immigrants, the municipalities needed to expend more resources in the construction of locations. But white municipalities were seldom willing to allocate resources, always considered limited, toward that end. The result was the squatting epidemic of the 1940s. A growing stratum of urban Africans had access to jobs but not to housing.[81] Others simply could not afford the available housing, given their meager earnings, and migrants' families could not gain access to hostels.

Resource poor but concentrated, squatters proved to be a militant group. As the numbers of squatters grew, city councils despaired. Official figures (whose tendency was to underestimate the problem) indicated that the squatter population, defined as those lacking approved and serviced accommodation, had by 1947 grown to more than a million, constituting at least 57.5 percent of the urban African population.[82] Because most squatters were legally employed, they could not be easily removed to rural areas using pass laws. However, municipalities could not just evict them from where they were unless they had a place to which to evict them. Several municipalities simply rescinded location regulations restricting one family to a house. But where they did not, squatters organized to keep municipal administrators and police at bay. The resulting movement highlighted the speed with which municipalities were losing control over both the housing issue and the squatting epidemic.

The first large squatter movement was organized by James "Sofa-sonke" Mpanza. At one time a court interpreter and at another a convicted murderer, Mpanza had the bold idea of breaking through an apartheid-defined urban geography by simply moving en masse to the open veld where houseless families could build themselves a shelter.[83] Exiting from Newclare and Cliptown onto vacant land in Orlando, Mpanza's Sofasonke ("We shall all die together") Party required all those who wanted to set up shelter on an allocated piece of land to swear allegiance to Mpanza and to pay a 2d. "entrance" and a weekly "rental" fee of 2.6d. In return, squatters were organized into committees "that appointed camp guards and provided crude sanitary conveniences." The squatters' movement began in March 1944. Mpanza's Sofasonke Party became the precursor of several efforts organized around similarly flamboyant individuals.[84] The squatter epidemic soon turned into an explosion, with camps emerging in peri-urban areas around the country, outside the scope of any legislation.

The rising tempo of urban protest in the postwar period compelled every force—whether on this or that side of the fence—to take stock of a fast-changing situation and to rethink its strategy. For the African nationalist movement, this led to a dramatic change in the center of gravity from rural to urban areas, from a focus on chiefs to urban strata as the locus of resistance, and from a preoccupation with constitutional methods to passive resistance and popular campaigns as the principal methods of struggle. Decades later, a free Nelson Mandela would reminisce on South African television that the squatter struggle was catalytic in setting off the debate within the ANC on the question of the focus, the methods, and the objectives of the struggle. As the partly elected but chief-dominated Native Representative Council adjourned its meetings indefinitely in the wake of the miners' strike—lamenting, "We have been talking into a toy telephone"[85]—the ANC became the locus of a wide-ranging debate on the strategy and tactics, principles and methods, of resistance. The debate on the identification of an appropriate social base for resistance and the efficacy of its methods centered in the Youth League of the ANC. Two developments within the ANC marked the onset of a new phase of resistance. The first was the adoption in 1949 of the Programme of Action, "the most militant statement of principles adopted by the ANC to date."[86] Reflecting this broad shift in geographical focus, program, and methods was a change in leadership, one that took place rapidly. The final point in that swing came a decade later, in 1958–61, with an organizational split that led to the formation of the Pan-Africanist Congress (PAC).

In the dialectic between resistance and repression, the municipalities had clearly lost the upper hand. The central state had to step in. Growing urban resistance exposed the inability of separate municipalities to cope with changing realities. The centralization of urban native administration was the state's attempt to overcome the weakness of separate and uncoordinated local authority responses to a resistance that no longer seemed to be a collection of discrete local phenomena. But there was no clear agreement on either the form or the program of that intervention. Differences crystallized in the form of two documents issued by two commissions, Fagan and Sauer, that preceded the 1948 election. Both agreed substantially on the immediate program but diverged fundamentally on the medium-term goal. The agreement was around the need to control African urbanization through a national pass system effected by means of a national labor bureau and population identification. But that is where the agreement ended. The Fagan Report saw African urbanization as inevitable, as it did the "increasing dependence of Africans on wage labour because the reserves could not support a growing population." Recognizing the "emerging class divisions within the urban African population," it called for promoting this trend within the framework of urban residential segregation. The Sauer Report called for reversing the trend toward African urbanization both by preventing it and by "removing the surplus population from towns."[87]

The National Party came to power in 1948 on a manifesto based on the Sauer Report. But the practical apartheid it implemented over the next decade could not just be a translation of Sauer's recommendations into policy.[88] To hold together the apartheid project, it had to take into account the interests of varied constituencies, particularly the labor requirements of the fast-growing manufacturing sector. Along the line, the National Party appropriated important elements of the Fagan strategy. Thus, as Evans has argued, the linkage that Verwoerd established between the trinity of housing, employment, and influx controls to combat the squatter epidemic ended up retrenching rather than eliminating the permanent section of the working class.[89] But the more practical apartheid accommodated the accumulation needs of different sections of capital, the more it widened the gap between economic strategy and its political project. For the economic strategy was modified to include the acceptance of a permanent African working class, whereas the political project became ever more rigid as it denied the legitimacy of expression of Bantu interests outside the framework of the many indirect rule authorities ranged across tribal reserves. In the process, it unleashed a tide of urban protest that it failed to contain.

By 1948 the Board of Trade and Industries was warning that "racial and class differences will create a homogenous proletariat which will ultimately lose all its earlier ties with rural community groupings which previously had influence and meaning in their lives." The result could only be "the detribalisation of large numbers of Natives"; the accumulation of "rootless masses concentrated in the large industrial centres" was surely "a matter which no government can sit back and watch." This point of view was echoed by the first minister of native affairs in the National Party government, Verwoerd. Declaring that "the position in the urban areas has become intolerable," he warned of the "social danger" of "detribalisation," which had removed "the tribal form of control" but left "nothing to replace" it. When the Native Affairs Department translated these injunctions into elements of practical apartheid, the attempt was to freeze the process of detribalization: classified as temporary urban residents, migrant workers were, in the language of an explanation given in Parliament, "periodically returned to their homes to renew their tribal connections"![90]

The point needs to be made over and over again that the slim victory of the National Party in the 1948 elections signaled a strategic shift whose significance was much larger than just a change in labor policy in response to changing employer needs. More than just tightening the grip on migrant labor and introducing measures to stabilize the core of industrial labor, apartheid involved a decisive shift in perspective as to how to come to grips with the problem of native control. The cutting edge of that shift was more political than economic. At the very time that the development of a militant nationalism signaled a shift from tribe to race as the locus of oppositional politics, statecraft moved in an opposite direction, from race to tribe as the guiding point in adapting its strategy of native control to a new situation. It was a change marked by two simultaneous moves: one involving a radical shift in the physical location of the native population, the other a reorganization of the state apparatus for native control. Those natives considered unproductive were flushed out from white farms and "black spots" in the rural areas, as from urban townships and shanties, to the reserves where homeland authorities were reorganized to administer fast-expanding populations through a traditional and autonomous system of rule. Meanwhile, the control of those who remained in the urban areas was removed from under disparate local authorities and was centralized under an apparatus of the central state, the Native Affairs Department. Apartheid had finally caught on to the secret of colonial control in Africa: indirect rule.

A comparison of native administration policy in the two eras, known in South African historiography as segregation and apartheid, will help make the point. In the era of segregation, though mediated through chiefs and headmen in different tribal areas, the administration of reserves was centralized under the NAD. Its writ covered every aspect of social life, from the allocation of land to the regulation of mobility to the administration of justice to the supervision of the domestic affairs of households to the relocation or reconstitution of entire communities. By law, the powers of the supreme chief could be devolved on any official employed by the department. In practice, it was the department that was the supreme chief in the reserves. In contrast, a decentralized form of administration by separate municipalities obtained for urban Africans. In the urban areas, the NAD was simply one of several authorities, and not the dominant one at that. In practice local authorities were autonomous in the administration of native affairs, for they regulated the entry, residence, and employment of Africans in urban areas. And they were far more susceptible to pressure from local employers eager to secure access to an expanding pool of cheap labor.

The reorganization of the state under apartheid was principally the recasting of the relationship between the central and the local state through two simultaneous and seemingly contradictory moves, but moves that made sense if understood in light of the overall problem of control over native affairs. Both moves are summed up in the dramatically altered position of the NAD. Apartheid removed the Native Affairs Department from rural areas and replaced it with a decentralized form of Native Authority administration. Together, the 1951 Bantu Authorities Act and the Bantu Laws Amendment Act of 1952 "went about systematically increasing the powers of the chieftaincy" while giving them financial powers to levy and collect taxes to finance their own costs.[91] Instead, the NAD emerged full blown in the urban areas where it effected a reverse development, replacing the decentralized form of control by municipalities with its own centralized control. In the process, it first subordinated and then entirely displaced local authorities in the administration of all aspects of Bantu affairs—all, that is, except health.[92] From a native point of view, apartheid combined a decentralized despotism (indirect rule) in the rural reserves with a centralized despotism (direct rule) in urban areas.

But the NAD did not come to administer urban Bantu affairs with a clean slate. It brought to bear on its new task the entire battery of lessons it had accumulated in the course of supervising indirect rule authority in the reserves. This is why the NAD did not simply forge a separate and racially distinct form of urban administration; it really altered the very basis of that administration. As administrative imperative expanded at the expense of the judicial process, judicial authorities were circumvented. As the institutional separation between the department as an administrative agency and the police was blurred, means of coercion came to be centralized within the department. The NAD even created subdepartments of labor and housing to tighten its administrative hold over township natives. Without underlining these institutional modifications it is not possible to understand the incredibly enhanced capacity of the apartheid state to effect the expanded program of influx controls and expulsion procedures—a program summed up in two fearful words, *forced removals.*

The systemic terror unleashed by apartheid in urban areas was the fist behind rolling waves of urban removal. Its point was to reverse the decades-long process of African urbanization; the grand design, wrote Tom Lodge, was "to restructure the industrial workforce into one composed principally of migrant labour." First set into motion in the western Cape in the late 1950s, this process unfolded on a national scale over the next decade.[93] One needs to remember that apartheid South Africa was a country artificially deurbanized. By 1990 half of South Africa's black population lived in the Bantustans, which together accounted for only 14 percent of the land in the country.[93] A large slice of this population was the victim of forced removals. It is estimated that forced removals uprooted more than 3.5 million people, or more than 10 percent of the South African population—labor tenants, farm squatters, and city residents—between 1960 and 1985.[94] In addition, a further 327,000 township residents were brought under the control of indirect rule Bantustan authorities as entire townships were incorporated into the boundaries of neighboring Bantustans, mainly KwaZulu. Nearly two-thirds of the country's African townships actually declined in size over the 1960s.[95] This is why, unlike in the reserves, where apartheid seemed more an administrative reform designed to restore the autonomy of tribal authorities, there could be no mistaking apartheid in the urban areas as anything but a frontal assault on the residual rights of the African population. My point is that this institutional modification, which fused power—administrative, judicial, and police—in a single administrative agency and its officers, was no institutional innovation. It amounted to creating white chiefs in urban areas: personnel who would dispense an administratively driven justice, a practice hitherto considered the hallmark of the administration of customary law in the reserves.

REFORMING INDIRECT RULE

It is helpful to recall that the introduction of indirect rule was a colonial reform. Faced with peasant resistance to colonial occupation, a resistance often led by clan leaders or chiefs, indirect rule was meant to hitch compliant sections from the traditional leadership of Africa to the colonial wagon and thereby broaden its social base. This reform mainly unfolded in the period between the two world wars. Its potential was exhausted in the aftermath of the Second World War when nationalist movements successfully linked urban protest against racial exclusion in civil society to rural movements against the uncustomary powers of Native Authority chiefs.

Faced with a political opposition that bridged the great gulf created by the bifurcated character of the colonial state—the rural and the urban—postwar colonial powers embarked on the first great reform of indirect rule. The point, once again, was to broaden the social base of rule by incorporating into the governing alliance the new social force on the colonial horizon: the native middle class. The method of the reform was electoral. Its program was to open the door to middle-class representation in the local state. The social objective was to weld together a coalition of traditional Native Authorities and elected middle-class representatives while keeping in place the customary authority of chiefs over peasants.

In countries where its point was either to preempt (Ivory Coast) or to sidestep (Kenya) the growth of militant nationalism, the reform survived independence. But where great nationalist movements successfully straddled the rural and the urban, a second phase of reform opened up after independence. Its point was to replace the Native Authority chief with the single-party cadre and thereby substitute an administrative with a political link between the urban and the rural. It is only when this political reform degenerated into a state edict that the accent shifted from party to state as the institutional basis of that link. With that, the intended reform of decentralized despotism degenerated into a centralized despotism.

Early resistance against the imposition of colonial rule was usually organized by clan leaders, who were often in direct conflict with missionary ideologues of the new order. But the agenda of such resistance was limited to restoring the independence of the clan, the ethnic group, or at most forging a localized united front of such groups. The best-known example from the period is the Maji Maji resistance against German colonialism in Tanganyika (1906–1909).[96] Like others, this resistance too was defeated. There followed—in the period after the First World War—a time of great popular demoralization, a crisis of civilization as it were. This was also the period of the triumphant proselytization of Christianity among peasant masses. Dubbed in official history as a period of stabilization of colonial rule, it was actually a period of defeat, of demoralization, and of the partial ideological incorporation of peasant masses inside colonial structures. The period of stabilization was not without protests. These were widespread. Peasant movements blossomed, against administrative forms and cadres brought in from outside. Depending on circumstances, they took on a variety of forms, usually ethnic or religious, but they were often neutralized by a simple reform. That reform was a simultaneous change in the institution of native control and in the face of its personnel: indirect rule. Later, as colonial rule consolidated, the point of reform was to deflate the institution of chiefship as the central state took direct charge of appointing and dismissing chiefs at all levels.

Starting with the French after the First World War, the Belgians in the 1920s and 1930s, and the Portuguese last of all, indirect rule had become the generalized mode of native control in the colonies by the 1950s. But the seat of indirect rule, the local states, was under great popular pressure by that same decade. The high points of anticolonial resistance were inevitably in places where peasant resistance built up against Native Authorities. Whether with the Convention Peoples Party (CPP) in Ghana, the Rassemblement Démocratique Africaine (RDA) in Guinea, or the Tanganyika African National Union (TANU), only those urban nationalists were able to forge a credible anti-colonial movement that could incorporate grievances against the local state into a wider movement and thereby rally peasant support to a countrywide cause. It is not really the central state but the decentralized despotism that was the local state that came under siege as the anticolonial movement surged ahead through the 1950s.

This is why the first wave of reform of indirect rule structures preceded independence and was the initiative of colonial powers. Key to this postwar reform was the introduction of elections so as to make room for middle strata in the local state: elected representatives rubbed shoulders with appointed traditional leaders in ethnically defined district councils. Meanwhile, on-the-ground administration remained a chiefly affair. The point of the reform, after all, was to weld together a coalition of traditional leaders and middle strata through a process of concession and conciliation short of doing away with ground-level despotism. The nature of that process is brought out in a recent study on local government reforms in Nigeria.[97]

The Nigerian reform is said to have been triggered by a dispatch from London on the subject of local government, requiring colonial authorities to introduce electoral reforms "in the shortest possible time." From the time it was implemented in the 1950s, the Nigerian reform proceeded as a single countrywide agenda that set a different pace for the north than for the south, so that while the electoral principle was introduced in the entire country, elected representatives were confined to a minority in the north but were allowed a majority in the south. The balance between the chief and the council in the range of Native Authorities was captured in two separate formulations: chief-in-council and chief-and-council. In the former, although the emir was required "to consult and act in accordance with the decision of his Council," he could as its chair still act against the majority in the interest of "order and good government." But in those Native Authorities constituted as chief-and-council, the emir as chair always had to act in accordance with the council majority. Both types of Native Authorities enjoyed considerable powers. The Land Tenure Law of 1962 gave them powers to issue rights of occupancy over customary land. Armed with a police force and a judiciary, they were empowered to make subsidiary legislation of three types: orders over persons in their locality; rules with respect to services in the locality, but only with government approval; and finally, instruments that concerned representation in subordinate councils.

The electoral principle held full sway in the eastern and western regions of the south, where powers were transferred to elected councils and local government created as an autonomous structure. Although the central government appointed a divisional officer "to serve as a guide and teacher" in the early stages, that officer was withdrawn by 1955. The result of this comprehensive decentralization, writes A. D. Yahya, was no less than a disaster. Elected councillors "never lived up to expectations"; once control from the center was relaxed, "Councilors misused their powers." As a result, "local government came to be associated with acts of widespread impropriety, inefficiency and corruption." Could it have been otherwise in a context where village-level chiefs continued to exercise absolute authority, thereby ensuring that decentralized councils operated with a minimum of popular constraint?

The corruption was documented by various commissions of inquiry. The result was public outrage. Following it, central control was reintroduced everywhere. When the military intervened in January 1966, its first act was to remove all elected councillors from councils. States were created and local government was reorganized. With the federal government embroiled in a civil war, the states had a relatively free hand in organizing internal matters. In the resulting diversity, one could still identify some common features. The mood was to break with the past, even if symbolically. In parts of the former Northern Region, the procedure of the Native Authority was said to be "irreconcilable and repugnant to the basic norms of democracy." Its name was changed. For the first time, traditional leaders found themselves a minority in council. In the former Eastern Region, community councils were created. Composed of elected or selected members, they were supervised by a field representative of the state government who wielded enormous powers. In the former Western Region, a council manager was introduced following popular riots against local government corruption and unaccountability in 1968. In this arrangement, the council manager was the chief executive of local government and was to run it as a general manager would a private limited company! Everywhere, the new authorities lacked the power to hire and fire staff. In response to widespread corruption, the decentralized and elected councils of the pre–civil war period had given way to tight control by newly created state authorities.

Local government was reorganized by the military in 1976. For the first time, a uniform system was created: local government now formed the third tier of government, after the federal and the state governments. In all councils, elected members were in the majority. Nevertheless, local government officials lacked administrative powers on personnel matters. As in the colonial period, the central state kept firm control over the hiring and firing of local personnel. At the same time, local government administration remained a dual and pyramidal affair. At the apex, elected officials consulted with "traditional authorities," say before appointing the chair of council, and "subordinate traditional authorities" ran village- and district-level administration at the base— more or less as they always had.

When the military handed power back to civilians in 1979, local government was for the first time constitutionally entrenched in the Nigerian political system. Yet the irony is that local government elections were never held once civilian rule was restored, even though the term of office of all councils elected in the military era expired in January 1980. In spite of the legal stipulation that new councils be immediately elected, they were replaced by appointed caretaker committees in most instances and sole administrators in some.

What had been achieved in these three decades of reform? To begin with, the social base of indirect rule was broadened with the entry of the middle strata. At the apex, rural traditional authorities were gradually restricted to symbolic and advisory functions as room was made for urban middle strata, whether through elections under the military or by appointment under civilian rule. Meanwhile, peasants on the ground continued to be administered as before, by a regime of chiefs and headmen. Second, electoral reform was never applied consistently to all levels of the state. Military rulers abrogated the electoral principle in the central state, but they introduced and upheld it in the local state; civilians did the reverse. Both, however, practiced village-level governance as a customary administration, of chiefs over peasants.

In the period after independence, the Nigerian path was broadly followed in the conservative states, where reconciliation between traditional leaders and middle-class nationalists was the order of the day. In Ivory Coast, this took on the character of a grand national coalition of urban-educated elites and rural Native Authorities. In a few instances like Sierra Leone after the antichief riots of 1955–56, this turned out to be a rescue operation for the Native Authorities.[98] Alongside the localized coalition-building was some degree of central control. Local authority elections were held in many countries, from Tunisia to Zambia, and Senegal to Sudan, but the new councils or committees were restricted to an advisory role.[99] Even where electoral reform was given some teeth, as in the Senegalese administrative reforms of 1960 and 1972, its bite was blunted by the central appointment of prefects and subprefects through whom the central government maintained its "tutelage" over elected local councils.[100] All in all, it was a reform very much in step with modifications to indirect rule administration introduced by the British in the fifties.

The rhythm of reform in the conservative states was a variation on the Nigerian theme. Notwithstanding the partial introduction of electoral reforms—by civilians at the center and the military at the local—the customary administration of chiefs over peasants continued. What appeared as a game of musical chairs, a back-and-forth movement between civilian and military regimes, represented a change within a broader continuity: from a decentralized civilian despotism to a centralized military despotism! Whereas the shift to a centralized despotism appeared as a naked military regime in the conservative states, it was much more the effect of a failed effort to uproot and transform indirect rule in the radical states.

Whereas conservative states followed the direction of the postwar colonial reform, radical states moved to erase the legacy of colonialism that was indirect rule. So in countries like Guinea and Tanzania in the sixties and Mozambique in the seventies, chiefship was abolished and replaced by centrally appointed party cadres. Many observers have argued that the administrative change was formal: in Tanzania, for example, the chief (*jumbe*) was simply renamed the divisional executive officer (DEO) or the village executive officer (VEO).[101] Like the chief, his duties were to enforce laws and to collect taxes. As the chief had done, he could take peasants to court for failure to pay taxes or failure to follow district by-laws on cultivation. But the change was not just in name. Alongside went a redefinition and limitation of powers. The newly established executive officer was an enforcement officer. Unlike the colonial Native Authority, he lacked the power to introduce bylaws or to adjudicate cases. Those powers belonged to the party cadre. Yet the shift from the colonial Native Authority to the postcolonial single party was neither just formal nor simply nominal.

The real shift was in the subordination of state administration to the will of a political party. It is not until this reform failed, until party supremacy over the state gave way to state-party rule, and a political process degenerated into administrative edicts that the party cadre appeared as a double agent—also a state agent—and overreached and extended his (and at times her) powers: simultaneously a representative of a political power and an enforcement officer. It is such a moment that was illustrated by a ground-level study in Rungwe District (Tanzania) which found[102] that the powers actually wielded by TANU cell leaders "exceed[ed] greatly the instructions received from Dar-es-Salaam, local government officials and TANU leaders." The cell leaders not only "settle cases," but also "impose fines and charge fees for arbitration." People "dissatisfied with the judgement of their own cell leader" may turn to a "court of appeal," only to find that the court is the same cell leader "alone, or in combination." As brought out in hearings to the recent Commission of Inquiry on Land, these village-level officials even used to detain peasants for up to forty-eight hours. Like the agent of the Native Authority, the party cadre too came to exercise a fused power.

If the Achilles' heel of the Tanzanian reform was that it elevated the single party above society, as its unaccountable representative, the same cannot be said—at least not formally—of the Mozambican reform, which began in the second year after independence.[103] Here the abolition of chiefship was coupled with the direct election of representatives to People's Assemblies in localities or subdistricts. By 1980, more than thirteen hundred elected assemblies had been formed in administrative localities and communal villages over the whole country. The limits of the reform became clear as it moved beyond the village level. All elections beyond the village were turned into an indirect affair. If the Mozambican reform expanded popular participation, it simultaneously limited representation to a narrow village-defined limit. Indirect elections went hand in hand with a key feature of indirect rule: fused power. From the top down, the party head was also the head of government in the locality and the president of the corresponding people's assembly. The party had "a key role in the selection of candidates to any organ." Fusion of power was the principle around which the party-state was constructed.

As custodians of a militant nationalism that had successfully bridged the urban-rural divide and posed colonialism hitherto its most serious challenge, radical leaders tried to institutionalize the political gains of the nationalist struggle into a single party. However, this attempt to reform the bifurcated state from above did not succeed. Lacking in democratic content, it carried forward the colonial tradition of fused power and administrative justice. We will later see how, faced with a peasant resistance to a top-down development program, persuasion and politics degenerated into extra-economic coercion. As that happened, the center of gravity of the radical party-state shifted from the party to the state. The bitter fruit of a failed attempt to transform decentralized despotism turned out to be a centralized despotism.

CHAPTER FOUR

Customary Law: The Theory of Decentralized Despotism

COLONIALISM claimed to bring civilization to a continent where it saw life—to borrow a phrase from a context not entirely unrelated—as "nasty, brutish, and short." Civilization here meant the rule of law. The torchbearers of that civilization were supposed to be the colonial courts. The courts were intended neither just as sites where disputes would be settled nor simply as testimony to effective imperial control; rather, they were to shine as beacons of Western civilization. Yet no sooner was this claim made than it lay in shreds as power was forced to find ways of controlling multitudes on the ground. The history of that moral surrender was one of a shift in perspective and practice, from a civilizing mission to a law-and-order administration.

The judicial system that evolved in the colonies bore a remarkable similarity. Though names may differ, it was everywhere a bipolar affair. At one end were the courts of chiefs and headmen, courts of the first instance to which natives had ready and easy access, courts that dispensed justice according to customary law. At the other end was a hierarchy of courts cast in the metropolitan mold, courts designed to solve disputes involving nonnatives. The intermediate category consisted of tribunals staffed by white officials, called commissioners in British colonies and commanders in French ones, who listened to appeals from chiefs' courts and who were charged with the general administration of the native population. In this bipolar scheme, customary justice was dispensed to natives by chiefs and commissioners, black and white; modern justice to nonnatives by white magistrates.

The dualism in legal theory was actually a description of two distinct, though related, forms of power: the centrally located modern state and the locally organized Native Authority. The hallmark of the modern state was civil law through which it governed citizens in civil society. The justification of power was in the language of rights, for citizen rights guaranteed by civil law were at the same time said to constitute a limit on civil power. The key claim was that this form of power was self-limiting. Against this description was the reality: the regime of rights was limited and partial. Citizen status was not conferred on all within the ambit of civil society. The primary exclusion was based on race.

In contrast to this civil power was the Native Authority. It governed on the basis of ethnic identity. The Native Authority was a tribal authority that dispensed customary law to those living within the territory of the tribe. As such, there was not a single customary law for all natives, but roughly as many sets of customary laws as there were said to be distinct tribes. Customary law was not about guaranteeing rights; it was about enforcing custom. Its point was not to limit power, but to enable it. The justification of power was that it was a custodian of custom in the wider context of an alien domination.

Against this description was the reality: customary law consolidated the noncustomary power of chiefs in the colonial administration. It did so in two ways that marked a breach from the precolonial period. For the first time, the reach of the Native Authority and the customary law it dispensed came to be all-embracing. Previously autonomous social domains like the household, age sets, and gender associations—to cite three important instances—now fell within the scope of chiefly power. At the same time—and this is the second breach with the precolonial period—any challenge to chiefly power would now have to reckon with a wider systemic response. The Native Authority was backed up by the armed might of the modern state at the center. We will later see that just as civil society in the colonial context came to be racialized, so the Native Authority came to be tribalized. To the racially defined native as the other in civil society corresponded the ethnically defined stranger in the Native Authority.

In this chapter, I will be concerned with three issues. The first is the domain of the customary. Who were the natives who were supposed to live by custom? What were the courts through which custom came to be enforced? And what were the sources of this customary law? My second objective is to understand the process by which the customary came to be defined, particularly so in a context marked by a rapid shift in both the perspective of colonial powers and the situation of different groups among the colonized. Confronted first by the need to create order and then to enforce development among conquered populations, the ruling concern with law rapidly gave way to a preoccupation with locating and boosting those who would enforce the law. At the same time, this late-nineteenth-century transition from slavery to colonialism turned out to be a period of radical dislocation for different strata among the colonized. Instead of a traditional consensus about custom, it signified a time of rapid change and much contest over the customary. Yet colonial powers presumed an implicit and unchanging consensus over the customary. Who then really came to define *custom* and how? Third, given this divided legacy, of laws modern and customary, what was the promise and the limit of the legal reform effected in the post-colonial period?

THE DOMAIN OF THE CUSTOMARY

What did *customary* mean? And who were the natives to which this justice was to apply? The answers to both questions are indeed revealing, for legal pluralism in this instance was more an expression of power relations in a colonial society than a recognition and tolerance of any multicultural diversity. Colonial pluralism was basically dual: on one side was a patchwork of customs and practices considered customary, their single shared feature being some association with the colonized; on the other side was the modern, the imported law of the colonizer. In countries like Nigeria, where external influence was not limited to European powers but included Islamic sources, the law sought to remove all ambiguity: section 2 of the Native Courts Law of colonial Nigeria provided that "native law and custom includes Moslem law."[1]

Conversely, *native* was used not to mean a person whose life had historically been governed by the customary law in question, but as a blanket racial category. It is instructive to look at how the courts in Nigeria defined the term *native*. At first glance, there seems to be a range of definitions: according to the Western High Court Law, a native was simply a Nigerian; the Northern High Court Law distinguished between natives and nonnatives and remained silent thereafter; the Eastern High Court Law revealingly defined a native as a "person of African descent."[2] But all ambiguity was removed in section 3 of the Interpretations Act, which applied to the federation and northern Nigeria; according to this act, the statutory definition of the term *native* included "a native of Nigeria" and a "native foreigner." Further, a "native foreigner" was defined as "any person (not being a native of Nigeria) whose parents are members of a tribe or tribes indigenous to some part of Africa and the descendants of such persons, and shall include any person one of whose parents was a member of such tribe."[3] The point was no doubt to cast the net wide enough to catch within its fold every person with any trace of African ancestry. The objective was to arrive at a racial definition, not a cultural one. Similar racially governed formulations were found in other colonies. In Lesotho, section 2 of the General Law Proclamation spoke of customary law as "African law" to be "administered" to all "Africans."[4] Following a survey of the operations of Swazi customary courts according to the terms of section 3 of the Swazi Courts Act 80 of 1950, Khumalo concludes that these courts have civil jurisdiction over all "Swazis," meaning "a member of the indigenous population of Africa who is a Swazi citizen attached to a chief appointed under section 4 of the Administration Act 79 of 1950."[5] Pointedly excluded are all Swazi citizens of non-African descent. In Botswana the law simply defines the jurisdiction of customary courts as covering all "tribesmen"![6]

Yet customary law was not a racial catchall. The native and the tribesman were not the same. Natives were disaggregated into different tribes. Each tribe had its own customary law, which the leadership of the tribe had the power to enforce. The notion of the ethnically defined customary was both deeper and more differentiated than the racially defined native: it grounded racial exclusion in a cultural inclusion. The natives denied civil freedoms on racial grounds were thereby sorted into different identities and incorporated into the domain of so many ethnically defined Native Authorities.

The domain of customary law was confined to customary courts, being the lower courts. "Native customary law, in my view," opined a British judge in a West African case, "is more or less in the same position as foreign law and it must be established by an expert before courts other than the native courts."[7] Who, then, had the authority to establish this "matter of fact" rather than "matter of law"? What were deemed to be the authoritative sources of customary law?

On this question, there was no clear agreement and often an amusing confusion. In both British- and French-controlled territories, superior court judges, whether European or African, "often sat with African assessors who informed them what was the customary law in question."[8] That, however, still begs the question: who would qualify to be an assessor? Opinions varied. To Goldin and Gelfand, authors of *African Law and Custom in Rhodesia*, for example, the answer was obvious: "The African knows his laws, not as a result of study, but by virtue of being and living as an African."[9] Yet the matter was hardly as simple and straightforward. As Governor Cameron confided to a visitor to Tanganyika, "the difficulty after a period of disintegration is to find out what their system was. *They* know perfectly well but, for one reason or other, they may not tell you."[10] A Portuguese authority on the subject thought he had found a way out of the dilemma. Unlike "the common law [which] should be applied by a qualified jurist," he argued, "the questions relative to usages and customs should be judged by the administrator because it is he who is conversant with the local custom and the dominant mentality."[11] The same authority was compelled to add: "For this purpose he is assisted by two natives who inform him on the local law." The famed British administrator-anthropologist Rattray agreed. In calling for "the retention of all that is best in the African's own past culture," Rattray admitted: "The main difficulty lies in the fact that we and the educated African alike know so little of what that past really was."[12] But "those few who possess the requisite knowledge . . . are illiterate, and in consequence generally inarticulate for practical purposes, except when approached by the European who has spent a life time among them and has been able to gain their complete confidence." As to why that should make the literate European indispensable but rule out the literate African, he never explained.

Presumably the illiterate native was the more pristine, just as the literate African was the more contaminated by alien worldly influences percolating through the written word. But even if the anthropologists considered the illiterate native a more reliable authority on customary law, that authority was surely seen in the nature of a primary source, to be sifted through, analyzed, its internal contradictions smoothed over, its gaps and lapses filled in, all to arrive at a coherent, consistent, and comprehensive secondary formulation. Still, it was not every native, not even every illiterate native, who was presumed to know customary law. For as many an experienced administrator and knowledgeable anthropologist suspected, it was more or less a truism that "real customary law was in the mind of the oldest men (or even of the dead) and that the new elders did not know it properly."[13]

With modern law there was no such problem; it was easily imported and read. For the British brought with them the common law, the doctrines of equity, and the statutes of general application that were in force in England at a particular cutoff date: in the case of Ghana, 1874; Kenya, 1897; Nigeria, 1900; and so on.[14] The French exported their civil code and other sets of legislation to their possessions. The Belgians went so far as to enact a simplified version of the mother code, calling it the Code Civil du Congo. On top of this imported law, there was the body of statutes promulgated by the colonial state.[15]

This dual system of justice was at the heart of indirect rule, and some variation of it came to be in every African colony. The pacesetter in these matters, as in others related to indirect rule, were reforms Lugard introduced in northern Nigeria. Three key statutes defined the nature of the judicial system in colonial Nigeria.[16] The first was the Native Court Proclamation. Under it, the resident in charge could set up four grades of native courts, with the highest sitting under the presidency of the paramount chief. The paramount chief's court had "full and unlimited jurisdiction to adjudicate in all civil matters or to try all criminal proceedings in which the chief's subjects were parties." For the subjects, there was to be neither a right of representation nor a right of appeal to a court presided over by a British judge or a political officer—no matter how serious the charge or the penalty involved. The paramount chief who presided over this court as the supreme native judicial authority was, in addition, the same paramount chief who sat as the supreme native administrative authority under the Native Revenue Proclamation!

The second statute defining the judicial system in the colony was the Provincial Courts Proclamation. A provincial court was set up by the high commissioner of the protectorate and was empowered to hear all cases involving nonnatives. Required to administer English common law, the doctrines of equity and the statutes of general application in force in England on 1 January 1900, these too were no nonsense courts that neither admitted lawyers nor were required to follow strict English legal procedure. To the nonnatives basking under the tropical sun in a nonsettler colony, they offered an English version of African customary law. The pride of place, the jewel in this thorny crown, was the supreme court of northern Nigeria, set up under a third statute. As befits a crown jewel, it was required to follow strict legality and strict technicality, complete with the right of legal representation for all parties involved, but its writ was limited to only the two cantonment areas of Lokojo and Zungeru. The crux of the matter was that more than 99 percent of the judicial work in the protectorate was carried out beyond its purview, in courts run by nonlegal administrators, whether native or European.

In French colonies, too, there were two parallel court systems, one French, the other native.[17] French courts were presided over by French magistrates, who judged according to French law, and were used in all cases involving a French citizen. Cases involving only subjects were the preserve of native courts. Under the era of direct administration, however, chiefs gradually were deprived of judicial powers, which were transferred to European administrators: a 1903 decree limited police powers of chiefs to a fine of 15 francs and five days in prison; another decree from 1912 limited their competence only to matters of conciliation; and yet another decree from 1924 conferred the chair of the court of first instance to a European official, usually a clerk. The native court of the second instance was presided over by none other than the cercle commander, this all-powerful administrator-judge, or his deputy or any other European official designated by the governor. Although customary law continued to be dispensed in these courts, it was given legal recognition only by the court of appeal at Dakar, the supreme court of French West Africa, in a 1934 decree. The court recognized the African village as a legal entity with customary rights and the village chief as the defender of those rights.[18] In the Italian colony of Somalia, state recognition of the customary came much earlier: royal decree no. 695 of 1911 stipulated that Italians be governed by Italian law and Somalis by customary law.[19]

The dispensers of customary justice were the cadres known as chiefs. The term needs to be understood in a broad sense, stripped of all racial connotations: chiefs were really nonspecialized, nonlegal administrative personnel whose broad portfolio also included judicial functions. As such, they should be seen to include both native chiefs and white commissioners (British) or commanders (French). Unlike magistrates' courts, which were staffed by professional lawyers and cordoned off by high tariff walls (fees) and a remote location, the commissioners' tribunals were an informal affair, with easy access and nominal fees. Like the courts of chiefs and headmen, of which they formed the upper tier, the commissioners dispensed a form of justice that was informal, inexpensive, and efficient. Defined by the powers and role of the office they occupied, the commissioners were really the white chiefs of colonial Africa.

DEFINING THE CUSTOMARY IN A
CHANGING CONTEXT

If the customary law dispensed in the courts of chiefs was presumed to be known by "the African . . . by virtue of being and living as an African" (Goldin and Gelfand), "by the administrator because it is he who is conversant with the local custom and the dominant mentality" (Moreira), by "illiterate natives" as transmitted to "the European who has spent a life time among them and has been able to gain their complete confidence" (Rattray), or by the "oldest" of the "elders," who then defined the substantive law? There were at least three sets of contenders with claims over defining the customary: the central state, the officials of the local state (the chiefs), and a range of nonstate interests. Everywhere, the claim of the central state set the limits to the customary in the form of a "repugnancy clause." Under French and Belgian systems, this limit was set unambiguously as the requirements of "public order and morality."[20] In some instances, the formulation came close to being crass: a law passed by French authorities in Senegal in 1912 stipulated that colonial law replace traditional law when the latter was "contrary to the principles of French civilization."[21] The Portuguese, too, had a formulation that clearly spelled out their claim to being both the custodians of "humanitarian" principles and the holders of power; the decree of 1954 that formally subordinated natives to custom and nonnatives to the common law required that custom not be "contrary to public order, that is, to the principles of humanity, the fundamental principles of morality or to free exercise of sovereignty."[22]

In British-controlled Africa, the colonial power simply claimed to be a custodian of general "humanitarian" notions of right and wrong. The standard formulation thus required that customary law be applicable if "not repugnant to justice and morality" (Kenya, Malawi), "not repugnant to natural justice and morality" (Southern Rhodesia), not repugnant to "natural justice, equity and good conscience" (Ghana, Nigeria, Sierra Leone), or not repugnant to "justice, morality or order" (Sudan).[23] Rarely did the British admit that the law must also safeguard the exigencies of power. Such a rare instance is found in the Evidence Act in Nigeria, which stated that no custom "contrary to public policy" would be enforced.[24] Similarly, the charter issued to authorize the colonization of Rhodesia required the high commissioner to "respect any native [civil] laws and custom . . . except so far as they may be incompatible with the due exercise of Her Majesty's power and jurisdiction."[25] The same illuminating phrase can be found in the Native Courts Proclamation of 1942 in Bechuanaland.[26]

What kind of limit did the repugnancy clause set in practice? The overriding constraint stemmed from the reality of defending power. At the beginning of colonial rule, a clear distinction was made between the civil and criminal aspects of customary law: the former was to be tolerated, the latter to be suppressed. The official justification was that "humanitarian" consideration to eliminate "evil" required that chiefs be deprived of any criminal jurisdiction, for chiefs were no doubt the source of much "evil" in Africa. Not only did this appeal to Victorian sensibilities, it also made much practical sense, for any attempt to restore the old institutional order was bound to be chief centered. The colonial power understood very clearly that dealing with crime was first and foremost about social control and the exertion of power. "Criminal law," pointed out the minister of justice and defense in Rhodesia, is all about "wrongs against the government and against the community," whereas "civil law deals with relationships between individuals." Even if "the criminal law . . . does not conform to the ideas of the people who are ruled," the real point was that "the government could not tolerate any attempts against its own custom, its own law, against itself, that is to say." The chief justice of the supreme court of the Federation of Rhodesia and Nyasaland agreed: "This is a matter in which we feel our law should prevail, because we feel that when it is a question of something which wrongs the whole community—and that roughly is the definition of the word 'crime'—it should override all other considerations, and that is why we distinguish between criminal law and civil law."[27]

Rhodesia was a colony with a difference. Even when the existence of native law and courts was officially recognized in 1937, the courts were expressly denied criminal jurisdiction. This was different from other British colonies, where once the question of law and order was settled and colonial rule became relatively stabilized, chiefs did indeed receive limited criminal jurisdiction. For indirect rule, as Lugard recognized, would mean little if it did not give chiefs the "power to punish." Rhodesia, however, was much more like the Cape or those French colonies where native resistance to colonial rule had been intense and sustained. The specter of the Matebele Kingdom and the resistance it spearheaded continued to haunt settler memories. The problem was not just to crush such a resistance, but to prevent its resurgence. From the point of view of the settler-dominated state, the "exercise of criminal jurisdiction was thought to be (and in fact is) a significant instrument of social control, and its removal could go far towards making Ndebele resurgence impossible."[28]

It is not that Victorian notions of right and wrong played no part in setting practical limits to customary law. They did, in matters such as slavery, mutilation, polygamy, and bride-price; but they were subordinate to political considerations, and for that reason, they were always negotiable. French colonial authorities made a distinction between the end of the slave trade and that of slavery. The former was adhered to more or less strictly, but not the latter. After all, as we will see, the end of slavery was followed by the "rosy dawn" of compulsions. The abhorrence of mutilation—and this too we will see—did not stop any colonial power from resorting to corporal punishment as an integral part of customary law. The Boer and the British authorities in South Africa who righteously denounced polygamy as female slavery and bride-price as "purchase in women" had no qualms about legislating a customary code that treated women as perpetual minors subject to a patriarchal chief-dominated authority. We are, after all, talking of an era when English common law gave husbands controlling power over wives and the state and judicial authorities extraordinarily severe powers over those categorized as vagrant, idle, or disorderly.

Some colonial administrators, like Robert Delavignette in French West Africa, thought an arrangement that coupled customary law with a repugnancy test was riddled with contradictions. "What are these principles" of civilization to which "native law" must not run counter, he asked, "if not those of the Code?"[29] In other words, if the repugnancy test were consistently applied—so ran the logic of Delavignette's argument—the code would sooner or later have to govern all relations, whether native or nonnative. But one thing should be clear. The repugnancy test was never construed as requiring that the law in the colonies, common or customary, be consistent with the principles of English law or the Code Napoléon. Such a requirement would have sounded the death knell of administrative justice. The point of the repugnancy test was to reinforce colonial power, not to question it. One study of court cases in colonial Nigeria concludes: "It is clear that the courts decide whether a particular rule is to be rejected for repugnancy largely in an *ad hoc* manner."[30]

Conflict over the Customary

If in practice the repugnancy clause was a way of enforcing the exigencies of colonial power, does it mean that—within those limits—substantive customary law was really decided by the colonized, was really the reflection of a traditional consensus that preceded the imposition of colonialism, and continued through it as the result of some kind of benign neglect? This could not have been, if only for one reason: the dawn of colonialism was a time of great social upheaval through most of the continent. Its most dramatic manifestation was the rise of conquest states in the nineteenth century. Their defeat liquidated the political power that had stabilized conquest-based claims. The end of slavery eroded or made uncertain an entire range of claims on the services of subordinates, from formal slavery to slave marriages. The onset of migrant labor provided young men with ways of earning cash and thus with an alternative to "service-marriage," an institution through which elders who controlled access to wives could claim a range of services from young men as prospective suitors. Instead of a consensual traditional notion of custom, the colonial era really began in the midst of conflicting and even contrary claims about the customary.

The content of customary law is difficult to understand outside this context of conflicting claims, many reflecting tensions hardly customary. These tensions were grounded in two intersecting realities: on the one hand, while an old regime of force (legal slavery) was eroding, a new one (colonial compulsions) was just as surely taking its place; on the other hand, while nineteenth-century commodity markets in slaves and artisanal products were fast shrinking, new colonial markets in wage labor and export crops were expanding just as quickly. Both those with and without claims in the old order sought to establish claims in the new one. The onset of colonial rule combined with new conditions—increased mobility and increased stratification—to generate new and contradictory claims. Not surprisingly, every claim presented itself as customary, and there could be no neutral arbiter. The substantive customary law was neither a kind of historical and cultural residue carried like excess baggage by groups resistant to "modernization" nor a pure colonial "invention" or "fabrication," arbitrarily manufactured without regard to any historical backdrop and contemporary realities. Instead it was reproduced through an ongoing series of confrontations between claimants with a shared history but not always the same notions of it. And yet—and this is the important point—the presumption that there was a single and undisputed notion of the customary, unchanging and implicit, one that people knew as they did their mother tongue, meant that those without access to the Native Authority had neither the same opportunity nor political resources to press home their point of view. In the absence of a recognition that conflicting views of the customary existed, even the question that they be represented could not arise.

To get a sense of how deep-seated was the conflict over the customary, we need to grasp how radical were the dislocations that marked the onset of colonial rule. At least three sets of tension-producing developments interlocked and made for a single overarching process. The source of this triple dislocation lay in broad political, economic, and social changes: the process of state formation, the development of markets, and far-reaching changes in gender and generational relations. The impact of colonial rule in each instance was nothing less than dramatic.

We have seen that nowhere in nineteenth-century Africa had the territory-based claims of the state singularly triumphed over kin-based claims of lineages. Everywhere, and not just in the nonstate societies, kin groups contested with and balanced the claims of state authority. The onset of colonial rule tipped the balance decisively in favor of state authority. This was particularly evident in kin-based societies, where every person had depended on kith and kin to protect life and property—for there was no other authority to turn to before colonial rule created one. It was also true, however, where hierarchical authority (chiefship) had preceded colonialism, for the consolidation of colonial power went alongside setting up a parallel court structure that would not only recognize individual rights, but also do so with a sweep so exclusive as to include even the domestic realm. In her study of the Kilimanjaro region in Tanzania, Sally Falk Moore argues that customary disputes brought to the chief's court in the colonial period "were probably decided in pre-colonial times at home, that is, in the social fields in which they arose."[31] Whereas the practice in the precolonial period was for chiefs "simply [to] announce the decisions of the [age-grade] assembly," the colonial chief "presided over" the assembly and "made the decisions," in the process phasing out the role of age sets. With the onward flow of colonial rule, the tendency was for chiefly power to become consolidated, if only for one reason. The operation of the chief's court "was permeated by the knowledge that the colonial government could be relied on to supply excessive force behind chiefly authority": the chief "could turn any recalcitrant over to the colonial authorities by falsely accusing him of breaking the rules of the colonial government," or he could "manipulate those rules to deprive individuals of opportunities to work for cash by executive fiat."

If native courts provided an alternative authority to that of the kin group, the cash economy also made it possible for some to escape obligations to one's kin. The beneficiaries of the new legal order came from diverse social strata. At one end were new and relatively prosperous peasants whose springboards were offices in the local state and opportunities in expanding market agriculture and whose vision often coincided with a more individualized notion of rights. At the other end the expanding money economy and market-based relations often generated a rising spirit of independence among those women and (junior) men who but yesterday were locked in servile relationships. Sometimes this led to a coalition of old victims and new beneficiaries around commonly advanced claims. Take the example of kin groups where households—persons and property—used to be inherited upon the death of the husband but where women and children often refused to be so inherited. Among the Langi people in northern Uganda, as among many others, such an inheritance used to be the right of the male sibling of the deceased. The former wife (*lako*), once inherited, was known as the *dako*. Although inheritance broadly continued to be practiced, women struggled for the right to choose a partner, even if within the confines of the kin group; in time widows won the right to refuse to be inherited by the husband's brother, in favor of a preferred—usually a better-off—member of the larger kin group.[32] Consider also "the typical circumstances of the migrant labourer who remitted his earnings home to his mother's brother who invested them in the purchase of cattle"; the resulting conflict as to whether the cattle "belonged to the individual whose earnings bought them or to their matrilineages" was often resolved by the new courts in favor of the younger man alone. As new property demanded new rights, old institutions (chiefs) newly recast recognized them, in the process emerging triumphant over other similarly traditional institutions (kin groups) more or less bypassed in the constellation of a new power. As Martin Chanock concludes in his brilliant study on law, custom, and social order in colonial Malawi and Zambia "economic individualizing and jural individuation went hand in hand."[33]

The spread of market relations, however, did not always lead to greater individual freedom for all concerned. When it came to conflict-producing and tension-ridden relationships, freedom for one could be only at the expense of another. This was often the case with the marriage bond between male migrants on the move and female agriculturists bound to village communities under the grip of a chief. As migrants appealed to tradition, chiefs often—as in Southern Rhodesia[34]—imposed punishments for adultery and enforced paternal control over marriage. In migrant labor zones, women could and did turn into cash crop–producing peasants, but their workload often increased alongside diminishing freedoms and increased compulsions.

In spite of the tendency of colonial texts to collapse the customary and the tribal into a single noncontradictory whole, there was seldom a clinical separation of tribes or even a homogenous internal culture in these times of great change and tension. The tendency was for a more or less mixing of tribes and an internal differentiation that went alongside varied and even conflicting practices within the same tribe. Not only were the boundaries of ethnicity blurred and elastic, there was often little that was traditional about tribal boundaries drawn by colonial administrators, as we have already seen. As Chanock asks with reference to those conquest states where patrilineal authority had often incorporated many a matrilineal peoples into expanding state systems, whose custom was considered law—the patrilineal rulers or the matrilineal subjects—and therefore a reference point for the tribe?

How a customary relationship between the sexes came to be forged gives a better idea of the nature of forces whose interaction shaped that outcome. The beginning of colonial rule was marked by a combination of forces predisposed toward improving the position of women, even if each had its own reasons. Missionaries were appalled at the institution of polygamy and bride-price. Settlers, too, were convinced that polygamy allowed the native male to live in sloth and idleness and was at the root of their labor problems. An astute writer in the *Natal Witness* of 1863 poked fun at the "alliance between the missionary and the labor-needing colonist, to alleviate the sufferings of the native woman," and suggested that both were interested in the abolition of a custom "which materially interferes with the object for which they have respectively left their mother country."[35]

This alliance, however, did not last long. Once again, as law sought to establish order and the central state looked for allies to consolidate its hold over local spaces, perceptions changed. By giving rights to sons and women, wrote the British administrator Charles Dundas in 1915, European law "falls like a thunderbolt in the midst of native society"; "all precedent and custom are cast aside, and the controllers of society are disabled." The British had "loosened the ties of matrimony," "freely granted divorces in favour of frivolous girls, and permitted them to run from one man to another, heedless of the bad example thereby set."[36] As they sought out the "controllers of society," the search for good laws gave way to one for effective authorities. As they came to appreciate the possibilities of control in the customary, their interest focused more on customary authorities than on customary law. As the substance of the law was subordinated to the quest for order, the claim to be bringing the "rule of law" to Africa became handmaiden to the imperative to ground power effectively. With this slide into pragmatism, colonial powers were usually content to let customary authorities define the substantive customary law. These authorities were the officials of the local state, with some variation between settler and peasant colonies. Where customary law was not codified, local initiative was inevitably greater. In the settler colonies there was great interest in codification; in the free peasant economies, this interest did not surface until after the Second World War. It is in the latter that, subject to the repugnancy clause, customary authorities came to have a disproportionate influence in shaping the substantive law.

Chiefs as Customary Authorities

The customary authorities were the chiefs. Stripped of military power and losing control over long-distance trade, chiefs faced the new era with great anxiety. Take the example of Chagga chiefs in the Kilimanjaro region of Tanganyika.[37] As most of their old sources of income dried up—from warfare to cattle raiding, from slave trade to ivory trade—chiefs desperately looked for and created new ways of earning extra income. Court fees were one means; extra-economic and extralegal exactions were another. Whatever the combination, a German observer of the pre–World War I period estimated that "the chief was paid seven times as much as the colonial government in this process."

Alarmed at how old service-yielding claims were disintegrating, chiefs were in a strategic position to seize the initiative under the new order. To do so, they claimed as customary every right that would enhance their control over others, particularly those socially weak. Central to this was the right of movement or settlement and sometimes even the right to claim children. In the increasingly stagnant pool of freed persons that this created over time, chiefs could glimpse multiple possibilities; the old slavery, with its innumerable gradations, from outright control to slave marriage, was giving way to the new clientelism, also with its multiple gradations. The chiefs were not alone in this quest. At different times, they were joined by different strata seeking to protect or gain privilege: free men in relation to women, the propertied in relation to the propertyless, seniors in relation to juniors, those indigenous against migrant strangers in their midst.

The fact that custom should be shaped by those in control of customary institutions was nothing new. The new thing about the colonial period was, to begin with, the privileging of a single institution—chiefship—as customary. Conferred the power to enforce their notion of custom as law, chiefs were assured of backup support from colonial institutions—and direct force, if need be—in the event they encountered opposition or defiance. Customary law thus consolidated the non-customary power of colonial chiefs. Should it be surprising that this power came to enforce as custom rules and regulations that were hardly customary, such as those arising from a newly expanding market economy? The courts in Kilimanjaro thus penalized as a violation of the customary any failure to pay taxes or school fees, to observe price controls or obtain a marriage certificate, to terrace certain lands or to keep away from cultivating land alongside streams.[38] As they were turned into an enabling arm of the state power, the courts not only enforced authority as such, but were often key to setting up a colonial export-import economy. The orders of agricultural inspectors and veterinary officers on the Kilimanjaro were enforced by native courts through fines and jail sentences. Take, as one instance, the case of peasants who were fined in 1947 because they failed to plant cotton with seeds provided by the Native Authority.

The case of colonial Malawi and Zambia illustrates the incredible range of rules that gave Native Authorities criminal jurisdiction.[39] These rules did not only control "drinking and the carrying of weapons and freedom of movement"; they went so far as to regulate "villages' cleanliness and sanitation, control of infectious diseases, control of fire, road-making, tree-felling, limitations, tax registration, reporting of deaths, grass-burning, the killing of game and other administrative matters." The rules were often technical to the point of minutiae. Rules on tree cutting, for example, "encompassed and defined such matters as the width of tree which could be cut and permitted distances from roads and rivers," and similarly with "rules on the use of streams and control of diseases." The more technical the specification, the more objective would seem the justification and the more infallible would appear the authority in question.

The administration and the courts moved like a horse leading a cart. As administration became established, its demands were enforced under the threat of penal sanctions. More and more activity previously considered civil now became criminalized with a corresponding increase in the number of criminal prosecution in the courts. The number of convictions in colonial Malawi rose from 1,665 in 1906 to 2,821 in 1911 to 3,511 in 1918. Two-thirds of the latter were for new statutory offenses that had nothing to do with custom: of 8,500 convictions realized in 1922, 3,855 were "for offenses against the Native Hut and Poll Tax Ordinance of 1921," 1,609 for "leaving the Protectorate without a pass," and another 705 for "offenses against the Employment of Natives Ordinance." A decade later, a second category of convictions appeared alongside those for failure to pay tax, breach of a labor contract, or insisting on free movement. That year, 776 were convicted for offenses against the Forest Laws, 387 for violating Township Regulations, and 227 for breaches of the tobacco and cotton uprooting rules. Could there be a better illustration of the law functioning as an administrative imperative?

By the late 1930s, administrative control had taken on the proportions of a stranglehold. In one colony after another, peasants were being ordered to leave their homes in the interest of soil conservation, to destroy ("destock") herds so as to restore the balance between livestock and grazing land, and to uproot subquality coffee trees to improve crop husbandry. None of this was being done by the central state; all of it was being enforced on the command of Native Authorities, everywhere instructed by European advisers. Take, for example, colonial Tanganyika, where Native Authorities were given powers to make orders (section 9) and rules (section 16) for "the peace, good order and welfare of the natives" under the 1927 Native Authorities Ordinance. In agriculture the power to make orders covered not only the "protection of trees and grassland" and "the control and eradication of animal and human diseases," but also "the increase of food production." In 1930 these powers "were greatly added to" by specific orders of the governor. The regulation "related to every conceivable aspect of farming practice and land use." There were orders "on everything": from "anti-erosion measures (compulsory tie-ridging and terracing, de-stocking, control over grazing, etc.)" to "improved methods of cultivation (destruction of old cotton plants, mulching of coffee, etc.)," and from the practice of "animal husbandry (cattle-dipping, etc.)" to methods "designed to prevent famine (compulsory production of some famine crops such as cassava or groundnuts)." The fiction was that rules were locally formulated and imposed by the relevant Native Authority in response to local conditions and needs, but "the fact that so many of the individual Orders were couched in more or less identical terms" led at least one analyst to conclude that they were issued "invariably at the instigation of the Administration."[40] Not surprisingly, "complaints against regulations went hand-in-hand with criticisms of chiefs and the chiefly system," and revolt brewed as "enforced agricultural change" gathered pace.[41] Whereas the rationale was inevitably technical, the effect was life draining. Behind the mask of indirect rule lay the day-to-day routine—customary— violence of the colonial system.

Should it be surprising then that *enforcing custom* became a euphemism for extending colonial administration and developing a colonial economy? Run by native administrators, native authority courts were supervised by another set of administrators, only they were European. The Native Courts Proclamation in Nigeria, for example, set up native courts without spelling out their procedure or practice, except for empowering the district commissioner to make the relevant rules. When the rules were so made, they "were not exhaustive so the courts were left to the District Commissioner's administrative guidance."[42] It was the administrator in charge who defined the uncodified customary law. Lawyers, however, were kept at bay, out of courts. The whole point of indirect rule was "to find a chief and build a court around him."[43]

Customary law was never concerned with the problem of limiting state power, only with enforcing it. Liberal theory emphasized the double-sided character of law, that while it came from the state it also restrained power. Power was said to be grounded in consent. State command was presumed to be rule bound, not arbitrary. This was the meaning of the claim that civil society was framed by the rule of law. None of these claims, however, sounded sensible where power sought to secure order through conquest, not consent. In such a context, the triumph of techno-administration under the guise of indirect rule through customary law was nothing but a retreat into legal administration. That retreat was indirect rule. "The separation of judicial and administrative power," rationalized Lugard at one point, "would seem unnatural to the primitive African since they are combined in his own rulers." And at another point, just a few pages later, he conceded the necessity: "In a country recently brought under administration, and in times of political difficulty, occasions may arise when the strictly legal aspect may give way to expediency."[44]

Under colonial conditions, respect for the law was really respect for the lawmaker and the law enforcer, often the same person. Consider, for example, the daily routine of the British district commissioner of Tunduru in southern Tanganyika.

> D was in the habit of going for a walk every evening, wearing a hat. When, towards sunset, he came to the point of turning for home, he would hang his hat on a convenient tree and proceed on his way hatless. The first African who passed that way after him and saw the hat was expected to bring it to D's house and hand it over to his servants, even if he was going in the opposite direction with a long journey ahead of him. If he ignored the hat, he would be haunted by the fear that D's intelligence system would catch up with him.[45]

In the French colonies after the Second World War, for example, a native who passed an administrator and failed to salute him risked the confiscation of his head dress and its deposition in the office of the cercle commander's office.[46] The 1920 "reforms" in Ghana made it a crime to "insult a chief," to "drum," or to "refuse to pay homage to a chief."[47] In a similar vein, the KwaZulu Legislative Assembly proposed in 1976 to increase the fine for insolence from R 4 to a maximum of R 100. In the event, the central state actually outdid the chiefs; it permitted the ceiling to be raised even higher, to R 200. But a member of the assembly argued that increasing fines "would not change the insolent behavior which exists in the community because we normally find that people who are disobedient to their chiefs are poor people." Not being in a position to pay fines, he argued that the poor should be meted out corporal punishment for insolence.[48]

The injustice that commissioners and chiefs administered was infinitely flexible: if a transgressor had property, he would be fined; if not, he would receive lashes in the nearest marketplace. Corporal punishment was not only an integral part of the colonial order but a vital one. In the Portuguese colonies, the *palmatoria*, a punishment delivered by means of a beating on the hands, became the symbol of the colonial legal system.[49] The French, the British, and the Boers preferred to administer the strokes of a hippopotamus hide—called the *manigolo* in Malinke, the *kiboko* in Kiswahili, and the *sjambok* in South Africa—on parts of the body less exposed but more sensitive.

Much has been written about the French colonial system of the *indigénat*, but inevitably it has been exceptionalized as a specifically French practice, and an early one at that. Its origin lay in an early colonial presumption that almost all the whites "had the authority to inflict punishment" on any native. Formalized as the indigénat in Algeria in the 1870s, the system was imported into French West Africa in the 1880s.[50] A decree of 1924 limited this generalized white privilege "to officials representing the public powers, administrators and their clerks." The privilege was then extended to nonadministrative chiefs for whom the "ceiling" was fixed at five days' imprisonment and a fine of 25 francs. The decree limited the offenses for which subjects could be penalized to twenty-four, "but their variety was such and their definition so loose that the effect was arbitrarily to cover anything." It gave the administrator a list of motives, "among which he could simply take his pick, and be sure of finding one that would suit a subject he wished to punish." In Guinea, for example, it included a penalty for anyone appealing the decision of an authority: "complaints or objects, knowingly incorrect, repeated in front of the same authority after a proper solution has been found." In Senegal it included penalties for "negligence to carry out work or render aid as demanded," for "any disrespectful act or offensive proposal vis-à-vis a representative or agent of authority" (including a failure to salute a passing administrator), or for "speech or remarks made in public intended to weaken respect for French authority or its officials" (including songs or "false rumors").[51] So marked was popular outrage against the indigénat by the time of the Brazzaville conference in 1944 that de Gaulle felt obliged to acknowledge publicly the need to abolish it.

Call it white privilege, rule by decree, or administrative justice, the point about the indigénat that set it apart from normal practice in the colonies was only that it crudely and brazenly put on the law books as rules the gist of day-to-day practice in the colonies. For was not the whole point of administrative justice to let administration operate unfettered by judicial restraint? Take, for example, the following list of charges taken from the Fort James court book:

- four lashes for "wasting time instead of buying food";
- five to ten lashes for "sitting around fire instead of working";
- one man was fined for "absenting himself from hospital while under treatment";
- another man was fined for "singing near the native church at 11:30 P.M.";
- some were fined for "being late to work";
- others were fined for "gross disrespect";
- two men were fined five shillings each for "constantly running away at the approach of the Boma official."[52]

How different was the practice in a British colony from the French indigénat? Was not the point to teach the recalcitrant a lesson, to ensure they learned to respect authority the next time around?

Listen to the testimony of those with direct experience of this rough-and-ready justice. A Dahomey newspaper reported in 1935: "Every day men and women, even those who owe nothing to the fiscal authorities, are arrested, lashed together and beaten under the pretext of refusal to pay their taxes. . . . Many of them, to comply with the payment of their taxes . . . pawn their children."[53] Around the same time, a Senegalese journal illustrated the kind of customary authority which it was a crime to oppose.[54] Salif Fall was a canton chief whose way of recovering overdue taxes was to tie up all the natives who could not produce a tax receipt during his inspection tour; "these unfortunates were then whipped in sight of the whole village till they bled, and, as a more effective reminder of the canton chief's authority, their sores were smeared with wet salt through the good offices of the Diaraff."

In words not very different, another newspaper described what it meant to live in a British colony, with its "denial to natives of the principles and procedure of British courts" while "subjugat[ing] the judiciary to the executive," under an authority that "invest[ed] District Commissioners" otherwise "innocent of English law and practice" with "powers of life and death in the provinces over natives of whatever standing without any trial by jury or the right to retain counsel" while "detest[ing] . . . educated natives as the *bete noire* that haunts its political and autocratic dreams," under an order that prescribes "public floggings of general offenders stripped naked in the public markets" while "maintain[ing] . . . so-called 'white prestige' at all costs." This powerful indictment of administrative justice in colonial Nigeria was published by a native paper, the *Lagos Weekly Record*, in its official tribute to Sir Frederick Lugard, the architect of indirect rule, on the eve of his retirement in 1919.[55] Two decades later, another Nigerian newspaper reported a meeting of the resident with representatives of various tribal unions and societies in the district, held in the Enugu High Court to discuss the question of the Enugu Native Court: "It is noteworthy that the general feeling of the meeting was against having anything to do with a native court for Enugu. . . . We ourselves have always been entirely lacking in enthusiasm for these so-called 'native courts.' In our opinion the scandal of bribery and corruption permeates the whole system and we see little likelihood of there being any improvement in this respect."[56] But having a native court was hardly a matter of choice, for written into the legal system of every colonial power was the distinction between subject and citizen. The prototype subject was the free peasant, ruled indirectly through an administrative cadre that was both native and European, purporting to work through traditional institutions that in reality were a mishmash—of practices severed from their original context, imposed by the colonial power, or initiated by officeholders—dispensing a customary justice that should more appropriately be understood as a form of administrative justice.

DERACIALIZATION AS POSTINDEPENDENCE REFORM

If customary law and the office of the chief, native or white, cannot be seen as a simple continuation of indigenous, precolonial forms of control, it is also true that this ensemble—the system of indirect rule—did not simply cease to be with independence. Nor was it just reproduced thoughtlessly or without restraint. The anticolonial platform of the 1950s often combined a demand for a unified legal system with a new-found respect for customary law as the embodiment of a much-maligned tradition. In this context, the call for a unified legal system meant a creative blending of customary and modern law and a single hierarchy of courts open to all as citizens. Such, indeed, was the agenda set by a conference of judicial advisers who met at Makerere University in 1953.[57]

But legal reform did not await political independence. It came as part of a larger reform of the colonial system undertaken in response to the great anticolonial movement of the postwar era. Anticolonial protest brought to center stage a debate that had been going on for decades within metropolitan circles, pitting administrators against lawyers, and conservatives against liberals. While administrators stood for efficiency, and in its name a "simple and speedy justice," lawyers called for "the transplanting of the technicalities of English criminal law and procedures." Professional legal criticism of administrative justice came to a head in the early 1930s with the appointment of the Royal Commission of Inquiry into the Administration of Justice in Kenya, Uganda and Tanganyika Territory in Criminal Matters. Chaired by H. G. Bushe, the legal adviser to the Colonial Office, the commissioners found it "fundamentally unsound" that "district officers should rest their prestige on their powers to judge and punish, and should base their judicial functions not on legal training and strict application of the laws of evidence but on their general knowledge of African life."[58]

The rising wave of anticolonial protest tipped the scales in favor of lawyers. The postwar reform of customary law proceeded along two lines: codification to blunt its arbitrary edge and professionalization of legal cadres while introducing a single unified appeal procedure to soften its administrative edge. Codification had been the preoccupation of settler regimes, concerned with limiting the autonomy of local state officials. It clearly had a double edge: while narrowing the scope for local initiative, codification also put the initiative in the hands of the central state. Codification as colonial reform began in 1938 when the government of the Bechuanaland Protectorate commissioned Schapero's *Handbook of Tswana Law and Custom*.[59] More books on African legal rules followed in the postwar era. Prominent among these was the work of Cory, who developed a method of recording customary law while working for the Tanganyika colonial administration.[60] This trickle of reform turned into a stream in the late 1950s as Britain moved into the decade of independence. Based at the University of London and inspired by earlier "restatements" prepared by the American Law Institute, an ambitious project, "The Restatement of African Law," was launched in 1959. It covered the countries of Commonwealth Africa and aimed at codifying the core of customary law: the law of persons, family, marriage and divorce, property (including land), and succession.[61] A parallel initiative attempted to build linkages between customary and modern courts, almost completely isolated from one another in the interwar period. Attempts were made in the 1950s to give high courts "a revisionary jurisdiction over native court proceedings" while attempting a shift of personnel "of the native courts from the traditional chiefs and elders to young lay magistrates with some basic training in law."[62]

To the radical leadership of the anticolonial movements, however, these appeared as no more than timid efforts at a late window dressing. Nothing less than a surgical operation that would unify the substantive law, customary and modern, into a single code would do. The militant edge of the anticolonial movement would be satisfied with nothing less than equal citizenship for all under the law. But soon it became clear that this was a herculean task, daunting and even utopian under the circumstances. Ironically, the first step in postindependence legal reform was a continuation of the preindependence reform process. Its starting point was the narrower agenda for the unification of courts and not of the substantive law.

Broadly speaking, the reform of the court system proceeded along two lines. The minimalist tendency was content to stay with the colonial reform, retaining the dual structure of customary and modern courts while providing for a single integrated review process. The resulting linkages between the two court systems could be limited to the apex (as in Chad, the Central African Republic, and Zaire in the 1960s), or they could be effected at various levels (as in Togo).[63] The native courts were renamed, as either African courts (Kenya) or simply lower or primary courts. A variation of the reform was effected in Nigeria, where the supervisory and review powers of administrative officers were done away with and lawyers were admitted to top-grade customary courts and to customary appeals in higher courts. But lawyers continued to be barred from most customary courts, which were the vast majority of tribunals in the country.

The maximalist reform aimed at a unified court system. This was the major tendency in the former French colonies and in the more radical of the Anglophone countries. Niger, Mali, and Ivory Coast simply abolished all customary courts. So did Senegal. Ghana followed suit in 1960, and Tanzania in 1963. The Tanzanian reform is perhaps the most far-reaching: the language of the primary courts is Kiswahili; in theory, it has jurisdiction over all cases; also, in theory, lawyers are admitted to all courts. Yet in practice primary courts—the lowest level in the triple-tiered hierarchy of the unified court structure—"have broader competence in cases of customary law than in those of modern law."[64] Similarly, in Senegal, a country considered a pacesetter in progressive legal reform in Francophone Africa, "no special court is set apart for the adjudication of customary cases," but "the jurisdiction of the courts of the justices of the peace is limited to minor cases in modern law, while it extends to all cases of customary law."

A unified court system without a simultaneous unification of substantive law was clearly still a long way from realizing the nationalist dream of "equality before the law." Neither did a unified court system mean that its several levels were now governed by a single and uniform set of procedures. To effect that would require a vastly expanded body of professional jurists. Not surprisingly, the managers of independent states soon discovered the advantages of customary courts in terms of their nonprofessionalism and accessibility. The problem was that the agenda of creative synthesis that would transcend the limitations of both customary and modern courts, while incorporating advantages of both, had been replaced by a triumphant modernism: the modern court was considered the desirable goal, but so long as resources were beyond reach and peasants remained "backward," the customary was accepted as a compromise, inevitable but hopefully temporary.

Thus the restatement initiative, based at the School of Oriental and African Studies (SOAS) in London, began to gain adherents among African governments; by 1966 these included Kenya, Malawi, Gambia, and Botswana.[65] The SOAS initiative was very much a continuation of colonial notions of the customary. Restatement retained its tribal flavor. In Malawi, for example, even "where two or more ethnic groups inhabited the same district," an "attempt was made to present significant differences between their laws" and to "re-present the material by ethnic groups."[66] Also, although the law was restated in written form, it was not codified, leaving a degree of initiative in local hands. But the restatement was seldom so simple an exercise as to involve no more than a transcription of oral into written custom. Anthropologists who examined the restatement process, as in Kenya, argued that the outcome was more "a set of ideal statements as to how the law should be administered" than "a reflection of contemporary Kipsigis customary law."[67] This was even more so in Tanzania, where restatement was part of a wider reform process; a single unified body of customary law cutting across ethnic boundaries was written and codified. Restating thus involved ironing out differences between ethnic practices and arriving at a single norm restated in a single law.[68] Henceforth, "unification" referred not to a process whose object was to arrive at a single body of law applicable to all, whether customary or modern, but to a more restricted process that aimed only at a unified body of customary law applicable to all ethnic groups!

Yet a third variant obtained in countries such as Ghana and Senegal.[69] Both attempted to arrive at a single body of law enforced by a single system of courts. Yet in both cases the written law contained customary alongside modern rules. In Senegal, for example, "78 officially recognized bodies of customs, chosen from 33 different ethnic groups, were applicable in the courts."[70] In African legal discourse, this attempt to join the customary and the modern into a single body of law was termed integration. All three variants, however, shared a common dilemma, for all tried to overcome the colonial legacy formally rather than substantively. Whether customary rules were simply restated in writing or were also codified through unification or whether they were integrated into a single body of law, the distinction between the customary and the modern remained. Both the courts and the parties to a dispute had to choose between two sets of rules in case of conflict. On this score, African countries divided into two: those which continued with the colonial tradition of a presumption in favor of the customary and those which reversed it.[71]

The latter group were the modernizers. Among their ranks were found a core, the radical anticolonialists, determined to bring to an end the colonial legacy with the proverbial surgical stroke. More than any other states, two officially Marxist-Leninist states exemplified this tendency: Ethiopia and Mozambique. Whereas the Mengistu regime in Ethiopia simply abolished the customary by implementing a radically modern civil code,[72] the example of Mozambique under Frelimo is of greater interest, for it claimed to have employed a strategy of reform more political than administrative, arriving at "a uniform judicial structure applying a uniform set of legal norms" but through a process that depended "to a large extent on a flexible and non-coercive relationship between the formal and the informal sectors of justice." This claim is made in an eloquent defense of the Mozambican road by two of its participants, Albie Sachs and Gita Welch.[73] The secret, argue the authors, lies in understanding change as the result of a "process," a "protracted struggle," in which "the objective is never seen to be that of destroying the old, but of transforming it, of developing the aspects that are positive and eliminating the aspects that are negative." The point, we are told, is to "ensure as far as possible that the people should be at the center of the process, so that the rate of advance in creating new structures is conditioned by the capacity of the people to assume new values."

But can a democratic political process result in a uniform outcome— not only "a uniform judicial structure applying a uniform set of legal norms," but more so "the remarkable achievement of the community courts" applying a uniform family law throughout the country[74]—under an incredible diversity of conditions, both historical and contemporary? Part of the answer lies in the modified version of "revolution from above" summed up in the earlier claims: the people are said to be at the "center of the process" only to the extent that they "condition" its "rate of advance," not its outcome! The outcome, the substantive law, is a given. What "facilitate[s] the attribution of a single set of rights and duties to all," Albie Sachs assures us, is that the substantive law sums up no more than the demands of "simple justice." After all, "the problems which tend to give rise to family conflict tend to be the same independently of how the family was constituted: men abandoning their wives, excessive drinking, physical abuse, sexual problems, financial stress, sterility, incompatibility of temperaments and so on." In such situations, "simple justice" means recognizing that a "wife-beater is a wife-beater, and it does not matter whether he paid lobolo, or is a Christian or a Muslim or a non-believer."[75]

The demands of simple justice are then summed up as a series of "orientations" that the "judges receive on how to deal with family disputes," and these "constitute the principles equally applied to all unions." One such principle, for example, is to "facilitate the departure of a wife from a polygamous union." To be sure, since the relationship between the "formal and the informal sectors of justice" is said to be "flexible and non-coercive," there is "no attempt to penalize practices regarded as wholly incorrect"—"such as polygamy and child marriages"—but the "orientation" contains a strong presumption against these. "In all parts of the country," Sachs and Welch assure us, "independent of what was permitted by local tradition, the judges will regard it as wrong for a man to take a second wife." "He will not be punished for so doing, but his first wife will have a judicial remedy if she so chooses, and any determination in divorce proceedings made about the division of property or the custody of children would not be influenced by any claim he might make or imply to the effect that his religion or ethnic background permitted polygamy."[76]

The consequences of this simple justice are hardly this simple, for a presumption in favor of the first wife in a polygamous marriage is not simply a presumption against the polygamous husband; it is equally a presumption against the rest of the wives in the polygamous marriage. To entrench the rights of the first wife is simultaneously to erode the rights of the rest. This lesson can be drawn both from Victorian attempts of Boer republics to "abolish" polygamy in turn-of-the-century South Africa and from radical nationalist attempts to reform tradition in postindependence Ghana. The Volksraad of the Orange Free State recognized the "customary law of inheritance" but "only in administering estates of *de facto* monogamists." "Tribal marriages" were invalid in both the Transvaal and the Orange Free State. The supreme court in the Transvaal "ruled that polygyny was inconsistent with the general principles of civilization."[77] None of this was very different from the eventually abortive postindependence bill in Ghana, which "sought to withdraw legal recognition from all but the first wife,"[78] and so on with the so-called noncoercive way of abolishing *lobolo*, bride-price; for although "there is no legal prohibition of the payment of cattle by way of *lobolo*," at the same time "no one can go to court to argue that cattle so promised have not been paid, or cattle so paid should be restored." Sachs concludes with a straight face: "the state does not interfere." What is to be the likely consequence of such an orientation? Surely, the flourishing of the "informal sector of justice," with its provisions (at least in the patriarchal societies) for ensuring that lobolo is both paid when customary and returned when customary.

If that is the case, one would have reason to doubt the claim that the Law on Judicial Organisation, passed in 1978, had within a decade been the instrument of realizing a "uniform family law" within all of Mozambique, "from the Ruvuma to the Maputo." To be sure, our authors also do concede a nonuniform outcome. "The new court system and the new forms of family law are most deeply rooted," we are informed, "in the areas where new relations of production and new forms of social organisation are most evident, namely in the communal villages in the countryside, and in the more strongly organised residential areas in the towns."[79] The communal villages "constitute more than 10% of all inhabitants of the countryside." In some of these villages, in Nampula, for example, where the family system was matrilineal, women "were reluctant to leave their traditional family villages where . . . they could count on a degree of protection from their kinfolk." "To move to a communal village," however, meant "entering a mononuclear relation with their husbands." One does not have to read much more to get to the root of the women's reluctance: in some villages, "some men left their original wives and children behind and entered into new 'monogamous' marriages in the communal village."[80] In this case monogamy becomes just another name for male license to shed a wife as a snake would shed its skin. And the "new forms of social organization" turn out to be a transition from a matrilineal to a patrilineal family organization, and the "orientation" a presumption against matriliny.[81]

The Mozambican reform was not without its positive side. But the gain was very much local: in the "people's tribunal at the lowest level," the system of chiefship was eliminated, and "the judges were elected from among the local population on the basis of their common sense, feeling for justice and their knowledge of the revolutionary principles contained in the Constitution."[82] As with colonial courts of chiefs, no lawyers were allowed; "all procedural formalism [was] reduced to the minimum." But not so in the higher courts, in the district, provincial, and national levels.[83] This means that poor people who won a case in a people's tribunal could easily find the tables turned in case of a review in a higher court if they could not afford a lawyer. But even if the lower court was no longer the customary court oriented by the chief, it was now a people's tribunal oriented by a judge whose "knowledge of the revolutionary principles contained in the Constitution" was an important qualification for election. That orientation and that knowledge, part of the revolution from above, was the key to the substantive justice administered in the new tribunals. As our authors disarmingly state, "The state sector at its best should represent all that is new, that transforms, that helps to establish a new consciousness"[84]—indeed a far cry from the principle that "the people should be at the centre of the process."

A less dramatic but no less drastic legal reform—from above—was introduced in postindependence Tanzania. Both family law and land law were "the subject of special legislation which either wholly or partly removes them from the jurisdiction of the normal court system." The reform channeled land disputes to land tribunals, four of whose five members were appointed by the ruling party (TANU) and the Ministry of Law and Settlement. Appeals were to go directly from the tribunal to the line ministry "without passing through any other courts." Family controversies, however, were to be handled by arbitration tribunals, all of whose five lay members were "appointed by the TANU Branch Committee having jurisdiction over the ward."[85]

I will put the legal reform in its wider political context in a later chapter. My interest now is in exploring the thread that links together the experience of the radical African states. This was the presumption that all one needed was a proclamation from the summit to change the flow of life on the ground. Were not the radical African states the true inheritors of the colonial tradition of rule by decree and rule by proclamation, of subordinating the rule of law to administrative justice so as to transform society from above? One radical regime after another carried out drastic changes, but mostly on paper. This is how Ghana tried to end polygamy and Ethiopia decreed an end to customary law. In a similar spirit, Tanzania proposed—as did a conservative state like Malawi— "the replacement of a matrilineal system of succession by a patrilineal one."[86] If the vision of change was audacious, the presumption that all that was needed to effect it was the stroke of a pen was breathtakingly naive. If the conservative regimes held up one part of the colonial tradition, recognizing African society as no more than an ensemble of tribes, each with its own customary law and thus with the right to be judged by its own law, the radical regimes took their stand on the ground that for all persons to be equal before the law, the law must be modern! It was a perspective best summed up in Samora Machel's well-known call: "For the nation to live, the tribe must die."[87] Just as they decreed a unified society—in the form of a single party, a single trade union, a single cooperative movement, and a single movement of women or youth—the radical regimes decreed a single body of substantive law. Whereas the conservative states were content with continuing the colonial legacy of a customary decentralized despotism, radical states tried to reform that legacy, but in the direction of a modern centralized despotism.

The result, predictably, has been an ever-widening gulf between what is legal and what is real. One cannot remove matriliny or polygamy or bride-price by legal fiat. One cannot even do it with matters that lacked a deep historical standing, so that, whereas legislation required that "the law of contracts of England" be "generally applicable" throughout Kenya, "in practice the customary law of contracts is still recognized and enforced in African courts."[88] Not surprisingly, matters reached a point at which some jurists were alarmed that if judgments "are based upon principles dictated by the central government and at odds with well-established and recognized rules of the local customary law, there is good reason to expect less resorting to the state judiciary." "The nullification of the judicial process on the part of a substantial element of the rural population," concluded this particular jurist, "is a serious danger."[89]

This, however, is not to say that no meaningful legal reform took place with independence. It did, but the main tendency of the reform was not toward the democratization of the legal system inherited from colonialism, but toward its deracialization. Racial barriers were dismantled and a formal equality was observed. Often chiefs' and commissioners' courts were abolished, and their functions were transferred to magistrates' courts. All litigants were formally given a status of equality before the courts, and the debate on legal reform was restructured—in the erstwhile colony as in the metropolitan countries—around the question of access to justice. It was a reform that summed up progress in the first phase of African independence, as it did in the "independent" homelands of South Africa.

Deracialization meant that the social boundary between modern and customary justice was modified: the former was in theory open to all, not just to nonnatives; the latter governed the lives of all those natives for whom modern law was beyond reach. Although independence deracialized the state, it did not democratize it. Although it included indigenous middle and even working classes within the parameters of the modern state and therefore potentially in the ranks of rights-bearing citizens, thereby expanding the parameters of civil society, it did not dismantle the duality in how the state apparatus was organized: both as a modern power regulating the lives of citizens and as a despotic power that governed peasant subjects.

One needs to grasp fully both the general achievement of postindependence reform and its outer limit, and within those boundaries the different outcomes. Deracialization signified the general achievement; it was a tendency characteristic of all postindependence states, conservative and radical. The outer limit of postindependence reform was marked by detribalization, a tendency characteristic of only the radical states. Whereas customary law continued to be ethnically flavored in the conservative states, enforcing an ethnic identity on the subject population through ethnically organized Native Authorities, customary law in the radical states was reformed as a single law for the entire subject population, regardless of ethnic identity. The decentralized despotism characteristic of the conservative states was deracialized but ethnically organized, whereas the deracialized and detribalized power in the radical states tended toward a centralized despotism. We will see that the latter has turned out to be the more unstable of the two, generating a demand for decentralization which—if pursued in the absence of democratization—is likely to lead to a despotism as generalized and as decentralized as it was in the colonial period.

The situation of those subjected to customary law and indirect rule through the institution of chiefship cannot be grasped through a discourse structured around the question of legal access. Unlike the urban poor who live within the confines of the modern civic power—the law-defined boundary of civil society—whose predicament may be grasped as a de jure legal equality compromised by a de facto social inequality, a formal access to legal institutions rendered fictional in most cases by the absence of resources with which to reach these institutions, the situation of the rural poor is not that of lack of access or reach, but the actual law (customary law) and its implementing machinery (Native Authority) that confront them. Their problem can be grasped not through an absence or remoteness of institutions, but through institutions immediately and actually present. That ensemble of institutions, the deracialized regime of indirect rule, is best conceptualized as a subordinate but autonomous state apparatus.

CHAPTER FIVE

The Native Authority and the
Free Peasantry

I HAVE ARGUED that the notion of the customary was not unique to the African encounter with Western colonialism. Distinctive to that encounter, though, was the scope of the customary. Stretched beyond personal law to include land and thereby rounded off into a complete circle, the customary provided the basis of a political despotism. Assured of customary access to land, the free peasant household was only partly subject to the influence of market forces. Beyond that, nothing short of force—customarily sanctioned—would breach this partial autonomy. The Native Authority in charge of enforcing custom came to signify the seat of a decentralized despotism. A distinctive feature of this form of the state was that market and force appeared as complementary twins, not as alternative ways of organizing economic life.

CUSTOMARY LAND TENURE

Could it be that in defining land as a customary possession colonial powers were simply acknowledging the existing state of affairs in their newly acquired possessions? After all, was not private property in land more the exception than the rule in precolonial Africa? To answer these questions simply in the affirmative or the negative would be misleading, for to acknowledge the absence of an institution—such as private property—is not the same as to come to grips with an existing institutional context.

The absence of private property in land needed to be understood contextually. In most parts of Africa, land was relatively plentiful, "easily taken up and as easily abandoned."[1] In such instances, it made little sense for rulers to "reward officials and followers by gifts of landed estates." This does not mean that private estates tied to state offices did not develop; they did. Where livestock flourished, for example, "estates in cattle supported state officials." "Where special conditions encouraged generations of men to cultivate the same land," however, as in some of the West African states "where agricultural settlements had existed for perhaps four thousand years and where systems of agriculture based on long-term fallow rotation were commonly practiced"—or in

some of the intralacustrine kingdoms of eastern Africa or the Lozi Kingdom in central Africa—landed estates did develop as attachments to office. The important point is that changing conditions often made for
changed practices and notions; thus, for example, where shifting cultivation gave way to settled agriculture, a family usually farmed a landhold-
ing for generations, in the process consolidating exclusive rights of cultivation over it.[2] Similarly, "before the imposition of colonial rule,"
"much of the arable land in the most populated regions" of West Africa
"had been turned into estates controlled by descent groups."[3] The point
is that there was no necessary contradiction between notions of community rights and corporate and individual rights: the existence of one did
not necessarily preclude that of others. This is why in trying to grasp
rules of access simply in terms of the absence of "private property" in
land, colonial powers ended up with a customary notion of tenure that
involved at least three important distortions.

The first was a notion of community rights so one-sided as to be at
loggerheads with any meaningful understanding of individual rights.
Colonial powers brought with them "European concepts of legal tenure
which they were prone to interpret as universal legal principles applicable everywhere"; and in particular, concluded the anthropologist Elizabeth Colson, "they assumed that the full range of land rights covered by
the concept of proprietary ownership must exist in Africa as in Europe."[4]
From this point of view, a right had to be exclusive. It was difficult to
entertain the notion of multiple rights in land. Thus "if no private person appeared to hold such rights over a given area, then they assumed
that the rights must vest in the political unit whose members used the
region." Thus arose a notion of a community right in land as a right
both proprietary and exclusive.

If the community was the customary proprietor over communal land,
then who was to exercise this right of proprietorship? The definition of
customary authorities who would exercise the right to allocate community land for household use involved a second distortion: hitherto ritual
powers were confused with proprietary rights. Throughout nineteenth-
century West Africa, there were found earth priests "representing the
first settler," who in "transform[ing] unoccupied waste into human
habitation and cultivation was assumed to have come to terms with the
power of the earth." These earth priests were acknowledged "both in
highly developed states and among people who recognized no other
form of community office." The tendency was for communities to recognize ritual offices reflecting the different uses to which land was put:
in Central Africa, there were earth priests, priests of the bush, and priests
of the waters; in East Africa, there were also priests of the cattle. An
interpretation that earth priests "were holders of the land rights of the

community" misrepresented their role, for "they were leaders of ritual and not allocators of land or rulers of men."[5] However, as Snyder put it with reference to colonial Senegal, the notion that priests had proprietary interests in land was really ideological. It formed the basis of a larger colonial construct: that the power to allocate use rights in "the land belonged to chiefs."[6]

And finally, there was a third distortion, which identified the community with the tribe and thus defined all migrants not belonging to the tribe—all strangers—as without a traditional right of access to land. In 1903, for example, the laws of Lerotholi, named after the then paramount chief in British Basutoland, prohibited the allocation of land to non-Basotho.[7] The Native Reserve Commission of 1927 in colonial Zambia explained its perspective as follows: "In selecting the reserves we are recommending we have endeavoured to adhere to the principle that they should be tribal or for a portion of a tribe."[8] Similarly, reserves in Kenya, as in Rhodesia or South Africa, were demarcated along tribal lines. The Native Authority (Control of Alienation of Farmland to Strangers) Rules of 1948 in Nigeria required strangers to obtain a license from the relevant Native Authority before they could farm.[9]

Yet in most precolonial African societies where status and wealth accrued to those who could attract dependents or followers, "'strangers' were welcomed—as wives, clients, 'blood brothers,' settlers or disciples—because they enhanced the prestige and often the labor force of the head of a household, kin group or community."[10] As a result, communities were more often than not multiethnic. In such a context, to identify community with tribe was to sow the seeds of much tension.

These three distortions—the community as customary proprietor of land, its appointed political leaders as holders and executors of that proprietorship, and the right of access to community land on a customary basis as tribally defined and therefore excluding strangers—in fact turned into many pivots around which developed a specifically colonial notion of customary land tenure. It now became "policy that all owners of land should be found" and "that such owners must be protected against exploitation by being denied the right to dispose freely of their interests." It also became "axiomatic that only a community could own land." Elizabeth Colson called this body of law governing "the allocation and use of land . . . customary, though untraditional."[11]

In grounding the powers of chiefs in the right to allocate customary land for use, customary law tended to fortify the position of Native Authorities. This much became clear in time. And inasmuch as it stood the passage of time, customary land tenure must be understood as not simply the result of a set of conceptual confusions, but as a policy that was reproduced because it was politically warranted. Let us take one example to underline this point.[12] When the West African Lands Committee was convened in 1912, evidence was brought before it "that Yoruba chiefs had no claims to land other than that belonging to their own families." Yet the committee—whose report was never published—stressed "the political importance of upholding 'pure native tenure.'" For land tenure, it argued, "was the foundation of native rule," so much so that "together they stand or fall."

Although the development of a customary land tenure was the main trend in colonial Africa, it was not the only one. There were also curative moments in Africa's colonial encounter. Customary law regulated access to land in the vast plains that stretched between the Sahara and the Limpopo, but there were also pockets and enclaves dominated by landlords and agrarian capitalists. Whereas the agreements that created a landed class had an Indian resonance to them, the shrinking "reserves" from which settlers pumped out land and labor had very much a New World ring about them.

Indigenous Landlords

The best-known Indian-style land settlement in Africa was the Buganda Agreement of 1900, which transformed a section of the precolonial ruling class of the Buganda Kingdom into a landed aristocracy.[13] The agreement covered all land then in use and some not in use: 10,034 square miles were distributed among the royal family and the greatest of the chiefs, and another 8,000 square miles were to be divided among lesser chiefs and notables—initially numbering 1,000 but increased to 3,700 persons in 1905. Through this transfer, large masses of peasants living on that land were turned into rent-paying tenants of *mailo* (mile-owning) landlords. Besides the landlords, there also mushroomed a class of European planters for whom every peasant who grew cotton for sale was one fewer laborer for hire on the cheap because he had another way of earning cash to pay tax. But the days of planters were limited. On the one hand, the crash of commodity markets that followed the First World War taught the colonial state that planters could survive adversity only if they were granted lavish subsidies; on the other hand, peasants proved to be a far more reliable and cheaper source of long-staple cotton, a commodity in great demand by the Lancashire textile industry in the decades following the American Civil War. In another decade, the growth of peasant production had run against the wall of landlord ambitions. As landlords took to extracting ground rent (*obusulu*) and commodity rent (*nvujo*) from tenants, the latter began to reduce the cultivation of commodity crops (cotton) and en masse joined a movement of clan heads (the *Bataka*) demanding a revision of the 1900 agreement. The colonial response was to clip the wings of the landed class through a land reform law that both limited the rent landlords could collect from tenants and gave tenants security of tenure, including the right of inheritance. That protection, however, was limited to three acres. Its social consequence was not an agrarian bourgeoisie, but an internally differentiated free peasantry. That land reform bill, the 1928 *Busulu* and *Envujjo* law, was a corrective measure by a stabilized colonial power.

The land reform law was the product of a decade-long rethinking over land policy, organized as a series of official conferences beginning in 1914. By 1922 the Governor felt confident enough to conclude a dispatch to the colonial secretary on the mailo system in Buganda: "It has become clear that the system is a dangerous one." That same year, the conference of provincial commissioners resolved as follows: "The Provincial Commissioners consider that it is a matter for deep regret that the idea of 'freehold' and 'landlordism' should have been introduced into the Protectorate by the Uganda, Ankole, and Toro Agreements, and would urge that this disastrous mistake should not be perpetuated in districts where the government has not committed itself by such unfortunate contracts."[14] By 1931 the Colonial Office was able to crystallize the cardinal points of land policy in Uganda and communicate them to the governor: (a) "noone to have grants of land in freehold"; (b) "no grants of 'official estates' from the occupants of which tribute can be expected by the holder of office"; instead, peasants must pay "tribute to the Protectorate government by which it is returned to the native administration and used together with the normal rebate of poll tax as a fund for the payment of salaries and pensions to chiefs"; and (c) "peasants to be secured in their holdings." In a nutshell, the policy reform aimed at neither freehold nor landlordism, but a land-secure free peasantry paying tribute to the state.

When the French moved to indirect rule policies in the aftermath of the First World War, they too introduced corrective measures where earlier they had reinforced indigenous landed property. In the Sherifian state of Morocco, where the social base of colonial rule was a landed class, indirect rule was introduced alongside customary tenure in land. To date, more than five million of seven million hectares of total arable land are made up of so-called collective lands. At the same time, a dual system of rule cordons off the collective areas from the rest of the country.[15]

Settler Capitalists

The free peasantry faced social extinction where it was confronted by a land and labor-hungry agrarian bourgeoisie of settler origin. Such a bourgeoisie, however, failed to get a firm hold over political power and thus over the institutionalized apparatus of force. Its aspirations were checked by a double barrier: peasant resistance and the conflicting demands of other sections of capital. In a colony like Kenya, the ambitions of an agrarian settler class seeking to appropriate a free peasantry were checked by a peasant rebellion: the Mau Mau. The Mau Mau may have lost militarily, but the settlers were defeated politically. At the heart of post–Mau Mau settlement was the Swynnerton Plan, a corrective program of land redistribution whose social objective was to expand the ranks of the peasantry. But the redistribution the Kenya Land Commission recommended, and the government accepted, was not mainly to dispossessed individuals or groups, but involved adding blocks of land to "tribal reserves." "The 'final solution' of the Kikuyu-European land conflict," Sorrenson summed up in his study of the Swynnerton Plan, "was seen in tribal terms."[16]

In the Portuguese colony of Mozambique, the colonial state mediated between the conflicting demands of Portuguese settlers for land (and labor) and those of South African mines for reserves that would be home to migrant-supplying peasant communities. The 1929 statute on native policy in the Portuguese colonies defined a native as "part of a community ruled directly by a chief, and subject in the first instance to African customary law." Part of that custom was "access to communal land." The communal reserves, inalienable to private owners, had been demarcated by law in 1918. Their size was increased fourfold in 1927.[17] The reason there were so few "civilized" Africans in the Portuguese colonies—five thousand in Mozambique by 1950—is not just that it was difficult to attain that status; it was also that an African *civilisado* lost all rights in communally held land.

Unlike settler farmers who sought to flush out land and labor from peasant communities through an ongoing and endless series of Kaffir wars, the demand of mining capital was for self-reproducing peasant communities (reserves), which would at the same time supply them with migrant labor in ongoing cycles. The point about the South African land law of 1913 is not just that peasant communities were confined to 7.13 percent of the land area—an allocation doubled by the Native Trust and Land Act of 1936—but that there was a repeated effort to create and hold reserves in which land was held in customary possession. The Natives Land Act of 1913 was the occasion of a wave of forced removals of

Africans from "white land," graphically described at the time by the black intellectual Sol Plaatje.[18] Contrast this with Kenya, where the trigger to the Mau Mau uprising was settler attempts to appropriate squatter land and turn it into farm-tied labor. Not surprisingly, then, when the Tomlinson Commission recommended in 1955 that freehold tenure be granted to the African population in the homelands on condition that it be "adequately used" in the interest of "development," the government rejected the proposal. In the words of Verwoerd, it "would undermine the whole tribal structure."[19] This political imperative made for a "stark tenurial dualism"[20] between peasant reserves and settler farms in the labor reserve colonies: in the farms, tenure was freehold or long-term leasehold; in the reserves, it was customary. The point of the customary was to contain migrant labor within a communal hold. Central to the labor policy of apartheid in the 1950s and 1960s was a consistent endeavor to expand the scope of migrant labor beyond servicing mines, to serving manufacturing establishments, so that it would periodically—and finally—return to reserves, now upgraded to ten homelands.[21] The complement of a free peasant is migrant labor, not a full-blown proletariat.

It is customary access to land that defines the free peasantry in Africa as distinct from small peasants elsewhere. It is also this ongoing access that gives it autonomy and makes of it a self-reproducing free peasantry. Although the fact of this autonomy is captured in the literature on exit option, its meaning is not. For a customary access to land does not mean that such a peasantry is uncaptured; it means rather that its productive activity is only partly shaped by market forces. To subordinate that activity further to an external demand—but without turning land into a market-governed commodity—is possible only through force. The other side of autonomy in this case is a regime of force. The fact that this regime is labeled customary does not make it any less coercive. To understand the nature of forces that shape the system of free peasant production, we need to understand the combined impact of markets and compulsions, two influences that we habitually tend to see as opposites. In this arrangement, however, force is not the prehistory of markets; it is its complementary twin.

The regime that enforced compulsions was known as the Native Authority. Its agent was the chief. Sanctified by customary law, the power the chief wielded was organized as fused power. To unravel and differentiate it would be to evoke suspicion, to keep it intact would be to maintain trust—such was the logic of the high priests of indirect rule. The holders of this power, however, should not be understood as mere functionaries who simply translated into executive action directives received from above. In a way, the autonomy of the free peasantry was reflected in the autonomy of the power to which it was directly subject, the Native Authority. The chiefs who were in charge of forcibly extracting labor and its products from free peasant households were also in a position to extract tribute from the same households. Besides the salaries they earned from the central state, the chiefs also had an autonomous source of revenue: personal tribute.

To say that the chiefs were autonomous is not to say that they were independent. It is not to claim that they did not act as intermediaries in implementing directives from the center, nor that they were not supervised by organs of the central state, even closely. Their claim to independence was embedded in the demand that they be recognized as traditional and therefore hereditary authorities. This was a claim rejected by every colonial power as soon as its rule was stabilized, for every colonial power jealously guarded the right to appoint and remove a functionary. But once appointed, the personnel of the Native Authority were left to their own devices, unless they failed to keep order, to carry out orders (which included the demand for public labor and compulsory crops), or to balance their books. The autonomy and the power of the Native Authority came to be crystallized in a decentralized despotism.

MARKETS AND COMPULSIONS

Historians used to assume that commodity production in Africa began with colonial rule. Prevailing notions took it for granted that indigenous economies were of a subsistence character and that trade began as the result of an external impact: Arab, Indian, and European. Seldom did they ask how it was possible for foreign traders to exchange bulk at the coast without the presence of internal traders who could first accumulate the bulk to be so traded. Postindependence historical work has effectively criticized this assumption, in the process retracing the history of trade and markets in Africa before colonialism.[22]

What, then, was the impact of colonialism on the market economy? At first glance it would seem to be in the deepening of markets, particularly for export crops and imported necessaries. This one-sided, outward-looking integration into the world economy was emphasized by dependency theorists. But dependency theorists also tended to turn the historical fact of the external character of capitalist relations introduced in the colonies into some sort of a theory of original sin whereby capitalism, not only in its origin but also at every step in its development, must continue to be an external imposition. This attempt to read the development of processes into their origin is not only reductionist, but also ignores an important historical fact. Commodity relations in Africa predated colonialism.

Yet dependency theorists grasped an important historical fact. As the exchange economy developed, peasants came to depend on markets—in varying degrees—for their survival. This was true of their day-to-day need for manufactured consumption goods, ranging from humble items such as salt and soap to relatively more sophisticated ones like sugar, cloth, medicine, and formal education. In turn, they came to depend on (foreign) markets, in which they sold industrial crops (cotton, coffee, tea, pyrethrum, and groundnuts). The dependence was even more pronounced of their productive activity. Although in lean times a peasant could forgo the use of manufactured consumables, even salt and soap, this was not as easy with producer goods, like the ubiquitous hoe, without which the cycle of production could not be set into motion. Walter Rodney wrote that the African peasant went into colonialism with a hoe and came out of it with a hoe;[23] he should have added that the hoe with which the peasant went in was locally made; the hoe the peasant came out with was imported!

The other side of this partial dependence was a partly eroded tendency toward self-sustenance. The sway of market forces was limited so long as land tilled by peasants remained a customary possession, for on that land, alongside the crops they sold, peasant households also harvested the staples they ate. Like everything customary, access to land was in practice subject to a tug-of-war, in this instance between traditional kinship authorities and the newly appointed chiefs. Not withstanding this tussle or the requirement to pay a customary tribute, the free peasantry retained access to the land it cultivated.

The partial dependence on markets was not uniform throughout the peasantry. The commodity economy was also the soil that differentiated the peasantry into various strata. Initially accidental features, whether demographic (size of the family), topographic (soil fertility), or locational (nearness to markets or lines of communication), could spin off into cumulative processes leading to either advantage or handicap, enrichment or impoverishment. Each step in this contradictory development presented different peasant households with either an opportunity or a constraint, depending on whether the household had a labor surplus or was labor deficient, enjoyed a surplus of implements (or farm animals) or was implement poor, could marshal a surplus of land or was land deficient. Thus peasant households were divided on the basis of those who employed extra hands to supplement family labor and those who did not even have the number of hoes needed to set all available hands into simultaneous motion and were compelled to sell some of their laboring capacity to meet immediate needs; between those who rented out oxen and plow and those implement poor who hired them; and sometimes between those who rented out surplus land and those who leased land because they did not have enough.

Several commentators on the African countryside have assumed that there could be no meaningful social differentiation within the free peasantry so long as land remained plentiful. But land is only one component of the labor process, whose other ingredients are labor and its implements. My studies in Uganda show that peasants with formal access to sufficient land may still find themselves land poor because they do not have access to the implements necessary to set into motion all the labor at the disposal of the family. Thus peasant households owning roughly similar plots of land may still find themselves in different socioeconomic locations because some are implement poor and others are not.[24]

The process of differentiation did not develop entirely on free rein. Both the tempo and the direction of development were shaped by the character of political (state) power. The differentiation of the peasantry was the end result of two related processes: the competition characteristic of local markets and a variety of impositions forced on the peasantry that tended to accelerate the impoverishment of the rural poor in particular. Just as in the realm of the political and the juridical, so in the economy, too, the nonmarket was hardly the traditional, the sum and substance of kinship relations; it was kinship relations subordinated to the demands of a new authority. The productive activity of peasants was shaped not by the market economy and the "economy of affection"—to use Goran Hyden's quaint phrase—but by the force of the market and the compulsion of force. The overall impact of colonialism in economic relations was contradictory, both facilitating and constraining market expansion. The free peasant economy lay at the interstices of markets and compulsions.

The distinction between market relations and direct compulsions is not quite that between force and its absence. After all, the "dull compulsion" of market forces assumes the presence of force "in the last instance"; it is possible only where a legal and political authority (institutionalized force) guarantees the reproduction of property rights and the sanctity of contractual obligations. The distinction is rather between the direct intervention of force into the very process of production (extra-economic coercion) and its indirect and external presence to ensure the legal basis for the reproduction of commodity relations. Neither should the history of force be taken as the prehistory of markets in their infancy, as assumed in much of the literature on African economic history. So long as the peasantry remains in customary possession of land, it retains a degree of self-sufficiency that can be breached only from without, by organized force or a chance catastrophe. When I asked a capitalist farmer in northern Uganda to identify the critical period in the family's accumulation in the village, she responded: "What helped us was the famine of 1980. People were hungry and they sold us things cheaply. That is when we really started buying."[25] Catastrophe, however, is irregular. The period between catastrophes is punctuated by force. It envelops peasant households like a web of exactions, ranging from forced labor to forced crops to forced contributions to forced removals.

FORCE AND THE STATE

Given that economic life in the African territories was generally precapitalist at the end of the nineteenth century, there was hardly a labor market from which to employ workers. Still, it is ironic that in a period whose moral thrust was defined by a growing campaign against slavery, all colonial powers seemed to have arrived at the same solution in the face of this dilemma: unfree labor. If international convention had abolished the slave trade, they reasoned, this was not quite the same as abolishing slavery. If an end to the slave trade diminished local supplies of labor, the shortage would be filled by various types of unfree labor—and so it was. Resort to unfree labor marked the practice of all major colonial powers: Belgium, France, Portugal, and Britain.

It was none other than Mark Twain who drew popular Western attention to this "organized system of plunder and outrage" built on "the most diverse imposts in labor or in kind" in King Leopold's Congo.[26] However, these did not end with the termination of King Leopold's personal overrule. Belgium's passage to direct colonialism served only to rationalize and institutionalize these practices in law, not to eradicate them. Early colonial legislation permitted sixty days of forced labor a year, reduced in 1955 to forty-five days; it could be called upon for compulsory cultivation or for public works.[27] The provision was rewritten into law after independence. The 1969 ordinance required every peasant household to contribute forty-five days of labor a year for "educational work"; furthermore, this limit could be exceeded "if there is urgent work to be done."[28]

Besides the Congo, Belgium controlled the twin colonies of Ruanda and Burundi. How the ensemble of forced practices shaped the daily misfortunes of a peasant is clear from the following observation by a missionary at Rugari (Burundi) in 1932:

> During the visit of the Resident . . . I remarked that the rains being a
> month and a half late and the natives having waited impatiently to plant

their crops, it would be unwise to stop them from doing it by imposing numerous labor levies which would do nothing to prevent an immediate famine: coffee campaign, manioc campaign, eucalyptus campaign, buckwheat campaign, public works (the dispensary at Kinazi and elsewhere), etc., etc. I pointed out that in addition there was in the area an epidemic of abscesses, condemning sometimes as many as five people in a household to inactivity.[29]

From 1887 onward, the French began to establish "freedom villages" along the length and breadth of occupied Sudan. To these villages, they brought all categories of slaves: those who had escaped from enemy territories, those taken from their masters either as punishment or for political reasons, those paid for by the French exchequer but not yet sold, and finally those few set free by the more liberal of the planters. For these wretched occupants, the emancipation from slavery was hardly the end of unfree labor. A note penned in 1894, found in the Bamako archives, described their condition: "Gangs of wretched men dying of hunger or on the brink of death, tired and yet, for example, forced to provide all the forced labor for the post and circle porterage."[30] Another French commentator noted that freedom villages in reality "provided an excellent solution to the problem of finding porters and labor gangs; in any case, it was greatly superior to the system of going out armed looking for people every time they were needed, only to have them escape the first moment they were not being watched."[31]

These villages were widely used to supply labor for individual Europeans and for the missions and to provide wives for soldiers. When the supply from the combination of unsold, captured, and freed slaves could not meet the prevailing demand, the French administration was not averse to forcing labor from the surrounding free population. G. Deherme, traveling through French-occupied West Africa in 1908, recorded one such instance: "In one district that I passed through, a custom had arisen that when a village could not or would not give the whole sum imposed [as taxes], a child would be taken and placed in the so-called freedom village until the tax was paid."[32] Not surprisingly, the appellate "freedom villages" did not stick with the local population; they called these "villages of the commander's slaves." To get an idea of how widespread unfree labor was at that time, one only has to look at French statistics of the period: a report issued in 1904 estimated that 2,000,000 out of the 8,250,000 inhabitants of French West Africa fell under the category "non-free."[33]

Freedom villages were progressively disbanded between 1905 and 1910, not because forced labor was done away with, but because it was successfully generalized as colonial occupation was consolidated. In the

French colonies of West and Equatorial Africa, all taxpayers were required by law to do statute labor, unless they could buy themselves out. Recorded in the books as basically ten to twelve days a year, this official limit was rarely adhered to. Because every canton was taxed according to its registered population, labor days owed by those absent or deceased were divided among those present. Should a task be considered of "urgent necessity" by the authorities, it could always be added on; a refusal by the population was sure to invite collective punishment.

In the early decades, forced labor was required not only for cultivation and public works, but also for head porterage. Because of inadequate and scarce means of transport, all export goods were produced in zones situated less than three hundred kilometers from the coast. Colonies farther inland were organized as labor reserves. Thus the farther inland a location, the more the accent on forced labor for head porterage—the "pipe heads" (*"têtes de pipe"*), as the forest exploiters called them. In those inland subsistence economies, there came into being a category of forced labor that was in addition to the obligation of statute labor. It met the demand of companies and big public works and became a way of fulfilling assorted taxes. This phenomenon was particularly marked in the concessionary economies of French Equatorial Africa, where as much as 40 percent of the male population between the ages of twenty and forty were recruited for work in the forestry and mining concessions in the 1920s. Coerced labor went alongside high mortality rates. In one three-year period, of 1,000 men recruited from a single division in Gabon, 182 died and a further 395 failed to return home.[34]

The central state, the plantations, and the mines do not exhaust the list of those who devoured coerced labor. Yet another category was made up of those demanded by the local state, personified by the native chief and the white cercle commander. In each agricultural area, peasants were required to till a communal field whose produce went to maintain the chief and his men. Over and above this traditional field of the chief, the police also demarcated another—the commander's fields—which the peasants were required to cultivate and which the police periodically checked at different stages of the agricultural cycle.[35]

Every time a European in charge at the local district office issued an order for recruits to be rounded up, it was open season for the local hierarchy, from various grades of chiefs to messengers to doctors and nurses. The following account written in 1942 and found in the national archives of Cameroon makes the point graphically:

> The *Office du Travail* said to the head chief: "You must give me forty men." His eyes shining, he called to the village chiefs to pass on the mes-

sage: "They want sixty men from me. Give them to me, quick." The village chiefs decide among themselves how many each should give to supply the sixty men. "I can give ten." Then he calls his messengers and tells them in secret, "Give me fifteen men." Then the messengers, armed with their trusty whips, set upon the villages and seize anybody they meet by day or night. In huts and in fields, they hunt men. Showing no pity, they hit and wound, but so much the better. "You want to be freed? Then give me a chicken. Give me five francs. You haven't got any? Hard luck." They take as many as they can in order to free as many as possible in exchange for remunerative presents. How they enjoy the recruiting season!

The demand for labor grows as it is passed down the chain of command. The Office du Travail calls for fifty men from the head chief, who asks for sixty from his six village chiefs, who in turn demand ninety from their messengers, for whom it is an opportunity for an open season "to take as many as they can in order to free as many as possible in exchange for remunerative presents." But the opportunity for gain is not yet exhausted. It reopens as men are taken up the chain of command, and those who can afford to are invited to buy themselves out. Let us pick up the story with the sixty men assembled before the head chief.

Then the same business of buying out starts all over again: "Who would like to give me a present? Anybody who gives me a goat will be free to return home." Even if the sacrifice is enormous, people prefer it to the certain ruin of going to work in a plantation. "Me, I'll give you a goat," says one man. "I don't want your goat," replies the chief, who for a long time has had his eye on the wife of the wretched man.

Those who have managed to buy themselves out do not go free, not that easily, and not yet. Freedom is conditional, and the new condition is a stint in the head chief's plantation before they can be let go. As the "price of their freedom," they "spend between a fortnight and a month working in his own coffee plantations where they are locked up at night, are very poorly fed and are given a daily fee of 0.30 francs."

Meanwhile, the recruits who are being marched to the Office du Travail must go through a medical examination before they can be put to work. Like every other, this step in the recruit's journey is a minefield.

The doctor, if he is unscrupulous, sees all these terrified men arrive and says to himself: "The nurse can do this lot." What an opportunity for the nurses! For they too can say: "I'll pass you unfit if you give me a chicken." Another will be visited by a concubine who says: "This one's my brother. Don't take him. You can replace him with one of the sick men you have rejected."

Failing the medical, too, cannot provide instant relief. Those who failed "will be 'picked' after the medical, and instead of going home the men with rickets and hernia and the old man will go and work with the others who have bought back their freedom." This is how the head chief is "able to recruit his workforce as if it were a European plantation." But just in case one thinks this is the end of the saga, keep in mind the man who passes the medical and goes to work in the European plantation; he is told by the policeman under whose "watchful eye" he must work, "If you give me two francs, I'll replace you this evening with another." Sooner or later, every recruit must realize that he is caught in a Catch 22–type dilemma: without buying yourself out, you cannot escape the regime of forced labor in the European plantation, but if you buy yourself out, you cannot go free without a stint of labor in the chief's plantation.[36]

In the Portuguese colonies of Mozambique, Angola, and Guinea, too, obligatory labor (*xibalo*) on roads and harbors was combined with heavy taxes on the rural population, designed to force peasants to leave their lands and to work for the central state, the plantations, or individual settlers. The colony of Mozambique, for example, was divided into three regions: the south, the center, and the north. Over time, these came to coincide with three distinct economic zones: the north (Cabo Delgado, Niassa, and Nampula Provinces) a predominantly peasant economy; the center (Zambezia, Manica, Sofala, and Tete Provinces) a plantation economy; and the south (Inhambane, Gaza, and Maputo Provinces) a settler farm economy.

River Save, the dividing line between the south and the central regions, also marked the northern limit for legal recruitment of migrant labor for South African employers. Labor migration from Mozambique to the south began in the middle of the nineteenth century. Then it was a relatively minor affair, directed at first to meet the labor needs of Natal-based sugar plantations. But after 1897, labor migration became the subject of interstate agreements. The agreement of 1914 restricted the monopoly labor-recruiting organization, the Witwatersrand Native Labour Association (WENELA), to recruiting in the three provinces south of the River Save (parallel 22). Historically, the three southern provinces were nurtured as labor reserves, for both internal settler farms and for South African mines.

In exchange for hiring Mozambican workers on a large-scale and long-term basis, the Transvaal received access to the port of Maputo, which came to service its gold-centered mining and industrial complex. Portugal, in turn, collected an emigration tax on each migrant; in addition, one-third of a worker's salary was directly paid to the Portuguese state, which proceeded to double the hut tax, demanding that it be paid in sterling, and gave the remainder in local currency when the worker returned to Mozambique. Between 1908 and 1975, the annual recruitment of migrants from Mozambique fluctuated between a low of 74,000 and a high of 118,000.[37] These figures account for legal migration. There was also an illegal flow, substantial because it was attractive to both parties: the employer found it cheaper because he could evade taxes and formalities and in the bargain have extra control over workers, and the workers could choose their place of work and avoid administrative supervision. No one knows the exact size of this flow, but one scholar estimates that the numbers involved "may well have been as many as went through legal channels."[38] By the early 1970s, one out of every five adult male workers in the southern provinces was employed as a mine laborer in South Africa.[39]

To the north of the River Save, in central Mozambique, the Portuguese state leased out huge tracts of land to British, German, French, and Swiss concessionary companies, which established plantations for sisal, copra, sugar, and tea.[40] The concessions were made in the period of the Scramble, between 1888 and 1894. At a time when Portugal was claiming all of central Africa and was afraid of losing it, large-scale concessions provided a facade of effective occupation so as to hold on to as much of Africa as possible. The most successful and longest-lived of the concessionary companies was the Mozambique Company, controlled by British financial interests from the first decade of this century to 1941.[41] Withdrawing from all direct economic activity, the company became successful based mainly on its ability to supply contract labor to sub-concessionary employers. One statistic will suffice to illustrate how widespread the practice of contract labor was in areas under company control: an average of eighty-six thousand laborers were contracted between 1912 and 1916, amounting to "at least 25% of the population" of the area. The length of the contract was three months in 1917 but went up to six months a decade later.

In the first phase of Portuguese rule (1880–1926), the concessionary companies were given political and administrative powers in the central and the northern regions. These included powers to extract forced labor from the peasantry. With the installation of the fascist regime of Antonio Salazar in 1926 and a turn to economic nationalism, there was a marked shift in Portuguese policy. Foreign companies were henceforth restricted to the central region, but a concession still included control over labor supplies in the locality. As it assumed political and administrative powers that had previously been company prerogatives, the Salazar state introduced the forced cultivation of cotton in both the center and the north, mainly to supply raw materials for the expanding textile industry in Portugal. After 1930, the peasantry of the north was no longer a major source of labor for plantations in the center; I will later detail the regime of forced cotton cultivation that led to the development of a cash-cropping peasantry in the north.

The competition for labor intensified in the 1940s with the arrival of settler farmers. Unable to compete with wages offered by South African mines, settlers too came to depend on the provision of forced labor. The colonial state mediated the resulting contradiction by making a distinction between two forms of coerced labor, contract and *xibalo*: the former mainly for concessionary companies, the latter mainly for settlers. Unlike with contract workers, availing xibalo labor was the responsibility of the local state. Ex-*regulo* Edward Moses Timana described the system: "The *regulo* usually received a list handed down by the Administrator of Manhica with the number of men and women needed for *xibalo*. The demand varied from months to years. Although the list sometimes included labor for public works, more often in the case of Ilha Mariana, *xibalo* labor meant hard labor on private settler farms."[42] Officially, xibalo labor was defined as a six-month obligation to labor outside the family holding. To recruit this labor, the regulo was helped by native police known as *sipais*.

Although considered mainly a male obligation, women—held responsible for the forced cotton crop—were not always immune from it. When the shortage of labor was acute, as during harvest and weeding times, women too were roped in. Only those natives defined as evolved farmers—persons who could combine a minimum access to productive wealth with a connection to the regulo and the Portuguese administrator—were exempt from the demands of xibalo labor. Even though cross-border labor migrants were officially exempt from xibalo labor when they returned home between contracts, in practice this was not always honored. It was not unusual for migrants to reach home at the end of a contract, "only to spend the seven month period in the fields and swamps hiding from the *regulo* and the African police force, making it difficult for them to assist family farming."[43]

Contract work was stimulated by tax: it took an ordinary contract worker in the Inhambane District ninety-five days to earn the money with which to pay his annual tax in 1917. A person was free to contract an employer of his or her choice, but failure to do so opened the prospect of a forced contract, or worse still, "correctional labor": forced labor paid at a rate even lower than contract labor, meted out to all those who had committed an offense, such as "non-payment of taxes," "evasion of contract labor," or simple "vagrancy." On top of this, every person was liable to perform service for the central state, in public works, in the police, or as a carrier. The last was the most dangerous. For example, of the twenty-five thousand carriers recruited for the campaign against the Germans, only five thousand returned to their villages. When not in government service, an African had to carry a passbook (*cader-neta*), which recorded his labor and tax obligations. To move from the district, he needed both the permission of the chief and a passbook that was in order.

In all instances, the state provided the legal and institutional framework for forced labor.[44] The 1899 code held all Africans, male and female—except those under fourteen and the old—liable for work. The 1928 code introduced limits to the liability of women but specified that Africans had a "moral and legal obligation" to work. They could exercise a recognized trade or profession, "cultivate on their own account land of a specified extent," or contract themselves to an employer. Once in a while the central state introduced a law specifically designed to boost coercive practices under cover of legality. Thus, for example, decree no. 5076 of 20 March 1943 stated: "Any natives who have not paid taxes for any years up to the present must pay off the shortfall by means of corrective labor, in terms of the law currently in force."[45]

The differences between colonial powers stemmed both from the situation each faced on the ground and from the difference in the resources each could command. This latter fact clearly set the British, with a global imperial reach, apart from the rest. Faced with an acute labor shortage, the British could turn to a populous and older colony like India. "There can be no doubt," stated an official report on turn-of-the-century emigration from India, that "indentured immigration has rendered invaluable service to those of our colonies in which, on the emancipation of the Negro slaves, the sugar industry was threatened with ruin, or in which a supply of steady labor has been required for the development of the colony by methods of work to which the native population is averse."[46] The emigration of indentured Indian labor lasted for close to a century, roughly from 1840 to the 1920s. In the first phase, from 1842 to 1870, more than half a million indentured laborers were sent to various colonies, both British and French:

Mauritius	351,401	Other West Indian islands	7,021
British Guinea	79,691	Natal	6,448
Trinidad	42,519	French colonies	31,346
Jamaica	15,169		

These figures do not include the flow of indentured labor to the sugar plantations of Natal. That flow began in 1860, was suspended between 1866 and 1874 during the depression linked to the American Civil War, and was then resumed until 1911, when public protest in India led to its suspension.[47]

So pervasive was coercion in the colonies that even wage labor was framed by restrictive legislation, marking it semicoercive. In all British colonies, the central state regulated relations between employers and workers through local Masters and Servants Ordinances. Modeled on eighteenth-century British laws, these defined leaving or quitting work before the end of a contractually stipulated period as desertion, a punishable crime. In 1929, for example, the number of Africans charged and convicted in Kenya under the Masters and Servants (or similar) ordinances was higher than in any other British colony in equatorial Africa. In fact, the numbers of those charged were nearly three times, and those convicted nearly twice, the figures for Nyasaland, the colony second highest on the list.[48] The difference lay in the fact that Kenya was a settler colony in which the central state undertook to facilitate the labor requirements of local white employers—as it did in South Africa, and as did the French, the Portuguese and the Belgians for concessionary companies and settlers operating in their colonies. The system of labor recruitment and control in Kenya, argues Bruce Berman, "was probably the harshest of any British colony in West or East Africa."[49] A Native Registration Ordinance forced all African men between the ages of fifteen and forty to register with the administration and carry a passbook (*kipande*), which included space for employers to record the duration of employment, type of work, and wages received. The use of penal sanctions against the breach of labor contracts was upheld by all colonial governments. When a Labour Party government was in office, from 1929 to 1931, Lord Passfield (Sydney Webb) urged its abandonment. The response from the governments of east and central Africa was one of firm opposition; all of them considered penal sanctions essential to the maintenance of the labor force.[50]

How can one reconcile this state of affairs with the well-publicized fact that statutory forced labor was abolished, in British colonies after the First World War, in French colonies after the Second World War, and in Portuguese colonies in 1961? There were two reasons that coercion could continue as practice even if it was abolished by law. First, modern civil law in indirect rule colonies was presumed to apply to the domain of the modern civic power only, not to the customary practices of Native Authorities in the local state. In other words, so long as it was passed off as customary, the regime of force continued. Jean Suret-Canale quotes a cercle commander writing to the local magistrate on 12 January 1948, two years after the abolition of statute labor: "Subject: refusal to obey the canton chief. The accused [nine names follow] have refused to obey the canton chief of the village of N'Zapa (Guizima canton) who asked them to maintain and clear the paths. I shall be grateful if you will apply the sanctions provided in Articles 471 and 474 of the Penal Code for their opposition to duties involving the canton and its chiefs."[51] In other words, even if statute labor was abolished, the customary obligation to obey the chief was not.

Customary labor historically sanctioned by and undertaken for the village community—but now compulsory for the local authority—usually calculated as one day in a week, continued to be the practice in all colonies regardless of reforms in the modern law, and it continues to be the case today. In Zaire it goes by the name of *Salongo*. In Uganda it is called *Bulungi Bwansi*; in Ruanda, *Umugunda*; in Zambia, *Umulasa*; in Malawi, *Thangata*; and in Swaziland, *Imimemo*.

When an "emergency" struck—or when "development" so warranted—it was not unusual for Native Authorities to demand more than customary labor. In the Kilimanjaro district in the Tanganyika of 1930, a chief instructed a *baraza* (a large public gathering) that all males were "to go to Himo and dig the Himo irrigation channel," warning that if anyone failed to comply, "his goat would be taken, slaughtered and eaten by those who had done the work"; if a man had no goat, "he would get fifteen strokes in public."[52] In some places, as in other parts of Tanganyika, no such precolonial custom existed. In 1926, "after consultation with the elders of the various tribes living in Tanga District," the district commissioner informed his superior that "no native custom exists whereby any native can be required by tribal authorities to work without pay either in the maintenance of roads in his neighborhood, or in any other kind of work," since "the construction and maintenance of roads" were in the past "regarded as a menace to tribal safety," and yet such a "custom of unpaid road maintenance" was instituted by the Germans; since "this custom was a great benefit to all," he recommended that "it should be continued." Similarly, the district commissioner of the nearby district of Handeni recommended to his superior, this time in 1956, that the "Handeni Native Authority had decided to pass Rules" requiring that "all able-bodied men," excepting "persons in permanent and regular employment such as chiefs, teachers, personal servants, etc.," may be "called upon by their Native Authority to give up to thirty days free labor per year on essential public works which the Native Authority will be carrying out for the benefit of their people."[53]

Rarely did a countrywide statute from the central state stipulate forced labor as a requirement. The exceptions were to be found in settler colonies; for example, the Native Authority Ordinance in Kenya, which required every adult male to do six days of unpaid labor every three months.[54] The practice in nonsettler colonies was for forced labor to be the subject of Native Authority bylaws ("Rules"). From considering force an African custom, it was but a short step to considering Africans as accustomed to force—as, say, a European may be to reason. So prevalent was this notion that at times even a doctor, whose job it was to reduce human pain, took to force to secure compliance from patients, in the process consoling himself of its morality, since force would be applied by a customary authority with a traditional right to do so. Listen, for example, to a doctor who worked for the Huileries du Congo Belge in the "industrial villages" from 1927 to 1930: "When I felt that it was necessary to whip someone I ordered a native chief, a decorated chief, to do it because he had that right toward his subjects."[55]

The tendency was to work out a face-saving and conscience-soothing compromise between otherwise conflicting demands of morality and convention: force might be used if force was necessary, but it should be employed as far as possible by customary authorities, not white colonizers. "Let the Bour engage in whatever repression he judges necessary," the French governor counseled his field officers in Senegal, "but you will not accompany the Bour to Diohine when he goes there to punish his subjects."[56]

Second, the fact of compulsion was relativized by presenting the subject with a choice between two compulsions: forced labor and forced crops. Thus, when charges of "forced cultivation of cotton" in Uganda were laid before the London-appointed Ormsby-Gore Commission of 1925, the central state released a copy of the following telegram from its chief secretary to the provincial commissioner of Western Province to back up its claim that peasants grew cotton of their own free will:

> I am directed by the Governor that the line to be adopted is not one of definite pressure towards cotton production. Natives to be informed that three courses are open, cotton, labor for Government, labor for planters, but no attempt is to be made to induce them to choose any one in preference to the others. Only one thing to be made clear that they cannot be permitted to do nothing, and can be of no use to themselves or the country. Inform D. C. Mbarara accordingly.[57]

Unlike forced labor, the compulsion to grow crops was seldom the subject of international interest or debate. Yet it was widespread in the colonies. Forced crops need to be understood in the context of an agriculture from which surpluses have been constantly extracted but to which very little has been returned in the form of improved inputs, whether implements of labor, seeds, or fertilizers. The result is a simple arithmetical equation: to increase the agricultural surplus is simply to increase the input of labor in cultivation. In the short run, however, the quantum of peasant labor tended to be fixed, since the size of the peasant population was a given. Given this constraint, the only way to increase the production of export crops was to shift labor from producing food for local consumption to producing industrial crops for export. Not surprisingly, to effect this shift force was necessary. Once the application of force was successful and export production increased, however, there was just as sure a drop in food production. Sooner or later such a shift would register as famine. The colonial response, once again, was to apply force to effect a further shift: this time not from export to food production, but from protein-rich and labor-intensive food crops to high-starch but low-labor ones. The antidote to famine was generalized malnutrition! Once again, we can trace the overall regime of forced crops with examples from different countries.

The archtypical forced crop in the African colonies was no different from what it had been in the New World: king cotton. Branded on the popular imagination as the setting for New World slavery, the colonial cotton regime that followed the emancipation of slaves in the Americas was not of a remarkably different order. Thus, when the British devised a "Grow More Crops" campaign in Tanganyika in the midst of the Depression of the 1930s, this exhortation was accompanied by "considerable use of force": legal requirements about "minimum acreages of cotton to be cultivated" were backed up by "threats of conscription for those who could not pay tax."[58] During the same Depression, the governor of Nyasaland wrote the secretary for state "urging more punitive measures for breaching tobacco-growing regulations"; his argument was that "'obedience' needed to be enforced to ensure the 'moral development' of the growers." Two years later, in 1932, 227 peasants were imprisoned "for breaches of the tobacco and cotton uprooting rules."[59] "The amount of cotton produced in Upper Volta is in direct proportion to the amount of pressure put on the natives by the Administration," Robert Boussac, the renowned French industrialist, summed up as the gist of his colonial experience.[60] The proverb that condensed Victorian wisdom with regard to child-rearing, "Spare the rod and spoil the child," was also the dictum that guided official relations with the colonized peasantry. Along the way, there developed a corpus of state literature that lay blame for the low levels of production on the laziness of the African peasant, particularly the male, and the culture that encouraged it. To increase productive labor, a range of social rituals—from initiation rites to dances—were often circumscribed.

We have a remarkable record of the harsh cotton regime in the Belgian colony of Congo, in the words of a Belgian missionary who in 1943 lamented its effects to colonial officialdom. The cycle of forced labor begins with the distribution of cotton seed in October and November. To prepare the cotton field takes "heavy labour." The required amount of land must be brought under cultivation. But if there is "not enough land in cultivation" or if there are "some weeds in the field," the official response is "a violation, fine, jail, whip!!!"

> Cotton demands continuous maintenance because weeds grow quicker than cotton and woe to the Negro if his field is not neat; no more strolls and hunting parties, no more endless palavers at the chief's court, no more

palmwine drinking parties in which each family in turn invites everyone in, little clan feasts. . . . We have invented no better way of destroying native customs, a real taboo for the administration, than cotton.

The harvest begins in June and calls for "great care and constant presence": picked cotton "must be left out in the sun" in the village; a "little granary with a screen in front of pilings" must be built to store it; large baskets must be procured "to carry the cotton to market." The evenings too are busy, for the cotton must be cleaned, "dry leaves and other dirt must be removed, as must yellow capsules which did not fully ripen." To make sure the cultivator attends the market on days set in advance, "the police come to the village to alert people." Yet the officially set price in the market is low, "manifestly inadequate," for "in this forced culture, the black takes all the risks: drought (like this year), plant lice, caterpillars, insects, locusts, floods, poor land, the fluctuation of the world market, our savage has everything against him." But if one is to "fully explain the tendency to desert the village," one must take into account the entire regime of forced labor:

> Let us pass to the public works which the chiefship must carry out every year: keep the village clean, which in administrative terms means the clearing of grass, bushes and shrubs within 100 meters of the most distant habitation; clear the banks of any watercourse which goes through the village up to 100 meters above and below the village; construct and maintain a prison, clear the trails and local automobile roads, fix up the resthouse, construct one or more schools. All this is done before a large force of police who question the intentions of the person in energetic and unequivocal terms. . . . As we see, the native of the interior is badgered, those harsher would say, tracked down like an animal.[61]

Equally exceptional is the reply of the provincial commissioner, which gives us a rare glimpse into the levelheaded thinking of a white official of the local state, his freedom of action circumscribed by realities on the ground and orders from above. Rather than deny the facts of the case, the commissioner stresses the dual rationale behind the labor regime: first, that the cultivator has available at his disposal not only his own labor but that of the family, including "children from their 10th year"; and second, that even if "the native feels himself oppressed by a condition he does not understand," it is because "the charitable conditions" that underlie official motivation can become evident only through its "long-range effect." This latter explanation is worth reading in full:

> If we recall that our estimates of the time needed to carry out tasks [are] inspired by a normal schedule, but which is scarcely the custom of rural natives, if we consider that agriculture labour does not necessarily require

regularity, that there are empty periods when agricultural activities slow up, if we consider that outside the compulsory crops there are complementary food crops (manioc, sorgho, maize, millet, sweet potatoes, eleusine, beans), it is easy to understand that, in fact, the native is concerned with work almost the whole year and has only rare occasions to move around or to seek pleasures which once formed the essence of his existence. And when the missionary in the letter to which I alluded above says of compulsory crops "that they deprive the native of 11 months of liberty," excessive language is certainly evident, but the thought expressed means that the native is no longer to act as he wishes—that is to say, he sees himself more and more obliged to dismiss from his economic, domestic and social life whims, negligence, and improvidence, and to submit to more and more strict rules of order, perseverance and work. There is no doubt that the native feels himself oppressed by a condition he does not understand, of which he does not realize the charitable conditions or the long-range effect. But the way followed cannot be abandoned.

Cotton-purchasing zones had been organized in the Congo from the 1920s on. Each zone pitted a monopoly purchaser against tens of thousands of cultivators. The administration set the rules of the game, that is, the minimum price for the crop and the minimum area each cultivator had to work. This system was extended to palm fruits and rice in the 1930s. When European settlers took over African cooperative dairies in Oriental Province in a later period, it was also applied to milk products.

Cotton was not the only colonial crop. Others followed. Sometimes introduced as emergency measures in times of war or depression, they tended to come into general use in the period after. Such was the case with rubber quotas introduced in the French colonies just before the First World War.[62] The simplest way for distributing the quota was for the central state to apportion it to a cercle or a district, and then to leave it to the cercle commander to instruct and hold the canton chief responsible for fulfilling a given production target "under threat of prison or cancellation of their appointments." After the harvest, the produce was "often carried on men's heads over dozens if not hundreds of kilometers," weighed at the end of the journey, and paid "generally several times lower than the free market prices." André Gide cites the example of a subdivision in French Equatorial Africa in 1926, where the population was taxed ten tons of millet.[63] Not being growers of millet, they had to march three days and purchase it at double the market price.

The quota system was convenient and soon came into general use in the French colonies. It was applied to the compulsory cultivation of maize and cocoa-palm plantations introduced by Governor Angoulvant on the Lower Ivory Coast on the eve of the First World War. And so it was with cotton introduced by Eboue in Ubangi.[64] For those who failed to meet a quota, the "lesson" came inevitably "in the form of a fine, prison or strokes of the *manigolo*." For those who lived near the border of a different colonial power, there was an alternative beyond meeting a quota or learning a lesson for not doing so: to flee across the border. The most conservative estimate of the number of Mossi who fled forced cotton cultivation in Upper Volta, to the Gold Coast is one hundred thousand. It was estimated that in the years 1953–55 between three hundred thousand to four hundred thousand persons had fled from the inland French colonies of Niger, Upper Volta, and Mali to Ghana—and certainly many more to Nigeria—making up 40 percent of the labor force on plantations and 16 percent of the number of traders in the region.[65]

Whereas the British preferred to assign a compulsory quota (for example, an acre of cotton) to every peasant household and the French apportioned collective quotas pyramid fashion top down through a series of intermediaries, the Portuguese generally left it to the concession companies to supervise the quota system. Take the example of the Niassa Company in the northern region of Mozambique, a thinly populated area colonized only after the First World War. We have already seen that the peasantry of the north, like the one in the center, was subject to forced labor in company-owned plantations in central Mozambique in the first period of Portuguese rule. In the 1930s, the Portuguese introduced forced cotton cultivation throughout Mozambique. The system weighed particularly heavily on the northern region, where the cotton campaign was organized by the Niassa Company. In every locality, suitable land was selected, cleared, and demarcated into plots (*machambas*) for which a specified individual would be responsible. The plots were graded; in 1947, the largest one measured 1.2 hectares, and the smallest (to be worked by a woman over thirty-six years of age) 0.2 hectare. The cycle of planting cotton, weeding, and picking was "often supervised stage by stage by an official." It was estimated that in 1944, 791,000 people were involved in cotton growing alone in Mozambique. Many of them were likely to be women, since men would have been dragged off for xibalo (forced labor).[66]

The result of the shift from food to export crops was often an acute food shortage. Cotton in the company-organized machambas in Mozambique, for example, seems to have absorbed an average of 150 days in a year. The predictable result was periodic and devastating famines. Faced with this dilemma, officialdom tended to seek a solution through a further shift in the production plan of peasant households, once again by force, except this time from growing protein-rich and labor-intensive crops like simsim or millet to planting starch-filled and low-labor crops like cassava. This is why administrative decrees that specified the crops peasants must grow on how much land were not confined to export crops; they ranged from export to food crops. The same concession companies that organized compulsory cotton production in Mozambique also marked out machambas for food crops. The one reason they all had in common was the prevention of famine and thereby a crisis in export production.

This cycle can be traced in British colonies. As administrative pressure succeeded in increasing export production in the early decades of colonialism, there followed disastrous famines leading to major population losses. The pendulum then swung to the other extreme, as one colony after another instituted a food policy of "district self-sufficiency" combined with the compulsory cultivation and storage of "famine crops." The politics of "district food self-sufficiency" has been documented by Nyangabyaki Bazaara with respect to the district of Bunyoro in Uganda.[67] The point of food self-sufficiency was not to increase the level of food consumption to improve the health of producers; rather it was to even out periodic food shortages by cutting back on consumption in better times. "To meet the needs of any localized shortage," a conference of district commissioners in 1935 called for "communal granaries" to be set up. Regulations passed in 1946 required every household to set up "individual husband granaries." Chiefs were ordered to "stop all women from going to areas where economic crops are grown," for such a move "decreases food crops." "All women," the instructions continued, "must remain at their homes and grow much food crops." But the district commissioner was clear that the campaign to increase food production must be waged through "propaganda and education"; it must "on no account take the form of increased prices." But if increased food production was not to be a response to market incentives, it would have to be decreed administratively. Without higher incomes and improved technology, however, increased output could be obtained only by shifting to less labor intensive crops. That shift had become so commonplace by 1952 that even the District Team and Planning Committee noted that "the people of Bunyoro grew a larger and better variety of food crops 10 or 20 years ago than they do now."

Minimum-acreage laws for specified crops, food as well as export, were the usual stuff of direct administrative intervention in free peasant agriculture. Even though carefully supervised by an on-the-ground agent of the central state, such as the district commissioner, it was usually given legal effect by a Native Authority bylaw. Often the center did no more than suggest. It was left to the relevant Native Authority—and to the district commissioner under whose charge it operated—to translate a suggestion into specific rules. In December 1951, for example, the provincial commissioner in Tanga (Tanganyika) "suggested that Native

Authorities" might "require any person to cultivate land to such crops as will secure an adequate supply of food for the support of such person and those dependent upon him." A "Local Government Memo—1954" declared that whenever "there is or is likely to be such shortage of food" in an area, the relevant Native Authority may issue a bylaw "requiring any able-bodied male native to work on public works," including "irrigation works," or "to cultivate land . . . to such reasonable extent as the Native Authority may direct." The response of the Native Authority in the district (Handeni) was to pass a bylaw in 1956 requiring that "every house owner has to have one acre of cassava planted or two acres once a year of sorghum." Then it added: "He who fails to do so will have three months' imprisonment."[68]

One outcome of administrative coercion was that even the most technical of personnel in the local state tended to take on police duties. The *bwana shamba* (agricultural assistant) in colonial Tanganyika was more like a crop inspector who told peasants what, how, and when to grow on how much land. Similarly, the agricultural agents whose task it was to supervise the production cycle in industrial villages in interwar Belgian Congo were "inundated by circulars and letters" forever complaining about "the slow growth in production." They would "soon exhaust the legal means of forcing natives to work harder." The result: "The agricultural agent has become a policeman, fulfilling his duties without conviction and with resignation."[69] Not surprisingly, when anticolonial mobilization swept free peasant areas, it was seldom through agitation against the central state; its driving force everywhere was inevitably the outrage against administrative coercion by officials of the local state, whether the source of that fury was forced crops, forced labor, "betterment" policies like bench terracing or tie-ridging, cattle dipping, or destocking.

To preempt our discussion of the postindependence period, we may note that so long as forced crops remained a practice—as in Zaire, where the 1969 ordinance stipulated that peasant households cultivate a half-acre of cotton and another half-acre of cassava[70]—agricultural extension work remained more a matter of coercion than of persuasion. Two researchers in the Shaba copper belt of Zaire penned the following entries in their diary over a decade: "In one village a student reported that peasants consider the agricultural *moniteur* an agent of the police. Charged with agricultural surveillance, his visits result in fines. Peasants often flee when he appears in the village [1973]."[71] And then in 1983: "In 1979 an Agricultural Department official deplored this situation as a hindrance to agricultural development. Four years later, the policy was still in effect, but the official was gone." Across the border in Ruanda, the situation was hardly different.[72] For there, too, since colonial times, the agricultural extension officers (*moniteurs agricoles*) in the communes "enforced various rules regulating agricultural production: digging anti-erosion ditches on hillsides; proper planting and care of coffee trees; installation of compost piles; pruning of banana plantations." There, too, "anyone who ignores the regulations is subject to fines." Not surprisingly, "the population views the agricultural extension officer as a type of policeman."

Forced sales were often a corollary to forced crops, when grown for export. For example, complementary to the administrative compulsion to grow cotton was often its sale to a specified agency, whether a governmental or a private concession company. Perhaps the most elaborate supervisory arrangement devised for export crops was in French colonies with the spread of Sociétés Indégenes de Prevoyance (SIP, native provident societies) in the 1930s. The SIP operated under the ex-officio presidency of the local cercle commander. It was compulsory for peasant growers to pay membership dues to the SIP, which in turn advanced seeds to members at 25 percent interest, constructed wells and feeder roads, made loans, and during the Depression of the 1930s assumed responsibility for marketing their produce.[73] Compulsory sales of export crops became a general phenomenon in the British colonies following the Second World War, when statutory marketing boards were set up everywhere. Although justified as institutions designed to stabilize market prices for peasant growers by accumulating surpluses in good times and releasing them when prices were adverse, in practice these marketing boards functioned only to accumulate surpluses, paying growers consistently below the market price, whether the times were good or bad.[74]

A NOTE ON PASTORALISTS

The relationship between the state and pastoralists merits a separate note for one reason: the end result of compulsions for mobile pastoral populations has been so drastic as to destroy the very basis of a way of life. The African pastoralists are concentrated in arid and semiarid zones like the Sahel and Horn. In an ecological context where rainfall is not only low but also extremely unreliable—with its spread variable, usually concentrated into few rainy days—rain-fed agriculture becomes a high-risk activity. The mainstay of productive life is cattle keeping, for unlike crops, which cannot be moved except seasonally, it is possible for herds and herders to move in search of water and pastures.

Pastoral populations range from nomads to transhumants. Whereas nomads have no permanent settlement at all, with the entire family moving all the time, transhumants combine a permanent settlement with mobile cattle camps. The herds in the cattle camp are the backbone of the economy of transhumants, whereas the crop cultivated in the settlements is its necessary complement.[75] Mobility allowed pastoralists access to short-term grasses while conserving wetter, longer-term pastures for the drier season. Pastoral boundaries were thus more ecological than physical, more flexible than fixed. Mobility was the precondition not only for the optimal utilization of resources, but also for their optimal conservation. It was central to the sustainability of a nondestructive pastoralism.

I will take the example of one particular population of pastoralists, the mainly transhumant Karimojong of northeastern Uganda, to illustrate how the imposition of a regime of compulsions eroded the basis of an entire way of life in a few decades.[76] Redrawing of boundaries leading to loss of pastures, administrative restrictions on mobility, and confiscation of stock were the three dimensions of an official policy that spelled disaster for pastoralism as a nondestructive way of life. Between 1920 and 1940, herders in Karamoja lost about 15 percent of grazing land to fellow pastoralists in Kenya—whose more fertile pastures had been transferred to white settlers—as a result of an official redrawing of external boundaries.[77] Internal boundaries were also redrawn during that same period: on the one hand, district boundaries were redefined to transfer dry-season pastures to surrounding agropastoral populations (Teso and Lango); on the other hand, a clear separation was made between counties inside Karamoja. Border areas between counties were declared no-man's-land, a *cordon sanitaire*, as each "tribe" was allocated a county and asked to stay put in it.

The final object of official policy was to "resettle" pastoralists, really to convert them into agropastoralists, to pin them to the ground in the interest of maintaining law and order and ensuring an efficient collection of taxes. A new system of administration, comprising a hierarchy of chiefs, was put in place to implement this policy. Confronted with a social order marked by strong community traditions and community sanctions over decision makers (elders), the colonial power showed a marked preference for appointing marginal men, usually from outside the district, as chiefs. Laws were passed—the 1908 Native Courts Ordinance and the 1919 Native Authorities Ordinance—to give these chiefs a wide range of powers. A chief was not just a civil servant charged with implementing policy. He now had the power to make bylaws affecting "his" people. He also chaired the clan court, which had the power to impose penalties of up to two months' imprisonment. In sharp contrast to the socially defined position of elders, these new functionaries of the colonial order were unchallengeable from below. By 1919 the chiefs had managed to press into forced labor 40 percent of the adult male population of the district![78] It is these chiefs who were ordered by the district commissioner in 1920 to ensure that at least half the adult male population would reside in permanent settlements at any one time to provide an adequate source of labor for the government.

The policy hit so directly at the heart of the pastoral economy that it evoked widespread popular resistance. The high point of that resistance was the killing of a number of chiefs who had shown notable zeal in its implementation. Soon the policy was in shambles, but official efforts to contain pastoralists within fixed and ever-narrowing boundaries—now reinforced by a host of measures to quarantine cattle—continued. The cumulative result was to erode the mobility necessary for a nondestructive pastoralism.

By the 1930s evidence was beginning to pour in of sharp ecological decline as herders grazed their cattle on diminishing pastures. The official response was dual: on one hand, to alienate communities permanently from those natural resources most ecologically threatened; on the other hand, to reduce forcibly the stock of herds. The 1940s were a decade of demarcating forests as reserves, and the 1950s of setting apart game land as reserves. Attempts to reduce the numbers of cattle ranged from establishing official markets where prices were set to flush a specified number of cattle out of pastoral kraals to destocking campaigns and outright plunder whereby female cattle were openly confiscated.

Denied access to natural resources on which historically they had depended for their livelihood—an access they had come to regard as a historical right—communities responded with short-run "survival strategies" that amounted to no more than a plunder of these resources to meet immediate needs: cutting down forests, abandoning practices that allowed seasonal pastures to rest, and instead grazing them across seasons. Once the relationship between communities and surrounding resources was reversed—from custodianship to alienation—the stage was set for a real "tragedy of the commons." But even when the crisis was at its sharpest, pastoralists never formed a single, homogenous mass of victims. Alongside those who resorted to survival strategies faced with an onslaught of compulsions, and finally outright state terror, there was always a minority, however tiny, that turned this same survival impulse of the majority into an opportunity for enrichment. So developed the accumulation strategies of those few who, under cover of the same regime of state terror, offered safety and livelihood to many in return for a combination of services on the grazing ground and the battlefield. These services allowed them simultaneously to raid, graze, and trade, with neighbors and with the forces of the regime. Thus emerged, alongside consensus building by elders characteristic of pastoral communities, a regime of fire and brimstone organized by competing youthful warlords and camp commanders.[79]

CHANGES IN THE CUSTOMARY

The customary was not opaque but porous, not stagnant but dynamic. In spite of the solidity of the Native Authorities and the reinforcing power of the central state, both the dynamism of the market economy and the organized activities of diverse social strata gave the customary a fluid content. However, it is also true that so long as the customary form remained in place, it affected the operation of the market and the initiative of social forces while containing both within a customarily given tribal mold.

Because land was considered a tribal asset and access to it a customary right confined to members of the tribe, the first group of persons subject to a levy in return for the right to use land—no matter how temporarily—were migrant farmers, dubbed strangers. In customary Africa, land may not be bought, but it may be borrowed. Its ownership may not change hands, but its possession can. A practice that began with strangers, borrowing was easily extended to poorer members of the community as the population increased and internal differentiation developed.

Although the extent of these practices is difficult to quantify, a number of village-level surveys continue to document their prevalence and growth. Strangers in the Gold Coast were expected to make annual payments (*isikole*) to the chief and to the family from whom they borrowed land.[80] Polly Hill's studies of cocoa farmers in southern Ghana identified three types of strangers: two of these, the patrilineal and the matrilineal "stranger-farmers," were migrants.[81] Mosi migrants from the central plateau of Bourkina Faso were the largest group of strangers farming borrowed land in West Bourkina.[82]

A field study in the peanut basin of Senegal showed that legal prohibition of private land transactions notwithstanding, "there was a high incidence of borrowing and lending of land."[83] Borrowing was but the starting point in a process with multiple possibilities. "Share-cropping," argues a recent field study from Lesotho, has been "a common feature of agriculture in Lesotho for many decades" and "appears on the way to becoming a commonplace farming strategy."[84] In colonial Kilimanjaro, a farmer may have been unable to sell a title to land, but that did not prevent the transfer of possession for a fee.[85] "The circulation of land via borrowing, inheritance, leasing and pledging," concludes a recent collection entitled *Land in African Agrarian Systems*, "is a key characteristic of flexible indigenous tenure systems."[86]

The impact of customary relations on accumulation was contradictory. Inasmuch as it restricted access to strangers and accumulation by them, the customary facilitated the same by kith and kin. Take, for example, the 1975 Land Reform Decree introduced by the Amin regime in Uganda. Claiming to reform the customary in the interest of development, the decree introduced leasehold tenure for those pursuing development, a claim that had to be ratified by district land committees usually made up of local notables. The result was a mishmash of the customary and the leasehold: leases could be granted on large tracts of land, even hundreds of acres, to those who could establish a customary link to the land in question! With a customarily restricted access substituting for a market transaction, the land title was a usurpation for the peasants displaced from it and a steal for the new owner.

Yet the customary form was not simply a mask without relevance. Even if customary ownership did not prevent the transfer of right of use, it did hinder full-scale privatization by lending justification to multiple rights in land. Where land rights could be sold, so long as land was considered a tribal asset, migrant rights remained insecure and migrant populations highly vulnerable. Undergirded by short-run political alliances, property rights remained susceptible to a shift in alliances.

The changing content of the customary made for shifting social attitudes to the customary over time. Initially, the powerful, like chiefs, stood for customary tenure; after all, it gave them the right to allocate land for use. In Kilimanjaro in the late 1920s, chiefs viewed any land transfers as a threat to their own powers but then learned to swim with the tide, demanding that all transfers be approved by them to be considered official. Not surprisingly, approval required a gift of gratitude.[87] However, as the weight of market relations increased, the customary turned into a last line of defense for those on the verge of destitution. "With the commercialization of agriculture," concludes Martin Chanock in a recent survey, "communalism became the rallying point of the economically weak, and was assaulted by the powerful and the development-minded."[88]

But the division in attitudes was not simply between the weak and the strong, or the poor and the rich. It also cut through the poor, separating those who belonged to the tribe from strangers, and often men from women within the same tribe. If migrant laborers saw in the customary their strongest hope for holding on to a land parcel in the home village, so did those land-rich who hoped to retrieve borrowed land from stranger-farmers. Migrant farmers and women often stood out as victims of customary claims: if migrant farmers were rendered perpetually insecure by customary notions of land rights which defined them as strangers in a village, so were women when faced with a patriarchally constructed notion of tradition.[89] The division, sometimes on a class basis, occurred just as often along ethnic and gender lines.

POSTINDEPENDENCE RESONANCES: SWAZILAND AND TANZANIA

By the late fifties, a conference organized by the British Colonial Office on African land tenure acknowledged the existence of "landlord/tenant relationships" in the African colonies, varying in character "from informal 'borrowing' as, for example, in parts of Tanganyika, through share-cropping agreements to much more sophisticated arrangements with written 'leases,' which are virtually indistinguishable from English lease-holds and which are of frequent occurrence in part of West Africa." Yet the same conference one-sidedly resolved that "the traditional systems of land tenure and agricultural practice tended to be static," so that with "the introduction of cash crops" these systems "restrict economic development."[90]

In its postwar reform phase, colonial strategy cast the customary as antithetical to development. If tradition was backwardness, then development would have to be induced from without, or at least from above. The two moments of colonial ideology, defense of custom at the point of its consolidation and the promise of development at its point of crisis, were reproduced as separate and contrasting discourses by two varieties of postindependence African governments: one conservative, the other radical. Whereas the former sought to conserve an already-gelled apparatus of force—the Native Authorities—in the name of upholding custom, the latter sought to reform that apparatus so as to remove backwardness and fight tribalism, all in the name of development. The conservative variant reproduced the decentralized despotism character-istic of the colonial state, and the radical reform tended toward centralization. Initially premised on a political—and therefore voluntary—mobilization, this attempt at reform soon degenerated into a set of administrative decrees. In the process, this attempt to set into motion a "revolution from above" built on another colonial tradition: administrative justice and fused power. In spite of sharply contrasting self-images and environmental influences, each built on one strand from a common historical legacy, and each was best comprehensible as one distinctive outcome of that legacy. I will briefly illustrate this dual legacy within a shared colonial context through two brief postcolonial examples: Swaziland and Tanzania.

The proliferation of a regime of forced compulsions is brought out in several studies on Swaziland and is worthy of detailed consideration.[91] The discovery of huge gold deposits in the Transvaal, including the eastern areas bordering Swaziland, brought a swarm of speculators into the country in the final quarter of the nineteenth century. Transvaal's fertile soil and rich pastures also attracted settlers who sought land concessions from the Swazi aristocracy, which was all too willing to grant these in return for monetary gain. Between 1885 and 1889, practically the whole country had been concessioned away. Such was the background to its formal annexation by the South African Republic (Transvaal) in 1894. Boer rule was short lived, however. Following the Anglo-Boer war, Swaziland became a British protectorate. In the face of growing protest against land concessions, British authorities issued in 1904 a proclamation (no. 3) intending to "delimit land for sole occupation by the Swazi." In practice, however, the delimitation turned out to be more a recognition of land appropriated by the concessioners than its reappropriation and return to Swazis; in the ensuing 1914 partition, two-thirds of the concessions were converted into freehold, and only one-third were returned! Such a drastic loss turned land into a scarce factor and was decisive in the shift from cattle (bridewealth) to land as the basis of chiefly power. It was also a key catalyst to labor migration.

The response of the Swazi aristocracy was twofold: to plead with British authorities for a revision of the land partition, and to extort funds from the peasantry for a repurchase of appropriated lands. It is the latter strategy and its consequence that are of interest to our query. The Swazi aristocracy soon discovered a common interest with the colonial state in promoting the flow of labor migrants to South African mines. While the colonial state restructured its tax-collecting apparatus and stiffened the prosecution of defaulters, the Swazi Royal House set its own levy on each migrant, amounting to a neat one-quarter of the annual mining wage.[92] Citing the need for cash to buy back ceded lands, the king substituted money for the traditional labor gatherings (*imimemo*) when peasants were required to plow, plant, weed, and reap the harvest to be set aside for official visitors. Soon chiefs followed suit, demanding that peasants wanting access to land pay cash or cattle as "*Khonta* fees" (*kukhonta* refers to the process whereby peasants used to pledge allegiance to a chief to get access to land).[93] Soon levy followed upon levy. Forced contributions were now justified by a range of objectives: from building and maintaining schools to civics to other state facilities.[94] Newspapers reported threats from chiefs that failure to pay up would result in confiscation of cattle.[95]

The original levy had been justified as a continuation of *siswati*, the customary way, transmuted from labor to cash because of the need to buy back ceded lands; but tribute labor could not customarily be used for private gain. When asked by a researcher whether this was siswati, peasants responded by saying: "This is the custom today, though not in the past."[96]

Once the Native Administration Act of 1950 had formalized the powers of the monarchy and the chieftaincy, the repurchased lands were "allocated at the whim of the king."[97] Furthermore, a developmental initiative—institutionalized in the post–World War II period as the *Tinkhundula* system—not only restored tribute labor, but also substantially removed it from the control of the chief to that of the king's appointees. The *emasosha* (soldiers) age group in each tinkhundula (a cluster of villages) were "given a field to cultivate." The king appointed an *indvuna* (a chief) to run an *inkhundula*, and the indvuna was now empowered "to extract surplus labor from the chiefdoms attached to his *inkhundula*."[98] A field survey carried out in 1990 illustrated how strongly chiefship had been reinforced as a customary institution since 1950: "Almost all" Swazis who had access to land "render tribute to the chief where their fathers lived, though only half keep a house on nation land and only 17% live there exclusively."[99]

When contracted by the Swazi state to review the future of traditional land tenure, a South African social scientist recommended that it be maintained at all costs.[100] "The right to grant or withhold access to the Right of Avail," he pointed out, "obviously confers a considerable amount of political power on any individual or group that can exercise it." No doubt, "Swazi are well aware of this intimate connection between the control over land allocation by traditional authorities" and "the whole indigenous system of social control." Many are aware that "any change towards a system of more individualized tenure" would "inevitably result in a complete breakdown of the whole existing social order." Asked to contemplate what would happen "if individualized tenure were to be introduced," one Swazi observer had no doubt that "there would, in fact, be no need of chiefs and *indvunas*."

If Swaziland reproduced the colonial legacy proper, the Tanzanian experience was anchored more in the post–World War II legacy of colonial reform. If the former was a regime of compulsions highlighted as customary, the latter ended up justifying compulsion as a development imperative. The difference between them was within a shared framework, one of despotism, decentralized in the former case, centralized in the latter. To understand the centralized despotism that the Tanzanian experience turned into we need to bear in mind that it was the bitter fruit of a failed reform. No doubt the "developmentalist" text drew its inspiration from various and diverse sources, not least of which was Soviet-style "revolution from above."[101] My purpose, however, is to highlight its historical context and thereby to anchor shifts in ideology and perspective to a changing context.

To argue that force was characteristic of colonial administrative policy at all times would be to present a flat and one-dimensional picture. In the face of popular opposition, swings in policy were inevitable. This was as true of the colonial period as it was of the period after independence. As the colonial state sought to broaden the social base for reform in the face of nationalist agitation, the pendulum swung from administrative coercion to market incentives. In social terms, this represented a shift in accent from the mass of the rural poor to rich peasants, the so-called progressive farmers. Promising in 1957 that "the era of the big stick was over," the director of agriculture instructed his staff to "stop harassing common peasants" and instead "to persuade 'progressive farmers' to improve their operations," even if regretting that "it would take some time to reorient the agricultural staff towards new methods."[102]

But rich peasants could not be invented where they did not exist or were few in numbers. In less than a year after independence, the pendulum returned from "persuasion" for rich peasants to administrative coercion for the rural poor.[103] At a meeting of all district commissioners in Tanga Region in March 1962, the regional commissioner "felt that if the people failed to respond to persuasion and exhortation it might be necessary to resort to coercion." That same year in July, the Handeni District Council passed a resolution to the effect that "any person not participating in development projects should be punished by six strokes." Later in October, a government circular noted "that since some people were not adequately involved in farming, the central government had decided that the district councils should have by-laws by which these people would be forced to farm." The central government provided district councils with a model bylaw, which stated: "Any person who contravenes or fails to comply with the provision of these by-laws shall be guilty of an offence and shall be liable on conviction to a fine not exceeding five hundred shillings or to imprisonment for a term not exceeding six months or to both such fine and imprisonment." By March 1967, twenty out of fifty-eight district councils had bylaws requiring cultivation of one acre of a cash crop and one acre of a food crop. One bylaw even required "that during the planting season everyone should be in the fields from 10:00 A.M. till 2 P.M." Another local government circular, dated August 1967 and titled "Enforcement of By-laws," stepped up the emphasis on coercion for development: "The Ministry of Home Affairs has now agreed that enforcement of Local Authority By-laws is the concern of the police just as much as is the enforcement of any other part of the written law of the republic, and that the police will take an active part in enforcing them."

Two studies of Handeni District in Tanga Region, by Ingle and von Freyhold, cover the period from independence to the Arusha Declaration and *Ujamaa Vijijjini* in the late 1960s to the "villagization" of the late 1970s and give an idea of how central government directives percolated to the ground level. Besides the requirement that individual households cultivate a fixed quota of food and export crop, Handeni District set up block farms as part of its development effort. In a block farm, peasants worked communally and were paid communally. Block farms covered both cash and food crops; in 1965–66 the emphasis was on block cotton farms; in 1967–68 it shifted to block cassava farms. The whole administration of the party-state got in gear to realize this development effort. Even "contingents of national police" were brought in "with equipment that allowed them to move freely and rapidly throughout the countryside" (Ingle). On his part, the area commissioner made use of the forty-eight-hour detention power to discipline "the more outspoken opponents."

And opposition there was; according to Ingle, it was "fairly widespread but inarticulate." Among the more revealing protests was an anonymous letter sent to all civil servants, cell leaders, and agricultural field assistants in one ward in Handeni District. Its subject was the block farm.

> First, you never remember the problem of hunger. . . . It is three-and-a-half miles to the farm of three acres, one acre being for the wife. Try to consider at what time shall we cultivate maize? The wife has three children, only two of whom can walk. Now, when will she walk to the farm? Isn't this development plan causing hunger? It is sad that . . . there have been two people taken away, who are youths.
>
> Agricultural field assistant take care of your job. It is not just for you to go all around in the villages chasing people in their farms where they obtain their livelihood, and sending them to the roads arranging them as rail lines. I have more to say but we are citizens of Handeni. We are very sorry, therefore Agricultural Field Assistant ——, Agricultural Field Assistant ——, and the VEO and cell leaders, you take unjust action. If you are tired of your job, you better retire. It is unjust to force people to farm, farming is done willingly. As in relieving oneself, one is never forced, it would be a wonder if a person had to be told to go to the WC [toilet].
>
> Send this letter anywhere in Handeni. I am sorry the paper is small and insufficient I have much to say.[104]

The letter was delivered to the district commissioner, but no action was taken. Development continued as a priority, with force as its midwife. In the words of the regional commissioner of Tanga, speaking to a 1967 meeting of district councils, "The time of persuading citizens to work for their own benefit is finished. It's necessary from now to enforce them to work hard." Closer to the ground, a divisional executive officer told a women's self-help group in 1968: "What is necessary to get you to work in development projects? Do we have to bring the *kiboko* [an infamous rhinoceros-hide whip used since the Germans]?" Decreeing in a similar vein that henceforth "people would have to work every Saturday on a road construction project," a community development officer introduced himself as follows:

> I am new to this area, so it will be useful if I tell you something of my character. I am not a kind and polite man: I am cruel! If I see that government orders are not obeyed, I will know where to find you, and how to punish you. I do not care if you hate me, for me it is only important that the orders of the government are fulfilled. I know you are truly blind otherwise you would have appreciated more the progress that staff have brought to Bulumbia. Now we are going to make you rise from a long sleep. I have a strong medicine for this job, we will give it to all lazy people. It is better than the poison which you use when you want to kill somebody.[105]

In the decade that followed the proclamation of the Arusha Declaration in 1967, the local state resurfaced as the true locus of on-the-ground coercion. How effective decentralized coercion could be in a postcolonial state is illustrated by a glance at the transition from "ujamaa" to "villagization" in rural Tanzania. In 1967 a local government circular confirmed that the police would henceforth take an active part in enforcing local-authority bylaws, which was easier said than done, for there were hardly any police in the rural areas. A regional or area commissioner could exercise the option of calling upon the "field force," a special riot police, but this was not a realistic possibility at the village level. Yet even if without police, a village was sure to have a TANU Youth League (TYL) branch with many of its members drawn from frustrated local youth. The TYL was used in 1967–68 to administer the right dose of coercion so that the first ujamaa villages could be set up in Handeni District. Von Freyhold describes a typical operation.

> A house would be built in the village and as soon as at least one room was finished, a lorry would be brought from the district council, filled with TYL members and driven to a house in a traditional hamlet. The owner and all his belongings would be shifted to the Ujamaa village. . . . Some of the people who were moved into the Ujamaa village in this manner would leave after only a night, but most decided to remain to avoid any further trouble. During this period a security committee was formed. One of its tasks was to report those who openly criticized this manner of recruitment into Ujamaa.[106]

The interesting point is that the authorities at the center of the party-state resisted this trend to coercion once they got to know that the field force had been brought in to coerce peasants to move into ujamaa villages. The central committee of the party called a halt to all use of force in implementing ujamaa. By the middle of 1969, most of those responsible for the use of force had been transferred. The period after shows the return of initiative from party to state and central to local authorities as peasants resisted persuasion. At first village authorities used administrative pressure, short of outright violence. Even though the local rate had been abolished, it was announced that tax arrears would be collected—but only from those who had not moved into ujamaa villages. In some cases, extensive land rights were granted to residents of ujamaa villages only, thereby turning outsiders into squatters. Yet another way to increase pressure was to channel aid—usually medicine or water—selectively only to those in ujamaa villages. Matters got more serious when famine intervened, and famine relief was selectively distributed only to residents of ujamaa villages. One villager summed up the new situation: "Originally *Ujamaa* was only the policy of the Party and very few people followed. But now the Party, government and even God who sent the famine are all backing *Ujamaa*. So those outsiders have no chance of escaping *Ujamaa*."[107]

The lessons learned in Handeni District in 1968 were put to country-wide use between 1972 and 1975. Before that could be done, the district-level state apparatuses were strengthened through an ambitious "decentralization" program. Beginning with the creation of village-based militia in 1971, senior officials were "decentralized" to regions and districts. A similar reorganization of the party created a strong and well-paid party bureaucracy at the regional, district, divisional, and even ward level. Appointed by district officials, the party official "responsible for about 2000 households earned the salary of a primary school headmaster, and was far more influential than the (elected) chairman of any of the villages in his area."[108] Militia groups "were usually headed by army officers and their core normally consisted of government staff including messengers and craftsmen employed by the administration and frustrated rural youth who longed for jobs and status and to whom free uniforms and meals and the excitement of para-military campaigns were a welcome break in their wretched life in the villages." In many places, "they obviously functioned in much the same way as TYL groups had functioned in some parts of Handeni in 1968."[109] Together, the officials of the party and the local militia moved swiftly into action to execute the forced villagization of 1972–75. Report after report talked of instances like in Morogoro, where peasants were "bundled into the (army) lorries and dumped" at new ujamaa sites, or Iringa, where officialdom tried "to assure that people remained in the new villages" by making their former houses "uninhabitable by ripping out doors and windows and knocking holes in the mud walls or by setting fire to the thatch roofs," or Mara, where to be "mobilized" was to be "ill-treated, harassed, punished."[110]

What lessons can we draw from the Tanzanian experience? Does the prevalence of coercion mean that there was no significant difference between the Tanzanian and the Swazi experiences? Was the emphasis on making development—as opposed to enforcing custom—merely rhetorical? I do not think so. The Tanzanian experience was first and foremost an attempt at a reform of the bifurcated state, at linking the rural and the urban, through the apparatus of the party. When this attempt to develop through persuasion (ujamaa) failed, persuasion gave way to coercion, and the link hitherto made through the party gave way to one effected through the state bureaucracy. The Tanzanian decentralization of the mid-1970s was in effect a centralization: it decentralized officials from the central to the local state. As the state bureaucracy prevailed over party officialdom, ideology and persuasion gave way to administrative coercion and outright violence. The failed effort at development from above degenerated into extra-economic coercion.

A not very different trajectory unfolded in Mozambique over the next decade. The more Frelimo pursued a strategy of revolution from above, the more it was compelled to rely on administrative coercion and the more its policies came to resemble those of an earlier era. The deputy minister of the Family and Cooperative Sector specified the crops the cooperatives must grow; in one such instance, the minister ruled that "it was obligatory for each cooperative to grow cassava and sweet potato."[111] As state farms were established in the Limpopo Valley, the government not only took over abandoned Portuguese farms, but also appropriated peasant landholdings. Instead of receiving back the land that had originally been taken from them by settlers, the poor and middle peasants of the area found themselves ousted from their remaining holdings, only to become laborers and tractor drivers on land that had previously been theirs![112] In what must indeed have been a bizarre replay of events, forced labor reappeared as compulsory "voluntary seasonal labor" on state farms.[113] The more this practice was used to feed state and communal farms, the more it took on features characteristic of company plantations and settler farms in the Portuguese era.

"A main task of the party in the economic field," declared the Third Congress of Frelimo in 1977, must be "to promote and develop the communal villages . . . based on collective production that we aim to install in our country." As with ujamaa in Tanzania, the earlier communal villages were the result of voluntary effort; but with the limits of persuasion reached, the state sector moved on to coercion. So when the Limpopo and Incomati Rivers flooded in 1977 and 1978, displaced families were forcibly settled in communal villages in Maputo and Gaza Provinces, kept from returning from their farms afterward, and compelled to provide labor to adjacent state farms and cooperatives.[114] When "dissatisfied peasants" began to run away from these administratively established communal villages, representatives of the party-state initially "tr[ied] to establish compromises with the peasants." But when compromise would not work and peasants kept leaving as and when opportunity presented itself, Frelimo officials described the situation in the clinical language of officialdom: as a persistent "disaggregation" problem. These same officials then concluded that they had no choice but to take "recourse to force as an ultimate reaction."[115] The growing regime of coercion was dramatically illustrated with the mounting of a program of forcible population removal from urban areas in June 1983. Known as Operation Production, this program targeted the youth from the southern provinces—those who previously would have migrated to South African mines for paychecks to supplement meager farm earnings but now had to look for that same supplement in Mozambican cities to the north—and forcibly removed them to the countryside, "where they were supposed to work at state farms or cooperatives."[116]

MARKETS AND COMPULSIONS: A SUM-UP

The significance of extra-economic coercion—as of the market—is different for different strata of cultivators and herders. In a field research I carried out in a village in northern Uganda in 1984,[117] I carefully counted the number of hours a poor peasant household loses as a result of compulsions. It came to 15 percent of an average family's laboring time. The corresponding figure for middle peasant households was roughly 10 percent of family labor time, but for rich peasants it was of nominal significance when counted as a percent of labor time at the disposal of the family. As with any uniform tax on a population divided into strata or classes, the effect of the same compulsion on peasant households of different strata is necessarily regressive. But even where direct economic gain from a regime of compulsions may be nominal, its political significance needs to be kept in sight: every time such a demand is made and conceded, it turns into yet another affirmation of power relations on the ground.

The significance of market and nonmarket relations is not just different but actually contrary for the opposite ends of the differentiated spectrum that is the peasantry. The primary problem for the rich peasantry is agricultural prices in the market; for the poor peasantry, the main problem is a regime of compulsions at the local level. The same policy can therefore have a contrary significance for one as opposed to the other. Take, for example, the standard policy reform that accompanies Structural Adjustment Programs (SAP). Although it may give better prices to rich peasants in the market, it reduces the budget of local administrations and intensifies the regime of compulsions that squeezes the rural poor. In this context, privatization and democratization do not mean the same thing. Privatization in fact takes place at the expense of the rural poor. Rich peasant interests are better summed up in the demand for privatization, whereas poor peasant grievances can be addressed only by a broader movement toward democratization.

It would be a mistake to think of the relationship of markets and compulsions as one-way and unilinear, that over time the weight of market relations increases and that of compulsions declines. Markets often develop in a customary fashion: you may be able to sell a usufruct right in land, but only to a fellow tribesperson. Conversely, strangers may borrow land from landlords, who in turn will count on their customary right to take land back from strangers. So long as force is customarily able to intervene directly in the process of accumulation instead of simply undergirding the legal framework that enables it, it will make sense to invest resources in political relations alongside productive activities.[118]

My claim is not that the weight of extra-economic relations is as significant today as it was in the pre–Second World War period or that it is evenly spread throughout the continent. Far from it. In tracing the historical development of these contradictory relations, markets, and compulsions, my purpose is to highlight the context within which a particular form of power—the indirect rule apparatus of customary power—was forged. It is also to underline the fact that in this form of power market and force are not always contradictory constructs. The fact that the specific context can help us make sense of a particular form of power does not mean that the form of power cannot survive a change in context. For, clearly, the context has changed—markets have both expanded and deepened over this century—but the apparatus of compulsion has not withered away in response. Power does not self-destruct. Its tendency is to adapt to a changing context and simultaneously to try to shape it. The reform of political power requires an explicitly political reform. Only crude economic determinists can hope that market reform will automatically translate into a democratic reform. In underlining the decentralized despotism that was forged in the colonial period, my point is to pose the question of political reform.

Part Two

THE ANATOMY OF RESISTANCE

CHAPTER SIX

The Other Face of Tribalism:
Peasant Movements in Equatorial Africa

I HAVE ARGUED that there was a real internal difference between civil power over citizens and customary power over free peasants. That difference turned more on the political than on the economic. It was not a difference between capitalist and precapitalist or market and premarket formations. The free peasantry lives neither outside market relations nor simply within it. It lives, rather, on the interstices of the market and direct compulsions. The internal difference between civil society and the free peasantry, however, lay in the mode of rule characteristic of each: whereas civil society was governed directly by a civil power enforcing a civil law claiming to guarantee rights, the free peasantry was ruled indirectly through Native Authorities whose claim was to enforce custom through a customary law.

The claim to legitimacy of customary law was that it was tribal law, and of customary authorities that they were the tribal authorities administering tribal law. Tribalism then was the very form that colonial rule took within the local state. At the same time, the revolt against indirect rule also took a tribal form. For a revolt aimed against indirect rule authority was inevitably confined to its parameters. A democratic struggle against the authorities of the local state had to take the form of a civil war within the tribe, and so it did everywhere. The customary form of the local state made for a simultaneous reproduction of ethnic identities in the tribally based system of decentralized despotism and for their blowing up from within. My point is that modern tribalism has to be understood not only as a historical phenomenon, but also as one that is contradictory. It signifies both the form of rule and the form of revolt against it. Whereas the former is oppressive, the latter *may be* emancipatory.

An internal civil war, however, cannot exhaustively explain the phenomenon usually referred to as tribalism, for we all know that media references to tribalism accent more the interethnic than the intraethnic, the conflict between tribes and not that within a tribe. My point is not to deny the existence of the former, but to claim that the nature of conflict between ethnic groups in the larger polity is difficult to grasp unless we relate it to the conflict within a tribe. Without that connection, we will be left with no more than a tautology: different tribes fight because they are different.

Two clues can help us break out of this tautology and make that connection. Both are social effects of the customary. We saw in the last chapter how state enforcement tended to rob custom of its diversity, homogenize it, and equate it with the boundaries of the tribe. The other side of this flattening tendency was to pose—sharper than ever before—the problem of the ethnic stranger, for customary tenure effects a division between the peasant in the customary home and the migrant (stranger) peasant; the same customary right that underlines the security of the former's holding renders the latter insecure on borrowed land. The effect of customary law is to pit one against the other. The translation of that effect into a political divide is not inevitable. It depends, I argue, on the nature of a peasant movement and of the community it helps forge. Naturally, this point is best made where an ethnic civil war breaks out in a multiethnic context, such as the Luwero Triangle in Uganda, a context in which I will elaborate the point.

A second clue lies in the division between the peasant who remains home (predominantly female) and the one who moves to the urban area as a migrant worker (predominantly male). The migrant is wedded to the customary not only as a defense of rights, but also as a claim to privilege, however petty, against both those powerful who would appropriate him wrongfully and those weaker (wife and children) who may have rightful claims to "his" land. In such a context, the customary is a cloak that conceals diverse tensions: class, ethnic, gender, and generational. Perched on the ground of the customary, a migrant laborer may at the same time fend off a challenge to patriarchal authority in the household and resist the Native Authority in the local state. He may simultaneously embrace tribal politics in a multiethnic urban arena and fight tribal authorities in the rural homeland. The seeming inconsistency between these standpoints collapses once we realize that the possibilities of migrant politics are as multiple as the location of the migrant is contradictory. I will illustrate this with reference to migrant workers in South Africa in the course of this chapter and the next: in this chapter, to underline the context of a resistance to tribal authorities in the reserves; in the next, to highlight the shifting stance of migrants in an ever-changing urban political landscape.

To understand the phenomenon referred to as tribalism, it is necessary to explore and connect both of its dimensions: the intraethnic and the interethnic, tribalism as internal civil war and as an external tension between tribes. There is now a growing literature on the invention of tribalism in colonial Africa. Richly detailed as these studies are, they still offer a top-down and partial view of the creation of ethnic identities. To begin with, they understand tribalism as an effect of colonialism rather than the very form of colonial rule. Second, in understanding ethnicity exclusively as an artifact of colonial rule, they miss its other side: that ethnicity is also a form of the anticolonial revolt. In assuming that only those ethnicities are real which have always existed, they presume ethnicities to be transhistorical phenomena and thereby miss the fact that ethnicities have a social history. This is why, rather than conceiving of an ethnic identity as simply "invented"[1] by statecraft or "imagined"[2] by intellectuals, it would make more sense to speak of the "making"[3] of an ethnicity.

If this much makes sense, then one need neither be singularly alarmed by the mere sound of ethnic movements nor be moved into embracing them uncritically. The shift from the former to the latter perspective can be glimpsed from the changing vocabulary of Africanist social science: from a study of tribalism to that of ethnicity to that of identity. Each succeeding term gives the phenomenon increasing respectability by casting it within a more acceptable, human, and universal frame. Whereas the sound of *tribalism* was undeniably pathological, *ethnicity* is more placid, part of a value-free vocabulary on the way to reconciling itself with the object it claims to describe; but *identity* has more the ring of a personal quest, if not quite the sound of a battlecry.

Writings on the peasant question in Africa are of recent origin. Not long ago, a debate raged over whether peasants actually existed in Africa or whether Africa was the continent of tribesmen.[4] As late as 1972, Ken Post could complain that "most writers either evade this issue or display analytical uncertainty or forthrightly reject the term [peasant]."[5] Studies of peasant movements are even more recent. Inspired by a unilinear modernist perspective that counterposed state interests as national to any partial demand as particularlistic or sectarian, peasant movements were stigmatized as tribal and considered illegitimate per se. Taken as evidence of peasant pathology, there was a strong bent in the literature toward caricaturing its subject matter as some sort of an anthropological oddity. In the next section of this chapter—also its theoretical anchor— I will argue that it is not possible to grasp the democratic content of peasant movements without transcending the unilinear modernist perspective that counterposes social particularism to state universalism.

In the section called "Tribalism as Civil War," I try to illustrate the argument that tribal politics within the tribally based system of local despotism is actually a form of civil war. In other words, to grasp the democratic potential of a peasant movement it is necessary to understand it as an insurgent expression in an internal civil war. To make this point, I will draw from the experience of rural struggles in apartheid South Africa.

Whereas the tendency to caricature peasant movements as tribal has been the strongest among political scientists, anthropological studies were more an enclave phenomenon in defense of peasant autonomy and peasant initiative. But that disciplinary gap, which opened with the decade of independence, seems to be closing as the pendulum of Africanist political science swings from a state nationalist perspective to an anti-state romanticism. Methodologically, that shift is marked by a change of perspective, from a preoccupation with nation building characteristic of both the modernization and the dependency paradigms to a state–civil society perspective. The result has been either an uncritical embrace of all civil society movements as democratic, with the peasantry presumed to be part of a rural civil society, or an equally romantic celebration of peasant communities, without any reference to civil society. If the distinction between free peasantry and civil society is internal to the structure of both the colonial and the postcolonial state, however, how are we to come to analytical grips with the notion of a peasant community? Is an analysis of peasant community possible that neither glorifies nor dismisses it? In the section entitled "The Peasant Community" I focus on the experience of two insurgent movements, the Ruwenzururu and the National Resistance Army, both in Uganda. Thus I hope to underline the democratic potential in a reorganized peasant community.

To follow up the discussion of the democratic potential of peasant movements, I then explore in the next section how these movements address tensions internal to peasant communities—tensions generated by class, gender, nationality, and age relations—in the process magnifying, reproducing, modifying, or transcending them. To do so, I highlight the autonomy of peasant movements and focus on their internal relations. To illustrate the discussion, I return to the experience of the Ruwenzururu and the National Resistance Army in Uganda but also draw from that of the Sungusungu in northwestern Tanzania. Each example reinforces a common theme: the peasant community is internally divided and reproduced through internal struggles. For this reason, to focus exclusively on the dimension of tribalism as civil war and thereby to present a peasant movement as an unmitigated revolt from below against oppression from above is to indulge in mythmaking by presenting an aspect of reality as its totality. Each example highlights a particular combination of the variety of tensions—class, gender, age, and nationality—that make up the fabric of peasant communities. The main focus, though, is on the interethnic tension illustrated best by the experience of the NRA in the multiethnic context of the Luwero Triangle.

In the final section of this chapter, I join the discussion on autonomy to that on alliances. I do so to understand the outcome of peasant movements and the forces that shape it. My specific purpose, though, is to show how local and central democratizations have been used in the most recent round of reforms in postindependence Africa as regime strategies to offset and defuse each other by preventing the reappearance of the urban-rural link that characterized the independence struggle. To make that point, I trace the contours of the most serious attempt yet to dismantle the regime of indirect rule in the local state: that of Museveni in Uganda.

BEYOND A JUXTAPOSITION OF
TRIBALISM AND STATE NATIONALISM

A researcher looking for empirical information on peasant movements in Africa is inevitably led to studies on ethnicity. For a long time the field resembled a red hot furnace, with partisans busy digging out information to fuel a long-standing polemic. Its ferocity notwithstanding, both sides to the polemic seemed to agree on one point: national (multiethnic and countrywide) movements are legitimate in that they carry forward the legacy of the nationalist struggle, whereas tribal (ethnic and locale-specific) movements are illegitimate because they detract from national unity.[6] The disagreement focused on how to classify different movements, as national or tribal, and on where to lay the blame for tribalism in Africa. Could it be that the bifurcated nature of the state shaped under colonialism, and of the politics it shaped in turn, had now appeared in the theory that tried to explain it?

The two sides of the controversy can be summed up as follows. One recognized the existence of ethnically defined movements (tribalism) but saw them as some sort of a primordial carryover, a traditional or atavistic residue, to be cured or erased with the march of modernity.[7] The other viewed tribalism as the result of a modern conspiracy, either external or local. Those who saw it as a foreign-inspired conspiracy marshaled evidence to show that many of the tribes of Africa were an arbitrary colonial creation,[8] whereas those who held the roots of this conspiracy to be local traced them either to tactical maneuvers by the state to divide the people or to elite strategies to "use" popular allegiances to gain advantage for themselves.[9] Whereas the conspiracy theorists saw tribalism as a kind of cancer introduced from without and above, the primordialists regarded it as an ahistorical original sin afflicting African peoples from below. Both agreed that tribalism is a curse of which Africa must be rid.

In their original statements, the two sides were not only theoretically distinct, but also tended to coincide with clear ideological divisions: the Right seeing tribalism as an internal primordial affliction, and the Left arguing that it was in fact an external but modern conspiracy. In the second round, however, as the positions got restated, this neat division tended to get blurred. Two modified historical versions of the primordial position emerged. One argued that modern tribalism was actually unleashed in an earlier historical period, the era of state-sponsored slavery, when the "kinship corporation" was the only safety net available to fleeing "citizens."[10] A second version distinguished between "moral ethnicity" and "political tribalism," the former an unproblematized transhistorical constant and the latter its ever-changing historical corruption, the former hailed as an expression of the ethical purity of the community and the latter dismissed as its regrettable political pollution.[11] Finally, there appeared the argument that contemporary tribalism was really an example of the "modernity of tradition": a modern strategy to build coalitions in the struggle for power, by all those who seek power and position, regardless of social position, and who must do so by recognizing the tribe as the fundamental building block of African society.[12] Even in this modified version, the second round remained a restatement inasmuch as all participants in the controversy accepted that tribalism remained *the* problem of African countries.

The problem generally referred to as tribalism covers two distinct phenomena: one is a set of deliberate policies and the other the parameters of social movements and of ideologies specific to them. Whereas the former can be explained as the outcome of conscious decisions of regime or elite strategies, the latter cannot. A perspective that sees a social movement as a simple historical residue or as the unmediated outcome of a policy decision is incapable of explaining it, for it necessarily ends up denying the movement any social history. The constraints generated in the process are clear when we examine concrete studies that attempt to analyze tribal movements. A few examples will suffice.

In an article entitled "The Second Independence Movement in Congo Kinshasa," Nzongola-Ntalaja proceeds to differentiate political groups in colonial Congo on the basis of those ethnically based and those supraethnic: on the one hand, Kasa-Vubu's Alliance des Bakongo (ABAKO), Tshombe's Confédération des Associations Tribales du Katanga (CONAKAT), and the Kalonji faction of the Mouvement National Congolais (MNC/K); on the other hand, Centre de Régroupement Africain (CEREA) of Kashamura, Parti Solidaire Africain (PSA) of Gizenga and Mulele, and the Lumumba-led mainstream in the Mouvement National Congolais (MNC/L). The inadequacy of the differentiation becomes clear as the analysis proceeds. The assassination of Lumumba and the subsequent imposition of the Mobutu regime led to the development of the Mulelist guerrilla struggle in eastern Zaire. But the author is unable to come to theoretical grips with this phenomenon,

for the Mulelist movement represented a seemingly contradictory combination. The only organized expression of "a comprehensive programme of social transformation," it was at the same time a movement
that failed to "expand . . . beyond the areas occupied by the two ethnic
groups constituting the initial base of the insurrection, the Mbunda
(Mulele's ethnic group) and the Penda (Gizenga's group)."[13] Now,
from a perspective that differentiates political movements exclusively on
the basis of whether they are ethnically based or supraethnic—the former retrogressive and the latter progressive—the existence of an ethnically based but socially progressive movement must surely appear as a
contradiction in terms, leading to no less than an analytical cul-de-sac.

What is a better clue to the social character of a movement, its social
base and objectives or its geographical scope? Is it possible for a locale-
specific movement to be liberating? Or for a countrywide movement to
be repressive? The limits of the perspective that presents geographical
scope as key to understanding a movement—or ideology as its own explanation—are brought out fully in the controversy that surrounds the
historical significance of Mau Mau in Kenya. One side dismisses Mau
Mau as "a narrow tribalist affair" because it was organized mainly in the
Kikuyu nationality,[14] because it "aimed at a revival of Kikuyu culture,"[15]
or because Mau Mau songs "reflected Kikuyu values."[16] The other up-
holds Mau Mau as a national movement either on grounds of its
ideology (the "revolutionary" content of Mau Mau songs) or on the
grounds that it was actually supraethnic and therefore represented the
culmination of anticolonial struggles in Kenya.[17] The only work that
cuts through the polarity tribalist versus nationalist, because it incorpo-
rates the political and cultural history of the Mau Mau in its social history, is a recent study by Frank Furedi.[18] Furedi recognizes both that
Mau Mau was "an authentic voice of the Kikuyu have-nots" and that
"with Mau Mau, for the first time the mass movement acted independently of the educated middle class leadership" and "put to question the
existing socio-economic structures of society."[19]

Stepping aside from the question of whether Mau Mau was a strictly
Kikuyu movement or whether it gained significant support from various
Kenyan nationalities, does not the larger significance of Mau Mau lie in
its social basis and its demands? Did not the social base of the Mau Mau
in the "Kikuyu have-nots" and its struggle for "land and freedom"
underline its democratic content as opposed to its particularistic concern? Its thrust toward equality as opposed to privilege? Its significance
for the majority (the "have-nots") liberating and unifying as opposed to
repressive and divisive? The parameters of the Mau Mau controversy illustrate precisely the perspective that I am setting aside in this endeavor
to grasp the contradictory character of ethnicity.[20]

TRIBALISM AS CIVIL WAR

Around the same time as the Mau Mau, there erupted a string of rural revolts in apartheid South Africa. Their background is a set of reform policies, both economic and political, that were first formulated in the late 1930s but came to fruition with the Nationalist Party government in the early 1950s. By the 1930s, poverty appeared to many an observer as the outstanding fact of life in the reserves. The symptoms of that poverty were familiar: overgrazing and soil erosion, land fragmentation and declining crop yields. Neither were its causes remote. The relationship between the reserves where labor was reproduced and the mines where it was consumed was evident to participants on both sides of the political divide. "On the one hand the reserves have served as mating camps for the production of migrant labourers," wrote Govan Mbeki, the ANC's chief organizer in the Transkei, in 1962, "while on the other they have proved suitable dumping grounds for the physical wrecks whom industry discards in the same way as waste fibre is thrown away after its juice has been extracted."[21]

Nor was the Chamber of Mines unmindful of the umbilical cord that tied accumulation in the mines to production in the reserves. A confidential report on conditions in the largest reserves (the Transkei and the Ciskei) commissioned by the Chamber in 1937 warned: "Semi-starvation is a very insecure basis with which to build a permanent labour supply."[22] When faced with government commissions appointed to investigate the problem, however, the same chamber argued that it was constrained by necessity, that the availability of low-cost migrant labor was key to sustaining their fortunes: "The ability of the mines to maintain their native labour force by means of tribal natives from the reserves at rates of pay which are adequate for this class of migratory class of native but inadequate for the detribalised native is a fundamental factor in the economy of the Gold Mining industry."[23] Yet government commissions, three in all, found that the supply of this low-cost migratory class was not sustainable under existing conditions. Dan O'Meara quotes an early Second World War report, which concluded that "the vast majority of the recruits to the mines came from the landless in the reserves" and that, for most recruits, "reserve production is a myth."[24] A single fact illustrated the trend. The time migrants spent in the reserves between fourteen-month contracts was decreasing: those returning to the mines within a year comprised 56 percent of re-recruits in 1931 but had grown to 64 percent in 1943. The Fagan Commission (1948) elaborated on the crisis of the reserves. In the Ciskei, for example, it found 30 percent of families landless and 29 percent without any cattle. Many with cattle had no land and so could graze cattle only on common ground. The commission held these findings to be generally "true for the rest of the reserves." Yet a third commission (Tomlinson) lent its authority to this line of reasoning when it concluded that reserves would be able to sustain only 50 percent of their present population if conditions remained the same.[25]

Efforts to check this trend were to lead to a dramatic shift in government policy. Hitherto concerned with checking differentiation and accumulation through a one-man, one-plot policy, the government now decided that the way to increase the carrying capacity of the reserves was to accelerate its internal differentiation, between "full-time peasant farmers" and those who combined farming with migrant remittances. Legislated as the Betterment Act of 1939, this shift was effected through three key programs: villagization, conservation, and privatization.[26] Villagization was designed to separate migrants from full-time farmers and to herd the former into rural dormitory villages while keeping the latter on farms. In the name of conservation, the state took charge of resource allocation and use: as a long-run measure, it set aside land for afforestation and defined access to vital fuel sources like forests; to achieve a balanced use of grazing land in the short run, it introduced cattle culling. Both measures hurt the rural poor, who lacked the capacity to forgo access to resources in the short run in the interest of conservation in the long run. Forbidden to cut trees, to uproot bushes, or to plow near riverbanks, the marginal peasantry was moved from its customary holdings to plots on new trust land. The move from customary to modern plots and methods was in turn an effort to reorganize the reserves through their privatization.

The implementation of "betterment" programs was interrupted by the war. After the war, the National Party twinned these programs, now renamed rehabilitation, with a political reform designed to consolidate its intended beneficiaries. This reform was the 1951 Bantu Authorities Act, devolving greater local powers onto full-fledged indirect rule authorities in the tribal areas. Everywhere, tribal authorities were put in direct charge of effecting measures that would further squeeze the rural poor and create opportunities for the rural rich. Here, as elsewhere on the continent, indirect rule went hand in hand with direct coercion of peasant producers. Distinctive to this coercion was that it was effected by Native Authorities in the local state, not on-the-ground representatives of the central state. Conservation schemes, for example, were largely implemented by forced unpaid labor. "The fact of the matter is," boasted the minister in charge to Parliament, "that by making use of the services of the community we are carrying out the same works at half the cost estimated by the Tomlinson Commission."[27] As proof, he cited the cost of two similar dams, one that had cost the Smuts government £15,000 to construct, but the other, built by the apartheid regime, "at the cost of 800 pounds or 1000 pounds" with the help of "community services." But the monetary cost, too, was met through an added compulsion on peasants. In the Transkei, for example, direct taxation almost doubled between 1955 and 1959; in the country as a whole, the number of Africans convicted for failing to pay taxes jumped from 48,000 in 1950 to 179,000 in 1960.[28]

The impact of forced rural differentiation was further accentuated by forced removals from both urban areas and from so-called black spots—pockets of African peasant freehold farming scattered amid white-owned agricultural land. The effect was to increase population density in the reserves dramatically. To control more effectively the movement of the African population flushed out of white areas, labor bureaus were set up all over the countryside from 1949 on. New types of passes were issued, now incorporating photographs and fingerprints. In 1952 the requirement to carry passes was extended to African women. The majority of the reserve population was caught in a pincer movement. Antisquatting measures in white areas were a compulsion to return to the reserves, but betterment really turned into a compulsion to leave the reserves. These measures accentuated the crisis of the reserves rather than diminishing it. Simkins has argued with respect to the reserves that "one must locate the really dramatic decline in production per capita in the period after 1948 rather than in the period before that date."[29] As the promise of betterment for the rural rich turned into a real menace for the rural poor, particularly for migrants, the possibility of a total collapse of their rural base loomed large. Not surprisingly, the apartheid reform package did not just cut through rural society as a knife cuts through butter; it also set it aflame, pitting victims against beneficiaries.

Over two and a half decades, from 1940 to 1965, resistance in the reserves became more an attribute of life than an exceptional event. Names like Zoutpansberg (northern Transvaal) and Witzieshoek (northern Orange Free State) in the 1940s, Bafarutshe and Sekhukhuneland in the Transvaal of the 1950s, and Thembuland and Pondoland in the Transkei of the 1960s became explosive symbols of resistance. By identifying two common features that thread these events together, I hope to illuminate the dimensions of civil war that marked these revolts and the catalytic role of migrant labor in igniting and shaping a revolt against practices they considered a breach of the customary.

"In every instance of rural resistance recorded in the literature," concludes a recent analysis of rural struggles in the 1940s and 1950s, "the intervention of a migrant association is noted."[30] As urban-based migrants organized in response to a threat to their rural base, they brought home the lessons of resistance learned in urban South Africa in the

1940s and 1950s. The raw material the migrants weaved together to organize resistance inevitably consisted of the tribal associations they had long formed, both as a protective shield in their urban habitats and as a link with their rural homes. The most important of these were burial societies, but *stockvels* (credit associations) also featured in some cases. These "homeboy" networks in which migrants discussed issues of common concern were welded together by migrant activists into larger cultural organizations. Venda migrants on the Rand, for example, formed the Zoutpansberg Cultural Association (ZCA) in Johannesburg in 1939. The ZCA, in turn, gave the impetus to the formation of the Zoutpansberg Balemi (Plowers') Association (ZBA) a few years later in the reserve. Then there were the Rand-based migrants from Sekhukhuneland, who had begun to form burial societies in the 1940s. These societies gave flesh and blood to their struggle against betterment policies in the reserve in the 1950s.[31] The link was clear: "Migrants became organizers, taking the message of organization with them whenever they went home on leave during the ploughing season."[32]

One needs to bear in mind that the ethnically organized burial, stockveld, or cultural societies did not necessarily isolate their members from urban influences. They appear to have functioned more as a crucible bringing together a variety of influences. As they were initiated into the ways of the city, migrants also gained familiarity with various forms of urban resistance. They learned of tactics such as boycotts and demonstrations, and they became familiar with organizations ranging from trade unions to liberation movements like the ANC and the PAC, and even the Communist Party. Hirson writes of the rebellion in Zoutpansberg:

> None of this could have happened without the Zoutpansberg Cultural Association centered in Johannesburg. It had close links with the Communist Party, and had offices at Progress Buildings, where CPSA [Communist Party of South Africa] offices were situated. Maliba was obviously its most outstanding publicist and its main activist, but he could not have achieved as much as he did without his committee. The ZCA advised and supported the peasants, and provided leadership for the struggle. It took up the immediate complaints in the reserves, through the ZBA and it reached out towards the workers in the rural towns. . . . Through the ZBA, the entire population was brought into the struggle.[33]

Alpheus Maliba, the ZCA president, was a nightwatchman, a migrant worker from a village called Mjerere near Louis Trichardt. He was recruited into the Communist Party (CP) in 1936 and "encouraged to organize a peasant movement."[34] But Maliba was no exception. The young hostel-based workers who took the initiative in the 1950s to organize Sekhukhuneland migrants on the Rand into an organization called Sebatakgomo were led by Flag Boshielo and John Nkadimeng, both members of the CP and the ANC. Nkadimeng later recalled: "Sebatakgomo came about in 1954 . . . with the issue of culling cattle . . . the curtailment of land . . . and so-called soil erosion under the Bantu Authorities Act. . . . We felt that many things were going to be done to our people in the country and they were not sufficiently addressed. So we needed an organization, a group in the movement."[35] Similarly, the Bafarutshe migrants who lived in Johannesburg's Western Areas and in Pretoria's Lady Selborne stayed in close contact, with each other and with home, through the Bafarutshe Association. When women in the reserves were compelled to carry passbooks in 1957 and refused to do so, the men and women migrants of the Bafarutshe Association journeyed back home and took charge. They brought with them a new tactic, the boycott, "many of them having just lived through the exciting events of the Rand bus boycott."[36] In Witzieshoek, too, when resistance mounted in the face of cattle culling in the 1940s, the impetus came from the Vigilance Association formed by Johannesburg-based migrants. In turn, the Witzieshoek Vigilance Association was advised by the trade unionist William Ballinger.[37] Likewise, the Pondoland Revolt "was dominated by migrants who had been retrenched following the slump in the Natal sugar industry of 1959–60," as was the Tembuland Rebellion by "migrants who had been relocated to the reserve following the tightening up of influx control in the Western Cape." In both cases, "the migrant associations in the towns played an important coordinating role in the resistance."[38] The Pondoland migrants, concentrated in the western Cape, were strongly influenced by the PAC, which was "especially influential in the workers' hostels."[39]

The issues that ignited this wave of revolts were inevitably linked to two developments that gathered momentum in the late 1930s: betterment in the reserves and the tightening grip of influx control measures around the reserves. Whereas the second was specifically a South African development, the first echoed post-Depression and postwar development measures undertaken across much of indirect rule Africa through Native Authorities in the local state. In Zoutpansberg in the 1940s, as in Sekhukhuneland in the 1950s and Thembuland in the 1960s, the introduction of land-rehabilitation schemes meant the loss of customary land and of customary rights to cut trees and gather firewood and building materials. In the stony slopes of Witzieshoek, "one of the most inhospitable in South Africa,"[40] where little cultivation was possible and most peasants relied on stock for their day-to-day livelihood, cattle culling turned into a menace for the marginal peasantry. In Bafarutsheland, where the density of both human and cattle population was low and therefore the effect of betterment programs not immediately destructive, the catalyst for resistance was the compulsion for women to carry passes. In Pondoland, however, there was an entire constellation of grievances, from land reclamation to cattle culling to increased taxes to Bantu education. Everywhere, migrants experienced the onset of the apartheid era as a direct threat to access rights they had come to consider as customary and therefore a threat to their rural base.

Everywhere, the wrath of migrants turned on chiefs, who were the bearers of apartheid reforms—indirect rule—and who stood to benefit from these directly. This was the second feature marking these revolts. The "most obvious general feature of the rural revolts," Matthew Chaskalson concluded in a comparative study of resistance in the reserves, "was that they were directed against rehabilitation and/or Tribal Authorities and symbols of influx control."[41] The revolts were everywhere an antichief phenomenon. Not all chiefs were attacked everywhere. In many places peasants distinguished between bad and good chiefs, between those who gave in to the temptation for individual enrichment and those who stood alongside their communities, even if out of fear for their lives if they did not; in sum, between those who violated real custom and those who upheld it. In some instances, like in the Bafarutshe Rebellion, the anger of the rural poor was directed specifically against those chiefs seen as collaborating with the apartheid authorites: they beat up chiefs' bodyguards and set chiefs' houses on fire. In Witzieshoek, they seized the cattle of chiefs they saw as collaborating with central officialdom. A good chief, said the peasants of Sekhukhuneland, is a traditional chief. Their notion of a traditional chief was of a leader in some measure accountable to the peasant community. It was a relationship summed up in a single sentence: "A chief is a chief by the people" (*Kgoshi de kgoshi ka batho*). To ensure that relationship and that accountability, the rebellious peasants of Sekhukhuneland established a village-based assembly of commoners, called the Khudutamaga. It was an initiative they had taken once before, at the time of the Sebatakgomo Revolt of 1956, and it was the initiative that, as we will see, defined a common element in peasant opposition to indirect rule authorities.[42]

Where revolt took on the dimensions of an uprising, as in Pondoland, its target was the very institution of chiefship. The thirty Pondos sentenced to death in the aftermath of the revolt were sentenced for the murder of pro–Bantu Authority chiefs. Testifying before an official government commission, a member of a leading Bizana family gave this description of the revolt:

> The people showed a spirit of rebellion—they opposed all the measures which were for their own advancement. They rejected Bantu Authorities. One man stands up and gives orders, and then they start burning kraals. After the members of the Bantu Authorities were burnt out, they went

about burning the kraals of those sympathetic to the Bantu Authorities. Then the more progressive people in the location were burnt out. Before burning the huts they took everything out. It is the more well-to-do owners who have suffered like this. Even if the poor owners were sympathetic to the Bantu Authorities, they are not burnt out.[43]

The Pondoland Revolt was no doubt the most advanced of that era. Against Bantu Authority, it created a democratically elected authority of commoners: the Hill Committee, created in 1960, "rallied [the] majority of the tribesmen in the Binzana District into open struggle against the authorities and their henchmen." Committee meetings were attended by "thousands of peasants who came on horseback to chosen spots on the mountains and ridges." Thus the movement came to be known as *intaba* (the mountain) and other times as *Ikongo* (congress).[44] It was a movement that "expressly excluded chiefs and headmen from participation at all levels."[45] The first step was an uprising against the chiefly hierarchy, setting the chiefs' houses on fire. Then all those supporting Bantu Authorites were ostracized "in life and death," in all activities ranging from childbirths to funerals. It was a tactic that was to prove "very effective in reducing the number of collaborators." Mass demonstrations of "thousands of peasants took place on an unprecedented scale."[46] Gradually, from implementing the slogan "No cooperation with the authorities"—no payment of taxes and a boycott of white traders—this movement evolved embryonic elements of an alternative power: in opposition to the bush courts held by the chiefs, Ikongo set up people's courts, which resolved disputes between peasants without charging any fees.[47] The Bantu Authorities ceased to function.

The Pondoland Revolt shared a key feature with other peasant-based revolts, like the Ruwenzururu and the NRA-led guerrilla struggle in the Luwero Triangle. In all these cases, opposition was aimed at indirect rule Native Authorities; in the course of each uprising, peasant communities were reorganized on the basis of self-administration. Though ethnically defined, the struggle of peasants everywhere took on the dimensions of a civil war inside the ethnic group.

THE PEASANT COMMUNITY:
VILLAGE SELF-GOVERNANCE AS DEMOCRATIC REFORM

If the struggle against the local authority of the indirect rule state is necessarily ethnic—and religious where state formation evokes a religious sanction—what then is the democratic potential of popular insurgency in the ethnic civil war? To answer this question, I turn to two contemporary experiences from Uganda: the Ruwenzururu (1962–80) and the

National Resistance Army (1981–85). In both instances, my interest is in the political aspect of the reform. How does reform seek to reorganize those who govern and those who are governed: on the one hand chiefs in the local state, on the other peasants living as a community?

The Ruwenzururu

The Ruwenzururu was a peasant guerrilla movement on the Uganda-Zaire border at the prime of its activity from 1962 to 1980.[48] A movement of the peasants of the Bakonzo and Bamba nationalities living on the slopes of Mount Ruwenzori, it was organized in response to intense nationality oppression that led to land deprivation, language exclusion, and job discrimination through most of the colonial period. Although its political leadership came mostly from middle-class intellectuals like teachers, the social impetus came from the poor peasantry of the mountains. By the close of the colonial period, the middle-class intelligentsia that had for decades endeavored to negotiate representation in a reformed state structure had come to an impasse. Dissenting voices surfaced as the strategy of negotiations reached a cul-de-sac. The most prominent was that of Isaah Mkirani, a schoolteacher who had set up the Bakonzo Life History Research Society on the mountain slopes as early as 1954.

As independence approached in 1962, Mkirani called for a shift from negotiations to armed struggle; the Ruwenzururu movement was born, with headquarters in forests across the border in Zaire. In that forest, Mkirani made contact, and shared experiences, with Mulelist guerrillas. With the armed struggle but three months old, Mkirani was arrested. In 1964 he escaped and returned to the mountain to find the leadership of the movement once again preparing for negotiations, this time with the authorities of the independent Ugandan state. Mkirani renewed his call for an armed struggle. The next two years were the most innovative in the history of the Ruwenzururu. His back up against the wall, Mkirani carried out a series of reforms whose point was to create a reformed state structure on the mountain. With that reform anchored in the rights of the peasantry, he sought to organize peasant support for an independent guerrilla struggle. Implemented between 1964 and 1966, when Mkirani died, the reforms unlocked popular energies, which explain the tenacity with which the mountain peasantry defended itself, against all odds, in confrontation with the armed forces of the Ugandan state—until a compromise was finally negotiated in 1980. It is these reforms that are of particular interest to us. I visited some villages in the Ruwenzori mountains in September 1984 and had the opportunity to talk with several participants in the Ruwenzururu. My main source of information, though, was a peasant called Mzee Muhindo, a guerrilla in the movement from 1965 to 1968 and a representative in the subcounty assembly who spent two years (1968 to 1970) in jail before returning to the fold of the movement.

As the movement developed into a guerrilla struggle leading to direct confrontation with government soldiers, the rich peasantry poured down the mountain slopes to the relative comfort of the plains, and the poor peasantry became the backbone of the armed struggle. This is why the Ruwenzururu movement could not simply be conceptualized as the struggle of two nationalities, the Bakonzo and the Bamba, against "outsiders." It was at the same time a civil war inside each nationality: between the mountain dweller and the plains dweller, between initiatives anchored in poor peasants and rich peasants, between those organizing an armed struggle and those calling for peaceful methods of resolving conflicts. We will see that the organization of the Ruwenzururu was at the same time a recasting of relations internal to the peasantry and a reorganization of the peasant community. The armed struggle that came to be known as the Ruwenzururu movement combined features of centralization and decentralization, organizational forms at the same time democratic and antidemocratic. The overall form the movement eventually came to adopt was more or less a replica of the Toro monarchy that it confronted, but inside this shell it organized some remarkable democratic initiatives. Isaah Mkirani declared the Ruwenzururu a kingdom in 1965 and had himself crowned king. "Why did Isaah create a kingdom?" I asked Mzee Muhindo. "He was fighting a king. He could not fight him as a subject. Therefore, he had to become a king himself. But," Mzee Muhindo assured me, "the assemblies did not lose authority when Isaah became king." How true to reality was this claim?

The thrust of Mkirani's reform was to reorganize the relation between the new state power and peasant communities.[49] That reorganization turned around two concrete measures: a redefinition of the role of a state functionary (chief) and the constitution of peasant communities into popular assemblies with supervisory powers over state functionaries. The two legs of the reform were interconnected. The first led to an elementary separation of powers, and the second put in place popular checks over bureaucratic authority. The Ruwenzururu reforms disentangled the various instances of state power—legislative, judicial, executive, and administrative—that were fused in a single functionary and had hitherto made for the total power of the chief. This preliminary separation of powers left administrative and executive authority to the redefined chief and transferred judicial and legislative powers to newly elected popular assemblies. Furthermore, it made the new chiefs accountable to elected assemblies.

It is worth going over how chiefs were appointed, transferred, dismissed, and promoted in the guerrilla-held mountain areas. The process of appointment was specific to the level of bureaucratic authority. At the lowest level, the village, the chief was appointed by the community itself. The state played no role in it. Middle-level chiefs, for subcounties and counties, were appointed by the prime minister but had to be confirmed by the elected assembly at the level affected. A chief at the highest administrative level was appointed by the president/king, but only from among those who had been elected as councillors by the people. The chief was both an administrative and an executive officer. As an administrative officer, he functioned as a civil servant; and as an executive officer, he chaired the elected assembly. The assembly had the right to censure or to acclaim the chief. A chief who was censured had to be transferred or dismissed, whereas no chief could be promoted without the support (acclamation) of the assembly concerned. The reorganization so achieved gave effect to two principles: the separation of powers, even if elementary, and the right of elected bodies to act as watchdogs over state functionaries.

Popular assemblies were organized in a pyramidal form, with five tiers. The assemblies exercised both judicial and legislative powers: they arbitrated disputes in their area and made policy decisions on specified matters. The village assembly included all adult villagers and dealt mainly with issues internal to the village. The parish-level assembly comprised three representatives from each of its six constituent villages. Its concerns were mainly tax, housing, and education. The movement imposed a tax on every adult male. For example, in 1965, the government taxed every adult male on the plains 45 shillings, but the movement tax on the mountain was 25 shillings; in 1967, when the government tax rose to 60 shillings, the movement increased its tax to 35 shillings. In a situation where government soldiers often charged up the mountain, burning and sometimes bombing huts, the question of housing everyone and of what type of dwellings to build became a key issue. In that same context, the question of reopening schools and redesigning the curriculum became yet another concern of parish assemblies. The third and fourth level of popular assemblies were for the subcounty (*gombolola*) and the county. Every subcounty comprised three parishes and every county five subcounties. Their agenda focused on issues that lower assemblies found difficult to resolve. At the summit of this hierarchy of assemblies was the Prime Minister's Council, whose major concerns were specified as (a) local administration—customs, (b) education, (c) defense, (d) justice, and (e) culture and religion.

Representation in each assembly was by election. The village assembly sent three representatives to the parish, which in turn sent three to the subcounty, and so on. Of the three, one was always the administrative chief of the area. Practices on the ground reflected a contradictory mix. On the one hand, indirect elections, with each level functioning as an electoral college for the next, meant a watered-down democracy the higher one went up the representative ladder; on the other hand, great stress was laid on direct and participatory forms. A novel feature of representation was the principle of rotation of representatives. Assembly rules specified that each member must in turn represent the assembly at the higher forum. The point of the election was simply to decide on the order of the rotation. Representation became more permanent at higher levels. Most assemblies met once a week: the village assembly every Tuesday morning from 9 to 12, the parish assembly every Wednesday from 9 to 2; the subcounty forum had a double session (8 to 12, 1 to 4) every Thursday, and the county assembly had a similar double session every Friday. The Prime Minister's Assembly met for a week, but only once in three months. And then, finally, there was the President's Assembly. An irregular affair, it comprised the prime minister's elected cabinet and representatives of the military, alongside county chiefs, and met only when matters could not be resolved by the Prime Minister's Assembly. It had a maximum of two meetings a year.

The National Resistance Army

The very questions that we asked of the Ruwenzururu movement can provide us with clues in understanding the success of the National Resistance Army (NRA) in the period of its guerrilla struggle (1981–85) in central Uganda. What were the reforms that unlocked the creative energies of the peasant population of the Luwero Triangle? There is no evidence of any direct link between the two movements, but the real linkage lies in the similarity of circumstances: the National Resistance Army/Movement (NRA/M) too was compelled to address the question of building a state power with a difference in its liberated zones. To marshal the support of the peasantry against the Obote II regime, this form of power had to highlight the question of rights of the peasantry in the institutions it created. Its starting point was none other than the replacement of a form of power hitherto unchecked and fused with a system of checks and balances built on a differentiated notion of power. Here, too, the guiding principles were a separation of powers and popular checks on it. Unlike the Ruwenzururu, the NRA/M simply abolished the position of the chief. In place of chiefship, it created a system of resistance councils and committees. The Resistance Council (RC) was a gathering of all adults living in a designated area; like the popular assemblies of the Ruwenzururu, it had legislative and judicial powers. The nine-person Resistance Committee elected by this council was the counterpart of the chief; as with the Ruwenzururu, it exercised administrative and executive powers.

Like the pyramidal system of popular assemblies put in place by the *Ruwenzururu*, the RC system of the NRA/M was multitiered. Though the NRA/M did not practice a system of rotation of representatives at any level, it did give effect to the right of leadership in a more elementary form by stipulating that no individual could hold more than one responsible position. Finally, the NRA/M institutionalized the principle of popular accountability by giving every council the right to recall any member of its committee between elections.

Neither the popular assemblies set up by the Ruwenzururu nor the NRA/M's RC system should be seen as a continuation of precedents such as the colonially established councils or the Mayumba Kumi committees introduced by the Uganda National Liberation Front (UNLF) after the overthrow of the Amin regime. Elected councils were introduced by the colonial power in 1952 in direct response to the peasant uprisings of 1945 and 1949. Although set up at various administrative levels, these councils had a purely advisory capacity; they were supposed to function as popular props to organs of the state. It drew inspiration from the ten-cell system prevalent in Tanzania. Like it, the Mayumba Kumi committees had mainly a security function; and like the colonial councils, they served as popularly anchored supports to—and not checks on—state security organs.

Though anchored in separate historical experiences, both in location and time, the Ruwenzururu and the NRA/M came up with a similar innovation in the arena of rights: the right of peasant communities to organize as communities and to hold state officials accountable as communities. It was a departure from the accent on individual rights in received liberal notions. It was a response to a dual context. On one hand, market relations had yet to penetrate and disintegrate communities fully, so that they may in turn be re-created through voluntary associations; the place of work coincided in the main with the place of residence; the family was still a unit of not just consumption and reproduction, but also production; circumstances of birth prevailed over choice of association in shaping one's life possibilities. On the other hand, political power confronted peasant communities as authority fused in the person of a chief, one in a vertical chain of command. If there were elections, peasants could cast a vote for a representative of their choice in the central state but not for a chief of their choice in the local state. When one regime replaced another at the center, a new chief might be appointed, but chiefship continued as an institution. In this context the right of association would have an extremely limited practical significance if understood only as an individual right. To be meaningful, it had to be interpreted as a right of residence-based communities, not just individuals. This innovation was of particular significance to those who lived on the margins of civil society.

The significance of the Ruwenzururu and the NRA experiences needs to be grasped in its historical specificity. To wage a political struggle, both movements were compelled to confront and dismantle the indirect rule authority that was the local state. But the reforms introduced in the process should not be seen just as constituting a single-minded move toward a state form that would be the basis of civil society–type freedoms. From a civil society perspective, these reforms were contradictory. They saw both the differentiation and the fusion of power, and not just the former, as the basis of political freedom. Both experiences differentiated executive and administrative functions from legislative and judicial authority. At the same time, both were deeply suspicious of a professional judicial cadre and strove for a fusion of legislative and judicial powers in a single popular assembly.

If the civil war I am talking about was not always ethnic—since in some cases it was religious—the explanation lay in a different process of state formation. In an illuminating analysis of the Hausa and Yoruba peasantries in Nigeria, Abdul Raufu Mustapha brings out the significance of divergent state-formation processes in shaping the perspective of insurgent peasant movements.[50] The Rogo peasantry in Hausaland "has a strong historical consciousness of being *talakawa* and see themselves in opposition to the *masu sarauta* who controlled the pre-colonial state systems, and who allied themselves to the colonizing power under Indirect Rule." In this dichotomy, the talakawa were the oppressed commoners, and the masu sarauta the indirect rule aristocracies through whom colonial rule was mediated. With the broadening of the political process after 1966, a rich peasant stratum from the talakawa was able to dominate local political and cooperative activities through a historically derived "Islamic radical populism," organizationally anchored at first in the Northern Elements Progressive Union (NEPU) and later in its successor, Peoples Redemption Party (PRP).

The corresponding cultural division in the Alade peasantry of Yorubaland was not between commoners and aristocrats, but between a "knowledgable western-educated person" (an *omowe*) who is also "cultured" (*olaju*) on the one hand and "a bushman, rustic or an illiterate" (*ara-oko*) who is at the same time "uneducated or uncultured" (*ojududu*) on the other. Unlike in Hausaland, where precolonial state formation was "much more thorough-going," the state in precolonial Yorubaland "did not have quite the same scope for dominating society, for the relationship between the rulers and ruled was mediated by blood-based, land-holding lineages which limited the scope for the exercise of direct state power over the ruled, and provided a modicum of protection against the rulers." Thus, unlike in Hausaland, where colonial indirect rule authorities appeared like a continuation of precolonial aristocracies, the local state in colonial Yorubaland appeared more a transgression of precolonial power and authority in kin groups. Social mobility seemed rooted more in education than in the circumstances of birth. As a result, "the Yoruba peasantry has always had a greater attachment to communalist and autochtonous values and institutions."

In Hausaland commoners saw indirect rule mediated through a precolonial aristocracy as a violation of religious norms. The rich peasant-led opposition was expressed through a radical Islamic populism. In Yorubaland, where indirect rule was mediated through "patriarchal gerentocrats of the upper stratum in Aleda," peasants experienced it as a violation of kinship norms. Here, too, opposition was led by rich peasants but took the form of a "communal (ethnic) populism" expressed through the Action Group and its successor, the United Party of Nigeria.

I will return to the experience of the NRA, both to highlight further the significance of its democratic agrarian program of 1981–85 and to underline its retreat from that program in the post-1986 period, after some observations on the question of peasant community and peasant stratification. At this juncture, however, it is sufficient to note that only in the nationalist imagination, and not in real social history, can movements emerge full-blown as the Greek goddess Athena is supposed to have done from the head of Zeus. That is why the question we need to ask when assessing the democratic content of a movement is not just one concerning its geographical sweep, but also one that underlines the social character of its demands: Do they tend toward realizing equality or crystallizing privilege? Are they generalizable to other ethnic groups or can they be realized only at the expense of others? In other words, when do they signify a struggle for rights and when a demand for privilege?

STRATIFICATION WITHIN THE PEASANT COMMUNITY

The literature on ethnicity tends to characterize the peasant community as undifferentiated and homogeneous. It is at this point that the analysis of peasant movements in Africa finds common ground with the wider debate on the peasant question. The two sides of this larger debate can be summed up in the polarity community versus stratification. Does there exist a peasant community and thus a peasant economy? Or is the

community torn apart by a process of differentiation and class formation, leading to the development of propertied and laboring households
on each side of the social spectrum? The controversy came to a head in
the Russian literature on the peasantry: the stratification side was ex-
pounded in the writings of Lenin, whereas the communitarian position
was best formulated by the Russian populist Chayanov.[51]

In the preoccupation with peasant revolutions that followed the Chinese, Vietnamese, and Cuban Revolutions, the controversy appeared in
a new form. Those inspired by communitarian notions asked, Are peasants revolutionary or not? By contrast, those anchored in a stratification
perspective asked, Which peasants are revolutionary, poor, middle, or
rich? Particularly influential were the writings of Eric Wolf[52] and Hamza
Alavi,[53] who proceeded to answer—"middle peasants"—through the
analysis of a series of case studies. The same question was answered differently by Paige, who placed his wager on "share croppers and migratory estate labourers."[54] All three, however, share a common premise: it
is possible to define one group or another in the countryside as revolutionary, whatever the overall context.

Can a capacity, whether revolutionary or not, be innate in a social
group? Or is any such capacity the outcome of historically changing processes and relations? If the latter, can one then speak of perspectives or
capacities outside historical and social contexts? This is not to argue
against any comparative analysis; it is, though, to question comparisons
whose bases lie in an ahistorical structuralism, which ignore context and
thus dehistoricize the subject.[55]

The debate is of more than historical concern because it continues to
arise in contemporary writings, whether explicitly or not. The terminology may and does change: from "peasant community" to a "peasant" or
"domestic" mode of production to an "ethnic group" or simply "peasant economy" or "economy of affection." In all cases contestants confront a common dilemma: which is real, community (ethnic group) or
stratum (class)? Each then proceeds to uphold one side of this polarity.
My purpose is neither to try to resolve this debate nor to sidestep it. I
will focus on it to the extent relevant to the questions raised in this chapter, beginning with a few remarks on the nature of the peasantry.

All peasant strata—whether they hire or sell their own labor power,
rent land or any implement of labor, lend or borrow money—share one
central characteristic that makes of them all peasants: they own some
productive property and participate to some degree in the labor process
on the land.[56] The unity of labor and property comes together markedly
in the circumstance of the middle peasantry and begins to break up as
the peasantry differentiates. Yet no matter how eroded, this unity continues to be real with both the rich and the poor peasantry. When it
ceases to be so for a household, that household can no longer be said to

belong to "the peasantry." This is why there is nothing contradictory in talking of both a peasant community and of different peasant strata.

From this perspective, the distinction between peasant community and peasant strata appears relative; the issue cannot be polarized. The peasant community exists, but it is not homogeneous. It is a unity but a contradictory one. The first theorist to emphasize the relative character of this polarity in the African context was Amilcar Cabral. In "A Brief Analysis of the Social Structure in Guinea,"[57] Cabral sought to understand the specific mode of peasants' political action. He took as his point of departure peasant communities as historically constituted (the Balanta, the Fulani, and so on). He then proceeded to investigate the internal class character of each community, distinguishing between the class-differentiated feudal-type structure of the Fulani on the one hand and the kin-based social organization of the Balanta on the other. Although Cabral sidestepped the polarity ethnicity-class, the tendency in academia was otherwise: a chorus saw politics in Africa as an expression of an all-pervasive ethnic consciousness, and a few dissenters upheld the class point of view. One of the few works to break through this arid stand-off was Richard Joseph's study *Militant Nationalism in Cameroun*.[58] Joseph's investigation of the social base of militant nationalism in the Cameroon peasantry led him to identify peasants from two ethnic groups as centrally involved in militant nationalist protest: the economically poor peasantry of Sanaga Maritime and the economically advanced farmers (and traders) in the more developed regions of the Cameroon.

Cabral's focus was on understanding the involvement of local communities in the larger polity, but my interest at this point is in understanding how local communities reproduce themselves, for the peasant community cannot be understood as a given, a traditional constant dragged through historical time. My purpose is to show that peasant communities are constructed and reconstructed in practice through social struggles. Those struggles tend to be total, not just cultural/ideological, but social. There exist contradictory ways of reconstructing the peasant community. That is why to understand the social nature of a communal (tribal) movement it is necessary to underline its social basis. Let us take a few examples and focus on how different peasant movements lead to alternative conceptions of reorganizing the same community.

The Sungusungu

Between 1980 and 1983 the Sungusungu organized over some fifty thousand square kilometers of land in rural northwestern Tanzania, a region whose peasant inhabitants number more than five million.[59] In this region the cattle-owning peasantry has experienced decades of deprivation. Beginning with the rinderpest epidemic around the turn of this century, followed by the officially sanctioned destocking campaigns of the 1930s and 1940s that were codified in law in the latter decade, capped with the postindependence experience of cattle raids that intensified as the economic crisis of the mid-1970s set in, this peasantry has been a victim of varied forms of forced appropriations. The response to this last phase of the crisis, that of cattle raids, was contradictory. Rich peasants organized to protect property. They got each household to contribute 200 shillings to a common fund, the idea being to pay off state security personnel with the object of securing a selective protection of property belonging to contributing households. It was a response of which the poor could not partake simply because they lacked the money to secure protection.

The response of the poor peasantry was to form alternative organizations, highly decentralized, each confined to a village. Village-wide popular assemblies controlled a popular village militia (the Sungusungu) and dispensed popular justice. The militia groups either took over or simply sidestepped local security organs like police stations, but in all instances they took direct charge of protecting peasant communities from cattle raiders. Through this initiative, the Sungusungu reconstructed the peasant community, but the process of inclusion in this community was at the same time a process of exclusion from it. Who was excluded? From the point of view of our query, married women. The key activity of the Sungusungu was vigilante work, carried out by small organized groups of *makamanda*. Unmarried women could be included in their ranks, but married women were always excluded.

The Ruwenzururu

In contrast to the Sungusungu, the Ruwenzururu did include married women as members of the peasant community but only partly. Women (whether married or not) were encouraged to attend only the lowest assembly (the village), particularly when discussion focused on food policy. The popular assemblies remained a predominantly male affair.

Every oppositional movement is forced to call on reserves of energy, on new sources of strength, when its back is up against a wall. Depending on the social character of the movement, this may lead to a broadening of public discussion as previously unspoken issues are articulated and become the subject of public discussion or to a widening of publicly accepted parameters of organization as previously unorganized groups are mobilized and gain a public presence. This is why periods of intense conflict often tend to telescope social change into short durations.[60] From this point of view, the Ruwenzururu experience is worthy of note on two counts. I have already discussed the popular assemblies, remarkable for their democratic component. They combined two novel principles, the rotation of representatives and the right to censure civil administrators. The absence of women, however, must be considered the principal limitation of the Ruwenzururu experience.

The movement also achieved a second remarkable mobilization, that of youth. Defined as those between the ages of seven and eighteen, the youth were organized as scouts. Scouts worked on weekends to build schools for youth and houses for old women. They bought essential items (fish and medicine) from the plains and carried them up the mountains. They collected firewood and food for the watch camps and sounded alarms. A novel feature of the mobilization of youth, however, was their participation in the cultural sphere. Every assembly was charged with preparing songs that gave meaning to popular experiences. The youth memorized these songs and integrated them into cultural performances they gave at different assemblies. Just as with the Mau Mau, songs became the principal cultural form of the Ruwenzururu, and the youth its main cultural agency.

The National Resistance Army

The National Resistance Army/Movement did not just reproduce the experience of the Ruwenzururu, even if separately and independently. It made two further contributions, in my view of seminal importance. The explanation lies partly in the different social dynamics of the Luwero Triangle and partly in the ingenuity of its leadership, bathed as it was in global ideological influences. Let me elaborate. Unlike the slopes of Mount Ruwenzori, the region of the Luwero Triangle brings together an ethnically mixed population of peasants for whom it has been an ancestral home for generations and migrants who have settled in the region over decades. Immigrants came mostly from Ruanda, from the 1920s on in large numbers. According to the 1948 census, 34 percent of the population of 1,296,701 in Buganda were immigrants, mostly from Ruanda-Urundi.[61] The alliance between these two social forces, a settled Baganda poor peasantry and non-Baganda migrant peasants and laborers, had fueled the uprisings of 1945 and 1949.[62] This alliance was broken in the aftermath of the colonial reform of the 1950s, which facilitated a shift in political initiative from popular to propertied strata and a top-down remobilization of the tribe in the context of the colonial reform. It was a shift ideologically marked and organizationally consolidated by the rise of the Kabaka Yekka (King Only) movement in Buganda. In consolidating a Baganda tribal identity in the name of king and tradition and under the leadership of landed strata, the Kabaka Yekka targeted at a stroke two social groups as alien: Indian shopkeepers and ginners, and Banyaruanda migrant laborers. The resulting top-down alliance of classes and groups in the Baganda nationality held through the 1960s and 1970s; Buganda became the bastion of tribal politics constituted in a top-down fashion.

Just as the threat of famine helps a people discover new sources of food, struggle and adversity define creative moments in the history of social movements. In Buganda memories of the popular struggle of the 1940s had receded far into the dim recesses of memory. In the intervening decades, from the 1950s to the end of the 1970s, a new political culture had taken root. It was an orientation that distinguished between those indigenous and those immigrant, between those Baganda and those from elsewhere. Its telling effect was the building of a wall between the two social forces that had propelled the uprisings of 1945 and 1949. The political task that the NRA/M confronted in the Luwero Triangle in 1981 was no less than to re-create the social alliance that had propelled the rural uprising of the 1940s: between indigenous peasants and migrant strangers. To do so, it had to arrive at a new notion of rights, one that would include within its fold the entire working population of Luwero, whether indigenous or immigrant. It did this in practice by redefining the basis of rights from descent to residence: all adult persons had the right to belong to a council in their place of residence. Though the NRA/M at no point underlined the theoretical significance of this departure, it is clear that a residential qualification for rights is in reality a shift from descent to labor as the basis of rights.[63] But the rights of migrants were limited to the first tier in the multitiered pyramid that was the system of RCs. Yet the shift in the basis of rights from an exclusive and localized (descent) principle to an inclusive and generalizable (labor) one was of enormous significance in a land with substantial immigrant minorities.

On the basis of a notion of rights modified to suit a different social context, the NRA rebuilt the alliance between Baganda poor peasants and Banyaruanda migrant laborers. By so doing, the leadership of the NRA—even though it came from an ethnic group outside Buganda—also successfully undermined the political hold of conservative Baganda elite groups on the peasantry of the Luwero Triangle. No wonder that the Obote II regime tried to portray that guerrilla struggle as the spearhead of an "alien" resurgence, a core movement of migrants of Ruandese origin which posed a threat to all Ugandans. And when the guerrilla struggle continued to surge ahead, spilling over beyond Buganda in its second phase (1984–85), the regime tried to cast it as a tribal war of a minority (the Baganda), potentially a threat to the rest of the nationalities in Uganda. The contention did not hold. Why? The fact that the overall significance of this struggle was unifying and liberating, and not divisive and repressive, was demonstrated by its next phase. As the guerrilla struggle expanded from 1984 on, the NRA was able to build an alliance between the Baganda and the Banyoro, two nationalities that had been at odds with each other since colonial power had built on the nineteenth-century contention between the states of Buganda and Bunyoro-Kitara.

In its Luwero days, the NRA took yet another step forward in expanding the social parameters of participation in public affairs. This constituted a blow to yet another tradition, in this instance patriarchal. Its cutting edge was an expanded participation of women and youth in community affairs. No formal limits were placed on the right of a woman, married or unmarried, to participate in public affairs, including joining the army. In recognition of historical and cultural realities that gave women and youth the status of a political minority even though they were seldom physical minorites, two positions on the nine-person Resistance Committees were reserved, one for a secretary for women and the other for a secretary for youth.

Between principle and practice, however, there was a gulf. Although women and youth were granted special representation in each nine-person committee, all the way up the pyramid, the body that elected that representative was neither wholly nor even mainly female or youth; instead it was the entire council of adults. Whereas the electorate at the lowest level usually comprised a female and youth majority, at higher levels it was invariably composed mainly of adult males. Would a woman elected by a predominantly male body be a representative *of* women or a representative *to* women?

It would be naive to see these reforms simply as efforts to reconstitute and emancipate peasant communities from below rather than from above. As they strove to build effective political coalitions against established authority, both experiences were marked by contradictory tendencies: political emancipation alongside social conservatism. As indirect rule authorities were dismantled and the rights of peasant communities recognized, all strata and sections within that community experienced a newfound freedom. But as communities were reproduced, so were the internal hierarchies within these communities. Their spontaneous tendency was to contain the reform. The poor and the migrant, the women and the youth, were at the same time galvanized into action as they were contained within a reformed social hierarchy. We will later see that none of these reforms was permanent. Each was modified, nullified, or strengthened by the totality of the social movement of which the peasantry and the NRA were but two agencies. The point is that a reform in the character of local authority must remain partial and unstable so long as it is not reinforced by a corresponding reform in the central state.

ALLIANCES AND CONTRADICTORY OUTCOMES

There is a strong tendency in contemporary literature to idealize peasant political action. To take a recent instance, in *Social Banditry in Africa* Crummey uses African material to build on an argument originally put forth by Hobsbawm: that criminality is a form of protest, and banditry is its most common form in class-divided agrarian societies.[64] But social banditry has a contradictory character, shaped by its historical and social context. Crummey's chapter on the Shiftanat in Ethiopia provides the material to illustrate the point. At one point a form of individual protest, the Shiftanat later came under the direction of various factions of the Ethiopian nobility and took on the form of organized and regular theft. As such, the Shiftanat really became an institutional medium for competition between factions of the nobility. Put alongside other material in the same book, and the European material originally put forth by Hobsbawm, it is clear that the content of social banditry can and does vary from one context to another: in one instance it was a form of popular protest, and in another it provided the grist for an institutionalized competition between factions of a dominant class. For Crummey, however, "crime is inherently a form of protest." The contradictory potential of peasant political action is most sharply illustrated by the fact that even though it is a vehicle of popular protest, it has not been very difficult to incorporate peasant initiative into broader state strategies, turning it into a force for order and stability rather than transformation. This is why protest and incorporation need to be seen as part of the history of the same peasant movement.

Let me illustrate this point by returning to our case studies. First, the Sungusungu. From 1981 to 1983, the Tanzanian state tried all it could to penetrate the organization of the Sungusungu, to identify and deal with its leaders. When it failed, it concluded that the movement had no leaders; to put the same thing differently, the movement was so decentralized that the leaders may themselves have constituted an entire social movement! From this recognition followed a shift in state policy toward the Sungusungu. Starting from its official recognition as a popular militia, the Sungusungu was dramatically incorporated into state structures by 1986. At the outset, Sungusungu stood out as a truly popular militia in contrast to state-created rural militias. But this contrast did not last long. State reform began by according the Sungusungu a ceremonial role in official occasions; the makamanda of the Sungusungu began to appear as official guards for visiting state dignitaries. Soon Sungusungu was directly involved in the implementation of some of the most repressive state policies, such as the compulsory labor measures that went under the name *nguvu kazi*.

Yet another instance is the Ruwenzururu. In this case, too, there was a swing from repression to reform. For nine years (1962–1971) the Obote I regime made futile attempts to suppress it militarily; for another nine years (1971–1980) there was simmering revolt under the Amin regime; and eventually the Obote II regime came to the conclusion that incorporation was a more feasible and efficient alternative to direct confrontation. By granting separate districts to the two nationalities from which Ruwenzururu guerrillas were recruited and by transforming the leadership of the movement into the officialdom of the new districts, it finally succeeded in neutralizing the Ruwenzururu. The difference lay in the more political/analytical approach of the Obote II regime as opposed to the predominantly military methods its predecessors employed. Beginning with a deciphering of different tendencies in the leadership of the Ruwenzururu, the Obote II regime identified those more responsive to a negotiated outcome and defined concessions it could make short of a strategic defeat. Maate, the secretary of the movement in 1962, when Mkirani was its president, was appointed head of civil administration in the district. Lesser leaders in the movement followed by taking positions down the hierarchy of the local state. The decision in favor of a negotiated settlement was not made by an isolated faction. The issue was deliberated at every level of assembly of the Ruwenzururu. When the king (Mkirani's son) came down the mountain exactly twenty years after the guerrilla struggle had been launched, he was ceremoniously exiled with a scholarship to an American university. The political/civil leadership of the movement was integrated into a reorganized local administration and put in charge of the local apparatus of the indirect rule state. Only the military leadership, the chief of staff and some of his lieutenants, refused to join the compromise; they stayed on the mountain.

The result was a remarkably reformed local administration in the region of the Ruwenzururu but not any significant change either in the form of the local state or in the social conditions that defined peasant life in the region. When I climbed the mountain in 1984, the parish chief who greeted me had been a former minister of education in the Ruwenzururu. At a meeting organized to introduce me to the villagers, he sounded a welcome note that I have seldom heard from a chief: "If you are here for noble reasons, we welcome you; if not, it is regrettable!" At a reception that followed the meeting, I found that he was the only person not drinking alcohol. I wondered if he was a born-again Christian. "At a time when everyone is drinking, a responsible person must abstain," he answered. He then added, "Of course, my share of the alcohol has been set aside. I shall drink it later." These anecdotes highlight the difference that a reform in the face of officialdom can make to day-to-day encounters between peasants and petty officials, but they in no way change the more basic facts of life that shape the destinies of peasant families.

I am not arguing that either the Sungusungu or the Ruwenzururu failed. Obviously not. Both succeeded in attaining limited objectives: the Sungusungu in bringing cattle rustling to a halt, and the Ruwenzururu in getting district boundaries redrawn to ensure a measure of local autonomy for the Bakonzo and the Bamba nationalities. I *am* arguing, though, that these successes have a significance both limited and temporary: the reforms neither affected the productive relations that shape peasant lives nor altered the nature of central state power. This is why there is no exaggeration in the observation that, as they were incorporated into existing forms of state administration through minor reforms, these movements became custodians of the very order they had originally organized against.

What underlies the localized character of peasant initiatives? The fact that they are necessarily built around locally manifested contradictions. In the Africa of free peasants, where a customary access to land combines with customarily defined Native Authorities, the peasant's definition of the enemy is usually a functionary of the local state. This is not to say that there are no instances of local chiefs joining a peasant protest. There are, as we saw with South African movements. Put differently, peasant grievances can reflect degrees of opposition: their focus can range from bad chiefs to chiefship as bad. The local nature of the contradiction lends itself to resolution by a localized reform, which may or may not be effected through a significant political or social transformation.

Few would deny that peasant movements have had diverse outcomes. At times they have been incorporated into wider regime strategies through localized reforms, as with the Sungusungu and the Ruwenzururu. At other times they have stemmed the tide of settler domination and laid the foundation of state independence, as with the Mau Mau, just as they have constituted the social basis of armed struggles in independent Africa, as in Eritrea and Uganda. This diversity of outcomes is shaped by the nature of alliances that peasant movements enter into and into which they are incorporated. Allies of peasants have included upper classes from the precolonial period, as well as middle-class nationalists and revolutionaries. Take, for example, the alliance between the royal family and peasants in Gile (Mozambique) in 1939 which became the basis of a popular revolt against colonially appointed chiefs;[65] or the case of Buganda, where the post-1928 reformed state administration split the alliance of the royal family and the big chiefs, laying the basis for populist peasant uprisings that fought chiefs in the name of the king. But even when peasants' allies were middle-class intellectuals, the latter's ideological orientation could be as diverse as the democratic monarchism of the teachers who led the Ruwenzururu or the social radicalism of the Mulelists in the Simba uprising in Zaire.

Because the peasantry lacks a strategic perspective on the character of the central state, peasant movements can be incorporated into diverse alliances. Their potential is therefore contradictory. Scanning the role of the peasantry in Chinese history, Mao commented that peasant revolts often have been like bushfires, creating an occasion for one dynasty to replace another.[66] We are reminded of the institution of the Shiftanat in Ethiopia, which built on and incorporated peasant grievances in a ruling-class project. Peasant action can be incorporated into the strategic perspective of other classes, even if these contradict its own project. This is why central to understanding the political significance of peasant movements is the question of alliances. An alliance, however, is not manipulation. No matter how unequal, it contains a moment of reciprocity, a democratic moment. An alliance cannot be coerced. This much is clear from a reading of both Furedi's study of the Mau Mau[67] and Gebre-Medhin's study of Eritrea.[68]

Gebre-Medhin's study of the social basis of Eritrean nationalism elaborates the point. He explores the history of relations among various middle-class groups and sections of the peasantry. These relations came to change both parties to it. Through experience, sectors of the intelligentsia came to realize that peasants could be expected to defend only a social order signified by social reforms of meaning to them; a political struggle, in other words, had to go hand in hand with social reforms. What should those reforms be? And would agrarian reform not antagonize internal groups that may otherwise be predisposed toward supporting a struggle against external domination? The relationship between the struggle against external domination and internal agrarian reform became a contentious issue leading to a political split between intellectuals of different ideological persuasions.

The effect of a step-by-step agrarian transformation advocated by radical intellectuals was to transform the organizational capacity of different strata of the peasantry. In changing internal relations within the peasantry, the reforms shaped a peasant community of a different type. Both the capacity the peasantry realized and the capacity its actions helped fuel cannot be understood without focusing on the twin issues of the autonomous organization of the peasantry and the alliance between strata of the peasantry and other social groups. Autonomy and alliance are not mutually exclusive. The local autonomy of a community does not preclude its incorporation into an alliance whose significance may be not only wider and strategic, but also ultimately contradictory.

That localized reform and strategic incorporation can go hand in hand is clear from the most ambitious attempt yet to reform indirect rule. Although the first wave of postindependence reform had little effect in changing the structure of the indirect rule state, the same cannot be said of the reform wave of the eighties. Changes introduced by radical populist regimes like Qaddafi in Libya, Sankara in Bourkina Faso, early Rawlings in Ghana, and Museveni in Uganda sought to liquidate the indirect rule structures of the local state. Chiefship was either abolished outright (as in Libya and Bourkina Faso) or was limited to a purely administrative function (as in Ghana and in Uganda, where chiefship was reintroduced to guerrilla-held areas in 1986 in a modified form, one in which it was also retained in the rest of the country).

The reform makes sense if understood in a broader context, for the combination of limited democratic reforms at the local level and concentrated power at the top is increasingly characteristic of reforms that have marked the new breed of radical regimes in Africa. The driving force behind these reforms is not simply the strength of rural community–based resistance to the local state, but also the threat of urban civil society–based demands for representation in the central state. Put differently, these reforms are not simply a concession to rural revolt, but also a regime initiative designed to checkmate urban civil society–based movements, thereby forestalling the possibility of an urban-rural alliance reminiscent of the postwar anticolonial upsurge. Given the tribal nature of authority in the local state, the alliance is bound to take on a tribal form, including an alliance of tribal coalitions at the center—thus the tenor of official opposition to multiparty elections, claiming that it is no more than a mask for tribal resurgence. In such a context, localized reform in favor of the peasantry—"empowerment"—consolidates the social base of the regime, and monopoly of power at the top neutralizes middle-class contenders for leadership from within civil society. Rural reform is thus presented as a move toward a direct, participatory, and community-based democracy and is favorably contrasted to urban demands for a multiparty, representative, and individual rights–based democracy. Through a move that simultaneously reorganizes peasant communities on the basis of local self-administration and clamps down on the freedom of party organization at the center, the regimes in question fragment social forces while strengthening their own support bases.

The resulting change reforms the institutional basis of the local state while leaving intact the institutions of the central state. As a result, it is both partial and unstable, easily compromised or even liquidated with a shift or change in the character of the central power. The shift is observable in the case of Ghana, where the autonomy of People's Defence Committees was compromised—a fact reflected in a change of name from People's Defence Committees to Committees for the Defence of the Revolution, from organs of the people to organs of the revolution. The change in nomenclature could not have been more telling. The case of Bourkina Faso illustrates how swiftly a change of regime can reverse a reform in the local state. With the coup against the Sankara government, the Neighbourhood Associations were liquidated as chiefs returned to the countryside and political parties to urban areas. Like in the Nigerian reforms where the military abrogated elections to the central state but introduced them in local state organs, and civilians did the reverse, we have here a game of musical chairs: a multiparty opening at the top goes hand in hand with a chiefly closure at the bottom, whereas the introduction of village self-governance goes alongside a single or no-party closure in the central state.

The partial and unstable character of a reform confined to the local state is illustrated by the example of Uganda under Museveni. I have already discussed the significance of agrarian reform (the Resistance Council and Committee system) in understanding the strength of the NRA's peasant base in the Luwero Triangle. The introduction of the Resistance Council and Committee system to the entire country in the post-1986 period was the single most important political achievement of the NRA/M, for this measure dismantled the indirect rule regime at the local level and replaced it with village self-governance. The chief was stripped of judicial, executive, and legislative powers and reduced to the position of an administrative official. Organized as the Resistance Council, the village community was now the village legislature, also with adjudicative powers. The nine-person committee the village elected—whose members it had the right to recall between elections—held executive powers.

From the outset the RC system had imbibed a crucial weakness: although it recognized the existence of peasant communities, it paid no heed to social differentiation within these.[69] Its organizational principles emphasized one's place of residence but totally ignored differentiated work experiences within the local community. Instead of being a medium to build the organizational capacity of those strata of peasants with an interest in social reform, the tendency for the RC system was mechanically to reinforce the parity of relations shaped outside its parameters: those who were better organized outside the RC came to dominate the RC. A consistent feature of the RC system was that it came to stabilize peasant communities on the basis of leadership by its more prosperous members. Political reform went hand in hand with social conservatism.

In the post-1986 period, this weakness was joined to a second, as the NRM was unable to link its participatory reform at the village level with a representative reform at higher levels. When the NRM came to power in 1986, its organized base was restricted to no more than a third of the country. In recognition of a plurality of forces in the country, it created a broad-based government at the center, but in recognition of its own weakness, it was also concerned with denying village access to oppositional forces at the center. Instead of linking a participatory process at the village level with direct representation at all levels, it took the path of Frelimo, resorting to indirect elections beyond the village. The RC system increasingly came to reflect two tiers: one local, the other central; one on the ground, the other at the apex. The higher one went up the RC pyramid, the more watered down was the democratic content of the system. Elections were direct only at the first level. At all subsequent levels, voting was confined to an electoral college of representatives but was rationalized as realizing face-to-face participatory democracy. With elections indirect, the power of recall became meaningless.

The arrangement could not hold in the face of pressure for direct and multiparty elections at the center. This demand came from two quarters: Western countries on the one hand and local political parties and urban civil society organizations on the other. With a growing external debt, signified by a debt-service ratio that fluctuated between 70 and 90 percent in the early 1990s, external pressure for political reform could not be ignored. At the same time, the failure to follow up local state reform with an improvement in rural living conditions gave political parties an opening through which to address the peasantry, particularly in the zones of former guerrilla activity. If Bourkina Faso witnessed a return from village self-administration to indirect rule administration with a change of regime, Uganda shows the possibility of a similar shift as a regime under pressure looks for new and more effective allies to prevent middle-class urban opponents from forging links with dissatisfied peasant strata.

The regime conceded partly to this combined pressure, allowing for direct but nonparty elections to a constituent assembly. As direct elections broadened oppositional access to rural constituencies, the NRM found it difficult to hold firm the social alliance of peasants and migrants that it had forged in Buganda during the guerrilla struggle. The claim of opposition parties was that the migrants had won out in that alliance, and on an ethnic basis at that—for the opposition stressed the ethnic affinity between migrants and the leadership of the NRA/M—arguing that this explained the regime's failure "to deliver" to "indigenous" peasants. The question as to whether the regime would lose the Baganda peasantry to the opposition became real as elections to the Constituent Assembly approached. Confronted by an ethnic accusation, the regime sought an ethnic alliance. That was the restoration of kingship, *ebyaffe*. It was a shift effected with both eyes on the electorate in Buganda. The pact between the Baganda royalty and the NRM leadership was to keep political parties out of Buganda. To many, it was a replay of an earlier deal—the alliance between Uganda Peoples Congress and Kabaka Yekka on the eve of independence—which also kept the opposition party out of Buganda. For the king and his men (and some women), however, the pact was a beginning, not an end. The royal party wanted restoration of kingship to be a meaningful affair, not just window dressing. To be worthy of office, the king must have chiefs and land, but to restore the powers of chiefs meant liquidating council democracy where it was most meaningful, in the villages. Local rule in Uganda was once again at a crossroads, hovering between self-governance and indirect rule.

Can one argue that any of the above instances—Sungusungu, Ruwenzururu, or the Resistance Councils—represents peasant empowerment? If so, then our discussion should serve to underline two issues. First, the immediate outcome of the same empowering reform depends on relations internal to local communities. The same institutional reform can have varied outcomes because the peasantry is internally differentiated and the capacity of peasant movements is shaped by the strength of its social base and the nature of its political leadership. Second, in the absence of a wider strategy of political change and social transformation, the empowerment of local communities can be of only limited and temporary significance. In the African continent, where a key institutional legacy of the colonial period is the bifurcated state, a successful democratic reform needs to straddle both spheres. A successful political reform of the bifurcated state needs to be simultaneously rural and urban, local and central.

CHAPTER SEVEN

The Rural in the Urban:
Migrant Workers in South Africa

I HAVE ARGUED that tribalism is both the form of power and the form of revolt against it. The response to ethnically organized power in the local state is an ethnically defined revolt, except that while the holders of power in a Native Authority are ethnically one, the population subject to their edicts is more often than not multiethnic; indigenous peasants live alongside stranger peasants, more so in some localities than in others. Because the intraethnic civil war in the Native Authority unfolded in the context of an interethnic tension, one effect of indirect rule through Native Authorities was to fragment the ruled along ethnic lines.

My objective in this chapter is to illuminate the link between politics in the Native Authority and that in civil society. The effect of a decentralized customary despotism is immediately to impose two major tensions among the ruled: interethnic in the Native Authority and urban-rural in civil society. The key social link between the two spheres, Native Authority and civil society, is migrant labor. This was particularly true in settler economies. This fact was appreciated by Jan Smuts in 1929 and was the driving vision behind the agenda the Broederbond tried to implement in the late 1940s.

The migrant worker needs to be seen as the locus of all major social contradictions in such a context. Besides articulating the tensions generated by a market economy—those of class, gender, and age—migrant labor also came to be the focus of differences reinforced by the mode of rule that was decentralized despotism: the interethnic and the urban-rural. As such, it came to be the key link in a complex chain of social relationships. Moving like a conveyor belt between the rural and the urban, it was, to paraphrase Marx, a class *in* civil society but not *of* civil society.

There was no one particular way in which these differences came to be translated into political life. There were, and are, different ways of linking the rural and the urban. Each is class specific. Each, in turn, either exacerbates ethnic differences—and softens class contradictions—in the course of bridging the rural and the urban or softens ethnic differences and highlights class contradictions. In this chapter, I explore the social effects of two ways of linking the urban and the rural: trade union politics and the politics of political parties, both tribal and nationalist. Through a comparison of the two, I hope to highlight the critical role of political leadership and political choice in translating social facts into political ones. My point is that if the mode of rule introduces and builds on specific differences among the ruled, then the point of political activism must be both to recognize the starting point of resistance as shaped by the nature of power and to transcend its limits.

The point is brought out forcefully in the post-Soweto experience of popular struggles in South Africa. If apartheid was the consolidation of indirect rule authority—institutional segregation—then the scope of the authority was not confined to rural homelands but extended to enclaves in urban areas, particularly hostels. The population that straddled both regimes was that of migrant workers, with a home in the reserves and bed space in the hostels, for the migrant worker was a free peasant transported to an urban industrial setting. The negatively defined semiproletarian was in reality a peasant worker. The tensions generated between the rural and the urban—the free peasantry and the urban worker—should be seen not just one-sidedly as reflecting an antagonism between migrant and resident labor, but as bringing home one of several possibilities inherent in the migrant situation. How that tension would be resolved in practice, whether through conflict or through alliance, was shaped by the nature of political leadership.

To make this point, I will focus broadly on the migrant experience in South Africa, specifically the hostel-based Zulu migrants who were partisans in the hostel-based violence that engulfed the Johannesburg region in the early 1990s. I characterize these migrants as free peasants in an urban industrial setting. How can this be when many studies have shown that most migrants have subeconomic, marginal, or even nonexistent land in the reserves, even if this is—as we will see—more true for some reserves like Transkei and Ciskei than for others, like Zululand, where the agricultural economy is less eroded? I have only one reason for doing so. The free peasant, as I have defined the term, is a direct producer on land partly shielded from the impact of market forces—and to that extent subject to compulsion by Native Authorities—because of a customary right to land. Unlike migrants in other industrializing contexts, those in South Africa came from tribal reserves in which they had a customary right of access to land and to which they were forced to return periodically. Both the right and the compulsion were justified as customary. Even when this right was significantly emptied of content, as when migrants clung to no more than a customary but nominal patch, the notion of customary rights—as of customary patriarchal privilege— was key to understanding the ideological baggage a migrant brought from the rural to the urban context. Inasmuch as a customary right was understood, claimed, and defended as a tribal right, notions of the customary overlapped with and reinforced an ethnic identity.

Yet this chapter is not about the totality of either the post-1973 trade union movement or the ethnic violence that has been a feature of South African politics over the last decade. It is not even about the totality of the violence that began in Natal in 1987, a phenomenon that from all accounts unfolded as an ethnic civil war, an intraethnic contest in which protagonists on both sides were Zulu. The object of my inquiry is more specifically the violence that erupted on the Reef in 1990, a phenomenon that took on an intertribal dimension, with Zulu migrant workers most often found on one side of the battle line.

To make sense of this violence, I have found it necessary to trace the historical contours of the landscape, broadly understood as the migrant experience in South Africa. Like any query that zooms in on a subject through historical time, its parameters are broader at the outset but focused as it comes to embrace the subject. This is why this query sidesteps the experience of what is probably the largest single social constellation of migrant workers in South Africa, the miners. My interest is not the rural or periurban migrant, whether to farms or to mines, but the rural in the urban.

From the time an urban industrial experience became a significant part of African working life in South Africa, the powers that be used all the resources and experience at their disposal to insulate and immunize it as a potential cancer. Migrant labor was never just a source of cheap labor; it was at the same time semiservile and controlled. Every effort was made to turn urban hostels in which migrants lived into enclaves shut off socially and physically from surrounding townships, just as an effort was made to subordinate migrants inside hostels to a regime of indirect rule; but the more migrant links with the reserve were kept alive, the more effectively they functioned as conveyor belts between urban activism and rural discontent. We have seen that the possibility was realized most dramatically in the experience of rural revolt in the 1950s and 1960s, so that even when a regime of terror could put out the fires of urban revolt, as indeed happened in the decade that followed Sharpeville, the flame of revolt remained smoldering in the reserves, part of the experience of migrants. Not surprisingly, just as migrants carried forms of urban militancy from towns to reserves in the 1950s, so they did the flame of revolt from the rural to the urban in the coming period: the so-called decade of peace that followed Sharpeville came to an end with the predominantly migrant strikes of 1972–74, at first in Durban, and then on the Reef and the Cape.

The response of the state to migrant activism, and to the possibility of a migrant-township political link in the aftermath of Soweto 1976, was to build on the difference between the two experiences so as to turn a rift into a divide. To set up a Chinese wall between migrant and township populations was the key objective of recommendations contained in the reports of two government commissions of the time, Wiehahn and Riekert, the former recommending that unions be allowed to organize resident urban labor but not migrants, and the latter calling for stabilizing urban labor while tightening the screw of "influx control" on migrants. That strategy was immediately defeated because the new independent unions fought it tooth and nail. The strategy was later resuscitated, successfully, for a number of reasons. The march of industrialization opened avenues for African semiskilled labor and made deskilled migrants marginal, and the union leadership began to reflect this changing balance at all levels and deserted the hostels. The limited perspective of unions was reflected in the controversy within its ranks between workerists and populists: the former called for an exclusively workplace-based strategy of organization and the latter for joining workplace and community-based demands, and both understood by *community* the urban townships—and not the hostel or the reserves. As migrants became marginal in the union movement, the structural difference between resident and migrant labor came to coincide with a difference between organized and unorganized labor. This difference now took on the dimensions of a tension. As it propelled forward a protracted urban uprising, the community of the organized brooked no breach in the ranks of the oppressed. In the unfolding dialectic between resistance and repression, though, those organized were better equipped for self-defense, and those unorganized were exposed to retaliation. As the community of the organized moved to action that seemed to dispense with those unorganized, the tension between residents and migrants—or townships and hostels—was aggravated. Simultaneously, the South African state initiative to abolish influx control laws in 1986 showed a keen appreciation of the central weakness of the organized opposition to apartheid: by opening urban gates to a flood of rural migrants, it hoped to feed the urban-rural antagonism and reap the harvest. The tension, however, did not explode into antagonism, except at sporadic moments.

My point is that the violence was not inevitable. Although the ground that made the violence possible can be understood only if we grasp the history of social relations that underlay the structural difference between the two experiences, that difference did not have to result in open conflict. To understand why this did happen requires putting it not only against a historical backdrop, but also alongside a critique of political leadership under the circumstances. Zulu migrants, an important segment of the social base of the independent union movement in the 1970s, were turning to Inkatha and then to the Inkatha Freedom Party (IFP) by the early 1990s. Migrant options narrowed as key political forces failed to appreciate and respond to the migrant situation. Like the unions before, the ANC failed to appreciate migrant choices and perspectives: to important sections of the migrant community, the ANC's call for a conversion of hostels into family units sounded like a death threat to their urban base. Just as surely as migrants had hit back at the betterment policies of the apartheid state, policies that threatened their hold on a rural patch in an earlier era, so they retaliated against the ANC's call for converting hostels, a program that now threatened their hold on an urban patch. But the embrace between these migrants and the IFP was neither permanent nor total. In another few years, the same migrant activists began to take initiatives independent of the IFP, in spite of its opposition—initiatives that testified to the importance of political choice even in the most impossible-seeming circumstances. It is these initiatives that define new possibilities in the era that opened with the nonracial elections of 1994.

This chapter is divided into three sections. The first is a survey of different explanations of the violence on the Reef. I seek neither to dismiss nor to embrace them but to underline their limits and to build on their insights. The two sections that follow consider two ways of linking the urban and the rural, each with its different set of social consequences: the second section focuses on the post-1973 trade union experience and the internal uprising that followed Soweto 1976; the subject matter of the third section is the political parties, both the internally based tribal IFP and the exile nationalist ANC.

CONTENDING EXPLANATIONS

In 1986 the South African government abolished influx control and the compulsion for African people to carry passes. With that, a key piece of legislation symbolic of the apartheid order and regulating the movement of migrant labor was scrapped from the books. It proved to be the starting point of a far-reaching reform process, leading to the unbanning of exile movements (including the ANC and the SACP) in 1990 and the holding of nonracial elections four years later.

In retrospect, 1986 also seemed to signal the beginning of a campaign of terror whose triangular outline highlighted a growing tension between, and sometimes within, three types of African communities: townships, shantytowns, and hostels. The violence began in 1987 in Natal, pitting townships allied with the United Democratic Front (UDF) against Inkatha-allied shanties and hostels in waves of mounting violence that by any account took thousands of lives. In 1990 it moved to the industrial heartland of the Transvaal, the Reef, where embattled hostel dwellers, also said to be pro-Inkatha, confronted neighboring townships and shanties, and at times hostels, of ANC persuasion. Once again, the toll stood in the thousands.

The political dimension of the conflict provided the clue to many who set out to explain it. After all, had not the political reform also set in motion a competition between all major forces with ambitions to shape the new order? Were not both sides of the battle line clearly defined by political preference? If combinations shifted from Natal (1987) to the Reef (1990), with mainly shanties and hostels battling townships in the former and hostels pitted against shanties and townships—and sometimes other hostels—in the latter, did they not continue to reflect an Inkatha preference on this side and a UDF-ANC allegiance on the other? And was not the South African government, particularly its security organs long nourished by an anti-Communist and antinationalist diet, not an innocent referee but a party with a clear and definable interest in shaping the outcome of the reform process? Clearly, so the line of reasoning went, the explanation of the violence lay not really in the observable actions of its participants—the residents of townships, shanties, and hostels—but in the not-so-hidden agenda of far more powerful and clear-sighted forces that formed the backup in all instances. Here was a clear case in which one needed to pinpoint external agencies, the hidden hands, the "third forces" behind the string of conflicts.

"The onset of the Reef violence," argued the Johannesburg-based Independent Board of Inquiry (IBI), "was signaled by a series of attacks on the Sebokeng Hostel which began on July 22 1990. The violence rapidly spread to the East Rand, Soweto, the West Rand and Alexandra township. In each case non-Zulu hostel dwellers were driven out of the hostels which became armed fortresses from which attacks were launched against the surrounding community and squatter camps in particular. Where Zulu hostel dwellers resisted the call to violence, they too were removed."[1] Titled *Fortresses of Fear*, the board's report approvingly cited the findings of a delegation of the International Commission of Jurists that visited South Africa in March 1992: the hostels were indeed Inkatha barracks.[2]

"Behind the scale of brutality," argued the Pietermaritzburg-based Community Agency for Social Enquiry (CASE) in material prepared for the International Commission of Jurists, "is clear evidence that the violence erupts at points when it most weakens the ANC and its allies, and dies down dramatically when it would most harm the government of FW de Klerk."[3] To back up its claim that "the violence appears to be switched on *and off* at strategic moments," the CASE report drew up a trajectory of the violence against a backdrop of "political facts of life in South Africa." If the violence was orchestrated, who were its regulators? To answer this question, CASE identified winners and losers in this deadly game: on one side, the National Party government and Inkatha, on the other side the ANC. "In essence," concluded yet another report from CASE, "the level of violence appears to go down when it would harm the government, and up when it can hinder the government's opponents."[4]

In assuming that the beneficiaries of an event are necessarily its perpetrators, these reports were guilty of a highly deductive line of reasoning. It was like arguing that if the rains are heavy and umbrella makers make a lot of money, then somehow they must be responsible for the rain! Or, to move from the natural setting of the above analogy to the social setting of the Reef violence, even if the beneficiaries of that violence understood their interests fully and acted in line with it, what explained the fact that direct participants in this violence were so readily available for this manipulation?

This question has given rise to a second line of reasoning, whose emphasis is on the observable behavior of direct participants and not the hidden agenda of forces in the background. The methodological shift is from the political to the sociological. In the words of an eminent South African sociologist: "Sociological conditions, i.e., the social organization of hostels, marginalisation and alienation, predispose hostels to mobilization and consequently violence on the slightest signs of provocation. It is not that the hostel dwellers are inherently aggressive, but that the social conditions that they live under make them easy prey to political manipulation."[5] The IBI report quoted earlier spelled out the argument in some detail: "The closed nature of the hostel system and the existence of large concentrations of single men, creates the perfect terrain for coercion and forced recruitment. This terrain also affords the opportunity for rapid mobilization, instant meetings, and the preparation for the launching of armed attacks."[6] To this inert condition, the closed nature of a single-sex compound, the IBI report added another, which makes hostel dwellers "easy to organize and influence": "the hierarchical and coercive nature of hostel organization and the role of *indunas* (a traditional position of leadership)." Hostel dwellers are easy to manipulate because they live in a closed world, both on account of the barracklike conditions under which they live and because of their allegiance to an equally hierarchical tradition and culture—so went this mode of reasoning.

There is yet a third line of reasoning uncomfortable with the argument that hostel dwellers are caught up in a Pavlovian mice-in-a-cage type of dilemma or that they are unthinking traditionalists responding to the dictum of an age-old culture. It is an argument that lays stress on the hostel dwellers as a conscious agency, as responding to a changing situation. From unthinking traditionalists, we thus move on to hostel dwellers as thinking traditionalists, as interest-bearing agents making a rational choice. "The harsh reality," argued Mike Morris and Doug Hindson for a study initially prepared for COSATU's Economic Trends group, "is that racial, ethnic and class antagonism held in check under classic apartheid have resurfaced in the climate of liberalization and deracialization."[7] The reform of apartheid has facilitated "rapid urbanization" and "sparked off a struggle for space, land and residential resources, leading to the mobilization of communities along new lines based on emerging social divisions—race, class, age, language and ethnic origin." The same reforms "have accentuated rather than dampened conflict," for "economic liberalization has not been matched by political incorporation of the mass of the people into the national democratic process." Many attacks, whether from squatter camps or hostels, are in fact "crude booty gathering raids, with houses being plundered and consumer items carted off." The "conflict over resources" is thus "taking place over the distribution of the marginal resources left over for black residential areas whose inhabitants are rapidly expanding but with no parallel expansion of resources being made available to them." For these authors, behind the violence lies "the blunt compulsion of material forces," now liberated by a reform of apartheid. This argument has found an echo among several analysts.[8] Forcefully arguing for "the need to go beyond characterizing hostel dwellers as either victims or vanquishers," Lauren Segal agrees in more or less the same words: "The current violence is therefore about the poorer and more marginalized sectors of black society struggling to make a space for themselves."[9] Further, the strategy has been more or less successful, for "the violence has 'reorganized the urban landscape' in favor of Zulu migrants."

All of these explanations contain a grain of truth, and none can be ignored. The argument for the existence of third forces is compelling, but it cannot by itself explain the violence: conspiracies do exist, but that fact on its own cannot explain why some succeed and others fail. Sociological conditions in hostels do explain why its inhabitants are more disposed toward mobilization, as economic conditions in deprived communities explain the acute desperation that marks the quest to sustain life, but neither explains the ways in which people actually mobilize or act. Although material conditions do explain the constraints under which we make real choices in real life, they cannot by themselves explain the choices we do make within those constraints. The old argument between structure and agency, between sociological and historical constraint and human will, cannot be resolved simply by holding up one end of the pole.

Are the choices that we make then explained by our culture, whether conceived of as static and suprahistorical or as dynamic and changing in time? I doubt it, not because culture, or tradition, as it is often called, does not shape our interpretation of circumstances and events. It does. But culture is seldom as compact and singular as it is sometimes made out to be. Rather, it is full of tension, diverse and differentiated. To understand culture as an undifferentiated and noncontradictory whole is to presume a single outcome to situations of conflict, whether that outcome is explained as the result of a single initiative or a singular absence of one. True, we make our choices within constraints—economic, sociological, and cultural—but we do make them. It is tempting to read back from an event and to explain it as the necessary outcome of historically evolved circumstances or consciousness. Such a reading back obscures the element of choice that confronted participants at each step along this historical route.

I will make this point in this chapter through a brief analysis of the politics of migrant labor on the Transvaal. My historical overview highlights the two decades that opened with the Durban strikes of 1972–73 and closed with the hostel-centered violence of the early 1990s on the Reef. Along the line, there has been a dramatic shift in popular understanding of what migrants stand for. Today, migrants, particularly hostel dwellers, are seen to represent the rural in the urban, the force of tradition bursting through the straitjacket of impossible circumstances. In the 1950s, however, migrants were the cutting edge of antichief struggles in the countryside. They were understood as an expression of the urban in the rural. In the 1970s, to illustrate another shift, migrants were seen as the most militant sector of a fast-unionizing working class on the Reef. But by the early 1990s, they had turned into the soft underbelly of both factory-based unions and township-based civics. Why?

To answer this question, I will borrow liberally from each of the explanations I have critiqued above, for the economists are no doubt right when they claim that rapidly changing circumstances (not only material but also political) over which migrants have had little or no control have something to do with the violence in which many are engulfed. Unlike the economists, I will argue that it is not only changing circumstances but also changing perspectives and strategies that we need to understand

and evaluate. Although the strategies cannot be understood except as a response to circumstances, there were choices made along the way and lessons that need to be drawn. To those who emphasize the weight of material compulsion in a one-sided way I will uphold the necessity of political choice and political analysis.

The culturalists too are right in insisting that besides the force of inert circumstances, there exist a migrant culture and tradition that shape migrant options. In contrast to those who see this culture in the singular (say, "Zulu tradition"), I will emphasize the plurality and heterogeneity of tradition. I will argue that it is necessary to restore not only the element of historical dynamism in the understanding of culture, but also that of contemporary diversity and plurality. Put differently, tradition should not be understood as a cultural baggage carried through historical time. Rather, like notions of community that I queried in an earlier chapter, those of culture are also reproduced through struggles that pit diverse and even contradictory notions against each other. Only a profoundly political and historical understanding of culture, I will argue, can give us a meaningful idea of migrant options, of choices available and choices made.

THE 1970s:
RURAL MILITANTS IN URBAN AREAS

Migrant labor was semicoerced and semiservile. The institution predated apartheid; nor was it uniquely South African. In the era that promised the emancipation of African labor from slavery, it was an alternative form of labor to which labor-seeking mines, plantations, and farms in the African colonies could turn. The institution was set and kept going through a web of extra-economic compulsions.[10] The native was tracked and kept on course like a beast by one set of laws; not simply and directly with a whip as would be a beast, but through legally defined injunctions and prohibitions that left him—and eventually her—"free" to work as a migrant in one of the many laborious and dirty jobs most easily found in mines, plantations, or farms. The framework of migrant labor was put in place by another set of subsidiary institutions and injunctions. Central to these in South Africa was the Natives Land Act of 1913, which legalized the earlier theft of land, created a huge marginal peasantry, and left it with little option but to turn into a captive labor force. Then there was a complex set of pass laws that simultaneously prohibited blacks from moving about the country to get the best job on the best available terms in a free market and branded those without employment as vagrants. For those who did take on employment, there was the Masters and Servants Act, which made it a criminal offense to break a labor contract, and a panoply of labor legislation that prohibited blacks from doing skilled work in most workplaces.

For those caught up in it, cheap labor was an incredibly costly system. Assuming an average eighteen-month contract, D. Hobart Houghton calculated in 1964 that migrants would travel an extra 370 million miles a year in addition to the normal daily journey to work.[11] Legally entitled to be in an urban area only for so long as they were employed, hundreds were daily sent to jail by commissioners' courts for staying longer than seventy-two hours without the requisite permission or for failing to produce their passbooks on demand. An estimated seventeen and a half million black persons were prosecuted under the pass laws between 1916 and 1981.[12]

The basic law regulating migrant labor in South Africa was the Urban (Bantu) Areas Act, first put on the books in 1923. Section 10 defined the few blacks with legal permission to live in cities and large towns not as having a right to do so, but as exempt from the provisions of the act. For a black person residing in rural areas who wished to move to a city the law prescribed a definite path.[13] That person would first have to register as a work seeker at the local Bantu Affairs commissioner's office. If approved, the person would be granted permission by the commissioner to be absent from the district for a period of eleven months, being the duration of the work contract he would get in the city. The contract would be renewed for another eleven months if the employer agreed and the district commissioner's office granted permission to be absent from the "home" district for a second contract. Such a migrant's wife or children could not join him in the city, for they had neither a section 10 exemption nor jobs that could count as reason for being in the city; but should they decide to accompany or follow him to the city anyway, their chances of remaining undetected were slim because of regular pass raids by township police. The laws criminalized even the most humane of impulses, like parents and children wanting to be together, and then gave transgression of the law as reason for continual policing. So pass raids were supplemented by regular and frequent midnight police raids on township homes, to check permits and to ensure that everyone sleeping in the house was indeed registered at the local township superintendent's office and therefore eligible to be within the area. For a migrant to qualify for a right to live in the urban areas, he would have to complete ten consecutive eleven-month periods of residence in that city! Until then, he remained a migrant whom the law deemed to be single, eligible for a bed in a single-sex hostel. The bed ticket a migrant obtained from the superintendent's office was nothing to be scoffed at. It was a valuable possession, for the simple reason that the monthly rent for a hostel bed was on the average no more than 10 percent of that for a backyard shack (in 1990). Given their meager wages and the necessity to remit a sizable portion to the family back home, migrants had little choice but to seek hostel accommodation while in urban areas.

The demand for migrant labor was very much a function of employers' needs, but the structure of employment was undergoing a rapid shift in South Africa in the first half of this century. In the early decades, there was an acute and crass contest between mines and farmers over the control of migrant labor. While mines tried to organize a regular and directed flow through systematic recruitment from the reserves, the farms penalized and waylaid migrants "trespassing" on the way to mine centers, forcing them to work for varying periods by way of compensation. The farm-mine competition for labor from a single pool became the subject of many government commissions. One of the reasons farmers gave to the Farm Labor Committee of 1932 for the shortage of labor was the competition of the mines, which "has absorbed a large proportion of farm laborers." The Native Economic Commission of that same year noted that there was no way a migrant could fulfill both a farm and a mine contract in the same year, even if he was a temporary worker in both places, for the service period on farms was three to six months in a year, whereas that on a mine was counted as 270 shifts, "which necessarily takes more than 9 months to complete."[14] In the forties, however, with increased recruitment of Africans for the war effort and revolt brewing in the reserves, mines turned to areas neighboring South Africa to meet expanding labor needs. By 1946 only 41 percent of mining labor came from within South Africa's borders.[15]

The shift in the labor-recruitment priorities of mines did not mean that the woes of farmers diminished correspondingly. The structure of the South African economy was changing, and a new and formidable competitor was on the horizon. By 1930 manufacturing had surpassed agriculture in its contribution to national income, and by 1943 it had outstripped the contribution of mining capital.[16] Further, the expansion of manufacturing capital drew less from the reserves than it did directly from the farms, encouraging an outflow of labor from white farms to industrial urban centers. This flow was quantified by the Tomlinson Commission (1955) for the period between 1936 and 1951: it calculated that although 40 percent of "Bantu urban residents" came from "European farms and other rural areas," only 8 percent were drawn from the reserves.[17] The remaining half were made up of those drawn from "foreign centers" (23 percent) and "the natural increase of the towns themselves" (29 percent).

By the early 1950s, the African population of South Africa was to be found in three roughly equal groups: one-third in the reserves, another third in urban areas, and a final third on European homesteads.[18] Anxious to stop the flight of labor from farms to cities, the union of white farmers (the South African Agricultural Union) put forward a memorandum on native policy that called for a freeze of this threefold compartmentalization of labor between reserves, cities, and white farms.[19] According to this scheme, "the industrial group" would be "wholly cut off from the practice of agriculture as a means of subsistence," farm labor would be accommodated as "full time employees" on European farms, and "a category of unclassified Natives" would be accommodated in urban fashion in the reserves so as to serve "their own people in various capacities." "In this way the Native could be encouraged to develop on useful lines, and at the same time an enormous labor force could be released." Contrary to this were the demands of industrial capital, which received a strong hearing in the report of the Fagan Commission (1948). The conclusion of that report argued that legal or administrative compulsions designed to perpetuate the system of migrant labor "are wrong and have a detrimental effect." "The policy should be one for facilitating and encouraging stabilization."[20]

Many have seen the victory of apartheid and the National Party as the triumph of white farms and mining interests—once a political accommodation had been worked out between the two—over industrial and commercial capital. Certainly, the system of migrant labor not only continued but was reinforced with a tightened regime of controls around it. Apartheid did indeed end the flight of labor from white farms to urban areas. Others have argued that practical apartheid involved more of a compromise; even if white farm and mining demands shaped the major outlines of native policy, this was by way of accommodating the interests of manufacturing and commerce. Precisely when migrant labor was being further entrenched, the core of urban-based industrial labor was being stabilized.

The terrain of this accommodation was far more political than economic. As we have seen, the shift from segregation to apartheid involved two simultaneous moves: a reorganization of the apparatus of native control, in both the reserves and the townships, and forced removals to shift radically the native population to indirect rule areas. The apparatus of control that the National Party organized in the course of forced removals was indeed formidable. With a single-minded will and determination, this armed fist was used to smash every expression of militant resistance and eventually to ban nationalist organizations in the wake of Sharpeville 1960. The decade of peace that followed Sharpeville was a time of effective repression. Undergirded by systematic terror, industrial growth increased by leaps and bounds. During the 1960s, the GNP grew at 6 percent per annum; along with Japan, it was the highest growth rate in the world.[21] Financed by a massive influx of foreign capital, the accelerated expansion of industry led to a structural transformation that brought manufacturing, commerce, construction, and transport under the sway of a few monopoly houses.[22]

The leap in accumulation, however, could not be without a corresponding expansion in the growth of the industrial working class and a simultaneous upgrading of skills for many. The number of Africans working in manufacturing increased from 308,332 in 1960 to 780,914 in 1980. Taken as a proportion of economically active Africans, the growth was indeed impressive, from 7.9 to 14 percent.[23] A consequence of this growth was an increased employment of educated labor and a dramatic expansion in postprimary African education to feed the demand for it. It is urban-based migrant labor and township-based educated youth—the two native social strata that grew with the prosperity of the apartheid economy—that would bring to a close its much-heralded decade of peace through a spectacular resurgence of urban resistance.

Faced with a combination of forced removals that dramatically increased the insecurity of urban communities, of Bantu education that systematically organized a racially justified substandard education for school youth while dimming its last remaining hopes for individually based advance, and of the tightening grip of influx control that regimented migrant labor through prisonlike conditions, the urban African population responded with a tempo of resistance at once powerful and protracted, sufficient to send the apartheid state reeling into a crisis whose proportions far eclipsed that of the postwar revolt to which apartheid had originally been a response. But relatively spontaneous acts of resistance, however dramatic, could not lead to sustained organization on their own. For that to happen, a decisive change in the very perspective of resistance was necessary.

A Historical Shift

The year 1949 had marked a turn in nationalist agitation from constitutionalist to popular methods, from petition and representation to boycott and demonstration. Sharpeville nipped this development in the bud and called its wisdom into question. With organizations banned and leaders whisked into jail, activists moved into exile. Their ranks bristled with a fast-growing conviction that the only effective response to the armed terror of the apartheid state was the armed resistance of the oppressed. Repression sought to strip communities of militants by barricading them in jail, and exile flushed activists out from their home

setting—even if voluntarily and temporarily. Gradually but impercepti-
bly, out of the struggle and the debate of the mid-1950s and the early
1960s, the notion of the exile as a professional revolutionary came to
supplant the idea of resistance as a mass and popular activity. Originally
advanced as a form of popular struggle, even heralded as its most advanced form, armed struggle soon came to be detached from any notion of popular struggle. Dazzled by the glamour of Vietnam, and then
Angola and Mozambique closer to home, militants turned to armed
struggle as would the faithful to a messiah. The armed guerrilla, the
proverbial fish in water, was now said to be a professional revolutionary
who needed only popular support to succeed. Meanwhile, ensconced at
a safe distance, beyond the reach of both apartheid's terror machine
and the discipline of internal struggle, two influences that would otherwise have kept them fit and trim—instead drawing nourishment from
their ability to play a growing international apartheid lobby effectively—
liberation movements increasingly came to resemble proto–state structures waiting in the wing for a crisis to happen and for an opportunity to
govern.

That crisis and that opportunity, however, could not be the doing of
exile movements. The decade of peace bore eloquent testimony to that
political fact. To break through that silence of captivity required no less
than a radical shift in perspective, one that would set aside the near religious faith in exile revolutionaries and armed struggle and return to the
day-to-day endeavors of working people, to take these as the raw material from which to fashion a culture of resistance adequate to its own
setting and to rebuilding resistance organizations. When that critique
came, it was more in the way of a practical initiative than a conscious
theoretical departure. Even when their actions signaled a departure of
epochal significance from the imperatives of armed struggle, its youthful
bearers continued to pay homage at the altar of armed struggle.

The youthful activists of the 1970s systematically forged a new path
of liberation, even if they did not do so consciously. They remind one of
the great populist movement of late-nineteenth-century Russia in whose
flow middle-class intellectuals merged with "the people." The populists
of 1970s South Africa too came from a youthful student generation.
Surprisingly, they were both black and white. The black student activists
were in their tens of thousands. They spanned the entire gamut of the
educational panorama, from primary institutions to secondary ones and
to university. Increasingly, they moved under a single banner: Black
Consciousness (BC). The white student militants were but a trickle, the
left wing of the white student movement. Shut out of Black Consciousness organizations and black townships ("the community"), prophets
outcast, they searched for a constituency. And they found it in the ranks

of those migrant workers who were the moving force behind the strike movement of 1973.

Durban 1973 and Soweto 1976 were the two events that symbolized, dramatized, and concretized this shift in the perspective of resistance, for in spite of their obvious differences—the bearers of the Durban strikes were mainly migrant workers, whereas the militants of the Soweto uprising were a more socially amorphous group among whom the student youth stood out—there were some basic and significant similarities between the two events. Both relocated the locus of struggle from the external (exile) to the internal (home), the agency of struggle from professional revolutionaries to popular strata, and its method from armed violence to nonviolent agitation. Together, these signified a fundamental shift in the very conception of struggle.

This is why one thinks that the militant black and white students of the 1970s had more in common than they realized. None was keen to join any of the externally based organizations or to court state repression by proclaiming allegiance to any. Neither heeded an argument then fashionable in "liberation circles" that anything short of armed or underground struggle, anything that smacked of agitation for reforms or open organizational work, was tantamount to a recognition of the apartheid state and capitulation to it. Together, they shaped the agitational and organizational context that nourished the countrywide urban uprising of the eighties and out of which came most of its key cadres. It was that nonviolent uprising—and not the much-awaited armed struggle—which really defined the imperatives and split the camp of apartheid, creating a paralysis that ended only with De Klerk's initiative of 2 February 1990. The historic turn in perspective that began with Durban 1973 and Soweto 1976 in South Africa had its parallel in the *Intifadah* uprising that shook occupied Palestine in the eighties. It was a shift in the paradigm of struggle that preceded the one in Eastern Europe by at least a decade.

The 1973 Durban Strikes:
Toward Building an Independent Workers' Movement

Unlike the decade that preceded it, the 1970s seemed to herald a time of change in southern Africa. At the forefront of that movement were migrant workers, whose meandering lives and generally miserable working conditions seemed to knit the region into one. Just when the armed struggle registered its most spectacular gain with the collapse of Portuguese colonialism in Mozambique and Angola, a parallel movement signifying the onset of an era of internal popular resistance could be discerned. In December 1971 thousands of Ovambo contract workers in the South African–managed Namibian cities of Walvis Bay and Windhoek struck against the migrant labor system. In the following month, this protest grew into a general strike involving some twenty thousand migrant workers; linked to it was an insurrectionary peasant struggle in the densely populated northern Bantustan reserve of Ovamboland.

In 1972 were the Durban strikes. The industrial areas of Durban provided employment to a larger number of workers than any other single urban center in South Africa. This industrial workforce tended to be concentrated in larger factories, mainly textiles and metal. Beginning in October 1972, the strike spread from one industrial area of Durban to another, then throughout Natal, and eventually across industrial centers in the whole country. At its peak, from January to the end of March 1973—thus known as Durban 1973—"more black workers were involved in strike action than in the previous twelve years after Sharpeville."[24]

The strike movement was like a magnetic spark that attracted a variety of hitherto dispersed forces and welded them together in a single effort whose organizational outcome would be the independent black workers' unions. At the core of this were the workers themselves, mostly migrant. Despite their semiskilled status, 70 percent of African workers had a monthly income below the monthly household subsistence level of R 78.18 for 1973. The very slogans used by the protesting workers—"sifunamali" and "asinamali"—the absence of "mali" (money)—reflect a stark reality: "despite the gigantic strides of industry in the 1960s, and despite the creation and consolidation of mass production in Durban, the African working class was on the brink of starvation."[25] In spite of their numbing poverty, the tradition of resistance was possibly more alive among migrant workers. Certainly, the decade of peace had a longer stay in most urban areas than in the reserves.

The compelling force with which these workers broke onto the industrial and political scene in 1973 made them the focus of a number of initiatives from different quarters. The first of these were older organizers from the ANC and the Communist Party–linked South African Congress of Trade Unions (SACTU) of the 1950s. Many of these veteran worker leaders had just been released from political imprisonment.[26] The second were young university-based intellectuals. Mostly white, they were without any historical link with black industrial workers. They were able to forge that link with the assistance of "black organizers from the old SACTU unions who gave them access to black workers."[27]

The white student radicals came from the Wages Commission of National Union of South African Students (NUSAS), the parent white student body from which the first Black Consciousness militants had broken away. Shunned by black student militants and without an anchor in the townships, they looked for alternative avenues of involvement. Established in May 1972, the university-based Wages Commission, in the words of one of its founders, "brought together white students who were increasingly critical of the dominant liberal opposition because they believed it was ineffective and focused on race rather than class exploitation."[28] Around the same time as the Durban strikes of 1972–73, they set up a series of service organizations in key industrial centers: the General Factory Workers' Benefit Fund (BF) in Durban, the Western Province Workers' Advice Bureau in Cape Town, and the Industrial Aid Society in Johannesburg.[29] Like the Benefit Fund, which was formally established to provide social security for workers employed in Durban and Pietermaritzburg, it was "through the handling of menial but very important complaints, payslips, Workmen's compensation, UIF, etc. that these activists had some influence amongst the workers."[30]

The white student initiative influenced both the nature and the speed of the unionization that followed in the wake of the Durban strikes. Not surprisingly, when the Metal and Allied Workers Union (MAWU) was formed in April 1973 in Pietermaritzburg, its secretary (Alpheus Mthethwa) was an employee of the Benefit Fund.[31] A few months later, the National Union of Textile Workers was established in Durban. As more unions were formed, their committees incorporated members from the executive committee of the Benefit Fund, and their organizing staff came to include BF militants who had previous organizing experience. To influence the flow of unionization and to consolidate the outcome, the Trade Union Advisory and Coordinating Council was formed that October.[32]

Durban was but one center in the emerging unionization of black workers. The new unions displayed a variety of forms. At one end were the East London–based community unions, which believed it was impossible to separate workers' factory demands from their township problems. Known as the political unions, they boycotted registration and aligned themselves politically with the exile-based liberation movements. At the other extreme were the Durban-based industrial unions, which were not averse to registering under conditions that would guarantee them a minimal independence but stayed clear of any political alignment. In the middle were the Cape Town–based general unions, which shared the boycott stance of the former but also the tendency of the latter to stay clear of any alignment with political movements. By 1981 the industrial unions, organized as the Federation of South African Trade Unions (FOSATU), a bloc with ninety-five thousand members in 387 organized factories spread across Natal, the Transvaal, and the Cape, emerged as the dominant force in the independent trade union movement. It is to the perspective of those who fashioned the strategy and tactics of FOSATU unions that we must now turn.

The militant white intelligentsia that came out of the universities in 1972 to form service organizations had a disproportionate influence in the FOSATU unions. Often accused of "academic Marxism" and "workerism" by critics,[33] they in turn charged the same critics with a populist orientation that failed to draw relevant lessons from the checkered history of trade unionism in South Africa. Marking the course of that history, and etched as lessons in the historical memory of these militants, were experiences of two unions: the Industrial and Commercial Workers' Union of Africa of the 1920s and the South African Congress of Trade Unions of the 1950s.

The ICU was a general union in whose ranks could be found both workers and allied strata, from peasants to petty entrepreneurs, but the group that defined its core social base was migrant workers. At a time when opposition usually took the form of addressing formal petitions and sending deputations to the authorities, the ICU was marked by "its militant call for open defiance of pass laws, a minimum wage and equality of opportunity."[34] Beginning with an effort to recruit Cape Town dockworkers, ICU membership expanded in response to militant strike campaigns. It is the ICU that organized the 1920 work stoppage that involved forty thousand African mine workers. Estimates of ICU membership at the height of its popularity in 1927–29 vary widely, between one hundred thousand and two hundred fifty thousand. But there is general appreciation of the ICU's contribution to establishing a tradition of black worker resistance, as reflected in the notes of a worker member: "Although the initials [ICU] stood for a fancy title, to us it meant basically: when you ill-treat the African people, I See You; if you kick them off the pavements and say they must go together with the cars and the ox-carts, I See You. . . . When you kick my brother, I See You."[35] To university-origin intellectuals in the ranks of FOSATU, the real failure of the ICU was organizational: it "failed in its efforts to gain recognized trade union status in South Africa."[36] That failure was the outcome of methods of organization that put too much stress on the leadership while failing to organize the membership in durable structures. The lesson was to build shop-floor structures resilient enough to survive both state repression and leadership crises.

Unlike the ICU of the 1920s, SACTU was very much a meeting point of factory-based unions. By 1959 its thirty-five affiliates counted for forty-six thousand members.[37] The quality of these unions is a point of controversy: Were many of the new unions "hasty constructions, often the result of interventions by SACTU in industrial disputes," evidence of its "bureaucratic shortcomings"?[38] Or did SACTU actually build "strong factory-based unions . . . with some success,"[39] being "the first to call successfully for community support in the form of a consumer boycott"?[40] Or were these simply two sides of the same picture? More at issue for the independent trade unionists of the 1970s was SACTU's original agenda: to link factory-based economic struggles with broad political struggles. That strategy defined the conditions both of its success and of its eventual demise. Its best-known effort, the successful "pound-a-day" campaign for a living wage, received massive backing from workers in the Johannesburg, Vereeniging, and Port Elizabeth areas—with 70–80 percent staying away in response—as well as from the ANC. But SACTU's association with the ANC led to its repression alongside the ANC in the post-Sharpeville period, and eventually to its exile, also alongside the ANC. A full-time organizer from the early 1980s recalled the debates of the period: "The intellectuals said, don't go the route of SACTU, of being dominated by the nationalist movement which used it as a recruiting ground and denied it independence. . . . Don't trust nationalists who use workers' struggles."[41] Unions must be wary of the nationalist movement and maintain their independence; that indeed was the lesson that FOSATU intellectuals drew from the experience of SACTU.[42]

Intellectuals who become activists have had to learn time and again that no amount of drawing lessons from the past can immunize a movement against old controversies reappearing in changed contexts, and so it turned out to be with intellectual activists in the independent union movement of the 1970s. Of the two issues that proved contentious in the decade that followed, one was a matter of tactics, the other of strategy. The former concerned the question of engagement with the employers and the state, the latter of alliance with community-based and nationalist organizations. Was engagement with the state tantamount to collaboration, as the exile-based movements argued and internal populists echoed? And was any alliance with nationalism a capitulation of worker interests to middle-class aspirations, as workerists claimed? Or did both engagement and alliance depend on conditions and circumstances, thereby depending more on the *terms* of engagement and alliance than their mere fact? Put differently, was not engagement a prerequisite to expanding the legal space for action and organization in the short run, and alliance necessary to changing the very form of the state that defined the legal space for popular activity in the long run? Whereas the tactical question was resolved in the short run, the strategic question proved to be of longer-run significance.

At the outset, the workerist trend tended to predominate in independent union circles. Its strength flowed, first, from an astute grasp of imperatives facing a weak and embryonic union movement. How else were workers going to be persuaded to join trade unions except by the assurance that trade unions lead not to repression but to actual short-term gains? Rather than being a reformist capitulation or an unacceptable compromise, the struggle for concessions would surely be a source of strength that would allow the unions to grow and fight even more ambitious battles. But short-term gains could not be won if one avoided negotiations and engagement under any conditions.[43] "The non-collaborationists argued that to operate openly was to be a stooge of the state," recalls a workerist organizer of the period.[44] "We had a totally different tradition: we didn't mind using any structures provided we could maintain our independence. Workers' independence was everything that Western Marxism taught us."

The workerist perspective made much sense from the point of view of its predominantly migrant social base. It was not only that the struggle for short-term gains was particularly vital for migrants earning below-subsistence wages while being pulled under by the twin demands of subsisting in urban areas and remitting a portion of their earnings to their families in the reserves. It was also that the workerist aversion to linking up with community struggles had a diminished impact on the lives of migrants, whose links with townships were both tenuous and ambiguous. As we will see, workerists and populists alike had a notion of community that was restricted to townships. This limited perspective would return to haunt them a decade later in the era of hostel-based violence.

In the meantime, however, workerist-dominated unions steered clear of community and political organizations alike, practicing little more than a form of peaceful coexistence with them. Thousands of workers in Natal could thus belong to FOSATU affiliates and "at the same time (find) their political home in Inkatha." In line with this cautious approach, when the KwaZulu administration requested in 1982 that its civil servants not be organized, FOSATU obliged.[45] Through a negotiated accommodation with the powers that be and a deliberated distance from the political opposition, the workerist-dominated unions gained breathing space and room for organization. Through persistence and patience, they built an independent trade union movement—as the phrase goes, from the bottom up. It was a contribution of historic significance, but it was also one that was to pull the rug from under their own feet. As industry expanded and so did the unions, the nature of not only work and workers but also of the issues that assumed urgency and of the organizational perspective adequate to addressing them changed. In that changed context, both workerists and the migrants whom they first organized found themselves marginalized.

Independent Unions and Industrial Unionism

As a rule, the dirtier, the more menial, and the less remunerative a job was, the more likely it was to be filled by migrants. A personnel manager of a foundry confirmed: "Show locals the job and 95% never come back, migrants don't leave because they know it is the only job they can get, there isn't a rapid turnover here."[46] Workers at the same foundry agreed that "township people ran away from metal work and that migrants 'stuck it out' because they had no hope of being registered elsewhere." Not surprisingly, unions that organized metalworkers (MAWU), dock-workers (GWU), or food and canning workers (AFCWU) were predominantly composed of migrants.[47] A shop steward with MAWU in Durban in the early 1980s recalls that at least 50 percent of the workers in the metal foundries were migrants.[48]

In the late 1970s, the organizational strategy of FOSATU industrial unions was to target big factories with hostel-based workers. Explaining why that was the case, the Transvaal secretary of MAWU, then also a resident in Vosloorus Hostel, explained: "It is easy to get hold of everyone in a hostel. It is an advantage when you organize. They are close to each other, living in the same conditions. It brings together a lot of different factories, sometimes ten representatives in one room. And they preach unions to each other all the time."[49]

Being easy to reach because of concentrated numbers was only one side of the story. The other side was that migrants were actually more available for organization than they seemed to be in the 1950s and the 1960s. To account for this change, a union-linked intellectual gives two reasons: on the one hand, with "tightened influx control" and the "dumping of urban unemployed in rural areas," the "migrant economy was under great threat and there was need for more money"; on the other hand, migrants were "no longer as mobile," for "many were moving into semiskilled work and were a little more stable."[50] Organizers and workers seem to trace migrant militancy to their working conditions. "Migrants are more militant," explained one shop steward, "because they are in jobs where conditions are worse."[51] "The migrants do the hardest work in the world," explained another foundry worker. "The employer thinks he can do what he likes with them. So they must have somebody to stand up for them."[52] "Without the union, we were defenseless," confirmed a migrant worker at the Everite Hostel in Brackenfell near Cape Town to a General Workers Union organizer.[53] These responses are in line with the conclusions of the Riekert Commission that manual work in manufacturing industry was "unpopular with urban Africans," and that those with residence rights "would rather remain unemployed than accept work not to their liking, especially manual work."[54] The point, argued a metal foundry worker in the East Rand, was that section 10 workers with residence rights in the township had a choice, whereas migrants did not: "They didn't have to be committed to struggling, because they need only change jobs if they don't like their conditions."[55]

Important as they are, these sociological factors—the collapse of the migrants' rural base and the relative stabilization of work, the hostel as the locus for collective organizing, the lack of work-related choices for migrants compared with urban workers, and the absolute wretchedness of work with which the migrants were stuck—do not fully explain the success of the independent unions of the 1970s. They do not explain why migrants turned to unions and not to any other form of organization in their hour of need. Nor do they explain why they stuck to that choice with tenacity when faced with repression. To understand these issues we need to grasp the very nature of these unions, both in their strength and in their weakness.

Organizationally, the new unions of the early 1970s displayed a variety of forms. The most notable difference was in the approach of the general community-based unions and the industrial unions. This difference, in turn, was shaped by contrasting perspectives of their respective leaderships. The leadership of the community unions was more likely to come from black educated strata with a background in township struggles and a BC persuasion, whereas that of the industrial unions was provided by service organizations with a white intellectual leadership. The former laid stress on mobilization, the latter on organization. Both underlined the democratic nature of their separate practices: for the community unions, that democracy was most immediately participatory; for the industrial unions, it was representative. In practice, however, neither claim held in an unqualified way.

The most notable of the general community-based unions were the South African Allied Workers Union (SAAWU), based in East London, and the General and Allied Workers' Union (GAAWU), based in Johannesburg. Led by charismatic intellectuals, like Thozamile Gqwetha from SAAWU, they pioneered a form of political unionism driven by large-scale general meetings held in a city hall or a big cinema. Uninterested in a negotiated relationship with management, more at home with rallies and mass meetings than the day-to-day on-the-ground organization of shop steward structures, the community unions registered dramatic successes initially. Moving rapidly to mobilize workers across a broad front, they relied on extensive organizing and mass campaigning in contrast to the intensive methods of the FOSATU bloc. But when faced with state repression—which in the case of unions like SAAWU was indeed vicious—they also collapsed rapidly. In the absence of the depth and resilience of a highly textured organization, all that was needed was to remove a union's leadership to precipitate its collapse. Once the security police and the employers realized this, they followed a well-planned strategy designed to detach the leadership from the mass of following through nonrecognition, detention, harassment, and torture.

Although the organizational deficiencies of the community unions are openly and critically discussed in South African literature on the experience of the 1970s and early 1980s, the same cannot be said of the industrial unions that became the driving force of FOSATU when it was formed in 1979. Often the industrial unions combined the joint initiative and energies of union-based black organizers and service organization–based white intellectuals who doubled as union leaders. The division of labor between the black organizer and the white intellectual leader had a truly Leninist ring to it: the organizer worked full time, openly, inside the union, and was subject to worker pressure and criticism; the intellectual operated from outside the union, in a structure not only external but also secret, remote from worker pressure. Mike Morris, a backup who became a union leader in the early 1980s, recalls: "Whites had the idea whites should not be dominant in the unions . . . but it led to the worst manipulation, most vanguardist. Black full-time organizers received directions from outside. But whites were not paid, not controllable, couldn't be hired or fired. . . . Whites had a backup of whites, it was secret to everyone except the front line."[56] So when the front line was banned or detained or went into exile, the backup replaced it without a step being missed. "We would go to staff meetings, not worker control meetings. . . . Real decisions were taken at meetings of banned people, not really in open committees."

"We were really intellectuals who happened to be white," says Morris. And there is a ring of truth in that. Surely, the lopsided division between the intellectual and the activist, the theoretician and the practitioner, could be found in several contexts outside South Africa. Yet within the context of South Africa's racially defined structures of oppression, the division was bound both to reflect and to reinforce that same racially defined hierarchy. Ironically, but not surprisingly, when the issue came to the fore, it was framed more in terms of race than in terms of the relation between intellectuals and worker activists. Formed in 1980, and by 1984 the only rival federation to FOSATU, the Council of Unions of South Africa (CUSA) "rejected non-racialism in favor of 'black leadership' charging, with some justification, that there were too many whites in influential positions within Fosatu."[57]

Fortunately, Leninist vanguardism was difficult to translate from paper to practice in the South Africa of the 1970s, for the simple fact of

African union organization in the period before the law allowed African (or nonracial) unions to register was that a union needed a strong plant-based organization with active support and participation of the membership to survive.[58] Because discussions with management usually excluded union officials, factory negotiations became the preserve of shop stewards, who not only had to develop the skills and resources for the purpose, but also had to cultivate sufficient support on the shop floor to execute decisions effectively. This single fact may have saved the industrial unions from their own vanguardist leadership. It is in this context, more as a response to compelling circumstances than as the realization of a dream, more as an afterthought than as foresight, that the independent unions developed the tradition of factory floor democracy, with the shop steward as a democratically elected worker representative. Take, for example, the case of the Metal and Allied Workers' Union, one of the strongest industrial unions, which shifted "from a strategy of mass mobilization to a concentration on building shop steward structures in a few selected factories"—only in the late 1970s.[59] The point is that circumstances shaped the course that both the community and the industrial unions took. The difference may have been in the rather dramatic way in which circumstances registered their verdict on the former.

By the time FOSATU was established in 1979, the gains on the shop floor were indeed impressive. As they moved from the indirect rule regime to the post-1973 reform that brought management-controlled liaison committees to post-1976 plant-level agreements guaranteeing minimal worker rights and collective bargaining procedure, the independent trade unions were able to "roll back the frontiers of management control in a number of areas."[60] At the core of that democratic trade unionism was the shop steward. Subject to regular elections, the shop steward was bound by workers' mandates and thus had to report back regularly. This tradition, part reality and part aspiration, gelled in FOSATU when it was formed in 1979. The Policy Statement spelled out five conditions that would be required to ensure the functioning of FOSATU as "a worker controlled federation":

1. The Federation is controlled by majorities of worker representatives at all policy making levels.

2. Those workers must be the authentic representatives of organized factory groups who have the capacity to report back to and be controlled by the workers they represent.

3. The workers concerned will be primarily production workers.

4. No non-worker controlled bodies, e.g., service bodies like the IAS, will be represented on the Federation with the right to vote.

5.   Most of the activity of the Federation will take place at a regional level where workers can most easily exercise control.[61]

How much of this reflected practice on the ground and how much was a statement of unrealized principles is difficult to say. Certainly, the formative experience of the industrial unions suggests that it would be sheer naïveté to assume even a close fit between formal structures and statements of principles on the one hand and the reality on the ground on the other. To achieve even an approximate fit would have required nothing less than a protracted struggle. In the absence of a thoroughgoing and regular internal evaluation, one can only fall back on hindsight, taking actual outcomes as high ground from which to reflect on preceding developments.

THE STATE AND THE INDEPENDENT UNIONS: FORGING MIGRANT-RESIDENT SOLIDARITY

The Durban strikes of 1972–73 unleashed a strike wave that instead of tapering off exploded yet again in 1975, this time in East London on the eastern Cape. Together, these brought to a close the decade of peace during which the South African regime, even if an international embarrassment, had been left to its own devices; international pressure for reform mounted. When the Soweto uprising of June 1976 led to the stayaways of September, nothing less than alarm built up in official circles. The prospect of politicized strikes, of overlapping waves of struggle bringing together township residents and unionized workers, resident and migrant, seemed real.

This concern led to the appointment of two government commissions in 1977, the first (Wiehahn) to focus on labor laws, the second (Riekert) on manpower use. When the commissions reported two years later, their recommendations became the basis of a coordinated government policy that highlighted two sides of a single strategy: selective incorporation and control. Wiehahn underscored the dangers of continuing with the existing system.[62] If African unions remained unregistered, they would in effect function as "power groups" that would "force employers . . . to negotiate outside the statutory system" but without being subject to any official supervision. This would no doubt "constitute a rallying point for underground activity: an industrial relations problem would become a security problem."

The case for a reform of native labor policy having been made, the government moved to devise a new system based on a threefold scheme: first, following Riekert, an "insider-outsider" strategy that would further entrench the division between urban and migrant labor; second, a process of registration accompanied by controls that would effectively depoliticize the registered unions and contain their activity within the field of industrial relations; and third, a system of plant- and industry-level bargaining that would fragment union centers and neutralize their newfound strength on the shop floor. At every level, rights were to go alongside responsibilities, and privileges along with controls, but not for all. The point was to identify the main fissure in the mass of African laborers being organized by the new unions and to deepen it through a set of reforms whose effect would be to contain one side by isolating the other. That crack was the divide between resident and migrant labor.

The distinction between resident and migrant labor already had a legal basis in section 10 of the Black (Urban Areas) Act, which laid down qualifications to be met by Africans who wanted to reside legally in any town for more than seventy-two hours. The Riekert Report identified the holders of section 10 exemptions as the insiders, as distinct from outsider migrant labor. At the insiders, it aimed a package of reforms: for the resident urban worker, greater freedom to move between jobs and towns and a preferential access to semiskilled industrial and commercial work; for the small proprietors, an end to restrictions on the development of African trade; and for all, the legal status of permanent urban resident and the right to live in cities with their families.[63] At the same time, it called for a tightening of the regime of influx control at both ends of the cycle of migrant labor: in the rural areas, through tightened measures to validate migrant contracts by rural labor bureaus; and at the urban end, by introducing a preferential policy for the hiring of insiders and by imposing heavy fines on employers who did not observe the policy. The unemployed, who had been resettled and relocated as "idles and undesirables," would now be "repatriated" to the reserves.[64] To cap this grand design to split two sectors of African workers, the government adopted a minority recommendation from the Wiehahn Commission: that migrants (including "commuters" and "foreigners") be excluded from all registered unions.[65]

In using legal recognition to steer the union movement into safer and nonpolitical channels, the Wiehahn Commission had taken a leaf from the postwar history of British colonialism. Yet the outcome was different, mainly because the unions refused to follow the script. The government had intended to seize the initiative with its reform proposals, and, for the moment, it appeared to be succeeding. The immediate effect of the introduction of reforms was to set off a sharp rivalry among unregistered unions on the tactical question of engagement. The predominant trend in both Black Consciousness–oriented community unions and general unions was to call for a flat boycott of government reform proposals. In the words of the vice president of SAAWU, to register "would mean swearing an oath of allegiance to racially discriminatory laws."[66] The industrial unions, however, rejected both the call for an outright boycott and registration on government terms. Instead, they embarked on a protracted struggle designed to change the very terms of registration.

In an act of open defiance whose point was to coordinate and direct black worker responses to the report, the industrial unions set up the Federation of South African Trade Unions as a countrywide federation just a month before the Wiehahn Report was released. Because of the strong organization of migrants inside unions that included both insiders and outsiders, the carrot the government dangled before urban insiders did not bring forth the expected Pavlovian response. The period was marked by some impressive shows of unity. In two Cape-based factories organized by the General Workers Union on the Cape, for example, workers with city rights volunteered to accept entrenchment in order to save contract workers' jobs.[67] The giant metal workers' union asserted its right to organize migrant workers. It was a demand the government conceded early in September 1979. Two months later, in November, FOSATU decided to apply for registration, provided further conditions were met: "If their non-racial constitutions were met, if they were granted full and not provisional registration, if unregistered unions were allowed to function as before, and if registration was granted on a broad industrial basis and not in a fragmented localized fashion."[68] But even when they registered, the industrial unions initially refused to join industrial councils. They continued to organize on the shop floor and to demand plant-level recognition from individual employers. When this was not forthcoming, strikes broke out, all of them illegal, culminating in the strike wave on the East Rand in 1981–82.[69]

This wave of strikes proved to be a turning point for both employers and unions. In its face, employers broke rank. Whereas the Steel and Engineering Industries Federation (SEIFSA) stuck to the official position of no plant-level bargaining, individual firms such as Barlow Rand called for a more pragmatic approach, negotiating with unions if they were representative, even if unregistered.[70] The first plant-level agreements were signed during the strike wave of 1981–82. Ironically, the rolling strikes on the East Rand also showed unions the limitations of a strategy that would concentrate on individual plants at the expense of an industry-level perspective. As strikes broke out in factory after factory, the union found itself "overstretched" and "unable to coordinate the strike wave which broke up into isolated struggles in different factories." For many, like MAWU, the lesson was that "centralized bargaining would allow them to organize workers across the industry around common demands, thus overcoming the problems experienced in the 1981 strike wave."[71] The upshot was that industrial unions finally decided to join industrial councils.

The unions had clearly won this first round of battle with the central state. One result was the defeat of the insider-outsider strategy aimed at pitting migrants against urban residents. Yet the irony of the decade of the 1980s is that the split did occur, not because of a conscious political strategy on the part of the state, but as the result of subterranean social processes whose import and consequences the union movement did not prove equal to grasping. During that decade, the manufacturing unions gradually moved away from their hostel base. It was partly a response to the changing nature of work and workers, partly a result of changing perspectives within the union leadership.

MIGRANTS MARGINALIZED

Structural change in manufacturing coincided with union demands for upgrading skills and stabilizing jobs. With an increase in the scale and capital intensity of production in the 1980s, firms became more interested in a stable workforce and in continuity of production. The other side of the stabilization process was a contraction of the labor force. Employers took advantage of the change toward a better-skilled but smaller workforce to deal with strikes and strikers. They "moved towards mass dismissals . . . holding out for trials of strength." By the end of 1982, workers were being laid off in the metal industry. Over the next eight years, the industry's workforce was reduced by a quarter. Those who suffered were those most vulnerable, the unskilled and the migrant.[72]

A corresponding change was taking place in middle-level union leadership. The young, the educated, and the urban were beginning to take command. "As early as 1977," comments Phil Bonner, a labor historian active in FOSATU circles, "we observed the beginnings of change. We could see students whose education ended with the Soweto uprising coming into factories. They were more political and militant in a different kind of way. There was a definite ideological input of this group. It was more BC oriented."[73] The change really came after 1979, after Wiehahn and the decision by unions to register legally, which proved to be a turning point. Legality opened the floodgates of membership as thousands joined eagerly. FOSATU membership, ninety-five thousand as late as 1981, multiplied manifold in the next few years. By the time COSATU was launched in 1985, it had a signed-up membership of half a million. As union membership expanded dramatically, the numerical weight of migrants also diminished—dramatically. The unions began experiencing an acute need for a new type of leader, particularly one with some education. Continues Bonner: "Younger, urban militants began to move into leadership. Migrants went along. There were no strong pressures then. More and more factories were becoming less migrant. Above all, shop stewards and particularly branch leadership [were] more dominated by educated younger people."

Every gain the union movement registered brought a new problem in its wake. Collective bargaining was no exception. Moses Mayekiso, a veteran leader of the metalworkers, previously organized as the Metal and Allied Workers Union and now as the National Union of Metalworkers of South Africa (NUMSA), explained: "As we moved to industrial council negotiations from plant-level organization, we lost direct contact with workers and lost accountability. We abandoned our own tradition of organization where we were eyeball to eyeball with workers."[74]

Increased recession and redundancies hit the engineering industries, beginning in 1982. At the same time, there was increased politicization. Tough and important labor disputes got under way, but these had an undercurrent. A political differentiation was taking place in the labor force: while one group was being knit tightly through organization, another was being sidelined. Phil Bonner identifies the 1982–83 strikes at Scaw Metals in the East Rand as "an important moment in losing . . . migrants. You could see their interests not being properly represented, eclipsed by other constituencies. We could see migrants retreating into themselves, even when continuing to be union members, e.g., in Zulu ethnic associations."[75]

These trends came together with the economic recession of 1983–84. By 1984, unlike in the late 1970s, few leaders stayed in hostels.[76] In those early days, a militant worker fired by management would just as immediately be recruited by the union as a full-time organizer. As a result, many shop stewards, and even some organizers, had come from hostels. But as the composition of hostel residents began to change to include large sections of the unemployed, the departure of unions from hostels turned into a flight. "With the economic recession of 1983/4 . . . the established unions basically abandoned the hostels because of the rising number of unemployed workers residing in them."[77] "The trend," confirms Mayekiso, "was against migrancy. People were bringing in wives and kids and moving into shacks, particularly when influx control lifted" in 1986.[78]

The change in the perspective and practice of the leadership has to be put in a wider political context to be understood. The early 1980s were the setting for an escalating internal uprising in urban South Africa. Located across townships, the urban revolt expanded as it absorbed layer upon layer of resident workers. The real shift that took place from the mid-seventies to the mid-eighties was the political displacement of migrants from the mainstream, and even forefront, of the broad movement against apartheid. All other changes tended to reinforce this central political shift.

The growing strength of urban residents in the unions, among both members and shop stewards, gave rise to demands that unions move beyond strictly workplace issues to issues affecting the welfare of workers. These pressures were felt most acutely in the East Rand, where rapidly expanding unionization, particularly of metalworkers, was dramatically increasing the strength of FOSATU unions. It was a demand made most effectively within the ranks of shop stewards, at first through organizational initiatives that tended to bring together shop stewards on a community basis and later through a broader demand that the trade union movement throw in its lot with the mass movement, particularly as expressed in the formation of the UDF in 1983.

The first attempt to break through the organizational confines of the workplace was the formation of shop steward councils (SSCs) in northern Natal and the East Rand. The Germiston Council in the East Rand brought together shop stewards in the Wadeville-Katlehong area. These extraconstitutional structures were organized in response to a compelling need, for when the strike wave hit the East Rand at the end of 1980, there was an acute shortage of organizers. With only two FOSATU-organized factories, workers decided to form a shop stewards' council and plan organizational drives themselves. Thus was formed the Germiston Shop Stewards Council in April 1981. Its members met once every two weeks, and leading shop stewards held planning meetings every week in between. Through joint deliberations, they tried to devise a common strategy and organize common action. By the end of 1981, shop stewards from twenty-three factories were attending these weekly meetings. A strike in any one of these factories was bound to have a ripple effect through the mediation of the council, as indeed it did in the Germiston area in 1981.

The emergence of shop stewards' councils created a structure that for the first time straddled the community and the factory.[79] Even if its members were elected representatives from the shop floor, the council was community based: it brought together shop stewards in all unionized factories in a particular area. Inevitably, their Thursday evening meetings were not confined to grievances arising from the shop floor. Other common concerns reflecting life in the community—such as rent, the clearing of shacks from township backyards, and pensions—were also taken up. As experience accumulated, the SSCs devised their own guidelines. These expanded the objectives of SSCs, now "to forge links with community organizations to encourage solidarity between the community and the workers struggle."[80] The reach of councils soon extended beyond trying to win community solidarity for workplace demands. The trigger that got SSCs to champion community-based issues directly was the threat to demolish shacks in some of the East Rand townships. With a serious shortage of township houses and hostel beds, many workers had no option but to live in shacks. Soon the SSC was discussing ways of leading resistance to demolition.[81] In the process, the councils ended up highlighting the need for community-based structures.

Calls to link work-based class action with community-based mass action had been made as early as 1976, but they had not always been successful. Problems encountered in the process suggest the ambivalent character of the relationship between one section of the township population—students—and another from the workers' population—hostel-based migrants. This came out dramatically in the 1976 Soweto stayaways. In their August call for a stayaway, students seemed more concerned with ensuring that all sections of the community honor it than with organizing different sectors for a concerted effort. Their tactics "varied from persuasion, tearing up parts of the railway line which takes workers from Soweto to Johannesburg, stoning buses which carried workers to the city to jeering at workers who were seen going to work."[82] Often, when persuasion did not work, coercion became the order of the day. Thus, when residents of Mzimhlope Hostel in Soweto refused to heed the strike call, students simply set sections of the hotel on fire, in the process burning several rooms occupied by migrants. Not surprisingly, they fell straight into a police trap, for the police had been waiting for precisely such an opportunity. A week before the proposed stayaway, police had addressed hostel residents, had asked them "whether they had come all the way . . . to stay away from work," and had promised police protection "to those who wanted to go to work."[83] Police protection is precisely what they got when, according to the Johannesburg *Star* of 24 August, approximately a thousand migrant workers from the hostel "carrying butchers' knives, pangas, tomahawks, *intshumentshu* (sharpened spikes), kerries and stones" went into action. By the twenty-sixth, 26 persons were dead and 107 injured.[84] For two weeks following the end of the stayaway on the twenty-fifth, Soweto remained an arena of conflict. Toward the beginning of September, "large numbers of workers left the hostels in fear of revenge attacks."[85]

Did the conflicts take place because the hostel workers were Zulus, as many observers have seemed to suggest every time hostels were engulfed in violence? One needs to ponder a number of facts before accepting this as a convincing explanation of events, at least in 1976. First, only 15 percent of hostel residents in Mzimhlope were then Zulus; also, "there is no proof that they were the ones who attacked township residents."[86]

Second, similar tensions surfaced in 1976 and 1977 between townships around the Cape and hostels in Langa and Nyanga, where residents tend to be Xhosa rather than Zulu.[87] Even more compelling is the experience of the next Soweto stayaway, which was organized from 13 to 15 September 1976. Not only were there fewer signs of violence this time around, but hostel residents actually supported the stayaway. Could it be because the Soweto Students' Representative Council (SSRC) had distributed leaflets in Zulu, Sotho, and English throughout Soweto calling upon the workers to stay at home? And even consulted the remaining hostel residents?

The students' conviction that they were the vanguard of the struggle could not have melted away so quickly, and yet it did thaw in the face of experience. Certainly, both Soweto and the townships around Cape Town had been only marginally touched by the strike movement and the wave of unionization that had engulfed Durban, the East Rand, and East London in 1972–74. As unionization grew, however, it came to influence the perspective of township-based militants everywhere. The grassroots civics that developed in the early 1980s took a leaf from the experience of shop stewards in independent unions: they moved from spectacular but one-sided mobilization to organizing street and area committees.[88] By 1987, 43 percent of Sowetans were reporting the existence of such committees in their part of town.[89] Without this on-the-ground weblike organization neither rent nor consumer boycotts could have been undertaken in a sustained manner or on a widening scale, as they indeed were during the 1980s.

From the self-important conviction that they were the vanguard of the struggle, students turned to looking for effective allies by the mid-1980s. The leaflet that the Transvaal region of Congress of South African Students (COSAS) addressed to workers calling on them to support the 1984 stayaway spoke in a language very different from that employed by the students of 1976:

- *LIKE YOU WORKERS*: we want democratic committees under our control (SRCs) to fight for our needs.
- *LIKE YOU WORKERS*: we students are prepared to fight all and every dismissal from our schools.
- *LIKE YOU WORKERS*: we defend older students from being thrown out of our schools, just like you defend old workers from being thrown out of factories.
- *LIKE YOU WORKERS* demand free overalls and boots so we students demand free books and schooling. And students don't pay for books and schools. IT IS THE WORKERS WHO PAY.
- *JUST AS THE WORKERS* fight assaults against the workers in the factories so we students fight against the beatings we get at school. . . .

WORKERS, YOU ARE OUR FATHERS AND MOTHERS, YOU ARE OUR BROTH-
ERS AND SISTERS. OUR STRUGGLE IN THE SCHOOLS IS YOUR STRUGGLE IN
THE FACTORIES. WE FIGHT THE SAME BOSS' GOVERNMENT, WE FIGHT THE
SAME ENEMY. . . .
*WE STUDENTS WILL NEVER WIN OUR STRUGGLE WITHOUT THE STRENGTH
AND SUPPORT FROM THE WORKERS MOVEMENT.* . . .
Workers, we students are ready to help your struggle against the bosses in
any way we can. *But today we need your support.*[90]

When Neil Aggett, a Food and Canning Workers Union (FCWU) organizer, died of torture in February 1982, at John Vorster Square, Johannesburg's police headquarters, the FOSATU unions called a countrywide stayaway. This thirty-minute work stoppage was a midway point in
the confluence between workplace- and community-based action; although the issue over which it was called transcended workplace grievances, the action was limited to the workplace. The turning point in the
united student-worker action was 1984, the year the South African Defence Force entered the townships. The propelling effect that this event
had in escalating the level of mass action could be seen in the Transvaal
stayaway of 5–6 November 1984. This event far outstripped previous
stayaways in scale and importance. The number of workers who stayed
away was estimated by the Labor Monitoring Group (LMG) at between a minimum of 300,000 and a maximum of 800,000, whereas
government estimates put the number of students boycotting school at
400,000.[91] The stayaways seemed to snowball, becoming the cutting
edge of a growing mass movement. In the eastern Cape (Port Elizabeth
and Uitenhage) stayaway of March 1985, the same social actors propelled into motion in 1984 came together: unionized workers, students,
township residents, and unemployed youth.[92] Between 18–22 March,
more than 120,000 black workers stayed away from work in the Port
Elizabeth–Uitenhage area for at least one day.

It is tempting to read these events, as many have, as a triumphant
march leading to a silver cloud on the horizon, in the process missing
the dark lining on that cloud. Did not the stayaways of 1984 and 1985
lead straight to the founding of COSATU, "the largest trade union federation in South African history"? And then to mass action on an even
larger scale, such as in 1986, when "over one million workers heeded
nation-wide stayaway calls on May Day and June 16"?[93] The 1984 stayaway was triggered by students and brought out workers, including migrants. Phil Bonner recalls it as the time when "the needs of the two
constituencies began fracturing."[94] By the 1985 stayaway, there was a
growing debate within the FOSATU leadership about the wisdom of
unions linking up with community-based organizations to launch joint
action. The vice president of FOSATU criticized the stayaway as not

being in the interests of the working class. Instead, he argued, it was nonworkers who ultimately benefited: "White chainstores registered record takings on the Friday before the black weekend; black traders and shebeen owners made a killing during it; taxi drivers did extremely well since there were no buses; and only workers have lost out all together—they lost a day's pay, some lost their jobs, and they were left weaker and more divided than before."[95]

The debate was often acrimonious. With the 1983 formation of the United Democratic Front, the leading coalition of populist groups, and the refusal of FOSATU to join its ranks, its pitch increased. "Unions affiliated to the federation," said Joe Foster, FOSATU's general secretary, "had members who supported a number of political organizations—including the UDF, the National Forum and Inkatha—and to side with just one organization would divide their membership."[96] But FOSATU was caught between two stools. Afraid of being outnumbered and swallowed by community-based organizations, which were preponderant within the UDF, it still could not ignore growing pressure from its own ranks to take action transcending the workplace. Its attempt to do so alone, such as the 1984 campaign against the tricameral parliament, only increased the pressure from within.

Not surprisingly, the UDF-FOSATU debate turned into a debate within union circles, with opposing sides going at one another with increasing abandon. In this context the debate between workerists and populists developed, each accusing the other of caricature and name-calling. Leading workerist intellectuals argued against those "progressive trade unions" who "emphasize the need for intimate connections between the trade unions and the community."[97] This call, they argued, really reflected the relatively uncomplicated need of "smaller industrial areas served by a single township where the union has the resources to push community issues." For example, in "the rural areas of the Western Cape, the FCWU has taken on this role; in Uitenhage in the Eastern Cape, there is likewise a close relationship between the Motor Unions and the community organization, all but one of its executives being Volkswagen shop-stewards or members." When this strategy is mechanically applied to the more complicated situation in "the larger industrial areas served by several dormitory suburbs, different problems arise," for "here the community turns out to be nothing of the sort: it is several communities often segregated by race." Any "excessive orientation towards 'the community'" in such a context can lead to "serious problems": dividing workers along racial lines, reflecting the apartheid-imposed parameters on community life in South Africa. The conclusion was inescapable: the more the unions linked up with communities, the more they would be infected by community-based problems, reproducing community divisions in the workplace as well. Hence, "the only place to forge non-racial as opposed to multi-racial solidarity" in South Africa, concluded Phil Bonner, "would appear to be the factory floor."

The call for transcending localized action was not going to be stemmed by pinpointing the problems of united action, for the basis of this call was not an uncritical defense of any and every united action. Rather it was a practical understanding of the limits of localized action, as all key strata increasingly confronted not local adversaries like employers and school or community authorities, but the central state. Leading workerist unions like MAWU began to feel the pressure, both as a demand that the political line of the union be reconsidered and as attempts to form breakaway unions. The most notable was the 1984 split in MAWU.[98] Many of "the advanced shop stewards who were directly involved in the running of the SSC, or playing leading roles in the union and/or the Federation and benefiting from education programs," joined the breakaway United Metal, Mining and Allied Workers of South Africa (UMMAWSA) "out of a sense of frustration with MAWU." One leading shop steward argued:

> The situation of the worker in South Africa is that they are oppressed and exploited. The struggle goes beyond the factory gates. Workers must address themselves to the problem of rents, shacks, electricity tariffs, schools, recreation, etc. In FOSATU and MAWU workers have been openly discouraged from taking up these issues and political organizations have been openly criticized. We recognize that the trade unions are not political organizations. But for them (MAWU) to say no politics in the trade union is nothing else but to keep their politics of reformism inside the trade unions.

It is "a tribute to Fosatu's structures and principles," comments the COSATU historian Jeremy Baskin, that this challenge that began with its shop stewards on the Transvaal led to the transformation of FOSATU from within, and not to the growth of a rival trade union center.[99] The formation of COSATU in December 1985—with a half-million signed-up members and the National Union of Mineworkers (NUM) as its largest affiliate—was certainly the eclipse of the workerist line and the ascendancy of those populists who had called for the primacy of unified political action. Ironically, the impetus for unity had come largely from workerists.[100]

In retrospect, the formation of COSATU seems a time for sober reflection on the previous decade's experiences rather than an occasion to rally for a final confrontation. The failure to carry through such a comprehensive sum-up meant that weaknesses surfaced in the midst of celebrations, as crevices in what many had presumed was a solid organizational wall. Phil Bonner had been right in saying that there was not one model community for which one had only to find a fitting prescription, but he was wrong to think that the diversity of communities was limited to a racial diversity. Both workerists and populists shared a weakness: their notion of community was limited to the township. It reflected the urban dimensions of the struggle that had unfolded in the wake of Durban 1973 and Soweto 1976. Neither had a notion of community that could embrace the rural, let alone the most problematic expression of the rural in the urban: the hostels and its migrant residents. Ironically but not surprisingly, just as militants—from within unions and community organizations (civics) alike—were strengthening the link between community and workplace, a clear split was emerging between the workplace and the community as migrant workers understood it. It is instructive to read responses recorded by a team of researchers who interviewed hostel-based workers in a factory in the Thokoza area on the Rand in 1990.[101] The team found "the link between union organization and hostel life . . . to be virtually non-existent." The interviewees felt "that hostel issues were directly ignored by the union." One worker explained:

> No, they don't come to our hostel. We meet here in our workplace, that's all. It's not because they are afraid to hold meetings in our hostel, it's just because they are not interested. That's why we had a conflict with them because they always went to meetings in the township and make decisions that would affect us without consulting us. That is especially during stay-aways so that is what makes us not recognize their calls for stayaway.

The community-workplace split was, as the populists had rightly warned, also a split between economic and political concerns. "When we posed the question of COSATU's alliance with the ANC and the SACP," noted the research team's report, many "saw the activities of the union as being restricted to the workplace and thus they were unaffected by, or saw no significance to this alliance." In the words of one migrant, "I only joined NUMSA for their protection at the workplace and not their political alliance."[102]

By 1986 migrants and hostels had turned into the soft underbelly of unions and civics. This underbelly would be exposed in the 1990s. In the face of state violence, sometimes initiated but other times fanned by third forces, unions would be paralyzed. Worse still, civics would lose perspective. Moses Mayekiso, NUMSA's general secretary, reflected in 1993: "Violence was beyond our strength. Our mistake was not to expect it. We should have expected [that] capitalists would try to destabilize us."[103] Between this situation and the Durban strikes of 1972–73 there was a curious similarity. Once again, migrants had become a marginal force in the world around them. Once again, they were available for organization. That organizational impulse came in successive waves, targeting a section (Zulus) and not all, not just as workers but also as migrants from a particular ethnic group. It came first as a company union, the United Workers Union of South Africa (UWUSA), then as a cultural movement (Inkatha) that beckoned them to their rural roots, and finally as the Inkatha Freedom Party (IFP), a political party that tried to harvest their alienation from township militancy. Each wave, however, seemed to leave behind a trace of dissatisfaction. Not surprisingly, migrants who had been at the helm of FOSATU unions in the late 1970s did not prove to be an inert force, available to every next suitor on the horizon. Instead of simply embracing every external initiative, this time they took their own initiative. Perhaps that was their greatest tribute to FOSATU's decade-long endeavor.

THE 1990s:
MIGRANTS AS TRADITIONALISTS

In 1990 the ANC was unbanned along with other exiled political groups. All political forces understood that the political map of South Africa was soon to change. They moved into place to begin, as it were, a chess game. The initiative lay with those possessed of a wider vision, for the unbanning had the opposite of a ripple effect. Moving inward from an outer rim, the force of the transition seemed to take on board every group and tendency, if only to take stock of it. Like a litmus, it seemed to test every claim, if only to discard those found wanting. Widely expected to usher in an era of peace, the transition was marked by spurts of violence. The focal point of the tension was immediately the triangular relationship between townships, hostels, and shanties. Its strain and stress exploded into bursts of violence, gripping the Natal and the Reef on the Transvaal. At the center of this violence were hostel dwellers.

In the first half of 1993, I interviewed many of these, initially as part of a Durban-based COSATU research team charged with understanding "the needs of hostel-dwellers." That effort bore little fruit. Organizers from COSATU's cultural group undertook to introduce us—three researchers—to hostel residents. A workshop was organized, to be followed by several interviews. But the workshop never took place, for no more than a few hostel residents turned up. With the assistance of a union organizer, I persisted for the next month, but little happened. I was able to meet one male resident of Dalton Hostel and ten women living in Thokoza Hostel. When I expressed the desire to go into Thokoza Hostel, my hosts found it a difficult proposition to realize. Eventually I was "smuggled" in as a cabinet mover, for precisely twenty minutes. I could not pretend to be a nonchalant mover if I stayed any longer! I met the ten Thokoza women workers for several evenings of long conversations, as I did the one organizer assigned to me. Eventually I realized the reason behind my difficulties. Both Thokoza and Dalton were considered Inkatha hostels. It was not safe for an ANC- or COSATU-linked person to operate openly within their confines.

A little discouraged, I moved to Johannesburg. I had two options before me. Every hostel on the Reef seemed to be clearly earmarked: ANC or IFP. It would be easier to gain access to ANC hostels, but it would surely be far more interesting, I thought, if I could gain entry to IFP hostels. Through sheer chance, I made a contact through a friend in the Johannesburg Civic Association. That contact was the Secretary of the newly formed Transvaal Hostel Residents Association and turned out to be a key that would open many doors for me, for with the secretary, I was able to meet and interview several residents in two hostels, Wolhuter (Jeppe) in Johannesburg and Mzimhlope in Soweto. Both Wolhuter and Mzimhlope were considered violent hostels. Both had been in the flare of conflict in the Transvaal over the previous year. Both were occupied mainly by Zulu migrant workers, whether employed or not. Through conversations with some of these hostel residents I was able to glimpse the plasticity of tradition.

Inmates in a Limbo

A hostel is obviously not part of a migrant's work space. But neither is it quite a worker's domestic space, for one's family is not allowed in a hostel. Conditions in the hostel are not subject to collective bargaining as are those on the shop floor, but then neither is the hostel a private domain free from employer interference. Hostels, writes Mamphela Ramphele, are really "institutions and not homes."[104] They are part of "approved accommodation" where migrant laborers, male or female, were required to stay before the influx control laws were abolished in 1986.

The labor compound system as it emerged in the early years of diamond and gold mining provided the prototype for the hostel system on the Rand in later years. The model was the militarylike quadrangular compound in the De Beers diamond field, complete with a twelve-foot fence and a single large gate, enclosing living quarters and a few provision stores.[105] With workers communally quartered in prisonlike barracks constructed on mine premises, this system spread fast to other labor-intensive enterprises on the Rand and to the mines in Rhodesia.

As early as 1923, the Natives (Urban Areas) Act required municipalities to accommodate African migrant labor in towns and recommended that hostels be built for that purpose. According to section 6 of the Bantu Urban Areas Act, number 25 of the year 1945, hostels were to be considered "Bantu areas."[106]

Johannesburg has a total of fourteen hostels.[107] The first male hostel was built in 1913 on the southern edge of what was fast emerging as the central business area of "egoli," the city of gold. Called Mai Mai, it resembled mine compounds with short concrete beds built for Chinese laborers who had been imported in 1904 to work on the Witwatersrand Gold Mines. Most urban hostels, however, were built after the passage of the 1923 act, six between 1924 and 1946.[108] Soweto (including Meadowlands) has fewer hostels than does Johannesburg. The first of the eight Soweto hostels was Dube, built in 1955. From the outset, sites for hostel construction were chosen with one idea in mind: to ensure the separation and isolation of its residents from the township population. Understandably, hostel construction continued in spite of township opposition, including from assorted native advisory boards. One of these was Mzimhlope, built on the southeastern side of Meadowlands. By 1974 the West Rand Administration Board estimated that no less than 20 percent of all male residents of Soweto over the age of eighteen lived in urban hostels.[109]

It is incredible that the new unions never came to grips with the concrete situation of hostels. Even in the early stage when migrants were the bulk of active members in several unions, most considered the hostel as no more than a physical site for organizing workers around shop-floor issues. A few did try to raise hostel-specific issues. One of these was the General Workers Union, which in 1984 waged a bitter and protracted struggle around the issue of accommodation and the rights of workers as tenants at Everite Hostel in Brackenfell near Cape Town.[110] Yet at no time were hostel residents an insignificant number or their conditions anything less than scandalous.

Figures on hostel accommodation vary. South African government sources put at 402 the number of hostels under the control of provincial and local authorities throughout the country. The figure excludes all mine company hostels and some private ones, which are not registered with local authorities. Of this total, 135 are in the Transvaal, 216 in the Cape, 35 in Orange Free State (OFS), and only 16 in Natal. The distribution of hostels, however, does not reflect the distribution of hostel beds. Although fewer in number, Transvaal hostels tend to house a larger number of beds. The above source estimates the distribution of beds at 297,158 in the Transvaal, 50,158 in the Cape, 26,125 in Natal, and 24,904 in the OFS. But the number of hostel beds is difficult to pinpoint with accuracy. Unlike this official estimate, which puts the total at 308,345, a CSIR study estimates it at 529,784, with 59 percent in the Pretoria-Witwatersrand-Vereeniging region.[111]

The number of beds, however, is in no way equivalent to the number of hostel residents. A bed holder is a relatively privileged person when compared with others who may use the same bed. In the four Johannesburg hostels owned by the Transvaal Provincial Administration (TPA), for example, a recent study estimates that an average of 1.21 people share each bed in a single twenty-four-hour period.[112] According to the chairperson of the Hostel Residents Association at Wolhuter, one of the aforementioned four hostels, there are roughly 5,000 others living in the hostel besides the 3,218 bed holders.[113] The bed occupancy rate in the Cape Town hostels has been estimated at 2.6 per bed, and in Dalton Hostel in Durban the rate is said to be as high as 6.[114]

How do all these people fit in a bed that is no larger than a wooden bunk or a concrete slab? Bed occupancy rates obscure the distinction between bed holders, bed users, and squatters within the same hostel. The bed holder, the "owner" of the bed, is the person who controls its use. Conversely, a bed is the only space over which its holder has effective control. The bed users actually share the bed with the bed holder, and a squatter simply puts up in any vacant space in the hostel. The bed user pays the bed holder in services, ranging from cleaning to sex; squatters pay the hostel administration. In Thokoza Hostel in Durban, for example, there are 689 bed holders but more than 1,000 squatters.[115] A bed holder pays a monthly rent of R 17.10, a squatter R 15.

The hostel population is a varied lot. Many of the migrant workers are hardly temporary. The Hostel Residents Association found that the average length of stay in the Johannesburg hostels was five to six years. In some instances, though, "people had been there up to 30 years; some of them were even second or third generation residents," handing down a bed from father to son.[116] Ramphele found that the average length of stay in Cape Town was twenty-six years for male bed holders and twelve for female ones.[117] Long-term hostel residence, however, does not necessarily mean that links with the countryside have been weakened. The study of the Johannesburg hostels, for example, found that half of the residents earned less than R 600 a month; of this, R 253 was being sent home every month to support families.[118]

There is a large unemployed population in every hostel; some have just arrived from the countryside and are looking for a job, and others have been retrenched. Zulu, a resident at Dalton Hostel in Durban, explains: "I have my brother with me. He is looking for a job. I can talk to a night shift person for my brother to use his bed. People usually help."[119] Such persons survive on temporary work in the area, or they take to hawking in the hostel compound, selling anything from cigarettes to drugs to alcoholic beverages to *muti* (traditional medicine). "It is the visitors," says Zulu, "who often become tramps." Once influx control was abolished in 1986, the unemployed gained entry into hostels. Their proportion increased with the onset of violence. Research carried out in mid-1991 showed several related trends: an outflow of those fleeing hostel violence for squatter camps or backyard shacks, with "a significant number" even returning to rural areas; and an inflow of "large numbers of predominantly unemployed" persons.[120] In Mzimhlope Hostel in Soweto, the unemployed are estimated to be 30 percent of residents.[121] The estimate for Wolhuter is fifteen hundred persons.[122] A fast-expanding group, the squatters are already the majority in many hostels.

Although bed holders are the long-term migrant population of the hostel, visiting their homes in reserves at regular intervals, the same cannot be said for the squatter population. The squatter population of metropolitan areas expanded dramatically once influx control was abolished in 1986. The rural poor, previously kept at bay by force, took to their heels. For rural people, hostels were one of the few easily available shelters in a large metropolitan area. As they arrived in town, refugees fleeing violence or drought or just day-to-day misery naturally headed for points where they could find family members, relatives, village mates, or anyone who was familiar to shelter them while they learned the ways of the city and found a niche in it. Often thought to be residents of only shantytowns, the squatter population actually divides between shanties and hostels. Some indicators suggest that those in hostels may be even worse off than those in shanties. The Johannesburg study, for example, found that 36 percent of hostel residents were functionally illiterate, with less than a standard two (second-grade) education. This compares with a 16 percent functional illiteracy among residents of shanties in the PWV region.[123] The hostel squatters are a far more transitory group than the long-term migrants, both in their living and in their working habitats. They straddle town and country and are usually forced to turn to the informal sector to make ends meet.

At first glance, a hostel presents a sharp contrast to a shanty. The concrete-and-brick structure of hostels obviously withstands the assault of the elements much more effectively than can the cardboard and tin mix that are shantytowns, but inside this modern structure, few facilities work. The mistakes of reckless planning have been multiplied a hundredfold by wanton neglect over the decades. If you want to make an electrical connection, you must do it "from the top." If you want air to circulate, you must keep the windows open and risk the cold. Having built the hostel, the municipal authorities left its maintenance to the wits of occupants, who are responsible for its daily cleanliness and all repairs. In an exceptional act of regard for the welfare of hostel residents, the provincial authority built a swimming pool at Wolhuter in the early 1980s. This illustrated their remote understanding of what the residents most needed. "We only used it once, when it was clean," says Temba Nxumalo.[124]

Space is scarce, and there is hardly any privacy. For the privileged population of the hostel, the bed holders, the private domain is the bed area, usually 1.8 square meters of space. "I am a member of the ANC Women's League, burial society, church. I have a lot to read. There is no desk, nothing. You just sit on your bed and eat. The bed is your cupboard, your chair, your table. You come with your pot and put it on your bed," complains Christina, who lives at Thokoza Women's Hostel in Durban. Because of the absence of any privacy and the openness of communal facilities, hostel residents are an easy target for thieves. In some hostels, the concrete slab that is the bed operates like a bunk, which pulls up to reveal a hole—the wardrobe. Many hostels, however, like Thokoza in Durban, have no such arrangement. In such a situation, personal property must be left behind with the next shift when a resident goes to work. If clothing is washed and dried on a line, it often must be secured with a chain and a lock to prevent its theft. If one wants to change clothes, one must do it in front of others. The fact that residents often sleep in shifts means that there is always someone asleep and someone else awake; noise is a constant factor. "While one group is sleeping, the other is making noise, listening to music," says another resident at Thokoza.[125]

The absolute and inhuman lack of privacy impresses a visitor who passes by a washroom or a toilet. Across the long hall that is the communal toilet facility, one can see a row of men, ten or so in Wolhuter, seated with their pants down, each left to his own preoccupation, with neither a wall nor a curtain separating one from another or from the line of men having a wash. Stench pervades the entire space, for toilets often leak and stink. The kitchen, too, is communal, which means one must wait one's turn to cook and eat, and if the line is long and the hour late, one must choose between a meal and sleep for the night, or, more likely, the lights have gone off and one can no longer cook. "In that place," said a former hostel resident, "we were like cattle in a kraal."[126] When asked whether they would be prepared to pay more for privacy in a toilet or a kitchen, half said they would be willing.[127] The answer indicated the level of their desperation rather than of their earnings.

The lack of privacy goes with filth. As if to compensate for the subhuman conditions in which they live, hostel residents often dress immaculately. The contrast between personal cleanliness, even meticulousness, and the squalor that is the communal facility is striking. It was easy to think that this reflected the contrast between the personal and the communal, and so I too wondered until I got to Mzimhlope. Built in the 1950s like all Soweto hostels, Mzimhlope contrasts sharply with hostels like the M-1 in Alexandra built in the 1970s. The M-1 was designed with a single-minded focus on social control, complete with iron gates and fence, not only to enclose the hostel from the township, but also to cut off one section of the hostel from another. The gates between sections are electric and have control panels that can be used to shut off a section in case of trouble. Mzimhlope resembles a housing scheme for a poor community in its layout. There is no fence, no gate; attempts to build one have never succeeded. Toilets are communal but smaller: four in a row for one block. I saw two such communal toilet facilities. The first was unlocked, could be used by anyone, and was leaking, blocked, and smelly. Another was locked, with a key for each family, spotless, even if two of the toilets had no tops to sit on.

The system of labor control in the hostels was a small version of the indirect rule system on the reserves.[128] A hierarchy of mine officials was created to resemble that of chief, headmen, and heads of homestead in the reserve. In this system, the chief is the white hostel manager, the headman is the native induna, and the heads of homestead are the "door"-based *isibonda*. Unlike the induna or the police "boy" who was appointed by the hostel manager and paid, the isibonda was elected and unpaid. Both came from a particular ethnic group, since hostel residents were both concentrated and divided on an ethnic basis. The system combined the autocratic powers of the white hostel manager with elected "native" isibonda. The latter, "door" representatives, were usually elderly men known for their fairness and wisdom. The point of the system was twofold: to control movement in and out of the hostel and to keep peace between inmates. This reality, a modern barracklike structure in which the induna (headman) was the chief compound policeman and therefore chief assistant of the white hostel superintendent, also has to be understood as a fantasy of the hostel administration, who hoped that the hostel would be an extension of the reserve in which migrants would continue to live their lives as in tribal harmony—sleeping in communal quarters at night while submitting to tribal discipline during the daytime—so that the world outside may continue as a white world.

To what extent did the world inside the hostel correspond to this fantasy? Much has been written on group life within hostels, of how its pattern was shaped by the obvious fact that new arrivals had to be initiated by older residents, preferably by those who came from their home area. Burial societies, credit clubs (stockvels), musical groups, and even soccer clubs are said to have shared two features: they tended to bring together people from the same home area and to organize residents along a hierarchy of age. But the often unqualified presumption that elders played a conservative role in the hostels is open to question. It is true that the cluster of organizations active in hostels tended to recruit members by home area, but it is not true that the end result was necessarily to divide people by home area or to reinforce a traditional conservatism in their ranks. Take, for example, the rural-urban link described by William Beinart in his study of "M," a Mpondo migrant worker of the 1940s.[129] The age group associations that Mpondo youth belonged to defined a range of activities into which youth with a common educational background could enter as they shuttled between reserve and sugarcane fields or mines. Rather than bring the youth under the control of elders, they tended to spurn adult control. Rather than act as a transmission belt for reinforcing hierarchical authority on the mines and a one-dimensional cultural solidarity on the reserves, they tended to be hostile to the white administration and to the more literate youth. This migrant subculture coalesced around activities that were part welfare, part gang activity; part work solidarity, part cultural identity.

True, in the soup-can world that is hostel life, one needs to take note of the enormous pressures for conformity and of the tendency for residents to internalize the imperatives of an institutional life, somewhat in the manner of long-term prison inmates.[130] But the direction in which these pressures flow is not always a given, like a one-way traffic flow. Sociological conditions may dim the flame of political choice, but they never quite succeed in extinguishing it. One needs to recall the experience of the 1950s and 1960s, when burial societies and stockvels turned into springboards for migrant organization and action against Native Authorities in the reserves. Then, it was these home area–based associations that provided the crucible in which Communist Party and ANC organizers linked up with migrants agitated about changes at home. In a different period, the 1970s, these same associations provided a bridge between migrants and the independent trade unions. All the evidence points to one conclusion: few migrants joined the union individually, through the mediation of a union organizer; most joined in groups, recruited by their fellow workers or hostels.[131] If in the late 1980s and early 1990s the impact of these associations turned out to be different, this time providing a bridge to an entirely different type of politics, one of hierarchy and oppression couched in the language of culture and tradition, it could not be because this was their natural or spontaneous tendency, something that could not have been otherwise. It does, however, have to be explained.

The traditional in the hostel needs to be seen as a point of contact and not always a point of division, as a springboard for action that does not always reinforce existing hierarchy and authority. Its potential remains contradictory, as its understanding remains diverse and changing. To understand why one and not another choice was made at a given time, why one and not another notion of tradition triumphed at that time, we need to understand both the context and the text that shaped the outcome. The context in the early 1990s was twofold: the hostel-township relationship and hostel-targeted initiatives from wider forces like the ANC and Inkatha. The text was the response of the residents themselves.

HOSTELS AND TOWNSHIPS

From the moment hostels began to be constructed as enclaves within townships, the relationship between the two was tension ridden. The agenda of officialdom in constructing compounds that were both enclosed and set apart from their surroundings—physically, ethnically, and socially—could not have been more transparent. Not surprisingly, township residents opposed this stratagem. The township-hostel distinction translated beyond the place of residence to the place of work. As a worker without a right to reside in a township for more than seventy-two hours, the migrant had little choice and was found in the most menial and worst-paid jobs. At the workplace, migrants were the "ama-overalls" (those who wear overalls). In the eyes of a township resident, the migrant was a country bumpkin. He (and there were also some shes) may have been industrialized, but he was certainly no urbanite. The distinction became the butt of many jokes. An official of the Hostel Dwellers' Association related one of these to me, not without a hint of bitterness: An old man is standing on the station with blocks in his ears (Zulu markings). The intersuburban train comes and doors open. He has a lot of luggage. He puts some in and goes for the rest. Meanwhile, the train leaves. He then chases after the train to get his luggage back.

In times of conflict, the migrant is not just somebody without urban sophistication; more important, he is considered a transient, a person with a superficial stake in urban life, with his real home in the reserve. At such times, the hostel dweller must hide his identity in the township. He must be prepared to give a township address in a moment of need. "If I go to town, I make sure people don't know I am from the hostel. If they find out, their behavior changes—because they think I am not with them for long, I can bring them trouble," explained Zulu, who lives in Dalton Hostel in Durban.[132] Sometimes an incident takes on the status of a legend and is passed on from one migrant to another. One such incident happened to the chairman of the West Rand Hostel Residents Association in early 1992. When visiting "a certain area," he was

held up by an AK-47-wielding self-defense unit and questioned extensively. "That chairman was saved," the secretary of the Transvaal Hostel
Residents Association assured me, "because he gave an address in the
township."[133]

The attitude is often reciprocated by migrants, many of whom dislike
the rough-and-tumble life of townships and see in it little more than a
loss of humanity. Take, for example, the views of some of the women
residents of Thokoza in Durban.[134] Gugumolefe, who came to Durban
from the Transkei in 1976, says: "If I go out, I don't go to the township. I just don't like it. I am from a farm. It's just not in my blood. I've
got an aunt there. She calls me, but I just don't go there." Angeline
Gabayi, who came from the Midlands in Natal a few years earlier, agrees:
"I have no friends. My auntie lives in KwaMashu. I don't like township.
We don't see things with one eye. It causes a problem. I have a child of
eleven. . . . Township people have a habit of not liking children. If they
have cleaned their house, you must not dirty it. You have to keep your
shoes out. A child can create trouble."

The fact that hostel dwellers are usually single and male tends to exacerbate conflicts with particular sections of the township population. In
interviews with residents of Mapetla (Soweto) in 1991, a student found
that a large proportion (60 percent) of women from their mid-twenties
to their late thirties—as opposed to a smaller proportion (25 percent)
of men—found their relationship with hostel dwellers to be "very difficult and problematic."[135] They complained of "sexual harassment" and
"contemptuous behavior towards women." Sometimes the structural
difference in the position of the two groups simply means that what may
be a burning issue in the township may have little resonance in hostels.
Take, for example, education. Over the 1960s, a larger proportion of
township students began to come from working-class rather than middle-class families. At the time of the Soweto uprising, township workers
needed little prodding to move into action, since the students who were
being savaged were their own children. But for hostel dwellers, whose
families were in the countryside, education was a remote issue. When
one combines this with a perspective dominant among students in the
early stages of Soweto 1976, that students were the leaders of the struggle for tomorrow, one begins to understand how clashes between students and migrants could lead to incidents like the burning of hostel
facilities and migrant beer halls at Mzimhlope in 1976.

Although it is important to situate the township-hostel tension in the
structural and historical dimensions of that relationship, there is a growing tendency among those who write of contemporary hostel violence
to read back from it, to look for, find, and emphasize in a one-sided
manner only the conflictual aspect of the relationship. But the township-

hostel relationship was never as one-sided as it became in the late eighties. There were always linkages that bound the two in a reciprocal way, even if they were weak. It is true, as Mamphela Ramphele writes, that except for beer gardens, "hostels have no public facilities of their own" and "depend on the limited public resources of the surrounding townships for all their needs—schools, clinics, churches, playgrounds, post offices, police stations, shops, etc."[136] But in spite of its construction as "a uni-functional sleeping area," hostels never remained just that. The hostel was a source of services for a section of township residents.[137] It was a microcosm of a rural area, which provided urban dwellers with services otherwise difficult to find. Hostel dwellers brewed cheap country liquor, and township dwellers flocked to hostels to enjoy various exotically named concoctions: Ntaba-Zosizi (Mountains of Sorrow), Izingodo (the Forest), Uhamba-Nobani (Who Is Accompanying You), Umqomboti (African Wine), and Qhum-Mbekele (Standstill). If hostel dwellers could have access to Western medicine only in a township, township residents too could also easily avail themselves of herbalists and diviners in hostels. Before the decline in services shut the hot water tap in many hostels, "township males flocked to the hostel to use showers which were unavailable in the township." If playgrounds were to be found in townships, hostels were the venue of tribal dances every Saturday and Sunday, events that township residents of all ages and both genders witnessed and enjoyed. At the same time, the hostel was a sanctuary for shady characters avoiding the police for one reason or another; gambling was rife in hostels, as was the smoking of *dagga* (marijuana).

Relations between townships and hostels changed dramatically, first with the township uprising of the 1980s, then with the onset of hostel violence in the early 1990s. As the township uprising unfolded in its many dimensions, the unintended effect on hostel life was often negative. Rent boycotts, combined with apartheid "decentralization" reforms, brought municipality finances to an all-time low, and corrupt councillors sucked dry whatever meager funds were available. Services collapsed. As hot water stopped coming, pipes dried up, and maintenance ground to a halt. Whereas township residents could take the organization created in the course of the uprising as a starting point for taking collective control over common facilities, hostel residents were left standing by as the hostel structure began to crack. The hostel-township relation became even more one-sided.

With the end of influx control in 1986, "illegality" ceased to be an effective form of administrative control in hostels. Regular blackjack nightly raids in search of illegal residents ceased. Although replaced by municipal police, the presence of repressive forces diminished. A few years later, when the violence began, both the hostel administration and the police fled the confines of the hostel—as did a section of the hostel population. Criminals and smugglers were now in a position to take refuge in a hostel; in some cases, they were even poised to take control. The hostel, for example, could be a chop shop to which a stolen car could be brought, taken apart, and then sold, all in a matter of a few hours. It gave a peculiar twist to the hostel-township relation, but this twist was the result of a historical process. Those who read that outcome as evidence of a long-standing insider-outsider split were guilty of reading the past from the present, of deducing history from empirical reality. "This reduction of Soweto community into two communities, the outsiders and the insiders," argues Babylon Xeketwane, "is too simplistic."[138]

Official efforts to divide township insiders from migrant outsiders were an entrenched and long-standing part of South African state policy. There were many mediations between policy and its translation into reality. One such mediation was the resistance of those who were meant to be so divided and stood to lose by it, either in the short or the long run. We have seen that the independent unions fought hard and successfully the post-Wiehahn attempt to translate this distinction into a law that would make illegal the unionization of migrants. They fought hard for the unity of labor, migrant and resident, on the shop floor, but union attempts to restrict organization to the shop floor could not hold in the face of apartheid, which defined for the worker a state of unfreedom in every aspect of his/her existence, whether at work or at home. Although the workplace proved to be an effective starting point for worker organization, allowing unions to pick issues they were equal to handling, to define an enclave in which they could build and grow, it could not hold as a limit to that organization. Once defined as a static limit, it was seen as stunting growth. The more worker organization and strength built up, the more the limits of that distinction appeared artificial and constraining. Ultimately, the shop floor–community divide was considered a regrettable legacy of an earlier era. The COSATU unions warmly embraced community issues.

As unions moved to link shop floor with community issues, in the process joining hands with community-based organizations, there arose a problem because they did so selectively, for there was not one single homogeneous community, but several distinct and heterogeneous communities. Ironically, as they embraced township-based organizations— and as the center of gravity of popular revolt moved firmly into townships—unions withdrew from hostels. If union organizers erred through inaction, we will see that the homecoming exile movements—particularly the ANC—put forth a series of hastily changing demands, from emptying hostels so they could be occupied by returning exiles to "converting" them exclusively into family units to "fencing" off "violent" hostels, demands that seemed as so many direct threats to the fast-changing hostel populations. If the "betterment" policies of the apartheid state in the 1950s had threatened the rural base of migrants, ANC demands regarding hostel conversion threatened their urban base.

In a rapidly changing context where the isolation of hostels from surrounding townships grew as fast as the township uprising raged around hostels, at a time when not only the future of the hostel as a single-sex migrant institution but also that of the migrant as part of the urban landscape seemed to be at stake, migrant workers once again became available for organization by other forces. Unlike in the 1970s, however, and perhaps precisely because of the gains of that period, this time that availability was not at the point of work but at the point of residence.

I need to underline that the difference in circumstance between township and hostel—the structural difference—did not mechanically and inevitably translate into a point of tension that generated conflict. At the same time we will see that the assumption by township activists that political differences necessarily reflected an ideological disagreement—and never one in circumstance—initially led to tensions within townships and posed a challenge to the activists of the uprising. Where activists were able to learn from mistakes, overcome these tensions, and organize an effective township resistance, the tension reappeared as one between the organized township and the hostel outside its fold. I will show this in the case of Alexandra, one of the most politically dynamic townships in South Africa.

THE ALEXANDRA CIVIC AND THE M-1 HOSTEL

Alexandra, say its civic leaders, has a population of 350,000 living in 4.6 square kilometers. Fifty percent live in shanties. Alex was declared a hostel area in the 1960s. The M-1 was built in 1972. By 1989 there were three thousand residents. They came from different areas and nationalities. No single group was dominant, but the majority comprised Pedi, Tswana, Shangaan, and Venda. Then came Xhosa and Zulu. Unlike the East Rand—where a township serviced a particular industry and was easier to organize—Alexandra fed assorted industrial establishments and was barely touched by unionization in 1976. In this, it was more like Soweto.

Civic leaders trace the origin of the civic movement to the 1976 Soweto uprising.[139] Student grievances in 1976 went beyond Bantu education to highlighting other issues, such as the provision of services. Their exemplary courage was a catalyst that revived adult organizations, including those of women. The first civic, the Port Elizabeth Black Community Organization (PEBCO), was strongly influenced by a Black Consciousness perspective. Its example appears to have inspired both the Soweto Committee of Ten and the Alexandra Action Committee, the precursors to civic organization in Soweto and Alexandra.

Several key activists in the civic movement came from trade unions. In Alexandra the best known was Moses Mayekiso, who personified the course the independent union movement followed in the first decade of its growth. He arrived in the Johannesburg area in the late 1960s as a migrant seeking work in the gold mines. Later, when he worked in a Toyota plant and lived in a single-sex hostel, Mayekiso was recruited by MAWU. No sooner had he risen to being a shop steward in the union than Mayekiso was fired by the company in the course of a wage strike. It was then, in 1980, that the union took him up as a full-time organizer. Mayekiso's involvement in community action developed around two issues: housing and security. Union members lived in appalling conditions. Rent payment to township councillors seemed a thankless one-way flow, since no services were provided in return. The local authority was propped up by a security management system consisting of police and vigilantes. Through regular raids designed to identify both "illegals" and those who had not paid rent, they kept residents in the grip of terror. "It was difficult to live in Alexandra if your documents were not in order," Mayekiso told the court that tried him for treason years later.[140] "We would have to wake up at midnight and go to sleep in the veld so the police who raided two or three times a week would not arrest us."

The civic movement came to fruition as the government tried to stem the growing township uprising of the mid-1980s by clamping a selective emergency on the most troublesome communities, defined as "oil spots." One of these was Alexandra. "That emergency helped us to reach the very people we had failed to reach before, the nonactivists, because anyone on the street could be detained," explained a civic activist of the time.[141]

> People started identifying the enemy, and we also started organizing the civic. People were so mobilized in Alex that they virtually took control of all aspects of their lives. People went on anticrime campaigns and rid the township of all crime. Women could walk the township any time of the night. People evicted the police physically, threw them into police barracks, stopped paying rent to local authorities. Then we said, "Should we not form a body to which we should pay rent money, and from it pay teachers when they withdraw from DET [Department of Education and Training, the government authority in charge of African education]?"

"Ungovernability" was the context in which community-based organizations began to build "organs of people's power." Its starting point was an interim structure set up in 1986, called the Alexandra Action Committee. (AAC)[142] The AAC was a formation of activists, many of whom drew inspiration from the success of trade unions in building factory-level structures around shop stewards. Under the leadership of Moses Mayekiso—by then also the general secretary of the National Union of Metalworkers of South Africa, the successor to MAWU—the Alexandra activists set out to form yard, block, street, and area committees. "Prior to 1985, we had ad hoc structures," an activist from the period recalled.

> In 1985 we began organizing democratic structures. People in Alex live huddled together. Twenty families share two bucket toilets, one water tap. Communal services create tension. So, we formed Alexandra Action Committee, a forerunner of the civic, to elect yard, block, street, area committees, and then to organize the civic from the ground up. . . . Every three streets formed an area. . . . An area committee is seventeen persons. . . . Once every three months, the executive and the area committees met in the Central Executive Committee as the decision-making body of the civic."[143]

In the course of that protracted confrontation, Alexandra blew up in early 1986. A six-day war pitted residents against vigilantes and police. Along with four other activists, Mayekiso was arrested and charged with treason, accused not only of mobilizing popular resistance against the government-appointed local authority, but also of setting up "organs of people's power" to usurp that authority. Mayekiso and his four colleagues were held for nine hundred days and not released until 1989.

No sooner were its leading activists detained than the structures set up by the AAC collapsed. It is a tribute to AAC activists that they turned a sharp dip in their fortunes into an occasion for critical evaluation. The rethinking led to the realization that activism had been a youth project. With the notion that they were the vanguard of the community, the activist youth had set out to mobilize the rest of the community, but instead of being the result of persuasion and a stepping-stone to organization, mobilization was at times achieved through coercion and led to alienation. "Prior to 1985, we were operating in a haphazard way," recalled Richard Mdakane, the general secretary of the civic in 1993, in a self-critical mood.[144]

> A stayaway would just be called to commemorate June 1976. Many, even in the community, would not heed the call. We would coerce them. . . . We would get up at 3 A.M. to coerce people to make sure buses don't operate. It exposed us to the security system. It instilled fear amongst people, not respect. When we go to jail, our programs just die. And we go to jail easily because [we have] no open support from the community. . . . After many years, we realized that the civic was just the activists. Even the community was alienated. We were forced to rethink, to consider the whole community.[145]

Part of that reappraisal was the relationship between the community and hostels. "There were times we would call community meetings without hostel dwellers," continued Richard Mdakane. "Prior to 1985, relations between us and hostel dwellers were alienating. After 1985, the civic realized we couldn't wish the hostels away, and they were not there out of any fault of theirs. That's why we organized them also. We knew they would be affected by the boycott. That's why we went in to organize hostels."[146]

The Alexandra civic was unusual in arriving at the decision that it needed to organize hostel dwellers.[147] Philemon Machitela, who had lived in the hostel as early as 1976–77, when he worked as a driver in the bus transport company and was a chief head steward in the Transport and General Workers' Union, was charged with organizing the hostel in 1986, but his effort was cut short by the state of emergency. When conditions improved in 1989, he started to reorganize. "We created a hostel committee of seventeen members democratically elected by all the hostel dwellers," said Machitela. There were four floors in Madala Hostel. Each was divided into blocks, and in turn into kitchens. The hostel committee was the apex of a pyramidal structure that led from kitchen to block to floor. The civic's decision paid off. The elected hostel committee represented a broad cross section of residents. Of seventeen, more than half were Zulu speaking; most of these belonged to Inkatha.[148] When Inkatha organizers visited the M-1 and Madala hostels in October 1990 "to militarily organize the Zulu hostel dwellers," they were "driven out."[149] Alexandra was able to avoid much of the violence that spread across the Reef in the aftermath of unbanning in 1990.

But violence did come to Alexandra in 1992, and its focal point was the hostel. "One Sunday morning," recalls David Letsei, "we just saw an army of Inkatha coming in. They brought people from all hostels in the Reef. They intimidated, killed, and expelled hostel residents who disagreed and people from the surrounding community." The Inkatha "army" carried "traditional weapons" and was escorted by the police, but that army was not just an external force. Inkatha's ostensible purpose in busing people into Alexandra was to hold a rally. Philemon Machitela, the civic organizer in Madala, estimates the numbers attending the rally at around eight thousand, out of which, he says, not more than two thousand were residents of Alexandra; from these, "most came from the hostel." It being daytime, many of those unwilling to participate were able to leave the hostel. Others did not, claims Machitela, out of fear or ignorance. Some joined "because if they did not support village mates they would become a target," and others because "they were not aware this would be the beginning of violence."

This account, as put together from interviews with civic organizers, raises several questions: Even if many attended in ignorance of the real objectives of the IFP, why did they attend? What was the alliance of forces that enabled the IFP to capture the hostel, even if militarily, after it had failed to gain entry to it a year earlier? The timing of the rally provides a clue. It followed on the heels of the civic's signing an accord with the Transvaal Provincial Administration in February–March 1991.[150] Part of the accord was a demand for upgrading hostels to family accommodations. "From the time we signed a regional accord and before we could report to the community," explained Nkele Ntingane, the assistant general secretary of the civic, "the violence began. We were taken unawares."[151]

The idea that all hostels should be upgraded to family accommodations came from the civic and was first mooted in 1986. When the emergency ended in 1989 and the civic turned to organizing hostels, civic organizers put the idea before hostel residents. The reception was mixed. "People from rural areas were not happy," recalled Machitela. "They wondered whether they would be forced to bring their families or be kicked out." The civic organizers were skeptical of the legitimacy of the opposition, holding the low level of education of rural migrants responsible for their failure to agree fully: "It is very hard for such people to understand what we mean by upgrading a hostel into a family unit and to understand [the] rights of people." To its credit, the civic responded with a revised position: "We offered alternatives: family or bachelors. They were satisfied." Yet the regional accord the civic signed in 1991 contained no trace of that alternative. The compromise of 1989 was replaced by a flat call for an end to single-sex accommodation in hostels. Why? I asked Machitela. "This was a political issue," was the short reply. A year after the violence began, in 1993, civic leaders had not changed their tune: "The solution is for the hostel system to be abolished, to be converted into family units."[152]

The civic's conviction that single-sex accommodation should be abolished was no mere dogma. It could not just have been a prejudice of township family residents, for the Alexandra civic, unlike others, had taken the initiative to organize inside the hostels—because it clearly understood that a failure to do so would only weaken it in the face of an assault from hostile forces. The experience of the Alexandra civic organizers is important precisely because their conviction grew from a day-to-day experience in hostels. Recalling their decision that the only solution was for hostels to be upgraded to family units, Moses Mayekiso insisted: "It was not something forced. It was a freedom we wanted. They participated in their decision."[153] "We started with an identification of problems, overcrowding and privacy," explained Philemon Machitela. "You had to come up with an alternative. We could see people leaving a hostel to stay in a shack outside, so they could be with wife and family." The problem was that the situation changed radically once influx control was abolished in 1986. The shanty population grew dramatically. The more those hostel residents who wanted to live with their families moved into shanties, the greater was the likelihood that many of those remaining behind would also be exercising an option—for not living with families. It should not be surprising that when the IFP called for a rally to protest the regional accord, there was a divided response from the hostel population.

A tension, however, is not the same as an antagonism. Recalling the days of the stayaways, Mayekiso argued: "It's true that hostel dwellers were not keen. Youths would enforce these on communities, and sometimes friction came directly out of it. But that did not create antagonism—the violence—people still worked together."[154] True, even if conditions for peaceful coexistence in Alexandra had been stretched thin by the accord, that alone may not have been sufficient for Inkatha to turn a protest rally into an exercise of force leading to the occupation of the hostel. For that, it needed active police support, which would have been difficult without the backing of the political authority in the township, the councillors. Starting from an ambivalent position between the central state authority and township residents, councillors turned against township residents as they were challenged by a rapidly organizing civic. When the civic called upon councillors to resign, the councillors turned to Inkatha and in turn received promises of protection. Among the councillors, "the mayor was particularly unpopular; he had been brought from outside and had a bad record."[155] To dramatize their demand that councillors keep Alexandra clean, residents emptied buckets of excreta in his house. That same week, the regional accord was signed. The following Sunday, Inkatha buses rolled into town.

The Wider Political Context

The movement that began with Durban 1973 and Soweto 1976 took on the proportions of a general urban uprising as the 1980s came to a close. Few of its participants, however, sensed the limits of the movement. Few recognized that this protest, no matter how torrential, was confined to townships. It had yet to find a way to reach out to the countryside in the grip of indirect rule authorities and to the enclaves of that same authority in the urban areas. Though shaped by the nature of power in apartheid South Africa, it had yet to come to grips with its nature, let alone find the means to transcend the many ways in which power fragmented the circumstances and experiences of the oppressed population. In such a situation, a township-based uprising had little possibility of going beyond checkmating the central state authority in a seesaw process of mutual attrition and gradual decline. In such a context, following several cycles of repression and resistance, the central state tried to break through the stalemate with a reform initiative. That initiative began with the abolition of influx control laws in 1986 and led to the unbanning of all exile political groups in 1990. It heralded the possibility of a new political order and inevitably set into motion the forces that hoped to shape the new order.

One of these was the ANC in exile. Like many liberation movements of the postwar period, it was organized as a protostate. In spite of enormous prestige within the country, the ANC operated more as a symbol than an organization of resistance within South Africa. Unbanned and back home, the ANC began a learning process, a coming to terms with forces and conditions shaped by more than a decade of experience in internal revolt. Like most paths of learning, it was a course littered with mistakes.

Following the unbanning of February 1990, there was public expectation of thousands of exiles returning home in the near future. A few months later, political and civic leaders were addressing rallies and community meetings, calling on residents to vacate hostels and make way for exiles.[156] Following the Reef War of August–September 1990, attention shifted to another *cause célèbre*. The conversion of hostels into family units was held up as the panacea for hostel-linked violence.[157] Without a vision sensitive to the variety of interests involved in a conflict and therefore able to incorporate those nonantagonistic in an overall solution, the ANC ran the risk of responding to an unfolding crisis with one ad hoc solution after another. The dilemma was illustrated dramatically when the ANC and the government signed a "record of understanding" after a 25 September 1992 summit meeting to discuss the violence.[158] At the meeting, the two parties agreed to fence twenty-eight "conflict" hostels. Following the example of several hostels where such a solution had been attempted earlier, the fence was supposed to "prevent criminality by hostel dwellers and to protect them from external aggression."[159] Construction of the first fence was to begin no later than a month after the summit—on 22 October 1992. The hostels to be fenced included four of the five included in this study: the Madala (Alexandra), Mzimhlope (Meadowlands), Wolhuter (Johannesburg), and Thokoza Women's Hostel (Durban).

By then, the attitude to the ANC was fast becoming the main line of division between and within hostels. For those who saw no alternative to maintaining two households, one in town and the other in the country, the ANC looked more and more tied to township-based forces. We will later see that this option—a foothold in town and another in the reserve—was the most real for Zulu migrants from KwaZulu, where agricultural degradation was less advanced than in any other reserve. Some of those who came from Zululand were already members of Inkatha. But even for others who were not, Inkatha seemed the only force with a countrywide-claim opposing the ANC directly on the hostel issue.

To understand the stamina of Inkatha, one needs to start from the fact that it claimed to be carrying on the tradition of the preexile ANC in the post-Sharpeville period. This was no empty boast, confined to using ANC symbols and colors. In the seventies, when the leadership of one homeland after another was accepting an apartheid-negotiated "independence" and the fear of "homeland independence" gripped migrant communities on the Reef, the name Inkatha became synonymous with opposition to that independence. In the throes of that enthusiasm Inkatha began calling mass rallies and opening branches on the East Rand.[160] It was a time when many workers from Natal carried two cards: a union card and an Inkatha card. As late as 1978, a poll carried out in Natal townships showed that Buthelezi was more popular than Mandela.[161] It was, after all, in recognition of Inkatha's popularity among sections of workers that the workerists, then in ascendance in FOSATU, argued that unions should organize workers regardless of political orientation and were always reluctant to take a political offensive against Inkatha.

Inkatha's gradualist reform line came under fire during and after the 1976 Soweto uprising. Not only did this lead to a sharp hostility in relations with urban youth activists, but the tactical disagreement with the ANC eventually led to a political break in 1979 over "loyal resistance" versus "national liberation struggle." The year 1979 proved to be a turning point. Following it, Inkatha set about using the homeland state structure at its disposal to build a single-party political organization to rival the ANC in Natal. That endeavor brought it into a head-on clash with the growing urban revolt. In the first half of the 1980s, Inkatha clashed with urban youth time and again: with KwaMashu schoolchildren in 1980, the University of Zululand students in 1983, and Durban township youth in 1985.[162]

The youth-led urban revolt did not really grip the townships of Natal until the mid-1980s. To understand both why this was so and the totality of Inkatha's response to it one needs to recognize that black township administration in Natal was a direct extension of the indirect rule apparatus in KwaZulu. It was neither as localized nor as fragile as similar administrations on the Reef or the Cape. As late as the early 1990s, KwaZulu townships in Natal were run by councillors, half of whom were elected and the other half appointed by the KwaZulu government.[163] Given its control over a host of rights necessary to pursue life in a township, such as granting trading licenses or house sites or places in schools, Inkatha was well placed to coerce the allegiance of residents when necessary.

The lesson Inkatha learned from the resilience of "its" township administrations in the face of the growing revolt was to extend the apparatus of indirect rule from townships to surrounding shanties. With an annual flow of rural refugees estimated at one hundred thousand throughout the 1980s, Greater Durban was considered, in Anthony Minaar's words, "one of the fastest urbanizing areas in the world," its squatting population second only to Mexico City. Targeting this recently urbanized population, Inkatha began weaving shanty dwellers into a tribute-driven administration run by a hierarchy of warlords and indunas (headmen). The fact that the largest state-built township, KwaMashu, had been excised from the Durban municipal area and incorporated into KwaZulu in 1969 helped, for in KwaZulu, all that an African person who wished to settle on a patch of land needed was permission from the local induna. This bit of custom allowed the Inkatha-placed or -recognized induna to extract regular tribute from all squatters and in turn provide them with protection in the form of a private army of *impis* backed by the KwaZulu police. Often the tribute went beyond providing gifts or tax to getting a member of the household to serve as one of the impis.[164]

On the Reef, Inkatha adopted a different strategy to suit different conditions. It sought out those opposed to or ambivalent about the unfolding township rebellion and promised them protection in return for membership. The first group comprised councillors and businesspeople. Susan Rubenstein found that all the councillors in Vosloorus in 1992 were without exception either members or officeholders of the IFP.[165] Systematically, Inkatha encircled hostels the way a hunter stalks its prey, beginning by establishing control over taxi routes and hostel trade.[166]

Four months after its unbanning, the ANC called for the dissolution of KwaZulu and the KwaZulu police force. That same month, July 1990, Inkatha officially turned itself into a political party. From then on, the Inkatha Freedom Party concentrated on opening branches on the Reef. It targeted the largest hostels for membership, exactly as the independent unions on the Reef had done a decade earlier. Without the series of ANC demands regarding hostels—first that they be vacated for exiles, then that they be converted into exclusive family units, and finally that the violent ones be fenced—it is difficult to believe that the IFP could have secured more than a toehold in most Reef hostels. But simply to argue that the IFP was an unintended beneficiary of ANC decisions in a fast-changing situation is to fail to explain why a section of hostel residents embraced the IFP and why that embrace turned ambivalent. To understand that is the purpose of the final section of this chapter.

Inside Tradition

I have argued that there was a rapid change in the composition of the hostel population in the period following the abolition of influx control in 1986. At a stroke, this legislative reform made it possible for various sectors of the African population to express their preferences with their feet. As the leaders of the Alexandra civic noted, those wanting family units moved out of hostels and into shanties. Their departure created room for home-based relatives and friends escaping the grid of rural poverty. The renewed population was composed of those with firmer rural connections and a greater need for single-sex accommodation. The shift in the social composition of hostel residents was also reflected in a changing ethnic mix. Because the scope and tempo of agricultural crises varied from one reserve to another, different ethnic groups among migrants faced different choices.[167] The fact that agricultural degradation was most advanced in the Transkei and least so in KwaZulu meant that migrants from the Transkei were most likely to bring their wives. In such a situation, the demand for family housing could easily appear as a predominantly Xhosa demand, whereas that for single-sex accommodation could sound mainly Zulu. Not surprisingly, many Zulu migrants saw the demand for family units as reflecting the preference of Xhosa migrants who had taken on wives on the Reef. A second factor accentuating the ethnic character of the recomposing hostel population was the political dimension of the violence. The fact that violence created conditions for a tighter IFP grip over non-ANC hostels meant that hostel residents fleeing violence were predominantly non-Zulu, just as township residents fleeing violence in the reverse direction tended to be mainly Zulu. The Mzimhlope Hostel in Soweto dramatically illustrates this two-way flow. Over the decade, the ethnic composition of hostel dwellers changed as Xhosa migrants fled to the township and Zulu township residents sought refuge in the hostel, taking up vacant family units. Previously the third-largest group among hostel residents, Zulus now comprise a clear majority.[168]

Add to these criminal elements for whom a violent hostel is the best possible shelter from their prey and from the law, and one begins to understand why the fast-changing population of many hostels reacted with particular hostility to the demand that single-sex accommodation be abolished. Its immediate effect was to make hostel residents receptive to those willing to argue their case. That initiative came from the IFP and allied forces. Given the town-country nexus around which migrant's lives were woven, that case was best made in customary terms. Not surprisingly, the ears immediately receptive to the IFP voice were those of Zulu migrants far from home. Although the IFP may be seen as a beneficiary of the violence, it did not continue to reap that benefit in the face of continuing violence, for as the violence spread and the IFP was seen to be linked to it, those among Zulu hostel residents alarmed by the fast-deteriorating situation began to take an autonomous initiative. In this context, autonomy could not and did not mean autonomy from the ANC, whose supporters had already been driven out of IFP-linked hostels in the first phase of violence. It could only mean autonomy from the IFP, the only force that claimed the right to represent hostel dwellers, particularly those from Zululand.

Following the Reef War of August–September 1990, public attention focused on hostels. Behind sharply drawn lines, two political groups defended two sharply opposed proposals. For the ANC and allied forces, the answer to hostel violence lay in converting hostels into family units. For the IFP and its supporters, hostels had to remain as single-sex facilities and be upgraded as such. *Conversion* and *upgrading* were the code words for these opposite standpoints. Neither solution was predicated on the idea that hostel residents would want the right to choose between alternatives, let alone the possibility that they might have the right to participate in defining alternatives. Whereas the ANC claimed to represent some sort of a general will, the IFP advanced an identity claim, the claim to represent the specific needs of Zulu migrants.

To give teeth to that claim, the IFP backed an initiative to form an organization for hostel residents in the first year of its formation. Created in Natal, the self-appointed leadership of the South African Hostel Dwellers Association (SAHDA) claimed to represent all hostel residents countrywide and hoped to unite all those opposed to the abolition of single-sex hostel accommodations. Upon its formation, SAHDA sought an audience with government ministers so that it could present a memo stating its demands. The audience was to be in August 1991. In preparation for it, an internal draft memo was drawn up.[169] Later a completely rewritten version was submitted to the ministers concerned. The two versions are different not only in the manner of expression, but also in their emphasis. The draft memo is rough in expression but concise in defining its subject matter. It is concerned in its entirety with different aspects of a single issue, hostels and hostel dwellers. It explains the rationale for forming the association in a context where all but hostel dwellers have been consulted on the question of "doing away with or improving . . . or changing" the status of hostel units: "Most regrettable and irregular is the fact that the people concerned, that is, the hostel dwellers, have never, as a body, had their say, opinion and suggestion on a matter which directly concerns them." It calls for "democracy for hostel dwellers." Its line of reasoning makes sense from the point of view of hostel dwellers.

The document that was actually presented was not just a polished version of the draft. It was rewritten and had a total change in emphasis. The opening page and a half, an elaboration of the Ubuntu philosophy, carried the imprint of the IFP/Inkatha. All references to the need for self-representation by hostel dwellers were omitted. Instead, there was a denunciation of the tripartite party-union-church alliance that the IFP holds responsible for the continuing plight of the hostels. "SAHDA believes," the rewritten memo read, "that the campaign of the African National Congress (ANC) and its allied forces namely the South African Council of Churches (SACC) and COSATU to abolish the hostels is aimed at enforcing urbanization of the AFRICANS (BLACKS) and dispossessing Africans of their land."[170]

SAHDA failed to make inroads in the Transvaal, where the hostel question was at a boiling point in late 1990. The real challenge to SAHDA came not from the ANC, but from an initiative that arose from within the Zulu residents of Transvaal hostels. It eventually took a regional form.[171] In a situation where violence was spreading and unilateral accords were being signed by different parties, all except hostel dwellers, a top-down claim to represent an unrepresented constituency had difficulty holding. None of the Transvaal hostel leaders were represented in SAHDA, and they were "very upset about it."[172] From the outset, the effort in Transvaal was marked by three features that distinguished it from SAHDA and that were central to its claim to being the legitimate representative of Transvaal hostel dwellers.[173] The first was an emphasis on the autonomy of each hostel and on elections as the basis for representation. Residents' committees elected at individual hostels were brought together into subregional and then regional associations. Individually organized hostels in the Transvaal first came together as two separate associations, one on the East Rand and the other on the West Rand, and were then united under a single umbrella organization, the Transvaal Hostel Residents Association (THRA). The second feature was an emphasis on direct action, ground level and popular, through which to organize. To rally opposition to the 26 September 1992 fencing agreement between the government and the ANC and to back up its claim that "hostel residents' needs should determine hostel initiatives," the THRA initiated a rental boycott by hostel residents and organized protest marches. The third and final feature was an attempt to broaden its organizational base beyond Zulu hostel dwellers, by putting forth its demands as those of hostel dwellers, regardless of ethnicity. An initiative of Zulu migrants, the THRA consciously sought to develop a multiethnic constituency.

The internal context that allowed this initiative to develop was a collapse of indirect rule authority in hostels following the onset of violence. The municipal police, who had replaced blackjacks, and the white hostel administration fled the violent hostels in mid-1990. Barricaded and armed, these hostels turned into no-go zones for the police. But as criminal elements moved into hostels for protection, they gained an upper hand in organizing the internal life of hostels. Ironically, it is the first phase of violence that underlined the need for self-administration in the hostels.[174] Violence also shifted the balance of authority from the old to the young, making possible an alternative to age as a basis for influence and authority. Through these experiences, the secretary of the Transvaal Hostel Residents Association claimed, "Hostel residents got convinced that they needed a representative body."[175]

"We began organizing in 1990['s] end when they said hostels must be demolished," recalled Temba Nxumalo, the chair of the residents' association at Wolhuter.[176] Even under the indirect rule administration, there had existed a committee structure based on room, floor, and the hostel itself. All that remained was to turn upside down the principle on which these committees were established. Instead of being the appointees of the white hostel manager, the committees were now elected. Where did the idea of electing committees come from? I asked. Once the residents felt they needed their own association, "they picked up the cue from civics; they felt they needed their own civic."[177] The non-ANC, Zulu-dominated hostels organized first, because they felt threatened. The pro-ANC hostels, like the five at Sebokeng, were represented by the township civic. Why not use existing structures, such as the IFP committee in the hostel? "It was felt," responded Steyn, that "the hostel association had to be as apolitical as possible, because many hostels have multilingual residents; for example, [the] Thembisa Hostel has many Pedi-speaking people from northern Transvaal who don't necessarily support the IFP." Wesley Dhlamini, chair of the Meadowlands Hostel Residents' Association, which did not organize until 1992, confirmed: "We felt that at that time hostels were a national political issue. As hostel residents, we wanted it depoliticized. We wanted to talk for ourselves, not to allow political organizations to speak for us."[178]

The elected residents' committee, however, is not the only organized hostel group with a direct influence on how the hostel is run. There are at least two others: the traditional leaders and the local IFP (or ANC) committee. "Every traditional leader comes from a particular area. He is the eye of the chief from that area," Dhlamini explained. "He is to make sure they behave well." Through various activities, from ensuring that "someone is buried through burial societies" to organizing "traditional functions" and "meetings to promote traditional heritage," they "link rural and urban life so [that] there must be a balance." "They act as fathers of the area": "If the IFP committee or we have a problem or there is a conflict of interest between us and [the] IFP, they solve the problem." Appointed by the local chief, the induna was the extension of the indirect rule authority in the rural area. His job was "to look after the men in a particular area, to assert control, and to protect the particular chief's interest in the cities."[179]

Violence had a dramatic effect on the role of the traditional leaders. Between organizing traditional dancing on Saturday and Sunday afternoons and training young men in traditional weaponry, "their main function" was to ensure "the security of the area."[180] I met Albert Mkhize, the chief induna at Wolhuter. A robust and tall man of sixty-four years, he first came to the Reef from Natal in 1951, worked his way up as a metalworker, and by 1993 was a foreman at a construction site. He said his main duty was to "sort things out when there is fighting." I asked for an example.

> In 1991, the world started changing. Everything started moving. The violence started. All the Zulus must be finished, the Xhosa nation said. Now the Zulus starting to stand up. How come the king to be finished? Here, I started to tell the people: "You must not move, Zulu or Xhosa, must stay. If you move, there will be no place for you after the violence." . . . The hostel is very strong because it defends itself. Even if someone comes, my people can fight. My responsibility is to make sure the people defend themselves.[181]

As the indirect rule structure under the hostel supervisor collapsed, the indunas became the instrument through which the indirect rule structure from the countryside—particularly KwaZulu—was strengthened in Transvaal hostels. In the throes of the violence on the Reef, the induna system was in fact elaborated into a full-fledged military structure. Under the chief induna, a hostel was divided into regionally defined impis (regiments), each with an impi captain or fighting leader, who in turn had section headmen who controlled squads of *amabutho* (warriors). The terminology is derived from rural Natal and is evocative of the structure of the precolonial Zulu military machine. The violent hostels were effectively organized for security. The security system covered not only the hostel, but also the corridor that linked it with the world outside; in Meadowlands, for example, this is the road between the hostel and the suburban train station. A mobile car patrol monitored any armed movement between the hostel and the station. There was a system of self-policing, complete with warning systems. Any visitor from outside was asked to follow a particular route when going to the hostel.

Unlike the elected residents' committees, which tend to have roughly the same structure in different hostels on the Reef, the structure of traditional leaders varies from one hostel to another depending on the ethnic composition of the resident population. At Wolhuter, where the residents are predominantly Zulu, there are two Zulu indunas, and the senior Zulu induna is the chief of all indunas. The indunas from "the other nations are helping hands of these two," the chairman of the residents' association explained.[182] But at Meadowlands, where the Zulus are roughly half the population, "the leader of the traditional leaders' committee is democratically elected by everyone in the hostel."[183]

The third leadership structure within the hostel is political. This is the local committee of either the ANC or the IFP. In the Zulu-dominated hostels, it is the latter. Unlike the traditional leadership of indunas, which is tied to its area of origin, the political leadership in the IFP committee is not. Like the hostel committee, the traditional leadership tends to take a hostel-focused view of things, whereas the political leadership necessarily thinks of the hostel as one cog in a larger IFP structure. In Wolhuter, successive waves of violence brought out the tension between the traditional and the political leadership. In spite of their key role in organizing the hostel security system, the indunas at Wolhuter fully backed hostel residents when some of them took a peace initiative to the nearby Xhosa-dominated Selby Hostel with whom fighting had been recurrent over most of 1992.[184] Peace committees were formed and joint prayers followed. The IFP, however, was not enthusiastic about a locally worked out peace and felt that its powers were usurped. The Jacob Dhlomo initiative from Wolhuter took place in August 1992 and became the basis of a wide-ranging peace initiative.

"What's your solution for the violence?" I asked Mkhize, the chief induna at Wolhuter. He answered:

> What can I say? My solution is here. I make a peace committee. I go to people in other hostels. The church must go there and tell people the violence doesn't pay us. We must think of children and of tomorrow. . . . I don't like the political people. He is messing our time. Anyone without a job—politics. It has caused factories to be collapsed and jobs to be lost. Anyone, any political party. . . . Inkatha is a cultural movement. IFP is a political movement. Today, Inkatha is taken over by IFP. There are people believing they don't agree with IFP, but they are Inkatha. . . . Inkatha is more law, not burning.[185]

If the tension between the cultural and the political leadership was difficult to discern in the open, such was not the case with relations between the elected hostel committee and the IFP leadership in the hostel. Hostel residents realized they were caught in a wider political battle, one out of all proportion to the importance of the immediate hostel issue and one they could not hope to influence directly. Whereas the IFP was calling for upgrading hostel accommodation entirely as single-sex quarters, the ANC wanted the hostels either to be demolished or to be converted wholly into family quarters. A strong and growing feeling among residents was that their circumstances varied and that they needed not one alternative but a range of alternatives, a choice, which would not be possible unless they took matters into their own hands.

The conclusion that the interests of a political party and those of hostel residents may not always coincide was arrived at not through a solitary encounter but through a gradual accumulation of experience. Critical to this realization was the experience with township councillors, who joined Inkatha when faced with the urban revolt of the mid-1980s. On one hand, Inkatha-driven councillors enjoyed a support base in the hostels. On the other hand, they were corrupt and responsible for poor services, not only to townships but also to hostel residents. "We as residents' committee will see them [councillors] as useless, not providing what they are elected for," argued Wesley Dhlamini, chair of Meadowlands Residents. "But councillors are members of [the] IFP. So when we attack them, they say we are attacking [the] IFP!"[186] Matters reached a point of no return when one particular council, the Diepmeadow Town Council in Soweto, privatized the Diepkloof Hostel without the knowledge of residents, who found out only when developers moved in. It was an incident that came to make the rounds of hostels around the Reef and was sure to be cited in any discussion of relations between councillors and hostel residents. Yet whenever residents considered a rent boycott against the council, in the manner of the township boycotts, Inkatha—and after 1992, the IFP—would object. But in October 1992, when the Transvaal Hostel Residents Association proposed a rent boycott following the 26 September fencing accord between the ANC and the government and the IFP objected to the boycott as an unlawful tactic, the THRA simply went ahead.[187] After a boycott lasting three months, the THRA won its demands and began representing its members in the Regional Hostel Forum. The experience was summed up by the vice chair of the Meadowlands Residents Association. "We regard [the] IFP as a political organization. They can't represent people on civic matters. We need a civic body to represent the people."[188]

So when it came to discussions in the Regional Hostel Forum organized by the National Housing Forum, the Transvaal Hostel Residents Association maintained that the THRA—and not the IFP—was the legitimate representative for residents' interests. "Hostel committees are a threat to political forces, including [the] IFP," concludes Sakkie Steyn from that experience.

> The Regional Hostel Forum has been postponed for six months for one reason or another. Hostel committees are not a surrogate for political parties—nor civics. The argument of political parties is that our members stay in hostels and we have a mandate to speak for them. Our argument is that so do members of the Zionist Church or COSATU. Representation depends on issue. At the very organization of the association there was a very strong feeling of autonomy, that we are not a political group. Hostel leaders had felt manipulated by parties in the past. They realized that party policies don't always reflect [the] interest of people on the ground. There will be tension between national and local community matters. The whole question of hostels was going too national.[189]

Tension, however, does not always lead to antagonism. This was the point that Moses Mayekiso had emphasized to me with reference to relations between civics and hostel residents. To weave tension creatively into an overall relationship requires recognizing a community as a heterogeneous social mix with nonantagonistic interests and accepting the legitimacy of its different components. It was a lesson that the trade union movement had found difficult to learn. Driven into a corner, their call for hostel autonomy opposed by political groups within hostels, it was a lesson hostel activists grasped the way a drowning person does a rope. What lessons did you learn in the process? I asked several times. "The first lesson was that you can't exclude any of the leadership structures within hostels," explained Sakkie Steyn.[190] Election and autonomy are not enough. The challenge was to get a representation on the ground that would reflect "a cross section of interests, including areas and interest groups." The election process was organized with this objective in mind, and it took six to eight months to effect. Even then elected committees were found to be insufficiently representative. There was a tendency to nominate and elect those with a formal education: elected committees "were made up of a strong section of English-speaking young matriculants." Yet hostel activists understood from experience that "if traditional leaders had a strong grip on a hostel, no project could get off the ground" without them. "Lots of projects started by other people were wrecked particularly for this reason," confided the secretary. After much discussion, a decision was taken: "Some of the traditional leaders would have to be coopted depending on particular circumstances within hostels." The precondition to neutralizing the IFP's political ambitions within hostels was to accommodate "all leadership structures" that would support the demand for hostel autonomy. In some places, like Wolhuter, this meant coopting traditional leaders, who were no more than appointed agents of indirect rule authorities in the countryside. In other hostels, like Mzimhlope, the indirect rule appointees were subject to an electoral practice: the head of all the appointed indunas in the hostel was elected. In the course of this struggle, and through modest initiatives, migrant activists were managing to evolve a new tradition while changing received tradition from within.

Migrant activists were neither closeted from surrounding influences nor immune to a learning process. Although often hostile to township-based civics, they took a leaf from the experience of residence-based civics that were both elected and autonomous. While recognizing the legitimacy of traditional leaders—mainly representatives of the Kwa-Zulu-based indirect rule authority—they were learning to tame them: either by cooption in elected bodies or by reorganizing their internal relations on the basis of an electoral principle.

Yet one cannot escape the fact that the induna represented a nonprogressive link between the urban and the rural: in bridging the two as custodian of an authoritarian tribal tradition, he highlighted interethnic tension and downplayed popular and class interest. At the same time, in the hostel violence of the early 1990s, this tradition was not imposed on migrants from above; it was voluntarily reproduced from below. To make sense of this, one needs to keep in mind that the tribal—the customary that summed up the form of tradition that the induna stood for—was not only the language of force in the Native Authority, but also the only language in which a migrant could have access to rights in the Native Authority. In the absence of an alternative—and progressive— link between the urban and the rural, migrants had no choice but to embrace indunas while seeking to reform the tradition they represented. If the threat to their rural base that was the betterment policy of apartheid in the 1950s spurred migrants into a revolt against compliant Native Authorities, a threat to their urban base that was the ANC's demand for turning hostels into family units in the early 1990s explains their embrace of agents of the same Native Authorities. Both instances underline one cardinal fact; critical to the shaping of South African—and generally African—politics in the period that lies ahead will be the ways in which the urban is linked to the rural.

CHAPTER EIGHT

Conclusion:
Linking the Urban and the Rural

As THE DAWN of independence broke on a horizon of internal conflict, reconsideration of the African colonial experience began. Could it be that the African problem was not colonialism but an incomplete penetration of traditional society by a weak colonial state or deference to it by prudent but shortsighted colonizers? Could it be that Europe's mission in Africa was left half finished? If the rule of law took centuries to root in the land of its original habitation, is it surprising that the two sides of the European mission—market and civil society, the law of value and the rule of law—were neither fully nor successfully transplanted in less than a century of colonialism? And that this fragile transplant succumbed to caprice and terror on the morrow of independence?

With the end of the cold war, this point of view has crystallized into a tendency with a name, Afro-pessimism, and a claim highly skeptical of the continent's ability to rejuvenate itself from within. Whether seen as a problem of incomplete conquest or as one of unwise deference to traditional authorities, both sides of the Afro-pessimist point of view lead to the same conclusion: a case for the recolonization of Africa, for finishing a task left unfinished. Part of the argument of this book is that Afro-pessimism is unable to come to grips with the nature of the colonial experience in Africa precisely because it ignores *the mode* of colonial penetration into Africa.

Yet another set of questions coheres around a perspective that is not evolutionist but particularistic, whose impetus is not toward highlighting African "backwardness" but underlining its difference. That difference is said to be the tendency to fragmentation and particularism, hitherto held in check and obscured by a shared dilemma, colonial racism. Was not racism the general aspect of the African experience—its colonial and external aspect—and tribalism its particular, indigenous and internal, aspect? Generally emancipated from racism with the end of colonialism, did not Africa once again come to be in the grip of a specifically African particularism: tribalism, ethnic conflict, and primordial combat? Another part of the argument in this book is that it is too naive to think of racism and tribalism as simple opposites, for alien (racial) domination was actually grounded in and mitigated through ethnically organized local power. In the colonial period, ethnic identity and separation were politically enforced. Although forged through colonial experience, this form of the state survived alien domination. Reformed after independence, purged of its racial underpinnings, it emerged as a specifically African form of the state.

THE FORM OF THE STATE

Colonial Genesis

I have argued that to grasp the specificity of colonial domination in Africa, one needs to place it within the context of Europe's larger colonizing experience. The trajectory of the wider experience, particularly as it tried to come to grips with the fact of resistance, explains its midstream shift in perspective: from the zeal of a civilizing mission to a calculated preoccupation with holding power, from rejuvenating to conserving society, from being the torchbearers of individual freedom to being custodians protecting the customary integrity of dominated tribes. This shift took place in older colonies, mainly India and Indochina, but its lessons were fully implemented in Africa, Europe's last colonial possession. Central to that lesson was an expanded notion of the customary.

Britain was the first to marshal authoritarian possibilities in indigenous culture. It was the first to realize that key to an alien power's achieving a hegemonic domination was a cultural project: one of harnessing the moral, historical, and community impetus behind local custom to a larger colonial project. There were three distinctive features about the customary as colonial power came to define it. First, the customary was considered synonymous with the tribal; each tribe was defined as a cultural group with its own customary law. Second, the world of the customary came to be all-encompassing; more so than in any other colonial experience, it came to include a customary access to land. Third, custom was defined and enforced by customary Native Authorities in the local state—backed up by the armed might of the central state.

To appreciate the significance of this, we need to recall only one fact. Although the use of force was outlawed in every British colony in the aftermath of the First World War (and in French colonies after the Second), this applied to the central state and usually to European officials supervising Native Authorities in the local state, but not to the Native Authorities. For this, there was one reason. So long as the use of force could be passed off as customary it was considered legitimate, and—to complete the tautology—force decreed by a customary authority was naturally regarded as customary. No wonder that when force was needed to implement development measures on reluctant peasants, its use was restricted to Native Authorities as much as possible. In the language of power, custom came to be the name of force. It was the halo around the regime of decentralized despotism.

The customary was never singular, but plural. As far as possible, every tribe was governed by its customary law. Europe did not bring to Africa a tropical version of the late-nineteenth-century European nation-state. Instead it created a multicultural and multiethnic state.[1] The colonial state was a two-tiered structure: peasants were governed by a constellation of ethnically defined Native Authorities in the local state, and these authorities were in turn supervised by white officials deployed from a racial pinnacle at the center.

Another peculiarity of this form of the state was that the relation between force and market was not antithetical. It was not simply that force framed market institutions. It was more that force and market came to be two alternative ways of regulating the process of production and exchange. To the extent that the scope of the customary included land and labor, that of the market was limited. To flush either labor or its products out of the realm of the customary required the use of force. Clearly, there was and is no particular and fixed balance between force and market. Its degree remains variable: the customary was never a Chinese wall keeping the tide of market relations at bay; nor was it of nominal significance. The customary was porous. Within its parameters, market relations were enmeshed with extra-economic coercion. Free peasants were differentiated, and those better off were shielded from the regime of force.

Postcolonial Reform and Variations

Characteristic of Afro-pessimism, whether in its left-wing or right-wing version, is a "roots of the crisis" literature that reduces the past to a one-dimensional reality. The result is a reconstruction of the past as if the only thing that happened was laying the foundations of a present crisis. The result is not an analysis that appropriates the past as a contradictory mix, but one that tends to debunk it.

The core agenda that African states faced at independence was threefold: deracializing civil society, detribalizing the Native Authority, and developing the economy in the context of unequal international relations. In a state form marked by bifurcated power, deracialization and detribalization were two aspects that would form the starting point of an overall process of democratization. By themselves, even if joined together, they could not be tantamount to democratization. Together, this amalgam of internal and external imperatives signified the limits and possibilities of the moment of state independence.

Of this threefold agenda, the task undertaken with the greatest success was deracialization. Whether formulated as a program of "indigenization" by mainstream nationalist regimes—conservative or moderate—from Nigeria to Zaire to Idi Amin's Uganda, or as one of nationalization by radical ones, from Ghana to Guinea to Tanzania, the tendency everywhere was to erode racially accumulated privilege in erstwhile colonies. Whether they sought to Africanize or to nationalize, the historical legitimacy of postindependence nationalist governments lay mainly in the program of deracialization they followed. The difference between them, however, was an effect of the strategy of distribution each one employed. Whether the tendency was privatization or etatism, both strategies opened opportunities for nepotism and corruption, for clientelism.

In contrast to deracialization, the task undertaken with the least success was democratization. Key to democratization was the Native Authority in the local state: its detribalization would have to be the starting point in reorganizing the bifurcated power forged under colonialism. The failure to democratize explains why deracialization was not sustainable and why development ultimately failed. Without a reform in the local state, the peasantry locked up under the hold of a multiplicity of ethnically defined Native Authorities could not be brought into the mainstream of the historical process. In the absence of democratization, development became a top-down agenda enforced on the peasantry. Without thoroughgoing democratization, there could be no development of a home market. This latter failure opened wide what was a crevice at independence. With every downturn in the international economy, the crevice turned into an opportunity for an externally defined structural adjustment that combined a narrowly defined program of privatization with a broadly defined program of globalization. The result was both an internal privatization that recalled the racial imbalance that was civil society in the colonial period and an externally managed capital inflow that towed alongside a phalanx of expatriates—according to UN estimates, more now than in the colonial period!

But if the limits of the postindependence period were reflected in a deracialization without democratization, I will argue that the Achilles' heel of the contemporary "second independence movement" lies in its political failure to grasp the specificity of the mode of rule that needs to be democratized. Theoretically, this is reflected in an infatuation with the notion of civil society, a preoccupation that conceals the actual form of power through which rural populations are ruled. Without a reform of the local state, as I will soon show, democratization will remain not only superficial but also explosive.

MAINSTREAM NATIONALISM

The mainstream nationalists who inherited the central state at independence understood colonial oppression as first and foremost an exclusion from civil society, and more generally as alien rule. They aimed to redress these wrongs through deracialization internally and anti-imperialism externally. The new state power sought to indigenize civil society institutions and to restructure relations between the independent state and the international economy and polity.

In the absence of the detribalization of rural power, however, deracialization could not be joined to democratization. In an urban-centered reform, the rural contaminated the urban. The tribal logic of Native Authorities easily overwhelmed the democratic logic of civil society. An electoral reform that does not affect the appointment of the Native Authority and its chiefs—which leaves rural areas out of consideration as so many protectorates—is precisely about the reemergence of a decentralized despotism! In such a context, electoral politics turned out to be about more than just who represents citizens in civil society, because victors in that contest would also have a right to rule over subjects through Native Authorities, for the winner would appoint chiefs, the Native Authority, everywhere. More than the rule of law, the issue in a civil society–centered contest comes to be who will be master of all tribes. As a Kenyan political scientist once remarked to me, the ethnicity of the president is the surest clue to the ethnic tinge of the government of the day. This is why civil society politics where the rural is governed through customary authority is necessarily patrimonial: urban politicians harness rural constituencies through patron-client relations. Where despotism is presumed, clientelism is the only noncoercive way of linking the rural and the urban.

Confined to civil society, democratization is both superficial and explosive: superficial because it is interpreted in a narrowly formal way that does not address the specificity of customary power—democratization equals free and fair multiparty elections—and explosive because, with the local state intact as the locus of a decentralized despotism, the stakes in any multiparty election are high. The winner would not only represent citizens in civil society, but also dominate over subjects through the appointment of chiefs in the Native Authority. The winner in such an election is simultaneously the representative power in civil society and the despotic power over Native Authorities.

Tribalism is more one-sidedly corrosive in an urban context than in the rural one. Stripped of the rural context, where it is also a civil war, tribalism in urban areas has no democratic impetus. It becomes inter-ethnic only. This practice is not confined to propertied strata. We have seen that migrants who became involved in the inter-ethnic politics of civil society did so partly to protect customary rural rights. In the absence of the democratization of Native Authorities and the custom they enforced, the more civil society was deracialized, the more it came to be tribalized. Urban tribalism appeared as a postindependence problem in states that reproduced customary forms of power precisely because deracialization was a postindependence achievement of these states.

RADICAL NATIONALISM

The accent of mainstream nationalism was on deracializing civil society, but it is the radical regimes that sought to detribalize Native Authority. The institutional basis of that effort was the single party, the inheritor of militant anticolonial nationalism, which symbolized a successful linkup between urban militants and rural insurrectionary movements against Native Authorities. Militant urban nationalism was the social and ideological glue that cemented otherwise heterogeneous peasant-based struggles. From that experience arose the single party as yet another noncoercive link between the rural and the urban.

The single party was simultaneously a way to contain social and political fragmentation reinforced by ethnically organized Native Authorities and a solution imposed from above in lieu of democratization from below, for the militants of the single party came to distrust democracy, by which they understood a civil society–centered electoral reform. A democratic link between the urban and the rural was in their eyes synonymous with a civil society–based clientelism. Seen as the outcome of an urban multiparty project, clientelism appeared as the other side of a deepening fragmentation along ethnic lines.

Whereas multiparty regimes tended toward a superficial and explosive democratization of civil society, their single-party counterparts tended to depoliticize civil society. The more they succeeded, the more the single party came to be bureaucratized. As the center of gravity in the party-state shifted from the party to the state, the method of work came to rely more on coercion than on persuasion. Whether heralding development or waging revolution, the single party came to enforce it from above on a reluctant peasantry. Although depoliticization contained interethnic tensions within civil society—and as a consequence within the whole polity—the result of a forced developmental march was to exacerbate tensions between the rural and the urban. The single party turned from a mobilizing organ into a coercive apparatus; in the words of Fanon, militants of yesterday turned into informers of today. True, there was a significant break with the formal institutions of indirect rule, but there was no such break with the form of its power. An institution such as chiefship may be abolished, only to be replaced by another with similar powers. The ideological text may change from the customary to the revolutionary—and so may political practice—but, in spite of real differences, there remains a continuity in administrative power and technique: radical experiences have not only reproduced, but also reinforced fused power, administrative justice and extra-economic coercion, all in the name of development.

The reform of decentralized despotism turned out to be a centralized despotism. So we come to the seesaw of African politics that characterizes its present impasse. On one hand, decentralized despotism exacerbates ethnic divisions, and so the solution appears as a centralization. On the other hand, centralized despotism exacerbates the urban-rural division, and the solution appears as a decentralization. But as variants both continue to revolve around a shared axis—despotism.

THE LESSON OF OPPOSITIONAL REFORM

The two tensions the specific form of the African state generated, the interethnic and the urban-rural, have also been faced by oppositional movements. In chapter 6 we surveyed some rural movements, and in chapter 7 the urban movement in post-1973 South Africa.

These movements bring out the two dimensions of the ethnic question, the internal and the external. Because the context in which rural movements organize is more often than not multiethnic, they face a common question: is a resistance against a tribal Native Authority possible which does not at the same time exacerbate interethnic tensions within the resulting movement?

I have argued that a peasant movement in the parameters of a Native Authority is at the same time an ethnic civil war. Yet this should not be understood as a claim that every such movement is committed to rooting out the institution of chiefship. Of the South African movements we surveyed, only the Mpondo sought to implement a democratic program whose target was the institution of chiefship. The rest fell short of it, some more than others. But all of them, without exception, sought to redefine the notion of the customary, to limit the powers of chiefship within traditional constraints. If "customary" is the name that power gives to the untraditional force with which it arms Native Authorities, it is also the language of peasant movements that seek to reform the same

Native Authority in the name of a custom anchored in notions more historical and popular. When I speak of tribalism as civil war, my notion of civil war is a continuum along which muted tensions coexist long before they break out into open confrontation.

Notwithstanding the colonial claim that traditional Africa was a tribal checkerboard, with each tribe in its own place, we have seen that tribal culture was highly textured and elastic, with the stranger often present on rural ground. For no reason other than to expand their following, the tendency of chiefs was to encourage strangers to settle in their domain. With a state-enforced and tribally circumscribed notion of custom, two related changes occurred. First, the tendency was to homogenize and flatten cultural diversity within the tribe in favor of an official tribal version. Second, the imposition of a tribal law as customary, to be defined and dispensed by a tribal authority, necessarily turned the simple fact of ethnic heterogeneity into a source of tension.

If the rural movements I surveyed were all to some degree marked by ethnic civil war, only the experience of the NRA in Uganda brought out clearly the intertribal tensions that surface in peasant movements. As it sought to weld together a common oppositional movement in a context where settled and migrant populations rubbed shoulders, the NRA defined rights as an attribute not of citizenship but of labor. To say that rights belonged to all those resident in a locality, regardless of geographical or ethnic origin, was to say that all those who labor have a justifiable claim to rights. Once labor was understood as the life-sustaining activity of laboring humanity, and not as wage labor, the accent shifted from citizens' rights to human rights.

To view rights as an attribute of labor is also to transcend the opposition between customary law and civil law, for the opposition notwithstanding, customary law and civil law share a common premise. Both see rights as an attribute of individuals belonging to a common land-based community. The difference lies in the definition of the community. From the point of view of customary law, that community is defined in ethnic terms, as the tribe; from that of civil law, the community is a nation, whether defined ethnically or territorially. Both subject and citizen derive their rights, customary or civil, through membership in a *patri*: a tribe for the subject, a nation for the citizen.

Although the NRA was able to bring a creative insight into resolving the interethnic tension in its rural base, the Luwero Triangle, it found great difficulty in addressing the urban-rural tension from a position of power in the city. It saw urban civil society demands for a representational multiparty democracy—a demand reinforced by many Western donors—as a threat, both to its hold on power and to the unity of power holding the country together. It was faced with the old dilemma that had plagued single-party regimes. Would not a multiparty contest in the city be about not just who would represent citizens in the city, but also who would be the master of tribes in the countryside? Would not such a contest both exacerbate clientelism in civil society and extend it to the countryside, thereby also activating and reorganizing democratic politics around interethnic tensions?

If the failure of the NRA—at the time of this writing, in late 1994— was in making a transition from the rural to the urban, from democratizing Native Authority to democratizing civil society, that of the urban movements in post-1973 South Africa was the opposite. The independent unions successfully fought attempts by the apartheid state to drive a wedge between migrant and resident labor in the townships but remained prisoners of a civil society–centered perspective. Although they disagreed on many issues of principle, the workerists and populists inside the independent unions agreed on one thing: the community meant the township. If the IFP—and in retrospect, also the ANC—succeeded in bridging the rural and the urban in the context of a multiparty contest, it did so at the cost of exacerbating interethnic tensions in civil society. Whereas the IFP was an urban extension of a Native Authority–based organization that it sought to conserve, the ANC was unable to arrive at a program to democratize Native Authority; instead, it turned to embracing those in the Native Authority who were willing to join it in an electoral alliance.

The Ugandan case shows that the democratization of the rural and the local cannot be stabilized unless extended to embrace the urban and the central, and the South African case illustrates the other side of the same proposition: without a democratization of rural customary power, urban civil power must inevitably degenerate. So long as rural power is organized as a fused authority that denies rights in the name of enforcing custom, civil society will remain an urban phenomenon. Surrounded by tribally organized customary powers, urban civil society is subject to a dual pressure: deracialization from within and retribalization from without. We can see this reflected in the dilemma the ANC faced in the 1994 elections.

Without a presence in either the reserve or the hostel—and without a program for democratizing customary rule in either—the ANC could reach the rural only from above, through Native Authorities. Confined to waging a democratic struggle in the urban and reduced to reaching rural communities through its customary authorities, the ANC found itself trapped in a Catch-22 situation. Its only option of linking the urban to the rural was through a tribal logic: either an intertribal alliance or an intertribal conflict, or more likely both, an alliance with those who are friendly (such as the chiefs of the Congress of Traditional Leaders of

South Africa, CONTRALESA) and a conflict with those who are not (such as Inkatha). In either case, the structure of customary power would remain intact. This is the context in which the 1994 election assumed a significance both civic and ethnic.

Critical to the shape these elections came to assume were migrant workers, the social force that more than any other straddled the rural and the urban. Without a democratic reach to either hostels or reserves, the ANC remained alienated from hostel workers, the very reason Inkatha raced to embrace those Zulu as the custodian of their customary rights in KwaZulu, a custom it promised to defend with arms if necessary. The more successfully Inkatha executed this project, the more the tribal logic of customary authorities came to contaminate urban civil society. As the hostel-township-shanty triangle was engulfed by violence in the early 1990s, this fact registered on popular consciousness with the impact of an explosion. Unable to isolate Inkatha from its social base, the ANC explored a tactical alternative to a fast-expanding conflict. To defuse an intertribal collision, it settled for an intertribal alliance from above. The promise of that alliance was a federated civic power. Its price was unreformed customary power in the reserves. The compromised federal solution of South Africa closely resembled the one arrived at in Nigeria after the civil war.

A METHODOLOGICAL POINT

There is also a methodological significance to the argument advanced in this book. It is that issues of democracy and governance cannot be directly deduced from the analysis of a mode of production; nor can they be read off as prescriptions from a general theory of democracy. In grappling with the question of democracy and governance, I have both shifted perspective from the mode of livelihood to the mode of rule and argued that there is a historical specificity to the mode of rule on the African continent. This shift underlines a critique—more in the nature of a sublating than a simple negation—of two kinds of contemporary discourses, that of political economy and that of civil society.

The critique of the standpoint of political economy is clearest in my analysis of the South African experience. In South African studies, the finest fruit of the political economy perspective was the cheap labor power thesis: it argued that apartheid was functional to capitalism, critical to ensuring a regular supply of cheap labor power. I have shifted attention from the cheapness of labor power to its semicoercive and controlled nature, in the context of a broader shift, from a focus on the labor question to one on the native question. My locus of analysis has been less the mode of accumulation than the mode of domination.

More than a response to the question of securing cheap labor power in a semi-industrial setting, I have argued that apartheid needs to be understood as the outcome of an unending quest for order in a setting both semi-industrial and colonial. Without denying the importance of the semi-industrial context, I have illuminated the significance of the colonial context in understanding apartheid as a form of the state. Rather than debunk or discard the perspective of political economy, my purpose has been to build on its insights while questioning its holistic claims.

Whereas in South Africa political economists generated a rich debate on the role of the state in reproducing a regime of semicoercive labor, the same cannot be said of the political analysis offered by their counterparts to the north of the Limpopo. Their claim was that the problem of Africa is one of "backwardness," of precapitalist relations of production, of insufficient proletarianization; in sum a lack of "development."[2] The key to democracy, then, is development. Ironically, this crude reductionism still finds defenders on both the Left and the Right, from militants advocating a single-party solution to champions of an IMF-style structural adjustment.

No less convincing, however, is the multiparty discourse of the so-called prodemocracy movements in equatorial Africa. Unlike their single-party counterparts, theirs is an explicitly political discourse. But it has turned a concrete historical experience—of civil society in the West—into the basis of a general and prescriptive theory. It has thereby turned democracy into a turnkey institutional import. Arguing that the problem of Africa is the absence or weakness of civil society institutions, it speaks the language of exclusion and marginalization, unable to unravel the form of power through which large numbers of Africans—in many cases the majority—are ruled.

Both perspectives presume rural areas to be residual, signifying a lack and an absence. That absence may be defined as economic or as political; the rural may be seen as lacking in urban modes of livelihood or in institutions of civil society. Whether it is activists in the trade unions and civics of South Africa or their more liberal counterparts in prodemocracy movements to the north, both have failed to arrive at a political program that addresses the mode of power containing rural populations on the continent. In contrast, my emphasis has been more on the mode of incorporation than that of marginalization. It is an emphasis less on the regime of rights from which the colonized were excluded on grounds of race than on the regime of custom into which they were incorporated and through which they were ruled.

In an analysis concerned not just with the colonial legacy, but also with postcolonial attempts to reform it, the shift has not simply been from the labor question to the native question; it has also involved placing the native question in the context of a broader problematic, the subject question. In practice, this latter shift took place with independence, with the birth of a decolonized and deracialized state. With it, the duality native-nonnative gave way to another, subject-citizen. Inasmuch as reform in postcolonial Africa crystallized along two distinct paths, known as the conservative and the radical, one can speak of two subject prototypes. In the conservative states, which reproduced Native Authorities as the locus of a decentralized despotism, the prototype subject was stamped with an ethnic identity. In the radical states, which detribalized Native Authorities but where reform degenerated into a centralized despotism—most dramatically illustrated when the central state branded poor and unemployed urban residents as vagrants and forcibly repatriated them to their "home areas" in the countryside—the prototype subject was simply a poor inhabitant in the rural areas, a peasant.

My point, then, is not only that the mode of rule is not deducible from the mode of livelihood. It is also that the specificity of the political in the African experience lies not as much in the structural defects of a historically organized civil society as in the crystallization of a different form of power. This is why the point of democratization cannot be just a simple reform of civil society. It also has to be a dismantling of the mode of rule organized on the basis of fused power, administrative justice, and extra-economic coercion, all legitimized as the customary.

The antidote to a mode of rule that accentuates difference, ethnic in this case, cannot be to deny difference but to historicize it. Faced with a power that fragments an oppressed majority into so many self-enclosed culturally defined minorities, the burden of resistance must be both to recognize and to transcend the points of difference. If there is a lesson in the experience of oppositional movements—whether rural, such as the Ruwenzururu, the NRA, and the Sungusungu or the urban, such as the independent trade unions in post-1973 South Africa—it is that to create a democratic solidarity requires joining the emphasis on autonomy with the one on alliance, that on participatory self-rule with one on representational politics. In the specific circumstances of contemporary Africa, to create a democratic majority is to transcend two divisions that power spontaneously imposes on resistance: the rural-urban and the interethnic.

THE WAY AHEAD

The point of this book is that any effective opposition in practice, and any theoretical analysis that would lead to one, must link the rural and the urban in ways that have not yet been done. This is why Uganda and South Africa are the paradigm cases today. Uganda, though the home of the most serious attempt yet to democratize Native Authority, has been unable to address the democratic demands of civil society movements. In South Africa, though the home of the strongest and the most imaginative civil society–based resistance on the continent, reform has floundered on the walls of customary power. As paradigm cases, both allow one to see in one place phenomena that appear as fragmentary elsewhere.

What social forces can link the urban and the rural? The only successful attempt yet to bridge the two has been the militant nationalist movement that followed the Second World War. The political impetus of this movement came from the disenfranchised native strata of the towns. Whether the "verandah boys" of Nkrumah's CPP, migrant workers in many powerful trade union movements, or the "boatmen" of Cabral's African Party for the Independence of Guinea and the Cape Verde Islands (PAIGC) a decade later, they shared a common social position: they lay beyond the reach of customary law and yet had few entitlements to civil rights. Though in civil society, they were not of civil society.

Faced with a growing and militant nationalism, colonialism embarked on its most ambitious reform program yet. Part of that postwar reform was a stabilization of migrant labor. Colonial governments raised "bachelor" wages to "family" ones, technically upgraded and differentiated the work process, and extended official recognition to trade unions. A similar process unfolded in South Africa in the wake of the post-Soweto Wiehahn and Riekert Commissions, but the reforms were of limited significance. In South Africa the end of influx control brought a wave of migrants from rural areas to urban ones—mainly into hostels and shantytowns. To the north of the Limpopo, the "informal sector" burgeoned as a combination of economic crises and structural adjustment led to a shrinking domestic industry alongside deregulated markets. Today it is migrant labor—and those in the informal sector—that forms a class that is in civil society but is not of it.

The social role of migrants varies, depending on the political choices available to them. As the South African case demonstrates, that role can be progressive or nonprogressive. The point about the prodemocracy movement of today is precisely that it lacks a program for linking the urban and the rural on the basis of democratizing rural power, as the ANC in South Africa. In the absence of such a democratization, the customary will remain a rallying cry lining up urban-based migrants behind customary authorities in their ethnic homes and behind city-based champions of the customary—so as to defend customary rights, however residual these may be. In the linkage between the urban and the rural, the rural is the key. So long as the rural is not reformed, the perversion of civil society is inevitable. This is why the limits of the current South African reform are so serious.

The most serious attempt yet to reform the rural was, as I have already noted, that of Museveni in Uganda, following earlier and more partial attempts, Qaddafi in Libya, Sankara in Bourkina Faso, and the early Rawlings in Ghana. They all highlight one lesson: decentralized democracy confined to the local state is both partial and unstable. It harbors contradictory possibilities: the point of reform of rural power can just as easily be to link up with representative demands from urban civil society as it can be to check these. If the objective is an overall democratization, it requires a balance between decentralization and centralization, participation and representation, autonomy and alliance. But if it is to checkmate civil society, a one-sided glorification of decentralization, autonomy and participation will suffice because, in the final analysis, it is bound to exacerbate the breach between the urban and the rural. Yet it is precisely such a tendency that is a growing orientation in left-oriented intellectual thought, on the one hand opposing and upholding participation against representation, on the other championing autonomy against alliance. If the experience of oppositional movements and the record of regime strategies reviewed in this book are anything to go by, this tendency needs to be seen as a negative development.

Colonial legal theory justified the subordination of subjects to a fused power as the continuation of a customary law and gave it the name of indirect rule; in contrast, it termed as direct rule the racially defined exclusion of colonized persons from citizen rights guaranteed by civil law in a differentiated form of power that framed civil society. Postindependence governments seeking to overcome this duality took one of two alternatives: either preserving the customary in the name of defending tradition against alien encroachment or abolishing it in the name of overcoming backwardness and embracing a triumphant modernism. But if indirect rule characteristic of Native Authorities was anchored in participatory forms, however distorted, and direct rule over civil society in representational forms, however exclusive, then was not the point to transcend both through a creative synthesis?

The reform of indirect rule systems in postindependence Africa built on the practice of participation without representation. In the second phase of radical African governments—from Qaddafi and Sankara to early Rawlings and Museveni—this reform became the basis of dismantling authority in the local state without democratizing power in the central state. Each of the peasant movements considered in chapter 6 tended toward participatory reforms, but none was able to stabilize these on the basis of participation alone. Participatory forms ("empowerment") that stress the autonomy of a bounded group—only to undermine any possibility of an alliance-building majority-based representation—can justify and uphold the most undemocratic forms of central power. One only needs to look at the experience of self-initiated squatter settlements in South Africa: many began with an emphasis on participation and ended up with a warlord.

At the other extreme, there is the phenomenon of representation without participation. This is characteristic of a multiparty electoral reform whose target is the central state while leaving intact the decentralized despotism crystallized in the local state. Without an accent on participatory forms (and, as we will soon see, autonomy), the tendency is for representation to turn into its opposite: instead of a representation of popular strata in the state, the representative turns into an agent of the state power to popular sectors.

If democratic politics calls for joining participation at the local level with direct representation at higher levels, a similar perspective also needs to be forged when it comes to the relationship between autonomy and alliance. If the rationale for autonomy is the legitimacy and particularity of the local, then the fragmentation produced by a one-sidedly localized perspective underlines the need for alliance as a way to transcend it. And if participation and representation, autonomy and alliance, cannot be viewed in a one-sided opposition, neither can the customary and the civil. In spite of the practice of Native Authorities to justify their writ as custom, the customary was never a single, noncontradictory whole. Not only the Native Authority but also many peasant movements spoke the language of the customary. For every notion of the customary defined and enforced by the state, one could find a counternotion with a subaltern currency. A democratic appreciation of the customary must reject embracing an uncompromising modernism or traditionalism. As a start, it needs to disentangle authoritarian from emancipatory possibilities in both.

The point is neither to set aside dualisms that mark social theory nor to exchange one set for another more adequate to describing the contemporary situation. Rather it is to problematize both sides of every dualism by historicizing it, thereby underlining the institutional and political condition for its reproduction and for its transformation. Although theory cannot by itself transform reality, without a theoretical illumination reality must appear a closed riddle.

The fall of Soviet-type regimes in the late eighties was followed by an uncompromising critique of single-party regimes. In the African context, these have been followed by equally single-minded and prescriptive reforms embracing multiparty elections on the one hand and decentralization on the other. With every fresh round of lessons, however, we seem to lose historical depth. Once again, the impact of multiparty elections—in the absence of a reform of rural power—turns out to be not just shallow and short-lived, but also explosive. Too many presume that despotic power on this continent was always or even mainly a centralized affair, in the process forgetting the decentralized despotism that was the colonial state, and that is one variant of the African state today. In the absence of alliance-building mechanisms, all decentralized systems of rule fragment the ruled and stabilize their rulers. No doubt this is the great attraction of the current wave of decentralization—and the historical amnesia accompanying it—to Africa's current rulers.

But for the opposition that must take stock of social fragmentation as its historical starting point, it makes more sense to appropriate critically the experience of militant nationalism of yesteryears than just to debunk it. The strength of that experience lay in its ability to link the urban and the rural—politically. Its Achilles' heel was the failure to ground the link in an ongoing process of democratic reform, one with a focus on reforming the bifurcated state inherited from colonialism. Once in power, militant nationalists pursued reform in both civil society and Native Authority, deracializing the former and detribalizing the latter. But they reformed each sphere separately, and they did so from above. As reform from above substituted administration for politics, a bifurcated reform strategy re-created the bifurcated state. That failure corrupted a hitherto political link between the rural and the urban into a coercive one, cutting the ground from under their own feet. So the attempt to reform decentralized despotism degenerated into a centralized despotism, the other and more unstable variant of the African state.

The second round of reformers, those of the 1980s and 1990s, learned one lesson from their predecessors but also reproduced a limitation. They began the reform process from below, by dismantling Native Authorities and reorganizing village communities on the basis of self-administration. Detribalization was thereby joined to democratization, but in the local sphere only. Their dilemma is how to reform the center and thereby how to join the rural and the urban through a single—overarching but differentiated—reform process.

The record of state reform has been mixed. The tendency of African governments has been to play reform in one sphere against repression in the other. The result, inevitably, is a truncated reform. Of the two tensions aggravated by the form of the African state, the interethnic and the rural-urban, the latter is key. Hitherto, there have been two ways of linking the rural and the urban: the administrative and the political. The administrative link has turned out to be coercive. The political link has taken the form of a noncoercive clientelism. To bridge the rural and the urban through a politics both noncoercive and democratic, it is necessary to transcend the dualism of power around which the bifurcated state is organized. To do so requires that the nature of power in both spheres, the rural and the urban, be transformed, simultaneously. Only then will the distinction rural-urban—and interethnic—be more fluid than rigid, more an outcome of social processes than a state-enforced artifact.

Notes

Chapter I
Introduction: Thinking through Africa's Impasse

1. Christopher Fyfe, "Race, Empire and the Historians," *Race and Class* 33, no. 4 (1992): 22. A number of examples in this paragraph are taken from this particular article.

2. Allister Sparks, *The Mind of South Africa* (New York: Ballantine Books, 1991), p. 184.

3. Gen. J. C. Smuts, *Africa and Some World Problems, Including the Rhodes Memorial Lectures Delivered in Michaelmas Term, 1929* (Oxford: Clarendon Press, 1929), pp. 76–78, 92. I am thankful to Bernard Magubane for first suggesting to me that I would benefit from a reading of this text.

4. Ibid., pp. 99–100.

5. See Lord Hailey, *An African Survey* (London: Oxford University Press, 1936), p. 150.

6. Samir Amin, *Accumulation on a World Scale* (New York: Monthly Review Press, 1974).

7. Jean-Francois Bayart, *The State in Africa: The Politics of the Belly* (London: Longman, 1993), pp. 31, 21.

8. John Thornton, *Africa and the Africans in the Making of the Atlantic World, 1400–1680* (New York: Cambridge University Press, 1992), pp. 125, 182; for a critical review, see Jacques Depelchin, "Lumumba, Braudel and African History: Dismantling or Reproducing the Colonial Paradigm?" (African-American Studies and History, University of Syracuse, 1994, mimeographed).

9. Talal Asad, *Genealogies of Religion, Discipline and Reasons of Power in Christianity and Islam* (Baltimore: Johns Hopkins University Press, 1993), p. 4.

10. Bayart, *The State in Africa*, p. 268.

11. On "patrimonialism," see Richard Sandbrook, *The Politics of Africa's Economic Stagnation* (Cambridge: Cambridge University Press, 1985); and Thomas Callaghy, *The State-Society Struggle: Zaire in Contemporary Perspective* (New York: Columbia University Press, 1984); see also Patrick M. Boyle, "A View from Zaire," *World Politics* 40, no. 2 (January 1988): 268–87. On "prebendalism," see Richard M. Joseph, "State and Prebendal Politics in Nigeria," in *State and Class in Africa*, ed. Nelson Kasfir (London: Frank Cass, 1984); and Richard Joseph in *Perestroika without Glasnost*, report of the Inaugural Seminar of the Governance in Africa Program of the Carter Centre (Emory University, 1989, February 17–18), p. 12.

12. For a review, see Mahmood Mamdani, "A Glimpse at African Studies, Made in USA," *Codesria Bulletin* (Dakar, Senegal), no. 2 (1990): 7–11.

13. See Thomas Callaghy, "The State as Lame Leviathan: The Patrimonial-Administrative State in Africa," in *African State in Transition*, ed. Zaki Ergas (London: Macmillan, 1987).

14. See Goran Hyden, *Beyond Ujamaa in Tanzania* (London: Heinemann, 1980), and *No Shortcuts to Progress* (London: Heinemann, 1983).

15. Donald Rothchild, "Hegemony and State Softness: Some Variations in Elite Responses," in *African State in Transition*, ed. Ergas.

16. Crawford Young and Thomas Turner, *The Rise and Decline of the Zairean State* (Madison: University of Wisconsin Press, 1985).

17. Naomi Chazan, "State and Society in Africa: Images and Challenges," in *The Precarious Balance: The State and Society in Africa*, ed. Donald Rothchild and Naomi Chazan (Boulder, Colo.: Westview, 1988).

18. In a section entitled "New Historical Parallels" in his introductory chapter, Hyden underlines the significance of the transition to industrialism in Europe for "more important leads" to understanding the African experience: "It is likely that observations on the early phases of class formation in industrial society may contain more important leads to an understanding of African development today than contemporary parallels from other parts of the world, be it India, China, the Soviet Union or the United States" (Hyden, *No Shortcuts to Progress*, p. 22).

19. Callaghy, "The State as Lame Leviathan."

20. Hyden, *Beyond Ujamaa in Tanzania* and *No Shortcuts to Progress*. For a critique, see Mahmood Mamdani, "A Great Leap Backward," *Social Science Research Review* (Addis Ababa) 1, no. 1 (1985).

21. Hyden, *Beyond Ujamaa in Tanzania*, p. 9.

22. Both claims are implicit in Andrew Arato and Jean Cohen, *Civil Society* (Cambridge, Mass.: MIT Press, 1993).

23. In a bibliographical survey of the subject, John Keene has stressed the marginal character of the view that civil society is a timeless and ahistorical condition: in the words of its most prominent advocate, Thomas Paine, a "natural condition of freedom" that is a legitimate arena of defense against state despotism. John Keene, *State and Civil Society* (London: Verso, 1988).

24. For a discussion of mainstream views in contemporary North American political science that have failed to exorcise "the ghost of Hegel," see Robert Meister, *Political Identity: Thinking through Marx* (London: Basil Blackwell, 1990), pp. 222–36.

25. Jürgen Habermas, *The Structural Transformation of the Public Sphere: An Inquiry into a Category of Bourgeois Society* (Cambridge, Mass.: MIT Press, 1991).

26. Jürgen Habermas, "Further Reflections on the Public Sphere," in *Habermas and the Public Sphere*, ed. Craig Calhoun (Cambridge, Mass.: MIT Press, 1992), pp. 430, 453–54, 423, 424.

27. Geoff Eley, "Nations, Publics and Political Cultures: Placing Habermas in the Nineteenth Century," in *Habermas and the Public Sphere*, ed. Calhoun, pp. 325–26.

28. F. D. Lugard, *The Dual Mandate in British Tropical Africa* (London: Frank Cass, 1965), pp. 149–50.

29. For a detailed discussion, see Mahmood Mamdani, "State and Civil Society in Contemporary Africa: Reconceptualising the Birth of State Nationalism

and the Defeat of Popular Movements," *Africa Development* (Dakar, Senegal) 15, no. 3/4, 1990, 47–70.

30. From this perspective, there could be no better starting point than Samir Amin's classic statement of 1970. See Samir Amin, "Underdevelopment and Dependency in Black Africa: Origins and Contemporary Forms," *Journal of Modern African Studies* 10 (1970).

Chapter II
Decentralized Despotism

1. "The King's Speech," 1904, quoted in Cyril Ehrlich, "The Marketing of Cotton in Uganda" (Ph.D. diss., London University, 1958), p. 32.

2. Catherine Coquery-Vidrovitch, "The Political Economy of the African Peasantry and Modes of Production," in *The Political Economy of Contemporary Africa*, by Peter C. W. Gutkind and Immanuel Wallerstein, eds. (London: Sage, 1976), p. 91, quoted in Kwame Anthony Appiah, *In My Father's House* (London: Methuen, 1992), pp. 203–4.

3. Christopher L. Miller, *Blank Darkness: Africanist Discourse in French* (Chicago: University of Chicago Press, 1985), p. 5.

4. Basil Davidson, *The Black Man's Burden: Africa and the Curse of the Nation-State* (New York: Times Books, Random House, 1992), pp. 60–61, 86.

5. Ifi Amadiume, "Gender, Political Systems and Social Movements: A West African Experience," in *African Studies in Social Movements*, ed. Mahmood Mamdani and E. Wamba-dia-Wamba (Dakar, Senegal: CODESRIA, 1995).

6. George Padmore, *Africa: Britain's Third Empire* (London: Dennis Dobson, 1948), p. 113.

7. See Radhakrishnan Mukherjee, *The Problem of Uganda: A Study in Acculturation* (Berlin: Akademie-Verlag, 1949), ch. 2.

8. On Karamoja, see Charles Ocan, "Pastoralism and Crisis in North-Eastern Uganda: Factors That Have Determined Social Change in Karamoja," working paper no. 20, Centre for Basic Research, Kampala. 1992.

9. The democratic character of tribal organization was stressed by Mukherjee in his 1949 study of Uganda. In subsequent research concerning the "lineage mode of production," Rey has argued that elders constituted an exploiting class. Mafeje, following Meillessoux, has contended that elders were really custodians of patrimony/matrimony; they could not be considered a class, since they were under a kinship obligation to surrender power to juniors when the time came. Although Mafeje's observation has merit, it still remains partial: not all juniors graduated to being elders in time. Also, was not the social category "elders" predominantly if not exclusively male? See P. P. Rey, *Les Alliances de classes* (Paris: Maspero, 1973). Claude Meillessoux, *Maidens, Meal and Money: Capitalism and the Domestic Economy* (Cambridge: Cambridge University Press, 1975). Archie Mafeje, *The Theory and Ethnography of African Social Formations: The Case of the Intralacustrine Kingdoms* (Dakar, Senegal: CODESRIA, 1991).

10. Mukherjee, *The Problem of Uganda*. Mafeje, *Theory and Ethnography*.

11. For a historical sketch, see Mahmood Mamdani, *Politics and Class Formation in Uganda* (New York: Monthly Review, 1976), ch. 2.

12. James S. Wunch, "Centralization and Development in Post-Independence Africa," in *The Failure of the Centralized State,* ed. James S. Wunch and Dele Oluwu (Boulder, Colo.: Westview Press, 1990), p. 63.

13. David Welsh, *The Roots of Segregation: Native Colonial Policy in Natal, 1845–1910* (Cape Town: Oxford University Press, 1973), pp. 146–47.

14. Transkei Land Service Organisation, "Rural Local Government and the Transkei Region" (Umtata, 1992), pp. 5, 8, 17. ("This document has been prepared by Tralso researcher Andre Terblanche, who draws extensively from the communities that we work with. A special acknowledgment needs to be made of Monica Hunter's *Reaction to Conquest,* the classical anthropological study of the Mpondo, which provided much of the historical material.")

15. Richard Levin, *When the Sleeping Grass Awakens: Land, Power and Hegemony in Swaziland* (London: Zed Press, forthcoming), pp. 23–25.

16. In response to a tendency to idealize the libandla, an SPP memo argued: "The *libandla's* . . . form is unregulated and not subject to strict control in its membership day by day. There can be no formation of concerted opinion in these councils because at meetings the people making up the council may be different from those who attended the meeting before" (cited in Levin, *When the Sleeping Grass Awakens,* p. 25).

17. Mogopode H. Lekorwe, "The Kgotla and the Freedom Square: One-way or Two-way Communication?" in *Democracy in Botswana,* ed. John D. Holm and Patrick P. Molutsi (Gabarone: Macmillan, 1989), pp. 117–18.

18. L. D. Ngcongco, "Tswana Political Tradition: How Democratic?" in *Democracy in Botswana,* ed. Holm and Molutsi, pp. 46, 49.

19. It was common for the colonial state to underline the subordinate nature of mediating interests (king, chiefs, headmen) in colonies through pronouncements that proclaimed the priority of interests of the natives, but in a context where the custodian of that interest was presumed to be none other than the colonial state! Take, for example, the 1920 crisis in Kenya, where to underline the fact that settlers would not have the political control their counterparts in Rhodesia had succeeded in attaining, the colonial state proclaimed "the paramountcy of native interests"! See Mahmood Mamdani, review of *Colonialism and Underdevelopment in East Africa,* by E. A. Brett, *The African Review* (Dar es Salaam) 3, no. 4 (1973).

20. P. P. Molutsi, "The Ruling Class and Democracy in Botswana," pp. 106, 110, and P. T. Mgadla and A. C. Campbell, "Dikgotla, Dikgosi and the Protectorate Administration," pp. 53, 55; both in *Democracy in Botswana,* ed. Holm and Molutsi.

21. R. S. Rattray, *Ashanti Law and Constitution* (Oxford: Clarendon Press, 1929), pp. 401–7.

22. Hollis R. Lynch, introduction to John Mensah Sarbah, *Fanti Customary Law,* 3d ed. (London: Frank Cass, 1968).

23. Sarbah, *Fanti Customary Law,* p. 24.

24. Ibid., p. 21.

25. Lord Hailey, *An African Survey*, rev. ed. (1956), p. v.

26. Ibid., p. 589.

27. D. A. Low, *Lion Rampant: Essays in the Study of British Imperialism* (London: Frank Cass, 1973), pp. 4, 68.

28. Margery Perham, *Colonial Sequence, 1930 to 1949* (London: Methuen, 1967), pp. 65, 145.

29. George Padmore, *How Britain Rules Africa* (London: Wishart Books, 1936), p. 317.

30. Jean Suret-Canale, *French Colonialism in Tropical Africa, 1900–1945* (London: C. Hurst, 1971), pp. 80–81.

31. Nzongola-Ntalaja, "The Second Independence Movement in Congo-Kinshasa," in *Popular Struggles for Democracy in Africa*, ed. Peter Anyang' Nyong'o (London: Zed Books, 1987), pp. 116–17.

32. Sir F. Lugard, "Report on the Amalgamation of Northern and Southern Nigeria," 9 April 1919; see A.H.M. Kirk-Greene, *Lugard and the Amalgamation of Nigeria: A Documentary Record* (London: Frank Cass, 1969); see p. 70.

33. Padmore, *How Britain Rules Africa*, p. 317.

34. Lugard, "Amalgamation of Northern and Southern Nigeria"; see Kirk-Greene, *Lugard and the Amalgamation of Nigeria*, p. 72.

35. File on Apollo Kaggwa in Colonial Office, CO 536/141; quoted in *Politics and Class Formation*, by Mamdani, pp. 126ff.

36. *Mutendwa v. The Minister for Native Affairs*, 1927; see Bennie Goldin and Michael Gelfand, *African Law and Custom in Rhodesia* (Cape Town: Juta, 1975), p. 30.

37. Jean Suret-Canale, "The End of Chieftaincy in Guinea," in *Essays on African History: From the Slave Trade to Neocolonialism* (Trenton, N.J.: Africa World Press, 1988), p. 155.

38. Bruce Berman, "Structure and Process in the Bureaucratic States of Colonial Africa," *Development and Change*, vol. 15 (London: Sage, 1984), pp. 161–202, 178.

39. Sally Falk Moore, *Social Facts and Fabrication: "Customary" Law in Kilimanjaro, 1880–1980* (London: Cambridge University Press, 1986), pp. 97, 100.

40. Peter Geschiere, "Chiefs and Colonial Rule in Cameroon: Inventing Chieftaincy, British and French Style," *Africa* 63, no. 2 (1993): 154–55.

41. Quoted in Allen Isaacman, "Chiefs, Rural Differentiation and Peasant Protest: The Mozambican Forced Labour Regime, 1938–1961," *African Economic History*, no. 14 (1985): 27.

42. Suret-Canale, *French Colonialism*, p. 327. On the basis of perusing through "the thick file of complaints against the chiefs of the subdivisions of Dalaba," Suret-Canale has argued that there was nothing unusual or exceptional in this. The chief of Kankalabe, for example, was criticized "for collecting—in addition to the tithe on the harvest—a tax for the meal on the chief's birthday (10 frs per married man) and another tax for his entertainment (in money and goods)." See Suret-Canale, *Essays on African History*, p. 167.

43. Moore, *Social Facts and Fabrication*, p. 186.

44. See Mahmood Mamdani, "Forms of Labour and Accumulation of Capital: Analysis of a Village in Lango, Northern Uganda," *Mawazo* (Kampala) 5, no. 4 (December 1984): 44–65.

45. *Report of the Commission of Inquiry into Local Government System* (Entebbe, Uganda: Government Printer, 1987).

46. The rich empirical detail gathered by this study unfortunately remains at odds with its conceptual mold, which identifies taxation to exclude all extra-economic compulsions. So the researcher can argue without any hint of a contradiction: "Since Independence, however, the taxation systems set up by the colonial governments have been all but dismantled and particularly at the local level." See Jane Guyer, "Representation without Taxation: An Essay on Democracy in Rural Nigeria" (symposium entitled "Identity, Rationality and the Post-Colonial Subject: African Perspectives on Contemporary Social Theory," Columbia University, 28 February 1991), pp. xxxiv–xxxv, iii–iv.

47. All examples cited are in *An Appetite for Power: Buthelezi's Inkatha and the Politics of "Loyal" Resistance*, by Gerhard Maré and Georgina Hamilton (Johannesburg: Raven Press, 1987), p. 90.

48. Alastair McIntosh, "Rethinking Chieftaincy and the Future of Rural Local Government: A Preliminary Investigation," *Transformation* (Durban), no. 13 (1990): 29–30.

49. Michael Schatzberg, *Politics and Class in Zaire* (New York and London: Africa Publishing, 1980), p. 60.

50. Ibid., pp. 63 (table 14), 72.

51. Ibid., p. 79.

52. Ibid., p. 73.

Chapter III
Indirect Rule: The Politics of Decentralized Despotism

1. Cited in Welsh, *Roots of Segregation*, p. 12.

2. Ifor L. Evans, *Native Policy in Southern Africa: An Outline* (Cambridge: Cambridge University Press, 1934), pp. 9–10.

3. H. J. Simons, *African Women: Their Legal Status in South Africa* (London: C. Hurst, 1968), pp. 29–30.

4. Where there was no settler population, the transformation of land into a commodity did not have to go hand in hand with its appropriation, nor did it lead to the destruction and dispersal of the community. Note, for example, the case of the Lebu in Dakar. Mamadou Diouf, Personal Communication, 15 August 1994.

5. Ivan Thomas Evans, "The Political Economy of a State Apparatus: The Department of Native Affairs in the Transition from Segregation to Apartheid in South Africa" (Ph.D. diss., University of Wisconsin, Madison, 1986), p. 25.

6. Simons, *African Women*, pp. 29–30; see also Lord Hailey, *An African Survey*, pp. 419–42.

7. Simons, *African Women*, pp. 31–32.

8. Ibid., pp. 28, 31–32.

9. Doug Hindson, *Pass Controls and the Urban African Proletariat in South*

Africa (Johannesburg: Raven Press, 1987), pp. x, 15–16, 24; on the Masters and Servants Act, see D. C. Hindson, "The Pass System and the Formation of an Urban African Proletariat in South Africa" (Ph.D. diss., University of Sussex, 1983), p. 297.

10. Evans, "The Political Economy of a State Apparatus," p. 25.

11. See S.2 of law no. 28 of 1865.

12. Welsh, *The Roots of Segregation*, p. 242. Welsh writes:

> In 1890 a group of exempted Africans petitioned the government asking for medals that would distinguish them from unexempted Africans. The government agreed to the request and said that the medals would be made and sold to those who wished to purchase them. But in September 1891 Inkayiso reported that only a few exempted Africans had bothered to apply for them. According to Inkayiso the medals were too big and the cost too high. But more important, exempted people were loath to buy them because of the legislation which had whittled away their privileges. (P. 240)

13. T. W. Bennett, *A Sourcebook on African Customary Law for Southern Africa* (Cape Town: Juta, 1991), p. 62.

14. Saul Dubow, *Racial Segregation and the Origins of Apartheid in South Africa, 1919–1936* (London: Macmillan, 1989), pp. 115–16.

15. The argument has been made in a strong form, one that denies any difference between British and French colonial rule, by Berman, in "Structure and Process."

16. The Nigerian figures are from I. M. Okonjo, *British Administration in Nigeria, 1900–1950: A Nigerian View* (New York: NOK Publishers, 1974), pp. 26–27.

17. Ibid., p. 29.

18. R. C. Buell, *The Native Problem in Africa*, vol. 1 (New York, 1928), p. 361; quoted in Berman, "Structure and Process," pp. 197–98ff.

19. Robert Delavignette, *Freedom and Authority in French West Africa* (London: Oxford University Press, 1950), p. 18.

20. See Berman, "Structure and Process."

21. Robert Huessler, *The British in Northern Nigeria* (London: Oxford University Press, 1968), p. 7; both Van Vollenhoven and Robert Huessler are quoted in Berman, "Structure and Process," pp. 175, 182–83.

22. On "recaptives," see Davidson, *The Black Man's Burden*, pp. 23–33.

23. A. Adu Boahen, *African Perspectives on Colonialism* (Baltimore: Johns Hopkins University Press, 1987), pp. 17–18.

24. Malyn Newitt, *Portugal in Africa: The Last Hundred Years* (London: C. Hurst, 1981), p. 143.

25. Fyfe, "Race, Empire," pp. 15–16.

26. A. E. Afigbo, "The Establishment of Colonial Rule, 1900–1918," in *History of West Africa*, vol. 2, ed. J.F.A. Ajayi and M. Crowder (London: Longman, 1974), pp. 424–83; quoted in M. E. Betts (revised by M. Asiwaju), "Methods and Institutions of European Administration," in *General History of Africa*, vol. 7, *Africa under Colonial Domination, 1880–1935*, ed. A. Adu Boahen, p. 316.

27. Davidson, *The Black Man's Burden*, p. 41.

28. Fyfe, "Race, Empire," p. 16.

29. Boahen, *African Perspectives on Colonialism*, pp. 19–23.

30. Quoted in Low, *Lion Rampant*, p. 88.

31. Ibid., p. 22.

32. Berman, "Structure and Process," p. 175.

33. Quoted in John Iliffe, *A History of Modern Tanganyika* (Cambridge: Cambridge University Press, 1979), p. 325.

34. Okonjo, *British Administration in Nigeria*, p. 25.

35. Lugard, "Report on the Amalgamation," pp. 70–71.

36. Padmore, *Africa*, p. 117.

37. Iliffe, *A Modern History of Tanganyika*, pp. 323–24.

38. Ibid., p. 25.

39. Ibid., p. 330–32.

40. Quoted in Martin Chanock, *Law, Custom and Social Order: The Colonial Experience in Malawi and Zambia*, (London: Cambridge University Press, 1985), p. 112.

41. Terence Ranger, *The Invention of Tribalism in Colonial Zimbabwe* (Harare: Mambo Press, 1985), pp. 5, 8–9.

42. Suret-Canale, *French Colonialism*, p. 312.

43. Delavignette, *Freedom and Authority*, p. 72.

44. Robert Delavignette, "French Colonial Policy in Black Africa, 1945 to 1960," in *Colonialism in Africa: 1870–1960*, ed. L. H. Gann and Peter Duignan, vol. 2, *The History and Politics of Colonialism, 1914–1960* (Cambridge: Cambridge University Press, 1970), p. 267.

45. Delavignette, "French Colonial Policy," pp. 259–60.

46. Jean Suret-Canale, "The End of Chieftaincy in Guinea," in *Essays*, p. 150.

47. Lord Hailey, *An African Survey*, pp. 207–8.

48. Betts, "Methods and Institutions of European Administration," p. 319.

49. Suret-Canale, *French Colonialism*, p. 322.

50. Delavignette, *Freedom and Authority*, p. 31.

51. Lord Hailey, *An African Survey*, p. 339.

52. Donal B. Cruise O'Brien, *The Mourides of Senegal* (Oxford: Clarendon Press, 1971), pp. 33–35, 46, 65, 163–69, 173, 179, 186, 189.

53. This and the following paragraph are based on Christopher Harrison, *France and Islam in West Africa, 1860–1960* (Cambridge: Cambridge University Press, 1988), pp. 165, 180–85, 189–90, 196–98, 202–4.

54. This paragraph is based on O'Brien, *The Mourides of Senegal*, pp. 246, 218, 275–76, 266–67.

55. Bogumil Jewsiewicki, "African Peasants in the Totalitarian Colonial Society of the Belgian Congo," in *Peasants in Africa: Historical and Contemporary Perspectives*, ed. Martin A. Klein, (Beverly Hills: Sage, 1980), p. 48.

56. Lord Hailey, *An African Survey*, p. 228.

57. Newitt, *Portugal in Africa*, pp. 54, 100–102, 104–5.

58. Betts, "Methods and Institutions," p. 323.

59. Lord Hailey, *An African Survey*, p. 358.

60. Amos Sawyer, "Proprietary Authority and Local Administration in Liberia," pp. 157–58.

61. Emmet V. Mittlebeeler, *African Custom and Western Law: The Development of the Rhodesian Criminal Law for Africans* (New York: Africana Publishing, 1976), p. 17; the "Cape Principle" also operated in Lesotho. See Sebastian Poulter, *Legal Dualism in Lesotho* (Morija-Lesotho: Morija Sesuto Book Depot, 1979), p. 16.

62. Goldin and Gelfand, *African Law and Custom in Rhodesia*, pp. 30–31, 34.

63. Mittlebeeler, *African Custom*, p. 20.

64. Poulter, *Legal Dualism in Lesotho*, pp. 17–18.

65. Decree law no. 39.666 of 20 May 1954; see Poulter, *Legal Dualism in Lesotho*, pp. 229–30.

66. D. S. Kyona, "The Judicial Process in the Customary Courts" (typescript, University of Transkei, 1982), pp. 276, 283.

67. G. E. Devenish, "The Development of Administrative and Political Control of Rural Blacks," in *Race and the Law in South Africa*, ed. A. J. Rycroft, L. J. Boulle, M. K. Robertson, and P. R. Spillar (Cape Town: Juta, 1987), p. 30.

68. Simons, *African Women*, pp. 20–23. The same commision also recommended that "all Kaffirs should be ordered to go decently clothed," a measure that "would at once tend to increase the number of labourers, because many would be obliged to work to procure the means of buying clothing"; it "would also add to the general revenue of the colony through Customs duties." Thus all Africans were required by proclamation "to wear European clothes in Durban and Pietermaritzburg," and so they did. "All men resorting to the towns carried trousers ready to be put on as soon as they entered the borough"!

69. Ibid., p. 36.

70. Ibid., pp. 37–38, 44. It is worth looking at the wider consequences of this "reform," which greatly resembles the Mozambican reform of almost a century later:

> But lobolo is the method of validating tribal marriage. An attack on lobolo therefore involved an attack on marriage and the entire family structure. . . .
> The chiefs, to be sure, continued to settle lobolo disputes, but they could not enforce their judgments by a legal process. District Commissioners complained that the absence of redress in the courts turned women into prostitutes and had deplorable consequences on family life. . . . The children of a tribal marriage were illegitimate, and their mother was their natural guardian. (Simons, *African Women*, pp. 38–40)

71. Hindson, *Pass Controls*, pp. 31–32.

72. Quoted in Deborah Posel, *The Making of Apartheid, 1948–1961: Conflict and Compromise* (Oxford: Clarendon Press, 1991), p. 40.

73. Two features of the 1923 act are worthy of note. First, being exempt from registering contracts of service and carrying passes, women were still partly exempt from the repressive grid the act put in place for natives. At the other

extreme was a second feature of the act, crystallized in section 17: African men and women found to be "chronically unemployed or convicted of criminal offenses could be imprisoned, sent to labour colonies or back to the rural areas." See Hindson, p. 41; see also Evans, *Political Economy*, pp. 68–69. It is the two features of the 1923 act—separate administration for natives and forced repatriation to rural areas—that the National Party would build on to create apartheid. The difference was that the primacy of the race principle would be replaced by the primacy of the tribal principle, and thus native administration by Bantu administration.

74. Dubow, *Racial Segregation*, p. 108.

75. Quoted in ibid., pp. 110–11.

76. Gerhard Maré and Georgina Hamilton, *An Appetite for Power: Buthelezi's Inkatha and the Politics of "Loyal" Resistance*, (Johannesburg: Raven, 1987), pp. 27–28.

77. Simons, *African Women*, p. 54.

78. Luli Callinicos, *A Place in the City: The Rand on the Eve of Apartheid* (Johannesburg: Raven, 1993), p. 102. The estimates of the number of miners on strike range from "over 60,000" (Callinicos, O'Meara [n. 79]) to "between 70,000 and 100,000 men" (Hirson [n. 86]).

79. Dan O'Meara, "The 1946 African Mine Workers' Strike and the Political Economy of South Africa," in *South African Capitalism and Black Political Opposition*, ed. Martin J. Murray (Cambridge, Mass.: Schenkman, 1982), p. 361.

80. Tom Lodge, *Black Politics in South Africa since 1945* (Johannesburg: Raven, 1983), pp. 11–12.

81. Callinicos, *A Place in the City*, p. 37.

82. Quoted in Posel, *The Making of Apartheid*, p. 34.

83. Callinicos, *A Place in the City*, p. 37.

84. See A. Stadler, "Birds in Cornfield: Squatter Movements in Johannesburg, 1944–47," in *Labour, Townships and Protest*, by B. Bozzoli (Johannesburg: Raven Press, 1979); quoted in Evans, *The Political Economy of a State Apparatus*, pp. 124–25.

85. Debow, *Racial Segregation*, pp. 133–34.

86. Lodge, *Black Politics*, p. 26; see also Baruch Hirson, *Yours for the Union: Class and Community Struggles in South Africa* (Johannesburg: Witwatersrand University Press, 1989), pp. 187–88.

87. Evans, *The Political Economy of a State Apparatus*, pp. 59–61.

88. Deborah Posel has critiqued a commonly held notion of apartheid as a "grand plan" that was simply "transcribed from a ready-made blueprint with little further ado," its development "fundamentally linear and cumulative, each step building on the successes of the last." Instead, she argues for an understanding of apartheid "as having been forged through a series of struggles within and beyond the state, which forced the architects of state policy to adapt and revise many of their original strategies." See Posel, *The Making of Apartheid*, pp. 4–5.

89. Evans, *The Political Economy of a State Apparatus*, pp. 145–49.

90. All quotes in this paragraph are from *The Making of Apartheid*, by Posel, pp. 38, 61, 81–82.

91. Michael Neocosmos, "The Agrarian Question in Southern Africa and 'Accumulation from Below': Economics and Politics in the Struggle for Democracy" (Uppsala: Scandinavian Institute of African Studies, 1993), pp. 63–64; see also Matthew Chaskalson, "Rural Resistance in the 1940s and 1950s," *Africa Perspectives* (Johannesburg), n.s. 1, nos. 5 and 6 (December 1987): 99.

92. The displacement took place in 1971, when the department took over the regulation of the labor-control machinery from local authorities. Evans argues in his thesis on the subject:

My central claim is that in the 1940s the breakdown of the administrative relations between the Department of Native Affairs and the local authorities undermined the state's capacity to regulate African struggles in the urban areas and led to the erosion of the segregation state. These two sets of issues—relations internal to the state and African resistance—became entwined in a mutually reinforcing dynamic which the United Party government was unable to resolve. The restructuring of the Department of Native Affairs in the apartheid era was a response to these inter-related issues. (Evans, *The Political Economy of a State Apparatus*, pp. 13–14)

93. John Pickles and Daniel Weiner, "Rural and Regional Restructuring of Apartheid: Ideology, Development Policy and the Competition for Space," *Antipode* 23, no. 1 (1991): 8; see table on p. 9.

94. Estimates are by Platzky and Walker, quoted in "Emerging Urban Forms in Rural South Africa," by Dhiru V. Soni and Brij Maharaj, *Antipode* 23, no. 1 (1991): 61; see also Pickles and Weiner, "Rural and Regional Restructuring," p. 18.

95. The figures are from Lodge, *Black Politics in South Africa*, p. 321.

96. John Iliffe, "The Organisation of the Maji Maji Rebellion," *Journal of African History* 8, no. 3 (1967): 495–512; see also Iliffe, *A Modern History of Tanganyika*.

97. A. D. Yahya, "Local Government Reforms: The Military Initiative," in *Nigeria since Independence: The First Twenty-Five Years*, vol. 5, *Politics and Constitutions*, ed. Peter P. Ekeh, Patrick Dele Cole, and Gabriel O. Olusanya (Ibadan: Heinemann, 1989).

98. See Bayart, *The State in Africa*, pp. 125–26, 150–53, 171–73.

99. Dele Oluwu, "The Failure of Current Decentralisation Programmes in Africa," in *The Failure of the Centralised African State*, ed. Wunch and Oluwu, p. 88.

100. Sheldon Geller, "Self-Tutelage vs. Self-Governance: The Rhetoric and Reality of Decentralisation in Senegal," in *The Failure of the Centralised African State*, ed. Wunch and Oluwu, pp. 134–35, 140.

101. Michela von Freyhold, *Ujamaa Villages in Tanzania* (London: Heinemann, 1979), pp. 37–38.

102. H.U.E. Thoden Van Velzen, "Staff, Kulaks and Peasants: A Study of a Political Field," in *Socialism in Tanzania*, ed. Lionel Cliffe and John Saul, vol. 2 (Nairobi: East Africa Publishing House, 1973), p. 153.

103. Bertil Egaro, *Mozambique: A Dream Undone* (Uppsala: Scandinavian Institute of African Studies, 1987), p. 110.

Chapter IV
Customary Law: The Theory of Decentralized Despotism

1. A.E.W. Park, *The Sources of Nigerian Law* (Lagos: African Universities Press; London: Sweet and Maxwell, 1963), p. 65.

2. E. A. Keay and S. S. Richardson, *The Native and Customary Courts of Nigeria* (Lagos: African Universities Press; London: Sweet and Maxwell, 1966), p. 248.

3. Park, *The Sources of Nigerian Law*, pp. 102–3.

4. Poulter, *Legal Dualism in Lesotho*, p. 21.

5. Kyona, "The Judicial Process," p. 280.

6. Ibid., p. 279.

7. Judge Somerhough, J. in Chitambala v. R. (1957), 6 N.R.L.R. 29, at p. 39; quoted in Antony Allott, *New Essays in African Law* (London: Butterworth, 1970), p. 148; see also Kyona, "The Judicial Process," p. 37. "African customary law," argued Ollenu, a West African legal commentator, "was in a sense a foreign law which had to be proved in its own land, a law external to the main body of law enforced in the superior courts." See A. N. Allot, A. L. Epstein, and M. Gluckman, introduction to *Ideas and Procedures in African Customary Law*, ed. Max Gluckman (Oxford: Published for the International African Institute by the Oxford University Press, 1969), p. 14.

8. Allot, Epstein, and Gluckman, introduction to *Ideas and Procedures*, p. 14.

9. Goldin and Gelfand, *African Law*, p. 78.

10. Quoted in Iliffe, *A Modern History of Tanganyika*, p. 322.

11. Adriano Moreira, "Portuguese Territories in Africa: Customary Law in the Portuguese Overseas," in *The Future of Customary Law in Africa* (proceedings of the symposium organized by Afrika Instituut, Leiden, in collaboration with the Royal Tropical Institute, Amsterdam, Universitaire Pers Leiden, Leiden, 1956), p. 231.

12. Rattray, *Ashanti Law*, pp. vi–vii.

13. Chanock, *Law, Custom*, pp. 53–54.

14. A. N. Allott, *Essays in African Law* (London: Butterworth, 1960), p. 18.

15. Thierry Verhelst, *Safeguarding African Customary Law: Judicial and Legislative Processes for Its Adaptation and Integration*, Occasional Paper, no. 7 (Los Angeles: African Studies Center, UCLA, 1968), pp. iii–iv.

16. Okonjo, *British Administration in Nigeria*, pp. 46–50.

17. Suret-Canale, *French Colonialism*, pp. 334–35.

18. Delavignette, *Freedom and Authority*, pp. 91–92.

19. Catherine Besteman, "Land Tenure in the Middle Jjuba: Customary Tenure and the Effect of Land Registration" (paper 104, Land Tenure Center, University of Wisconsin, Madison, December 1990), p. 5.

20. "*Ordre public et bonnes moeurs* is a concept well-known to continental lawyers." See Verhelst, *Safeguarding African Customary Law*, pp. iii–iv.

21. Cited in Elise H. Golan, "Land Tenure Reform in Senegal: An Economic Study from the Peanut Basin" (paper 101, Land Tenure Center, University of Wisconsin, Madison, January 1990), p. 11.

22. Moreira, "Portuguese Territories in Africa," pp. 229–30.

23. See Park, *The Sources of Nigerian Law*, p. 72; Mittlebeeler, *African Custom*, pp. 9–10.

24. Section 14(3) of Cap. 16 of the Evidence Act. See Park, *The Sources of Nigerian Law*, p. 69.

25. Mittlebeeler, *African Custom*, p. 19.

26. Section 1 of no. 13 of 1942 stated: "'Native law and custom,' 'Native law or custom,' and 'Native custom' mean in relation to a particular tribe or in relation to any native community outside any tribal area the general law or custom of such tribe or community except so far as the same may be incompatible with the due exercise of His Majesty's power and jurisdiction or repugnant to morality, humanity or natural justice, or injurious to the welfare of natives." See Allott, *New Essays*, p. 146.

27. Mittlebeeler, *African Custom*, p. 21.

28. Ibid., p. 11.

29. Delavignette, *Freedom and Authority*, p. 88.

30. Park, *The Sources of Nigerian Law*, pp. 70, 72.

31. Moore, *Social Facts and Fabrications*, pp. 170, 104, 148–49, 108–9.

32. See Mamdani. "Forms of Labour."

33. Chanock, *Law, Custom and Social Order*, p. 36.

34. Terence Ranger, "The Invention of Tradition in Colonial Africa," in *The Invention of Tradition*, ed. Eric Hobsbawm and Terence Ranger (Cambridge: Cambridge University Press, 1983), p. 258.

35. Quoted in Welsh, *The Roots of Segregation*, pp. 43–44.

36. Chanock, *Law, Custom and Social Order*, pp. 149–50.

37. Moore, *Social Facts and Fabrication*, pp. 96, 97.

38. Ibid., pp. 185–86.

39. Chanock, *Law, Custom and Social Order*, pp. 113, 108, 213. The next two paragraphs are constructed from this source.

40. Lionel Cliffe, "Nationalism and the Reaction to Enforced Agricultural Change in Tanganyika during the Colonial Period," in *Socialism in Tanzania*, ed. John Saul and Lionel Cliffe, vol. 1, (1972), pp. 17–18.

41. Henry Bienen, *Tanzania: Party Transformation and Economic Development* (Princeton, N.J.: Princeton University Press, 1974), p. 38.

42. Keay and Richardson, *The Native and Customary Courts*, pp. 15–16.

43. Ibid., p. 21.

44. Sir F. Lugard, *Dual Mandate in British Tropical Africa*, 5th ed. (London, 1965), pp. 553, 539.

45. E. K. Lumley, *Forgotten Mandate: A British District Officer in Tanganyika* (London, 1976), p. 55; quoted in Ranger, "The Invention of Tradition," p. 216.

46. Suret-Canale, *French Colonialism*, pp. 164–65.

47. Beverley Grier, "Contradiction, Crisis and Class Conflict: The State and Capitalist Development in Ghana Prior to 1948," in *Studies in Power and Class in Africa*, ed. Irving Leonard Markovitz (New York: Oxford University Press, 1987), p. 38.

48. Maré and Hamilton, *An Appetite for Power*, pp. 89–90.

49. Albie Sachs and Gita Honwana Welch, *Liberating the Law, Creating Popular Justice in Mozambique* (London: Zed Books, 1990), p. 2.

50. Harrison, *France and Islam*, p. 194.

51. Suret-Canale, *French Colonialism*, pp. 331–32.

52. Quoted in Chanock, *Law, Custom and Social Order*, p. 108.

53. *Le Courier de golfe du Benin*, 1 March 1935; quoted in Suret-Canale, *French Colonialism*, pp. 346–47.

54. Dalaba Archives, Guinea, report of 9 January 1935; quoted in ibid., pp. 326–27.

55. 1–22 February 1919; in Kirk-Greene, *Lugard and the Amalgamation*, p. 271.

56. *Nigerian Eastern Mail*, 20 July 1940; quoted in Padmore, *Africa*, p. 117.

57. Bennett, *A Sourcebook*, p. 59.

58. Quoted in Chanock, *Law, Custom and Social Order*, pp. 50–51.

59. Chanock, *Law, Custom and Social Order*, pp. 53–54.

60. Verhelst, *Safeguarding African Customary Law*, p. 18.

61. J. O. Ibik, Malawi II, *The Law of Land, Succession, Movable Property, Agreements and Civil Wrongs*, Restatement of African Law Project, School of Oriental and African Studies, University of London (London: Sweet & Maxwell, 1971), p. vi.

62. E. Cotran and N. N. Rubin, eds., *Readings in African Law* (London: Frank Cass, 1970), pp. xx–xxii.

63. Verhelst, *Safeguarding African Customary Law*, pp. 2–4.

64. Ibid., pp. 4–6; see also pp. i, xv, 38.

65. Ibid., p. 19.

66. Ibik, *The Law of Land*, p. ix.

67. Michael Saltman, *The Kipsigis: A Study in Changing Customary Law* (Cambridge, Mass.: Schenkman, 1977), p. 106.

68. It should be noted that this too was a continuation of the practice of colonial reform in Tanganyika, where Cory "not only wrote down customary rules of law as he found them," but "also modified them where possible trying to achieve unification" (Verhelst, *Safeguarding African Customary Law*, p. 18).

69. Cotran and Rubin have argued that the Ghanaian experience differs markedly from that of other states, which, whether they seek unification or integration, go about it through simple abolition. In contrast, the Ghanaian case is seen as an example of a long-term process of assimilation: "It . . . envisages a dynamic process whereby, as extraneous forces such as a changing economy produce a greater degree of similarity in the laws of different units, individual rules of law which grow to be identical with one another are absorbed into the corpus of common customary law, by means of some clearly defined procedure. In many ways, this seems an admirable system." Yet they add that "although written into the law of one African country (Ghana) . . . unfortunately it has never been used extensively." See Cotran and Rubin, *Readings in African Law*, p. xxiii.

70. Verhelst, *Safeguarding African Customary Law*, p. 8.

71. The Tanzanians argued that they had overcome the racial dualism in co-

lonial practices, although not the dichotomy "customary" and "modern," by basing the choice on a "mode of life test" that put emphasis on the community of a party, not its race. See Poulter, *Legal Dualism in Lesotho*, p. 118.

72. The Civil Code of Ethiopia was drafted by Professor René David of the Sorbonne, who recognized that "its immediate and total enforcement is unlikely" and that it "represents" more "a goal to be sought rather than a crystallization of social conditions that exist." See Verhelst, *Safeguarding African Customary Law*, p. 26; A. Arthur Schiller, introduction to *Africa and Law: Developing Legal Systems in African Commonwealth Nations*, ed. Thomas W. Hutchinson et al. (Madison: University of Wisconsin Press, 1968), p. 15.

73. Sachs and Welch, *Liberating the Law*, p. 72.

74. Ibid., p. 17.

75. Ibid., p. 72.

76. Ibid., p. 73.

77. Simons, *African Women*, pp. 36, 40, 44.

78. Cotran and Rubin, *Readings in African Law*, p. xxv.

79. Sachs and Welch, *Liberating the Law*, p. 75.

80. Ibid., p. 70.

81. The nearest historical parallel to matriarchal resistance against patriarchal "communal" villages must be the nineteenth-century conquest of matrilineal societies by patriarchal conquest states, leading to the bonding of matriarchal women in "slave marriages."

82. Sachs and Welch, *Liberating the Law*, pp. 46–47.

83. In substantive law, the most dramatic example of a return to customary methods of justice—the simple justice of the colonial period—was the reintroduction of corporal punishment: "New legislation was introduced, which for the first time since independence imposed whipping as a method of punishment to be used in particular cases, and subsequent to that came examples of public flogging in different parts of Mozambique. And this was done in a way which was given maximum publicity." See Sachs and Welch, *Liberating the Law*, p. 112.

84. Ibid., p. 24.

85. Moore, *Social Facts and Fabrications*, pp. 161–66.

86. Cotran and Rubin, *Readings in African Law*, p. xxiii.

87. Sachs and Welch, *Liberating the Law*, p. 5.

88. Y. P. Ghai, "Customary Contracts and Transactions in Kenya," in *Ideas and Procedures*, ed. Gluckman, p. 333.

89. Schiller, introduction to *Africa and Law*, p. xviii.

Chapter V
The Native Authority and the Free Peasantry

1. Elizabeth Colson, "African Society at the Time of the Scramble," in *Colonialism in Africa*, vol. 1, *The History and Politics of Colonialism, 1870–1914*, by Gann and Duignan (1969), pp. 41–42.

2. John W. Bruce, "Do Indigenous Tenure Systems Constrain Development?" in *Land in African Agrarian Systems*, ed. Thomas J. Bassett and Donald E. Crummey (Madison: University of Wisconsin Press, 1993), p. 35.

3. Elizabeth Colson, "The Impact of the Colonial Period on the Definition of Land Rights," in Victor Turner, ed., *Colonialism in Africa, 1870–1960,* vol. 3, *Profiles of Change: African Society and Colonial Rule* (Cambridge: Cambridge University Press, 1971), p. 204.

4. Ibid., pp. 196–97.

5. Ibid., pp. 199–200; on French "colonial ideology that considered earth priests as having proprietary interests in land," see Francis G. Snyder, *Capitalism and Legal Change: An African Transformation* (New York: Academic Press, 1981), p. 274.

6. Thomas J. Bassett, "The Land Question and Agricultural Transformation in Sub-Saharan Africa," in *Land in African Agrarian Systems,* ed. Bassett and Crummey, p. 6.

7. Steven W. Lawry, "Transactions in Cropland Held under Customary Tenure in Lesotho," in *Land in African Agrarian Systems,* ed. Bassett and Crummey, p. 59.

8. Quoted in Robin Palmer, "Land in Zambia," in *Zambian Land and Labour Studies,* ed. Robin Palmer, vol. 1, National Archives Occasional Paper no. 2 (Lusaka, 1973), p. 59.

9. Lord Hailey, *An African Survey,* p. 789.

10. Sara Berry, "Hegemony on a Shoestring: Indirect Rule and Access to Agricultural Land," *Africa* 62, no. 3 (1992): 336.

11. Colson, "The Impact of the Colonial Period," pp. 196, 207.

12. Cited in Berry, "Hegemony on a Shoestring," p. 342.

13. See Audrey I. Richards, "Some Effects of the Introduction of Individual Freehold into Buganda," in *African Agrarian Systems,* ed. Daniel Biebuyuck (Oxford: Oxford University Press, 1963), pp. 271, 267; also see Mamdani, *Politics and Class Formation,* ch. 3, for details. Also see, by the same author, "Uganda: Contradictions of the IMF Programme and Perspective," *Development and Change* 21 (1990): 451–53.

14. See Mamdani, *Politics and Class Formation,* p. 129.

15. See Abdelali Doumou, "The State and Popular Alliances: Theoretical Preliminaries in Light of the Moroccan Case," in *Popular Struggles for Democracy in Africa,* ed. Peter Anyang' Nyong'o (London: Zed Books, 1988), pp. 48–77; see also Abdeslam Baita, "'Reversion to Tradition' in State Structures in Colonial Morocco," in *The Moroccan State in Historical Perspective, 1850–1985,* ed. Abdelali Doumou (Dakar, Senegal: CODESRIA, 1990), pp. 29–60.

16. Cited in Berry, "Hegemony on a Shoestring," p. 345.

17. Newitt, *Portugal in Africa,* pp. 101–2, 138–39.

18. See Henry Bernstein, "'And Who Now Plans Its Future?' Land in South Africa after Apartheid," in *When History Accelerates: Essays on Rapid Social Change, Complexity and Creativity,* ed. C. M. Hann (London: Athelone Press, 1994), pp. 161–87; see also Lord Hailey, *An African Survey,* pp. 691–92.

19. South African Institute of Race Relations, *The African Homelands of South Africa* (1973), pp. 79–80; quoted in "Towards a History of Nationalities in Southern Africa," by Michael Neocosmos (paper presented to the conference

"Dimensions of Economic and Political Reform in Contemporary Africa," Kampala, 8–12 April 1994), p. 21.

20. John W. Bruce, "Land Tenure Issues in Project Design and Strategies for Agricultural Development in Sub-Saharan Africa" (paper 128, Land Tenure Center, University of Wisconsin, Madison, 1986), p. 14.

21. See Bernstein, " 'And Who Now Plans Its Future?' "

22. On eastern Africa, for example, see G. N. Uzoigwe, "Pre-Colonial Markets in Bunyoro-Kitara," *Comparative Studies in Society and History* 14 (1972); John P. Pottier, "The Politics of Famine: Ecology, Regional Production and Food Complementarity in Western Ruanda," *African Affairs* 85, no. 339 (April 1986); David W. Cohen, "Food Production and Exchange in the Pre-Colonial Lakes Plateau Region," in *Imperialism, Colonialism and Hunger: East and Central Africa*, ed. Robert I. Rotberg (Lexington, Mass.: Lexington Books, 1983); see also Nyangabyaki-Bazaara, "Food Markets in Bunyoro-Kitara" (Centre for Basic Research, Kampala, 1991, mimeographed).

23. Walter Rodney, *How Europe Underdeveloped Africa*, (Dar-es-Salaam: Tanzania Publishing House, 1976).

24. For empirical data, see Mahmood Mamdani, "Extreme but Not Exceptional: Towards an Analysis of the Agrarian Question in Uganda," *The Journal of Peasant Studies* 14, no. 2 (1987): 199, table 2.

25. Mamdani, "Forms of Labour," p. 57.

26. Mark Twain, *King Leopold's Soliloquy* (Berlin: Seven Seas Publications, 1961), pp. 38, 74, 81–82.

27. Crawford Young, *Politics in the Congo: Decolonisation and Independence* (Princeton, N.J.: Princeton University Press, 1965), p. 11.

28. Schatzberg, *Politics and Class in Zaire*, p. 75.

29. J. P. Chrétien, with the collaboration of E. Mworoha (1973), "Rapport sur les migrations du XXe siècle en Afrique orientale. Le cas de l'émigration des Banyaruanda et des Barundi vers l'Ouganda," in "Commission Internationale d'Histoire des Mouvement Sociaux et des Structures Sociales, Enquête international portant sur quelques grands mouvement migratoires internationaux de la fin du XVIIIe siècle a nos jours" (Paris, mimeographed), pp. 16–17, cited in Jewsiewicki, "African Peasants, pp. 62–63.

30. Archives of the Government-General. Bamako. E 1/27/48 of 4 September 1894; quoted in Suret-Canale, *French Colonialism*, p. 67.

31. Quoted in Suret-Canale, *Essays on African History*, pp. 137–38.

32. G. Deherme, *L'Afrique Occidentale Française: Action Politique, Economique et Sociale* (Paris: Bloud et Cie, 1908), pp. 57–58; quoted in *French Colonialism*, by Suret-Canale, pp. 64–65.

33. The information on freedom villages has been culled from Suret-Canale, *French Colonialism*, pp. 64–65, 67, and Suret-Canale, *Essays on African History*, pp. 137–38. On statute labor, see Suret-Canale, *French Colonialism*, p. 252.

34. Berman, "Structure and Process," pp. 169–70; and Suret-Canale, *French Colonialism*, p. 244.

35. Suret-Canale, *French Colonialism*, pp. 229, 298.

36. Account of Mme Dugast in 1942, Archives nationales du Cameroun,

Yaoundé, cited by J. L. Dongmo, *Le Dynamisme bamiléké* (Cameroun), vol. 1, *La Maîtrise de l'espace agraire* (Yaoundé, Centre Édition et de Production pour l'Enseignement et la Recherche, 1981), pp. 122–24; cited in Bayart, *The State in Africa*, pp. 71–72. Also cited in Martin Kilson, *Political Change in a West African State: A Study of the Modernization Process in Sierra Leone*, (Cambridge, Mass.: Harvard University Press, 1966).

37. For a detailed analysis of the agreements, see Ruth First, "The Mozambican Miner: A Study in the Export of Labour" (Centro de Estudos Africanos, Universidade Eduardo Mondlane, Maputo, 1977, mimeographed), pp. 15–18. For detailed figures on the composition of the mining labor force in South Africa between 1904 and 1976, see table 2 following p. 25; see also Newitt, *Portugal in Africa*, p. 112.

38. Newitt, *Portugal in Africa*, p. 113.

39. The Rand mines were not the only employers of Mozambican migrant labor. As late as the close of the 1940s, two hundred thousand Mozambican workers were estimated to be working in Rhodesia. Besides, Mozambican migrants also went to the tea plantations of Nyasaland (Malawi) and the sisal plantations of Tanganyika. See Merle L. Bowen, *The State against the Peasantry: The Politics of Agricultural Change in Mozambique, 1950–1992* (forthcoming, University of Virginia Press); see ch. 2, p. 25.

40. Signe Arnfred, "Notes on Gender and Modernization: Exs from Mozambique" (The Language of Development Studies, New Social Science Monographs, Copenhagen, 1990), pp. 85, 88–89; Lars Rudebeck, "Development and Democracy: Notes Related to a Study of People's Power in Mozambique" (paper presented at conference entitled "The Formation of the Nation in 'the Five,'" Instituto Nacionale de Estudos e Pesquisa, Bissau, Guinea-Bissau, January 1986), p. 3; Bowen, "The State Against the Peasantry," ch. 2, pp. 21–22.

41. For information on the Mozambique Company, see Newitt, *Portugal in Africa*, pp. 77, 82, 116.

42. Bowen, "The State Against the Peasantry," ch. 4, pp. 6, 33–34.

43. Ibid., p. 14.

44. Newitt, *Portugal in Africa*, pp. 107–8, 115.

45. Sachs and Welch, *Liberating the Law*, p. 82.

46. See Reports from Commissioners, Inspectors, and Others (1910), vol. 27; *Report of the Commissioners on Emigraton from India to the Crown Colonies and Protectorates*, Parliamentary Paper, vol. 10 (1910), HMSO 5192, pp. 21, 3.

47. Lord Hailey, *An African Survey*, p. 387. Hailey also notes not-so-successful attempts by the French to import indentured labor from Cuba and China, and by the Belgians to do so from China, Barbados, and Liberia; see p. 1362.

48. For figures on Kenya, Nyasaland, Tanganyika, Uganda, Zanzibar, Gold Coast, and Nigeria, see table in Anthony Clayton and Donald Savage, *Government and Labour in Kenya, 1895–1963* (London: Cass, 1974), pp. 159–60; quoted in Berman, "Structure and Process," p. 196.

49. Berman, "Structure and Process," p. 196.

50. Chanock, *Law, Custom and Social Order*, p. 109.

51. See Suret-Canale, *Essays on African History*, pp. 169–70. On statute labor in general see Suret-Canale, *French Colonialism*, p. 252.

52. Moore, *Social Facts and Fabrication*, pp. 181–82.

53. Clyde R. Ingle, *From Village to State in Tanzania* (Ithaca: Cornell University Press, 1972), pp. 72–73.

54. Audrey Whipper, *Rural Rebels: A Study of Two Protest Movements in Kenya* (Nairobi: Oxford University Press, 1977), p. 107.

55. A. Debczynski, *Dwa lata w Kongu* (Warsaw: Dom Ksiazki Polskeij, 1928), pp. 249–50; and H. Gordzialkowski, *Czarny sen. Lwow* (Warsaw: Ksiaznica-Atlas, n.d.), p. 105; both cited in "African Peasants," by Jewsiewicki, pp. 62, 60.

56. Martin A. Klein, "Chiefship in Sine-Saloum (Senegal), 1887–1914," in *Colonialism in Africa*, vol. 3, *Profiles of Change*, ed. Victor Turner, p. 56.

57. *Report of the Ormsby-Gore Commission*, Cmd. 2387 (London, 1925), pp. 142–43.

58. Andrew Coulson, *Tanzania: A Political Economy* (Oxford: Clarendon Press, 1982), p. 48.

59. Chanock, *Law, Custom and Social Order*, pp. 229, 120.

60. Quoted in *The State in Africa*, by Bayart, p. 61.

61. B. Geldhof M. Schennicke, 15 May 1943. Archives de la sousregion du Tanganyika a Kalemie. The reply is in Inspection Report, Provincial Commissioner, Manono Territory, July–August 1943, Archives de la division Regionale des Affaires Politiques du Shaba, Lubumbashi; both are cited in "African Peasants," by Jewsiewicki, p. 66.

62. Suret-Canale, *French Colonialism*, p. 229.

63. André Gide, *Voyage au Congo* (Paris: Gallimard, 1927), p. 215; quoted in *French Colonialism*, by Suret-Canale, p. 229.

64. Suret-Canale, *French Colonialism*, p. 229.

65. Jean Rouche, "Migrations au Ghana," *Journal de la Société des Africanistes* 26 (1956): 33–196; quoted in *French Colonialism*, by Suret-Canale, p. 246.

66. On forced cotton cultivation in Mozambique, see Newitt, *Portugal in Africa*, p. 122; see also Isaacman, "Chiefs," p. 15.

67. Nyangbyaki Bazaara, "The Food Question in Colonial Bunyoro-Kitara: Capital Penetration and Peasant Response," (master's thesis, Department of Political Science, Makerere University, 1989), pp. 107–8, 114–16.

68. Ingle, *From Village to State*, pp. 47, 64.

69. Debczynski, *Dwa lata w Kongu*, pp. 249–50; and Gordzialkowski, *Czarny*, p. 105, both cited in "African Peasants," by Jewsiewicki, pp. 62, 60.

70. Schatzberg, *Politics and Class in Zaire*, p. 75.

71. Cited in Catherine Newbury and Brooke Grundfest Schoepf, "State, Peasantry and Agrarian Crisis in Zaire: Does Gender Make a Difference?" in *Women and the State in Africa*, ed. Jane L. Parpart and Kathleen A. Staudt (Boulder, Colo.: Lynne Reinner, 1989), pp. 96–97.

72. Catherine Newbury, "Ruanda: Recent Debates over Governance and

Rural Development," in *Governance and Politics in Africa*, ed. Goran Hyden and Michael Bratton (Boulder, Colo.: Lynne Reinner, 1992), p. 207.

73. Jonathan Barker, "Stability and Stagnation: The State in Senegal," *Canadian Journal of African Studies* 11, no. 1 (1977): 27–28; quoted in "Structure and Process," by Berman, pp. 170–71.

74. For Uganda, see Mamdani, *Politics and Class Formation*, pp. 247–53.

75. This relationship between herding cattle and cultivating crops is reversed in the case of agropastoralists, with the latter gaining primacy.

76. The material in this section is elaborated by Mahmood Mamdani, with P.M.B. Kasoma and A. B. Katende, in "Karamoja: Ecology and History," working paper no. 22, Centre for Basic Research, Kampala, June 1992.

77. In Botswana it is estimated that if one added together the land set aside for commercial ranching, national parks, and game reserves (and the newly proposed Wildlife Management Areas), the sum would amount to 41 percent of Botswana's total land area! See Bob Hitchcock, "The Future of Remote Area Development in Botswana" (seminar paper, National Institute of Research, Gabarone, Botswana, July 1988); quoted in "The Rights of Minorities and Subject Peoples in Botswana," by K. Datta and A. Murray, in *Democracy in Botswana*, by Holm and Molutsi, p. 69.

78. Department of Veterinary Services and Animal Industry, *Uganda Administrative Reports*, 1956–67, Moroto District Archives; quoted in "Pastoralism and Crisis," by Ocan.

79. For a detailed discussion, see Ocan, "Pastoralism and Crisis."

80. Berry, "Hegemony on a Shoestring," p. 343; Lord Hailey cited examples of strangers having to forfeit a third of their crop to the owner of the land (Lord Hailey, *An African Survey*, pp. 793–94).

81. Polly Hill, "Three Types of Southern Ghanaian Cocoa Farmers," in *African Agrarian Systems*, ed. Beibuyek, p. 203.

82. Mahir Saul, "Land Custom in Bare: Agnatic Corporation and Rural Capitalism in Western Bourkina," in *Land in Agrarian African Systems*, ed. Bassett and Crummey, pp. 81–85.

83. Golan, "Land Tenure Reform in Senegal," p. 29.

84. Steven H. Lawry, "Transactions in Cropland Held under Customary Tenure in Lesotho," in *Land in Agrarian African Systems*, ed. Bassett and Crummey, pp. 63, 67.

85. Moore, *Social Facts and Fabrication*, pp. 165–66.

86. Thomas Bassett, "Introduction: The Land Question and Agricultural Transformation in Sub-Saharan Africa," in *Land in Agrarian African Systems*, ed. Bassett and Crummey, p. 20.

87. Moore, *Social Facts and Fabrication*, pp. 111–12, 152.

88. Martin Chanock, "A Peculiar Sharpness: An Essay on Property in the History of Customary Law in Colonial Africa," *Journal of African History* 32 (1991): 71–72.

89. Fiona Mackenzie, "'A Piece of Land Never Shrinks': Reconceptualizing Land Tenure in a Smallholder District, Kenya," in *Land in Agrarian African Systems*, ed. Bassett and Crummey, pp. 194–221.

90. Colonial Office, "African Land Tenure," Summer Conference on African

Administration, seventh session, 28 August–1 September 1956, King's College, Cambridge, African no. 1186, pp. 21, 44.

91. Neocosmos, "The Agrarian Question in Swaziland," in *Social Relations in Rural Swaziland*, ed. Michael Neocosmos (Manzini: Social Science Research Unit, University of Swaziland, 1987), pp. 81–126; Richard Levin, "Is This the Swazi Way? State, Democracy and the Land Question," *Transformation* (Durban, Natal), no. 13 (1990); also Neocosmos, "The Agrarian Question in Southern Africa"; Levin, *When the Sleeping Grass Awakens.*

92. Levin, *When the Sleeping Grass Awakens*, pp. 47–49.

93. Ibid., pp. 19, 156.

94. Neocosmos, *Social Relations in Rural Swaziland*, p. 108.

95. Levin, *When the Sleeping Grass Awakens*, p. 57.

96. A.J.B. Hughes, "Land Tenure, Land Rights and Land Communities on Swazi Nation Land in Swaziland" (manuscript, Institute for Social Research, University of Natal, Durban, 1972), p. 134; cited in Levin, *When the Sleeping Grass Awakens*, p. 57.

97. Levin, *When the Sleeping Grass Awakens*, p. 155.

98. Ibid., p. 119.

99. Margo Russell, "African Freeholders: A Study of Individual Tenure Farms in Swazi Ownership," Working Paper, Land Tenure Center, University of Wisconsin, December 1990, p. 52.

100. Hughes, "Land Tenure," p. 239; cited in "The Agrarian Question," by Neocosmos, pp. 101–2.

101. On the ideology of developmentalism in Tanzania, see Issa Shivji's introduction to *The State and the Working People in Tanzania* (Dakar, Senegal: CODESRIA, 1986).

102. Von Freyhold, *Ujamaa Villages*, p. 35.

103. Unless otherwise stated, all material and quotes are from Ingle, *From Village to State*, pp. 65–66, 68, 69.

104. Cited in ibid., pp. 69–70.

105. Van Velzen, "Staff, Kulaks and Peasants," p. 157.

106. Von Freyhold, *Ujamaa Villages in Tanzania*, pp. 127, 37.

107. Ibid., pp. 128, 47.

108. Coulson, *Tanzania*, p. 254.

109. Von Freyhold, *Ujamaa Villages in Tanzania*, p. 56.

110. Coulson, *Tanzania*, pp. 250–51.

111. Merle L. Bowen, *The State against the Peasantry*; see ch. 3, p. 27.

112. Hermelle, *Land Struggles and Social Differentiation in Southern Mozambique* (Uppsala: Scandinavian Institute of African Studies, 1988), pp. 28–29; quoted in ibid., ch. 3, p. 13.

113. Bowen, *The State against the Peasantry*, ch. 3, p. 17.

114. Ibid., ch. 2, p. 39.

115. Rudebeck, "Development and Democracy," pp. 7–8.

116. Bowen, *The State against the Peasantry*, ch. 2, p. 34.

117. Mamdani, "Forms of Labour.

118. This last point is also made by Berry in "Hegemony on a Shoestring," p. 347.

Chapter VI
The Other Face of Tribalism:
Peasant Movements in Equatorial Africa

1. As in Ranger, *The Invention of Tribalism*.

2. As in Benedict Anderson, *Imagined Communities* (London: Verso, 1991).

3. As in E. P. Thompson, *The Making of the English Working Class* (New York: Vintage, 1963).

4. The debate has been excellently summed up and commented on by Archie Mafeje in *Codesria Bulletin* (Dakar, Senegal), no. 1 (1990).

5. Ken Post, "'Peasantisation' and Rural Political Movements in Western Africa," *European Journal of Sociology* 13 (1972): 223–51. For a survey of the literature, see Allen Isaacman, "Peasants and Rural Social Protest in Africa," *African Studies Review* 33, no. 2 (September 1990) 1–120.

6. Take a recent example from Botswana. A paper delivered at a conference on democracy in Botswana recapitulated the long history of the denial of rights and citizenship status to minority "subject" nationalities, which in turn have demanded anything from forms of affirmative action within existing state boundaries to separate statehood, just as often dismissed by the authorities as tribalist. Yet the only comment the paper could draw from conference participants was that "the author's emphasis on minority rights was divisive rather than promoting national unity which should be everybody's concern." See K. Datta and A. Murray, "The Rights of Minorities and Subject Peoples in Botswana: A Historical Evaluation," in *Democracy in Botswana*, ed. Holm and Molutsi, pp. 68–69; see also Holm and Molutsi, *Democracy in Botswana*, p. 154.

7. As early as 1963, Clifford Geertz advanced the thesis that tribalism in African politics is an inborn motivation and would therefore affect the motivation behind politics in Africa permanently. See Clifford Geertz, "The Integrative Revolution: Primordial Sentiments and Civil Politics in the New States," in *Old Societies and New States*, ed. C. Geertz (New York: Free Press, 1963). For a recent example, see D. W. Throup, *Economic and Social Origins of Mau Mau, 1945–53* (London, 1987).

8. This is the thread that runs through an otherwise excellent critique of some recent literature on tribalism by Aiden Southall, "The Ethnic Heart of Anthropology," *Cahiers d'Études Africaines* 100, XXV-4 (1985): 567–72.

9. "There is a real difference," argued Archie Mafeje in an influential article, "between the man who, on behalf of his tribe, strives to maintain its traditional integrity and autonomy, and the man who invokes tribal ideology in order to maintain a power position, not in the tribal area, but in the modern capital city, and whose ultimate aim is to undermine and exploit the supposed tribesmen." See Archie Mafeje, "The Ideology of Tribalism," *Journal of Modern African Studies* 9, no. 2 (1971): 258. A more strident and less nuanced version of this position can be found in John Saul's argument that tribalism is actually a direct manifestation of "petty bourgeois politics," being a "pathology" specific to Africa. See John Saul, *State and Revolution in East Africa* (New York: Monthly Review Press, 1977).

10. "If in Europe the response to the failure of the state to provide security

for the individual was the institution of feudalism," argues Ekeh, "in Africa the response to the violation of the citizenry by the state, in its sponsorship of the slave trade, was the entrenchment of kinship corporations." See Peter P. Ekeh, "Social Anthropology and Two Contrasting Uses of Tribalism in Africa," *Comparative Studies in Society and History* 32, no. 4 (October 1990): 660. In a recent update of this position, Basil Davidson has argued that this historical legacy has been reinforced by a modern development. Citing Peter Ekeh's analysis of the period of slavery, Davidson adds: "In just the same way, the predatory nature of the postcolonial or neocolonial state in Africa . . . has provoked self-defense by kinship ties or their bureaucratic equivalents and, with this, a corresponding subversion of the state by smuggling and related kinds of economic crime." See Davidson, *Black Man's Burden*, pp. 225–28.

11. See John Lonsdale, "Moral Ethnicity and Political Tribalism," in "Interventions and Boundaries: Historical and Anthropological Approaches to the Study of Ethnicity and Nationalism," ed. P. Kaarsholm and J. Hultin, occasional paper no. 11, IDS, Roskilde, 1994, pp. 5–50; see also John Lonsdale, "The Moral Economy of Mau Mau: Wealth, Poverty and Civic Virtue in Kikuyu Political Thought," in *Unhappy Valley: Conflict in Kenya and Africa*, ed. B. Berman and J. Lonsdale, vol. 2, *Violence and Ethnicity* (London: James Currey, 1992), pp. 315–504.

12. "Ethnicity," argued Masipula Sithole, "is a resource which those who aspire to positions of power and leadership have used when perceived to yield results." Then he added emphatically: "A worker seeking power will manipulate ethnicity no differently and the response of the ethnic constituency is likely to continue to be rational and selfish. To view a worker as behaving differently is romantic nonsense." See Masipula Sithole, "The Salience of Ethnicity in African Politics: The Case of Zimbabwe," *Journal of Asian and African Studies* 20, nos. 3–4 (1985): 190.

13. Nzongola-Ntalaja, "The Second Independence Movement in Congo-Kinshasa," in *Popular Struggles*, by Nyong'o, pp. 124, 131.

14. See W. R. Ochieng, "Review of Roots of Freedom, 1921–1963," *Kenya Historical Review* 4, no. 1 (1976); see also B. E. Kipkorir, "Mau Mau and the Politics of Transfer of Power in Kenya, 1957–1960," *Kenya Historical Review* 5, no. 2 (1977): 313–28.

15. R. Buijtenhuis, *Essays on Mau Mau, Contributions to Mau Mau Historiography* (Leiden: African Studies Centre, 1982).

16. Bethwell Ogot, "Politics, Culture and Music in Central Kenya: A Study of Mau Mau Hymns, 1951–56," *Kenya Historical Review* 5, no. 2 (1977): 115–34.

17. Maina wa Kinyatti, "Mau Mau: The Peak of African Political Organisation in Colonial Kenya," *Kenya Historical Review* 5, no. 2 (1977): 287–311.

18. Frank Furedi, *The Mau Mau War in Perspective* (London: James Currey, 1989), pp. 18, 138–39, 142.

19. Furedi's contention that "while organisationally independent, Mau Mau was ideologically indistinguishable from KAU [Kenya African Union] and moderate constitutionalists" (p. 138) is at odds with his equally firm insistence that Mau Mau "put to question the existing socio-economic structures of society"

(p. 18). It is ironic that Furedi is still caught up in the language of the very controversy whose parameters he succeeded in transcending epistemologically: he still uses the labels "tribalist" and "nationalist" as opposites, one derogatory, the other laudatory!

20. I do not wish to present a one-sided opposition between social perspective and geographical scope, only to uphold the former and dismiss the latter. Clearly, geographical scope is not unimportant: without a focus on the enclave character of the Mau Mau in Kenya, the Mulelists in Zaire, and the NRA in Uganda, it is not possible to explain their historical trajectory satisfactorily. My purpose, after all, is to question the one-sided opposition between the social and the geographical.

21. Govan Mbeki, *South Africa: The Peasants' Revolt* (London: Penguin, 1964), p. 67.

22. Francis Fox and Douglas Back, "Preliminary Survey of the Agricultural and Nutritional Problems of the Ciskei and Transkei," transcript, 1937; quoted in Lodge, *Black Politics in South Africa*, p. 262.

23. Quoted in Callinicos, *A Place in the City*, p. 101.

24. Quoted in O'Meara, "The 1946 African Mine Workers' Strike," in *South African Capitalism*, by Murray, pp. 367, 375.

25. Cited in Mbeki, *South Africa*, p. 75.

26. William Beinart and Colin Bundy, "State Intervention and Rural Resistance: The Transkei, 1900–1965," in *Peasants in Africa*, ed. Klein, pp. 294–300; Lodge, *Black Politics in South Africa*, pp. 262–65; Callinicos, *A Place in the City*, p. 50.

27. House of Assembly Debates, 9 May 1962; quoted in Mbeki, *South Africa*, pp. 98–99.

28. Lodge, *Black Politics in South Africa*, p. 266.

29. C. Simkins, "Agricultural Production in the African Reserves of South Africa, 1918–1969," *Journal of Southern African Studies* 7, no. 2 (1981); quoted in "Rural Resistance," by Chaskalson, pp. 50–51.

30. Chaskalson, "Rural Resistance," p. 54.

31. Peter Delius, "Migrants, Comrades and Rural Revolt: Sekhukhuneland, 1950–87," *Transformation* (Durban) 13 (1990): 9.

32. Callinicos, *A Place in the City*, p. 49.

33. Baruch Hirson, "Rural Revolt in South Africa, 1937–51" (post graduate seminar paper, Institute of Commonwealth Studies, London, 1976); cited in Chaskalson, "Rural Resistance," pp. 54–55.

34. Callinicos, *A Place in the City*, p. 49.

35. Delius, "Migrants, Comrades and Rural Revolt," pp. 9–10.

36. Lodge, *Black Politics in South Africa*, p. 275.

37. Ibid., p. 269.

38. Chaskalson, "Rural Resistance," pp. 54–55.

39. Lodge, *Black Politics in South Africa*, p. 285.

40. Ibid., pp. 271–72.

41. This study generalizes on the basis of an analysis of a number of revolts of different intensity, scope, and duration: Hurutse, Sekhukhuneland, Thembu-

land, Pondoland, Zoutpansberg, Witzieshoek, Ngutu, and Thaba Nchu. See Chaskalson, "Rural Resistance."

42. Delius, "Migrants, Comrades and Rural Revolt," p. 10.

43. Beinart and Bundy, "State Intervention and Rural Resistance," p. 309.

44. Mbeki, *South Africa*, p. 120; Ben Turok, "Pondo Revolt," (Congress of Democrats Publication, n.d., mimeographed), pp. 10–11, 14.

45. Evans, "Political Economy," pp. 246–47.

46. Mbeki, *South Africa*, pp. 131–33.

47. Ibid., p. 125.

48. A detailed analysis of the social and historical context of the Ruwenzururu movement can be found in Arthur Syahuka-Muhindo, "The Ruwenzururu Question: A Struggle for Democracy by Baamba and Bakonzo People of Western Uganda" (master's thesis, Makerere University, Kampala, 1989).

49. This account, based on my own interviews in September 1984, differs slightly from the one in "The Ruwenzururu Question," by Syahuka-Muhindo, pp. 277–84.

50. See Abdul Raufu Mustapha, "Peasant Politics and Democracy in Nigeria" (paper presented at the International Workshop on Social Movements, State and Democracy, New Delhi, 5–8 October 1992), pp. 20–29.

51. A. V. Chayanov, *The Theory of Peasant Economy*, ed. Daniel Thorner (Homewood, Ill.: Richard D. Irwin, 1966); V. I. Lenin, *The Development of Capitalism in Russia* (Moscow: Progress, 1962).

52. Eric Wolf, *Peasant Wars in the Twentieth Century* (New York: Harper & Row, 1969).

53. Hamza Alavi, "Peasants and Revolution," in *The Socialist Register*, ed. Ralph Miliband and John Saville (London: Mervin Press, 1965).

54. Jeffrey Paige, *Agrarian Revolution: Social Movements and Export Agriculture in the Underdeveloped World* (New York: Free Press, 1975).

55. For a similar viewpoint, see Furedi, *The Mau Mau War*.

56. Mamdani, "Extreme but Not Exceptional," pp. 191–225.

57. Amilcar Cabral, "A Brief Analysis of the Social Structure in Guinea Bissau," in *Revolution in Guinea: Selected Texts* (New York: Monthly Review Press, 1970).

58. Richard Joseph, *Militant Nationalism in Cameroun: Social Origins of the UPC Rebellion* (Oxford: 1977); also by the same author, "Radical Nationalism in French Africa: The Case of Cameroon," in *Decolonisation and African Independence: The Transfers of Power, 1960–1980*, by Prosser Gifford and Wm. Roger Louis (New Haven: Yale University Press, 1988).

59. For a detailed discussion, see Patrick Masanja, "Some Notes on the Sungu Sungu Movement" (Department of Sociology Seminar Paper, University of Dar-es-Salaam, 8 March 1984). See also Ray Abrahams, "Sungusungu: Village Vigilante Groups in Tanzania," *African Affairs* 86, no. 343 (April 1987): 179–96; and Horace Campbell, "Popular Resistance in Tanzania: Lessons from Sungu Sungu" (paper presented at the International Seminar on Internal Conflict, Makerere University, Kampala, Uganda, 21–25 September 1987).

60. In this context one needs to understand both the introduction of women

combatants in guerrilla struggles, from the Algerian National Liberation Front (FLN) to the Ugandan NRM, and their retreat from the public arena in the period after the guerrilla war!

61. Richards, "Some Effects," p. 268.

62. This analysis is in Mamdani, *Politics and Class Formation*, ch. 7.

63. When later translated—rather mechanically—from rural areas, where the sites of residence and work tended to coincide, to towns, where they did not, the principle of residence-based rights would have an opposite effect: to deprive laboring communities of the collective right of organization. For an elaboration, see Mahmood Mamdani, *NRA/NRM: The First Two Years* (Kampala: Progress Publishers, 1988).

64. Donald Crummey, ed., *Banditry, Rebellion and Social Protest in Africa* (London: James Currey, 1988); see also the review by Michael Watts in *African Economic History*, no. 16 (1987).

65. Isaacman, "Chiefs, Rural Differentiation and Peasant Protest," p. 35.

66. Mao-ze-Dong, "The Chinese Revolution and the Chinese Communist Party," in *Selected Works*, vol. 2 (Peking: Foreign Language Press, 1967).

67. Furedi, *The Mau Mau War*.

68. Jordan Gebre-Medhin, *Peasants and Nationalism in Eritrea: A Critique of Ethiopian Studies* (Trenton, N.J.: Red Sea Press, 1989).

69. For a critique, see Mamdani, "State and Civil Society in Contemporary Africa."

Chapter VII
The Rural in the Urban: Migrant Workers in South Africa

1. Independent Board of Inquiry, *Fortresses of Fear* (Johannesburg, 1992), pp. 1, 2, 4.

2. International Commission of Jurists, press release, 29 March 1992; cited in ibid., p. 9.

3. David Everatt (deputy director, CASE) and Safoora Sadek (coordinator, HRC), "The Reef Violence: Tribal War or Total Strategy?" 28 March 1992, in *Consolidated CASE Reports on the Reef Violence*, by David Everatt (Johannesburg, 1992), pp. 2, 4, 5.

4. David Everatt, "Who Is Murdering the Peace? CASE Research Statistics," October 1991, in ibid., p. 5.

5. Paulus Zulu, "Durban Hostels and Political Violence: Case Studies in KwaMashu and Umlazi," *Transformation* (Durban), no. 21 (1993): 22.

6. Independent Board of Inquiry, *Fortresses of Fear*, pp. 1, 5.

7. Mike Morris and Doug Hindson, "South Africa: Political Violence, Reform and Reconstruction," *Review of African Political Economy*, no. 53 (1992): 43–44, 46, 47, 51. This article is a revision of a report, first circulated in draft form at the meeting of the Economic Trends Group on 7 July 1991 in South Africa.

8. Often a study may contain more than a single line of reasoning. Paulus Zulu, for example, argues the following: "The conflict which has become political had its origins in the competition for scarce resources between the hos-

tel and the informal settlements around them." See Zulu, "Durban Hostels," p. 14.

9. Lauren Segal, "The Human Face of Violence: Hostel Dwellers Speak," *Journal of Southern African Studies* 18, no. 1 (March 1991): 213, 231.

10. See Sparks, *The Mind of South Africa*, p. 191.

11. Quoted in Eddie Webster, *Cast in a Racial Mold: Labor Process and Trade Unionism in the Foundries* (Johannesburg: Raven Press, 1985), p. 207.

12. Marie Wentzel, "Historical Origins of Hostels in South Africa: Migrant Labor and Compounds," in *Communities in Isolation: Perspectives on Hostels in South Africa*, ed. Anthony Minaar (Pretoria: Human Sciences Research Council, 1993), p. 3.

13. Anthony Minaar, "Hostels and Violent Conflict on the Reef," in *Communities in Isolation*, ed. Minaar, p. 24.

14. M. L. Morris, "The Development of Capitalism in South African Agriculture: Class Struggle in the Countryside," in *South African Capitalism*, ed. Murray, p. 286.

15. Lodge, *Black Politics in South Africa*, p. 262.

16. Murray, *South African Capitalism*, introduction to pt. 4, p. 240.

17. Tomlinson Commission report, 1955, p. 28; cited in Morris, "The Development of Capitalism," p. 288.

18. Martin J. Murray, "The Development of Non-European Political Consciousness, 1910–1948," in *South African Capitalism*, ed. Murray, p. 348.

19. Editorial, *Farmers Weekly*, 10 October 1945; quoted in Morris, "The Development of Capitalism," pp. 289–90.

20. Dan O'Meara has argued that the battle lines over the postwar evolution of native policy pitted industrial and commercial capital against mining and farming interests. The former "wanted a stabilized labor force to be financed largely by higher taxation of the new Free State Gold Fields," whereas the powerful mining sector "wanted the migrant system of cheap labor to continue and mining taxation reduced" (O'Meara, "The 1946 African Mine Workers' Strike," pp. 384, 385).

21. Jeremy Baskin, *Striking Back: A History of COSATU* (Braamfontein: Raven Press, 1991), p. 17.

22. The figures supplied by the Mouton Commission on monopolies (1977) showed that "a mere 5 per cent of the total number of firms in the manufacturing sector collectively accounted for 63 per cent of the sector's turnover; only 5 per cent of those in the wholesale and retail sector accounted for 69 per cent of turnover; 5 per cent of those in construction accounted for 63 per cent of turnover; and 5 per cent in transport accounted for 73 per cent of turnover." See Eddie Webster, "The Rise of Social-Movement Unionism: The Two Faces of the Black Trade Union Movement in South Africa," in *State, Resistance and Change in South Africa*, ed. Philip Frankel, Noam Pines, and Mark Swilling (Johannesburg: Southern Book Publishers, 1988), p. 177.

23. Anthony Marx, *Lessons of Struggle* (Cape Town: Oxford University Press, 1992), p. 193.

24. David Hemson, "Trade Unionism and the Struggle for Liberation in South Africa," in *South African Capitalism*, ed. Murray, pp. 710–11.

25. Ari Sitas, "The Flight of the Gwala-Gwala Bird: Labour, Politics and Culture in Natal's Labor Movement" (Department of Sociology, University of Natal, Durban, 1993, mimeographed), pp. 5, 13.

26. Isizwe, "Errors of Workerism," *South African Labour Bulletin* 12, no. 3 (March/April 1987): 52.

27. Mike Morris, interview by author, Durban, 22 June 1993.

28. Webster, *Cast in a Racial Mold*, p. 132.

29. Baskin, *Striking Back*, pp. 18–19; Webster, *Cast in a Racial Mold*, p. 132; Marx, *Lessons of Struggle*, pp. 194–95.

30. Two Trade Unionists, "Errors of Workerism: A Response," *South African Labour Bulletin* 12, no. 3 (March/April 1987): 65.

31. Webster, *Cast in a Racial Mold*, pp. 132–33.

32. Phil Bonner, "Focus on FOSATU," *South African Labour Bulletin* 5, no. 1 (May 1979): 7.

33. See, for example, the critique of workerism originally produced in a UDF publication and reproduced alongside a response from "two trade unionists" in the *South African Labour Bulletin*. Isizwe, "Errors of Workerism," and Two Trade Unionists, "Errors of Workerism."

34. Murray, "The Development of Non-European Political Consciousness," p. 336.

35. Quoted in Baskin, *Striking Back*, p. 8.

36. Murray, "The Development of Non-European Political Consciousness," p. 337.

37. Baskin, *Striking Back*, p. 13.

38. Lodge, *Black Politics in South Africa*, p. 193.

39. Baskin, *Striking Back*, p. 13.

40. Marx, *Lessons of Struggle*, p. 191.

41. Morris, interview.

42. "In the early 1970s, the new independent unions eschewed political action outside of production. They wished to avoid the path taken by SACTU which was closely identified with the campaigns of the Congress Alliance in the 1950s and was destroyed or forced into exile along with the rest of the Alliance by state repression in the 1960s." See Webster, "The Rise of Social-Movement Unionism," p. 179.

43. For an appreciation of this point of view, see Steven Friedman, "The Struggle within the Struggle: South African Resistance Strategies," *Transformation* 3 (1987): 58–59.

44. Morris, interview.

45. Colleen McCaul, "The Wild Card: Inkatha and Contemporary Black Politics," in *State, Resistance and Change*, ed. Frankel, Pines, and Swilling, p. 163.

46. Quoted in Ari Sitas, "From Grassroots Control to Democracy: A Case Study of the Impact of Trade Unionism on Migrant Workers' Cultural Formations on the East Rand," *Social Dynamics* (Cape Town) 11, no. 1 (1985): 39.

47. Phil Bonner, "Independent Trade Unions since Wiehahn," *South African Labour Bulletin* 8, no. 4 (February 1983): 20.

48. Qabula Alfred, interview by author, Durban, 11 May 1993.

49. Quoted in Webster, *Cast in a Racial Mold*, p. 209.

50. Phil Bonner, interview by author, Johannesburg, 10 June 1993.

51. Quoted in Webster, *Cast in a Racial Mold*, p. 211.

52. Ibid., p. 276.

53. General Workers' Union, "Workers' Hostels: An Issue of Control," *South African Labour Bulletin* 11, no. 8 (September/October 1986), p. 68.

54. Webster, *Cast in a Racial Mold*, p. 204.

55. Sitas, "From Grassroots Control to Democracy," p. 40.

56. Morris, interview.

57. Baskin, *Striking Back*, p. 30.

58. Bonner, "Independent Trade Unions," p. 31.

59. Webster, *Cast in a Racial Mold*, pp. 232–33.

60. Eddie Webster and Karl von Holdt, "Towards a Socialist Theory of Radical Reform: From Resistance to Reconstruction in the Labour Movement" (Ruth First Memorial Symposium, Cape Town, 17–18 August 1992, mimeographed), p. 7.

61. Bonner, "Focus on FOSATU," pp. 7, 21–23.

62. Sections of the Wiehahn Commission's report are quoted in Bonner, "Independent Trade Unions," pp. 17–20.

63. Lodge, *Black Politics in South Africa*, p. 337; Mike Morris, "State, Capital and Growth: The Political Economy of the National Question," in *South Africa's Economic Crisis*, by Stephen Gelb (Cape Town: David Philip, 1991), p. 44.

64. "Comment 1: Focus on Riekert," *South African Labour Bulletin* 5, no. 4 (November 1979): 2.

65. The second leg of the reform called for the existing industrial relations system to be deracialized so that unionized African workers would be at par with their white, colored, and Indian colleagues. "The operation of the law," argued Wiehahn, "should be extended to all those whose actions outside the law might disrupt industrial peace." The correlative of legal registration would be a set of controls designed to ensure that unions functioned as nonpolitical industrial organizations. Moreover, it would be an offense for unions to affiliate politically under the 1956 Industrial Conciliations Act.

The final and third leg of the reform package concerned the role of registered unions in industrial relations. Wiehahn hoped to keep unions out of plants by replacing liaison committees with works councils. Whereas the liaison committee was constituted by African employee representatives and management in equal proportion, the works council would be a multiracial but exclusively union affair in which representation would be based on formal equality between each set of separately unionized employees, those not unionized, and management. "Works Councils," explained a standard model from the Steel and Engineering Industry Federation, "are primarily advisory and consultative bodies and cannot by resolution or otherwise reverse or amend any instruction given by the management. Nor can they interfere with disciplinary measures."

To curb plant-level agitation, Wiehahn argued for collective bargaining to take place at the industry level. Agreements arrived at in the industrial councils would be binding; any breach would be a legal offense. The collective bargaining would pit employers' representatives against representatives of various registered trade unions, once again enjoying formal equality regardless of representativity. With small white artisan unions having the same representation as large black industrial unions, the point—once again—was to constitute an alliance of employers and white unions to block black unions. See Bonner, "Independent Trade Unions," pp. 19–20.

66. Quoted in ibid., p. 21.

67. Edwin Ritchken, "Trade Unions and Community Organizations: Towards a Working Alliance?" *Transformation* 10 (1989): 41.

68. Bonner, "Independent Trade Unions," p. 22.

69. Webster and von Holdt, "Towards a Socialist Theory of Radical Reform," p. 4.

70. Mike Morris, "Capital's Responses to African Trade Unions Post Wiehahn," *South African Labour Bulletin* 7, no. 1 (September 1981): 75–76.

71. Webster and von Holdt, "Towards a Socialist Theory," p. 8.

72. Ari Sitas, "The New Tribalism: Hostels and Violence" (Durban, 1993, mimeographed), p. 5.

73. Bonner, interview.

74. Moses Mayekiso, interview by author, Johannesburg, 15 June 1993.

75. Bonner, interview.

76. Ibid.

77. Anthony Minaar, "Hostels and Violent Conflict on the Reef," in *Perspectives on Hostels*, ed. Minaar, p. 29.

78. Mayekiso, interview.

79. For information on the councils, see Webster, *Cast in a Racial Mold*, pp. 237–38; Bonner, "Independent Trade Unions," p. 31; and Bonner, interview.

80. Mark Swilling, "Workers Divided: A Critical Assessment of the Split in MAWU on the East Rand," *South African Labour Bulletin* 10, no. 1 (August/September 1984): 103–4.

81. Ibid., pp. 104–5.

82. Archie Mafeje, "Soweto and Its Aftermath," in *South African Capitalism*, ed. Murray, p. 742.

83. Independent Board of Inquiry, *Fortresses of Fear*, p. 4.

84. Mafeje, "Soweto and Its Aftermath," pp. 743–44.

85. Wentzel, "Historical Origins of Hostels," in *Perspectives on Hostels*, ed. Minaar, p. 7.

86. Ibid.

87. Mamphela Ramphele, *A Bed Called Home* (Cape Town: David Phillip, 1993), p. 86.

88. Friedman, "The Struggle within the Struggle," p. 61.

89. Marx, *Lessons of Struggle*, p. 167.

90. Quoted in Mark Swilling, "Urban Social Movements under Apartheid," *Cahiers d'Études Africaines* 99, XXV-3 (1985): 378.

91. Jeremy Seekings, "Political Mobilization in the Black Townships of the Transvaal," in *State, Resistance and Change*, ed. Frankel, Pines, and Swilling, pp. 217–18.

92. Swilling, "Urban Social Movements," p. 370.

93. Webster, "The Rise of Social-Movement Unionism," p. 192.

94. Bonner, interview.

95. Swilling, "Urban Social Movements," p. 375.

96. "Trade Unions and the UDF," briefing in *South African Labour Bulletin* 8, nos. 8–9 (September/October 1983): 5.

97. Bonner, "Independent Trade Unions," pp. 33–34.

98. Swilling, "Workers Divided," pp. 117, 119.

99. Baskin, *Striking Back*, p. 31.

100. I am grateful to Bill Freund for this observation.

101. Segal, "The Human Face," pp. 204–5.

102. Ibid., p. 205.

103. Mayekiso, interview.

104. Ramphele, *A Bed Called Home*, p. 87.

105. Norman Levy, *The Foundations of the South African Cheap Labour System* (London: Routledge & Kegan Paul, 1982), pp. 38–39.

106. Sitas, "The New Tribalism," p. 2.

107. Minaar, "Hostels and Violent Conflict on the Reef," in *Communities in Isolation*, ed. Minaar, p. 44.

108. Babylon Xeketwane, "The 'War' on the Reef: The Political Violence on the Reef's Black Townships since July 1990" (B.A. Honors diss., University of Witwatersrand, Department of Industrial Sociology, Johannesburg, 1991), pp. 35–37.

109. Segal, "The Human Face of Violence," pp. 193ff.

110. General Workers' Union, "Workers' Hostels: An Issue of Control," *South African Labour Bulletin* 11, no. 8 (September/October 1986): 65–76.

111. Minaar, "Hostels and Violent Conflict on the Reef," p. 10.

112. Social Surveys, *Needs Assessment Study for Johannesburg Hostels* (1992, mimeographed), pp. 4–5.

113. Temba Nxumalo, interview by author, Johannesburg, 8 June 1993.

114. Minaar, "Hostels and Violent Conflict on the Reef," p. 66.

115. Daisy, interview by author, Durban, 19 May 1993.

116. Sakkie Steyn, secretary, Transvaal Hostel Residents Association, interview by author, Johannesburg, 4 June 1993.

117. Ramphele, *A Bed Called Home*, p. 31.

118. Social Surveys, *Needs Assessment*, p. 18.

119. Zulu, interview by author, Durban, 9 May 1993.

120. Susan Rubenstein, *The Story of a Hostel Project: A Special Report on Nguni Hostel at Vosloorus* (Johannesburg: Bernhardt, Dunstan, 1992), pp. 6–8.

121. Ngema Dumisani, committee member, Hostel Residents Association, interview by author, Soweto, 9 June 1993.

122. Nxumalo, interview.

123. Social Surveys, *Needs Assessment*, p. 17.

124. Nxumalo, interview.

125. Gugumolefe, *Interview*, Durban, 25 May 1993.

126. Quoted in Minaar, "Hostels and Violent Conflict on the Reef," p. 26.

127. Social Surveys, *Needs Assessment*, p. 21.

128. See Levy, *The Foundations*, pp. 39–41; Hirson, *Yours for the Union*, pp. 167–68; and Ramphele, *A Bed Called Home*, p. 60.

129. William Beinart, "Ethnic Particularism, Workers' Consciousness and Nationalism, the Experience of a South African Migrant, 1930–60," SSAC, vol. 13; quoted in Hirson, *Yours for the Union*, pp. 166–67.

130. The point is brought out inevitably and forcefully in sociological studies of hostel life. See Ramphele, *A Bed Called Home*, pp. 8, 13, 61; Zulu, "Durban Hostels," pp. 1–23.

131. See, for example, the results of the shop stewards' survey in Webster, *Cast in a Racial Mold*, pp. 210–11.

132. Zulu, interview.

133. Steyn, interview.

134. Gugumolefe, interview.

135. Xeketwane, "The 'War' on the Reef," p. 50.

136. See Ramphele, *A Bed Called Home*, p. 19.

137. Two accounts that I have read which break out of this one-eyed vision and present a relatively balanced picture are by Soweto-based students. See Xeketwane, "The 'War' on the Reef," pp. 49–50, 51–52 and T. Mthetwa, "Community, Urban Migrants and Workers" (third-year sociology essay, Sociology Department, University of Witwatersrand, 1990), as quoted in Segal, "The Human Face of Violence," p. 197.

138. Xeketwane, "The 'War' on the Reef," p. 54.

139. Richard Mdakane, general secretary, and Nkela Ntingane, assistant general secretary, Alexandra Civic Organization, interview by author, Alexandra, 7 June 1993.

140. "Profile," *The Star*, 1 June 1993, p. 9.

141. Mdakane, interview.

142. Philemon Machitela, organizer, Alexandra Civic Organization, interview by author, Alexandra, 11 June 1993.

143. Nkele Ntingane, assistant general secretary, Alexandra Civic Organization, interview by author, Alexandra, 7 June 1963.

144. Mdakane, interview.

145. In interviews with hostel workers and their representatives, discussions of the stayaways often evoked bitter memories of being coerced to abide by civic decisions. See, for example, this response from the secretary of the Transvaal Hostel Residents' Association:

> During the boycott, if people were caught buying, they would be made to drink the oil. Certain taxis would not pick up hostel people or just wouldn't stop at hostels. Eventually there were agreements whereby separate taxis catered entirely for hostel residents. The result was a very strong polarization of communities. Certain taxis, businesses, trains were branded as "off-limit" to hostel residents. . . . People in trains were forced to sing liberation

songs and toyi toyi by youngsters. At the interface between hostel and community, ANC-Inkatha, Zulu-Xhosa, there was high polarization. (Steyn, interview)

146. Mdakane, interview.

147. The Vosloorus Hostel in the East Rand is another instance where hostel dwellers participated in a joint community forum together with the civic association and other groups. See Rubenstein, *The Story of a Hostel Project*, p. 6.

148. Machitela, interview.

149. David Everatt, "Funeral Vigil Massacres: Mourning the Mourners" (material prepared for the Goldstone Commission, March 1992), p. 5.

150. Gavin Woods, "Hostel Residents—a Socio-Psychological and Humanistic Perspective: Empirical Findings on a National Scale," in *Communities in Isolation*, ed. Minaar, p. 74.

151. Ntingane, interview.

152. Mdakane and Ntingane, interview.

153. Mayekiso, interview.

154. Ibid.

155. David Letsei, interview by author, Johannesburg, 8 June 1993.

156. Minaar, "Hostels and Violent Conflict on the Reef," p. 30.

157. That "all single quarters in the townships will eventually be altered into family units" was promised by the minister of Constitutional Development and Planning in 1986 following the repeal of influx control. The next month, in June, the government announced plans to build two new single-sex hostels because "a demand for accommodation of persons on a single basis exists"! See Minaar, "Hostels and Violent Conflict on the Reef," p. 35.

158. For a text, see Minaar, *Communities in Isolation*, appendix D, pp. 252–54.

159. When F. W. de Klerk visited one such hostel (Marafe in Soweto) surrounded by a razor wire fence, the residents requested that it be removed, for "the fence will not prevent people from fighting. It can be cut if people are determined. . . . This fence is only here to create tension between us [hostel residents] and [township] residents. The residents actually make fun of us because we have been caged inside the very place we stay in. They see us as idiots." See M. Moroke, "Remove Razor Wire Fences—Hostel Dwellers," *The Star*, 25 September 1990, quoted in "Hostels and Violent Conflict on the Reef," by Minaar, p. 15.

160. Sitas, "The New Tribalism," p. 5.

161. Blade Nzimande, interview by author, Durban, 17 June 1993.

162. Morris and Hindson, "South Africa," p. 50.

163. Anthony Minaar, " 'Undisputed Kings': Warlordism in Natal," in *Patterns of Violence: Case Studies of Conflict in Natal*, ed. Anthony Minaar (Pretoria: Human Sciences Research Council, 1992), p. 60.

164. Ibid., pp. 68, 71–72.

165. Rubenstein, *The Story of a Hostel Project*, p. 6.

166. Sitas, "The New Tribalism," p. 7.

167. See David Everatt, interview with *Vrye Weekblad*, 8–14 May 1992, in

Consolidated CASE Reports on the Reef Violence; Minaar, "Hostels and Violent Conflict on the Reef," p. 25.

168. Wesley Dhlamini, chairman, Meadowlands Hostel Residents' Association, interview by author, Soweto, 14 June 1993.

169. "Memorandum for Presentation to the Honourable the Ministers of Law and Order and of National Health with a Delegation of SAHDA on the 5th August 1991 in Wachthius in the Ministry of Law and Order" (mimeographed), pp. 3, 4, 16.

170. Memorandum submitted by SAHDA to Minister Adriaan Vlok, Minister of Law and Order, and Dr. Rina Venter, Minister of National Health and Health Services (Pretoria, 1991-08-05, mimeographed), p. 2.

171. Unlike the Transvaal, an association had already been formed among hostel residents in the Western Cape in the 1983–85 period. The initiative to organize came from those who belonged to trade unions. Organized on the basis of elected representation inside and between hostels, the Western Cape Men's Hostel Association opened its doors to women hostel residents at its 1986 conference. See Ramphele, *A Bed Called Home*, pp. 89–92.

172. Steyn, interview, 4 June 1993.

173. See "Transvaal Hostel Residents' Association: Structures" and "Transvaal Hostel Residents' Response to the Record of Understanding Agreed to between the Government of the Republic of South Africa and the African National Congress on the 26th September 1992" (Johannesburg, October 1992, mimeographed).

174. Steyn, interview, 4 June 1993.

175. Steyn, interview, 9 June 1993.

176. Nxumalo, interview.

177. Steyn, interview, 4 June 1993.

178. Dhlamini, interview.

179. Minaar, "Hostels and Violent Conflict on the Reef," p. 28. Minaar, however, generalized one historical moment and argues that the triple structures in Zulu-dominated hostels—the hostel committee, the indunas, and the IFP committee—all reinforce "local Inkatha structures" under whose control they function.

180. Steyn, interview, 4 June 1993.

181. Albert Mkhize, chief induna, Wolhuter Hostel, interview by author, Johannesburg, 8 June 1993.

182. Nxumalo, interview.

183. Dhlamini, interview.

184. Khotso Kekana and Albert Nolan, "Making Peace from Below," *Challenge* (Braamfontein, April 1993): 2–4.

185. Mkhize, interview.

186. Dhlamini, interview.

187. Nxumalo, interview.

188. Ngema Dumisani, vice chair, Meadowlands Hostel Residents' Association, interview by author, Soweto, 9 June 1993.

189. Steyn, interview, 9 June 1993.

190. Steyn, interview, 4 June 1993.

Chapter VIII
Conclusion: Linking the Urban and the Rural

1. Notwithstanding Basil Davidson's claim to the contrary in *The Black Man's Burden: Africa and the Curse of the Nation-State.*.

2. Expressed in nonradical terminology, the problem is "the politics of the belly," to cite the title of Jean-Francois Bayart's latest book. It is a politics that he explains as "the rush for spoils in which all actors—rich and poor—participate in the world of networks." My point about clientelism is that it is more an effect of the form of power than an explanation of it.

PRINCETON STUDIES IN
CULTURE/POWER/HISTORY

High Religion:
A Cultural and Political History of Sherpa Buddhism
by Sherry B. Ortner

A Place in History:
Social and Monumental Time in a Cretan Town
by Michael Herzfeld

The Textual Condition
by Jerome J. McGann

Regulating the Social:
The Welfare State and Local Politics in Imperial Germany
by George Steinmetz

Hanging without a Rope:
Narrative Experience in Colonial and Postcolonial Karoland
by Mary Margaret Steedly

Modern Greek Lessons:
A Primer in Historical Constructivism
by James Faubion

The Nation and Its Fragments:
Colonial and Postcolonial Histories
by Partha Chatterjee

Culture/Power/History:
A Reader in Contemporary Social Theory
edited by Nicholas B. Dirks, Geoff Eley, and Sherry B. Ortner

After Colonialism:
Imperial Histories and Postcolonial Displacements
edited by Gyan Prakash

Encountering Development:
The Making and Unmaking of the Third World
by Arturo Escobar

Social Bodies:
Science, Reproduction, and Italian Modernity
by David G. Horn

Revisioning History:
Film and the Construction of a New Past
edited by Robert A. Rosenstone

The History of Everyday Life:
Reconstructing Historical Experiences and
Ways of Life *edited by Alf Lüdtke*

The Savage Freud and Other Essays on Possible
and Retrievable Selves
by Ashis Nandy

Children and the Politics of Culture
edited by Sharon Stephens

Intimacy and Exclusion:
Religious Politics in Pre-Revolutionary Baden
by Dagmar Herzog

What Was Socialism, and What Comes Next?
by Katherine Verdery

Citizen and Subject:
Contemporary Africa and the Legacy of Late Colonialism
by Mahmood Mamdani

Colonialism and Its Forms of Knowledge:
The British in India
by Bernard S. Cohn

Charred Lullabies:
Chapters in an Anthropography of Violence
by E. Valentine Daniel

Theft of an Idol:
Text and Context in the Representation of Collective Violence
by Paul R. Brass

Essays on the Anthropology of Reason
by Paul Rabinow

Vision, Race, and Modernity:
A Visual Economy of the Andean Image World
by Deborah Poole

Children in Moral Danger and the Problem of Government
in Third Republic France
by Sylvia Schafer

Settling Accounts: Violence, Justice, and Accountability
in Postsocialist Europe
by John Borneman

From Duty to Desire:
Remaking Families in a Spanish Village
by Jane Fishburne Collier

Black Corona:
Race and the Politics of Place in an Urban Community
by Steven Gregory

Welfare, Modernity, and the Weimar State, 1919–1933
by Young-Sun Hong

Remaking Women:
Feminism and Modernity in the Middle East
edited by Lila Abu-Lughod

Spiritual Interrogations: Culture, Gender,
and Community in Early African American Women's Writings
by Katherine Clay Bassard

Refashioning Futures:
Criticism after Postcoloniality
by David Scott

Colonializing Hawai`i:
The Cultural Power of Law
by Sally Engle Merry